*Rationality in
Science, Religion, and
Everyday Life*

Rationality in Science, Religion, and Everyday Life

A Critical Evaluation of Four Models of Rationality

MIKAEL STENMARK

University of Notre Dame Press
Notre Dame, Indiana

Library of Congress Cataloging-in-Publication Data

Stenmark, Mikael.
    Rationality in science, religion, and everyday life : a critical
evaluation of four models of rationality / Mikael Stenmark.
        p.   cm.
    Originally presented as the author's thesis (doctoral)—Uppsala
University, 1994.
    Includes bibliographical references (p. 383).
    ISBN 0-268-01651-8 (alk. paper)
    1. Rationalism.   I. Title.
BD181.S74   1995
128'.3—dc20   94-41140
                                                                          CIP

Contents

Acknowledgments

In completing this work, a revised version of my doctoral dissertation defended at Uppsala University in March 1994, I have incurred debts to many people. I am grateful to them for stimulating and critical discussions of ideas and preliminary drafts. It is two persons, in particular, to whom I am deeply grateful: Eberhard Herrmann, my mentor, who has read every draft and who has been throughout the time it took to complete this work a constant source of encouragement and inspiration; and Gary Gutting for making it possible for me to study one year at the University of Notre Dame and for taking time to read and comment on every chapter in this book.

Other people I would like to thank are: António Barbosa da Silva, Vincent Brümmer, Michael Byron, Carl Reinhold Bråkenhielm, Carl-Henric Grenholm, Jon Gunnemann, Robert Heeger, Werner G. Jeanrond, Anders Jeffner, Ingvar Johansson, Simo Knuuttila, Lars Koen, Ernan McMullin, Alvin Plantinga, Susan Poppe, Mark Sluys, Janet Martin Soskice, David Vessey, and the participants of the research seminar in philosophy of religion, Uppsala.

I would like also to express my debt to The Swedish-American Foundation and The Swedish Institute for providing financial support during my year at the University of Notre Dame.

Finally, I would like to thank my parents, Elon and Alice Stenmark, for love and support, and my wife, Anna Romell-Stenmark, for much more than words can say.

1

Introduction

Something that is characteristic of us human beings is that we form beliefs about a vast number of things and under certain circumstances change and reject some of these beliefs. What we encounter not only makes us believe certain things, it also makes us change what we believe. So part of being human is to have the ability to form, revise, and reject beliefs. These cognitive tools of ours are sometimes called *belief-formation* and *belief-regulation processes*. We might wonder about when it is that people form and regulate their beliefs in a proper, responsible, or reasonable way. We often say that to perform such and such an action is not a reasonable thing to do, or to think so and so can hardly be justified. When we ask these kinds of questions we are, in fact, dealing with issues of *rationality*. And we make this kind of evaluation of what people do all the time and in almost all areas of life. A central problem for philosophy is, therefore, to try to make clear what rationality is and under what conditions we should say that something is rational.

People form and hold beliefs in a lot of different areas or contexts, in science, religion, everyday life, politics, and so on. However, people in different places, cultures, and times acquire a lot of different and incompatible beliefs about all sorts of things. And sometimes we say or hear: "That was reasonable to believe for people living in the Middle Ages or that is reasonable for people of other cultures to believe, but not for us." Or alternatively, we say or hear: "This is what they believe in a primitive tribe, but that is not reasonable to believe"—and sometimes it is presupposed that what is reasonable is to believe as *we* do in a modern Western society. But what should we say of these assessments? Is rationality the same for all people and for all areas of life, or did rationality mean one thing then and another thing now and a certain thing in one area of life and something else in another? This is another question philosophers have to address and try to answer, whether this reasonableness or responsibility is the same in all the areas in which we form and hold beliefs or if it changes as we change areas or contexts. Another way of putting this is to ask whether the conditions for rational belief formation and regulation are the same everywhere or if they change with circumstances, and—if they change—to what degree.

Roughly, these are the questions that will occupy this study. Of course to be able to answer especially this last group of questions we need to know a bit about what rationality is, so that we know what to look for. On the other hand, I will claim, we cannot know what rationality is without examining some concrete instantiations of it in practice. Therefore, I will look at and compare three areas of human thought—science, religion, and everyday life. The focus will be on *beliefs* or *believing,* without, of course, assuming that that is all that is going on in these domains. In relation to these areas, four models of rationality will be developed and critically examined.

1.   Science, Religion, and Everyday Life

In *science*, scientists form beliefs about how different natural or cultural phenomena interact with each other They build theories about these phenomena and their interactions, and they try to assess which theories present these phenomena and their interactions in the best way. In this context we may wonder about what the conditions for accepting and holding on to a theory are—what the standards for theory-choice and theory-acceptance are.

Any proper model of rationality must, it seems, somehow deal with science and the kind of reasoning that goes on there. We have to ask ourselves what impact or status science has on the discussion of rationality. As Putnam notes:

> And if what impressed the Few about science from the start was its stunning intellectual success, there is no doubt that what has impressed the Many is its overwhelming material and techno-logical success. We are impressed by this even when it threatens our very lives.[1]

Science is taken by most models of rationality as something of a paradigm example of rationality in action. Science provides a test case of accounts of rationality. But we will see that the advocates of the different models that I shall present understand the paradigmatic status of science in different ways, and this has important consequences in our assessment of the models.

In *religion,* religious believers form beliefs about God (or gods) or the sacred and its relation to us and our situation. Religious convictions develop as the result of experiences of suffering and joy, of meaning and meaninglessness (or alienation), of guilt and liberation (or salvation), or the like. Creeds are created to express these existential experiences and sanction their proper solutions. New experiences confirm, undermine, or lead to the rejection of these beliefs or creeds; and new ones come in their place. In this context we may also wonder what the conditions are for accepting or rejecting a belief, and even more drastically, if any belief of this sort is rationally acceptable.

In *everyday life,* we form beliefs about other people—relatives, mates, strangers, TV stars, and so on, about our relationships to these people and how to communicate with them, about how to drive a car and bake a cake, and about thousands of other things. In this context we may also wonder about how beliefs are accepted, revised, or rejected, and about what standards of rationality ought to be used. In fact, this is the area of life in which we have most of our beliefs, and it is not optional whether or not we participate in it, as with science and religion. To abandon our beliefs of everyday life is in fact to give up life. Hence these beliefs are of great but ignored importance, I will claim, when developing an appropriate model of rationality. In this sense (though in a different sense than science) everyday beliefs are also paradigm cases of rationality in action, because a proper model of rationality must be able to make sense out of everyday life belief formation and regulation.

The question that I shall address is whether we can say that the ways of forming and holding beliefs in these three areas of life have something in common, and if so, we have to determine what it is that they have in common. Or are these human practices so different that nothing concerning how one should form and regulate one's beliefs in one of the practices has any resemblance to how one proceeds in the other practices? In particular, the focus will be on religious practice and religious belief: what standards of rationality, if any, should apply, and can it be rational to be religious or accept religious beliefs? More specifically, the questions I shall try to answer are:

1. What is rationality and under what conditions is something rational?
2. Is the notion of rationality applicable to religious and non-religious views of life? And if so, what standards of rationality are appropriate to use to evaluate that kind of activities or beliefs?
3. Is rationality the same in all areas of life, in all places, and at all times?

In addressing these questions I shall also try to spell out, to some extent, the relationship between rationality and related epistemic notions like *justification, knowledge, truth, evidence,* and *grounds.*

2.   Theoretical, Practical, and Axiological Rationality

What kinds of things can be rational? Obviously not trees, machine-guns, or planets. However, many things can be characterized as rational, for instance, propositions, beliefs, decisions, actions, behaviors, plans, strategies, persons, and so on. The fact that trees, machine-guns, or planets cannot be considered rational gives us a clue to when it is appropriate to apply the term "rational." We can say that in these cases the questions of rationality do not properly arise, and we can describe such situations with the term "a-rational." Another example is questions concerning taste, whether one likes blondes or brunettes, ice-cream or pizza. In these situations we cannot say that it is irrational to like blondes and pizza. Rather these questions fall outside the scope of rationality. Hence the terms "rational" and "irrational" describe situations in which the question of rationality does properly arise. The term "irrational" describes those cases when the demands of rationality (whatever they are) are violated, and the term "rational" those cases in which these demands are fulfilled.

Basically we can say that there are three contexts of rationality. Rescher writes that: "Reason can (and should) come into operation whenever we are in a position to decide what to do—whenever a choice or decision confronts us."[2] And philosophers have in general thought that the areas where we can decide what to do are those of belief, action, and evaluation. Hence the contexts of rationality are theoretical, practical, and axiological:

1. *Theoretical rationality* is concerned with what we (or some other kinds of beings) should believe or accept.
2. *Practical rationality* is concerned with what we (or some other kinds of beings) should do or perform.
3. *Axiological rationality* is concerned with what we (or some other kinds of beings) should value or prefer.

As we will see, however, some philosophers claim that questions concerning values, preferences, or desires fall outside the scope of rationality. But I will reject such a restriction and claim that people can be fully rational in their beliefs (more exactly, their *believings,* to use Chisholm's term)[3] or actions only if the ends or aims they try to achieve—via their beliefs and actions—are in their real interest. I shall also claim that axiological or evaluative rationality is of great importance when we try to determine whether it is rational to accept religious beliefs. In this, one of my main objectives becomes clear, that of *arguing against a too narrow conception of what "rationality" is all about.*

3.   Realistic and Idealized Models of Rationality

Rationality has to be *realistic,* at least so I will claim, in the sense that it cannot require more than what the supposed agent (or agents) can possibly be expected to do.[4] But what can reasonably be expected of someone depends on the agent's resources and circumstances. The thesis that rationality has to be realistic is expressed by what will be called the *axiom of reasonable demand*: one cannot reasonably demand of a person what he or she cannot (possibly) do. If rationality is realistic, this means that a proper model of rationality must take into account the constitution and the actual predicament of the agent. Typically, the agent is an actual being of some sort. Almost exclusively, the agents are then human beings, but they can of course also be real beings of other kinds such as highly developed animals. However, as we will see and surprisingly enough, the explicit or implicit agent of rationality discussed by philosophers is often a fictive being of some sort, a theoretical construction of some kind, like a purely epistemic being or an ideal observer.

Idealized models of rationality (or maybe better: *too* idealized models of rationality, since rationality always involves a degree of idealization), on the other hand, are those models which reject the axiom of reasonable demand—that ask of the agent more than what that creature can possibly do. Hence, idealizations are always relative to who the agent of rationality is supposed to be. If, however, rationality is realistic and we are interested in the rationality of the beliefs, actions, and evaluations of *human beings,* then we have to take into account the constitution and predicament of actual human beings when developing or examining existing models of rationality. A second main thesis of mine, maybe more radical than the first thesis, is a consequence of this understanding of rationality. It consists of the claim that *most conceptions of rationality proposed by philosophers have been far too idealized or utopian to apply in an interesting way to actual human agents like you and me.* In fact, if taken literally, they imply that human beings are usually irrational in what they do.

In particular, this understanding of rationality will lead me to reject one of the cornerstones in many, maybe most, models of rationality, *evidentialism.* Roughly, evidentialism is the view that it is rational to accept a proposition (belief, theory, and the like) only if, and to the extent that, there are good reasons to believe that it is true. More generally, rationality calls for proceeding on the basis of good reasons for whatever we do—believe, act, or evaluate. Essentially my argument for rejecting evidentialism is that if evidentialism is true, then we are irrational in believing most of the things we believe, which is an absurd consequence, and, therefore, we should reject evidentialism.

Instead, I shall try to defend a position that will be called, for lack of any better term, *presumptionism,* since its advocates claim that our belief-forming processes and their outputs (beliefs) should be *presumed* to be intellectually innocent until proven guilty. These processes and their products do not first need to be justified (given good reasons for) before it is rational for us to believe them. Instead, our beliefs are initially justified through the force of a presumption. It is rational, at least initially, to believe what our experiences or belief-forming processes lead us to believe. People are intellectually permitted to accept what they believe without good reasons that support them, as long as they do not know that good reasons against what they believe have emerged. So our initial attitude to our beliefs should not be skepticism, as the evidentialist claims, but trust—in fact, what else can we reasonably do? Basically, the argument I shall give for why we should accept presumptionism is that it does not waste unreasonably much of our limited cognitive resources. It does not—unlike evidentialism—create chaos in our thoughts and paralyze our actions if it is literally followed.

4. Philosophical Research Programs

So one thesis of mine is that when we consider questions of rationality we have to take into account *real* people, *real* science, and *real* religion, and so on, if we expect to be able to apply our models of rationality in these real-life domains. Much of my criticism against different accounts of rationality, concerning the possibility of applying them to science, religion, and everyday life, will be based on this claim. But must philosophers take into account empirical considerations of this sort when they try to construct a model of rationality? Is it not enough if they focus on strictly conceptual and logical matters? Behind these questions and the answers that are given to them, we can find a disagreement among philosophers deeper than the one about how we should proceed in issues concerning rationality. In fact, it is possible to distinguish three basic research programs in philosophy, concerning how to do philosophy properly, which not only apply to rationality but to any, or almost any, issue philosophers can address. These philosophical programs or methods I shall call the *formal*, the *contextual*, and the *practice-oriented approach*— that are applicable to rationality, explanation, science, religion, and so on.

The first two approaches can be seen as situated at each side of a spectrum and the third as an inter-mediating position. To make the differences among them clear I shall describe them as more extreme than they may typically be expressed or presupposed to be. But one's position is, of course, a matter of degree, and exactly where the formal approach becomes practice-oriented and the practice-oriented approach becomes contextual, or vice versa, is a difficult question and will at least for now remain an open question. However, despite this problem, it is not so hard to characterize pure or paradigmatic versions of them.

The advocates of the *formal approach to philosophy* (the *formalists*) claim that the formulation of adequate standards for assessing some aspect (in this case rationality) of activities such as science and religion can be done *independently* from the actual practices of scientists and religious believers. These standards should rather be arrived at by performing a purely conceptual and logical inquiry. On this account it is the philosophical standards or models that have epistemological authority not the practices themselves. And the aim for the formalist working with questions of rationality is to formulate a conception of rationality which would be appropriate for any reasoning being, which would be good no matter what practice the agent is involved in, and no matter what the world is like.

So, for instance, the formalist assumes that the problem of scientific rationality should be approached by developing a general characterization of rationality and then by understanding scientific rationality as a special, or maybe the only, case of it. The way to proceed is to first formulate a general model of rationality and then use it to formulate standards concerning the rationality of the claims made by scientists. No examination of the history of science or of the contemporary practice of science is needed as a basis for a recommendation of appropriate standards for scientific rationality.

The problem of the rationality of religious faith is approached by the formalists in philosophy of religion in the same way as their colleagues address scientific rationality in philosophy of science. If the formalists are negative towards religion they try to show that religion or religious belief does not satisfy these *pre-established* standards of rationality. On the other hand, if they are positive towards religion they use the same strategy but try to reach the opposite conclusion. However, what all of them have in common is that the actual practices of religion are, strictly speaking, irrelevant to the question of what the appropriate standards for rationality in religion should be. No examination of the history of religion or the contemporary practice of religion is needed as a basis for a recommendation of appropriate standards for rationality in religion. So suppose, for instance, the standards of rationality that the formalist recommends for religious belief imply that rational religious believers must be able to calculate the probability that their beliefs are true and believe them only to the degree the evidence warrants. If somebody were to object by saying that this is totally foreign for the actual practice of believers, the formalist would respond by denying the relevance of actual practice to the question of rationality.

While the advocates of the formal approach do not pay any serious attention to the actual practices, this is the key occupation of the defenders of the *social* or *contextual approach to philosophy*. *Contextualists* rely only on an examination of actual practices when formulating and justifying the standards for rationality. More precisely, the contextualists claim that the formulation of adequate standards for assessing some aspect (like rationality) of activities like science and religion is *totally dependent* on the actual practices of scientists and religious believers. Hence the ultimate ground for the justification of the appropriate standards of rationality in religion or science is constituted by the actual practices themselves. The aim of contextualists is not to determine whether scientific or religious belief can be rational, but to exhibit the standards of rationality already present in religious or scientific practice. So the rationality of religious or scientific beliefs is justified or explained not by philosophical standards but by the *preferences* of the scientific or religious community. Hence the ultimate authority for the formulation of standards of rationality is the activities, or better the participants of the activity themselves. The standards of rationality for assessing scientific and religious beliefs are embedded in the way of life, mode of life, discipline, practice, paradigm, tradition, lifeworld, narrative, story, or whatever it is called, to which the beliefs in question belong. The standards for the rationality of religious or scientific beliefs are *internal* to religion or science, not external to the practices—that is, in accordance with some universal and ahistorical epistemological standards.

The third approach, and the one I will try to defend, is the *practice-oriented approach to philosophy*. Practice-oriented philosophers seek to take into account the insights of the other two approaches while avoiding their shortcomings. Roughly, they claim that the problem with the contextual approach is that, if the actual practices are the ultimate basis for testing and justifying standards of rationality, we will have no epistemological basis independent of these practices from which we can assess the practices. It is not possible for someone who is not participating in a practice to evaluate the practice critically. (These problems will be discussed in detail in chapter 11.)

On the other hand, and again roughly, practice-oriented philosophers think that the problem with the formal approach is that it risks divorcing epistemology from the actual practices of science and religion. If the standards of rationality come only from purely logical and conceptual considerations that are unconstrained by the ends and assumptions of the actual scientific and religious practice, then the problem is to see how these standards are *scientifically* or *religiously relevant*. A purely logically developed and justified standard for rationality need not take into account the actual goals of the activities. Or formalists might specify standards for rationality that cannot be satisfied by actual practices. Both the philosophical aims and means might be utopian, wrong, or just irrelevant from the point of view of actual practices like science and religion. But, practice-oriented philosophers claim that whether an aim is utopian or not is something we have to learn in practice—by participating in or closely observing what is going on in a field, what people in it are actually trying to achieve, and what means they typically use to reach their ends. Our aims and means can and should be modified in the light of what is achievable for us and what is achievable might vary from one domain of belief or practice to another. Hence what we need is an approach that has *substantial contact* with the actual ends and means of science and religion but which at the same time allows somebody from the "outside" to assess them critically.

The practice-oriented philosopher takes the contextualist to be correct in that a precondition for evaluating the rationality of science or religion is that we must understand the actual practice of these activities. We need to develop an accurate account of science and religion. And this, practice-oriented philosophers think, places certain *constraints* on an appropriate model of rationality. However, there is also an element of truth in the formal approach, because it seems reasonable to claim that from a purely philosophical point of view some, perhaps *prima facie,* standards of rationality can be established. For example, one such standard might be that a belief must not be a self-contradiction. This shows *that* philosophical considerations are of importance, but of course not *how* important they are.

So practice-oriented philosophers claim that we have to take into consideration actual practices when constructing a model of rationality. But this does not mean that we simply have to accept the practices as givens—as the contextualists seem to do. The actual practices of science and religion are relevant for setting the appropriate standards for rationality, but they are not the only relevant considerations. The appropriate standards are the ones that acknowledge the epistemological significance of both the actual practices and the philosophical accounts that are proposed independently of such practices. The issue is neither purely empirical (or *a posteriori*) nor purely conceptual (or *a priori*), it is a combination. But according to the advocates of the practice-oriented approach, philosophers do not have the resources to be able to formulate a general model of rationality which lacks a careful look at some actual examples of rationality in action. So philosophy has to be *practice-oriented* but neither *practice-determined* nor *practice-independent*. Hence the only way to determine whether scientific or religious beliefs are rationally acceptable—and if they are rationally acceptable, in what way—is to take into account the actual practice of science and religion.

If we want to formulate these three philosophical research programs or approaches in more general terms, we can express them, roughly, in the following way (let *A* stand for aspect: rationality, knowledge, explanation, and the like, and *P* for practice—science, religion, everyday life, and the like):

1. *The Formal Approach:* The philosophical view that the conception of *A* is epistemically independent of the actual practice (or practices) *P*, where *A* is used.
2. *The Contextual Approach:* The philosophical view that the conception of *A* is epistemically totally dependent on the actual practice (or practices) *P*, where *A* is used.
3. *The Practice-Oriented Approach:* The philosophical view that the conception of *A* is epistemically dependent on but not exhausted by the actual practice (or practices) *P*, where *A* is used.

I think that most philosophical accounts of, at least, the standards of rationality for science and religion can be located somewhere on this scale or spectrum. All three approaches will be exemplified in what follows; in fact, it provides the main schema for the classification of the four models of rationality we will examine. The advocates of the first model are formalists, the defenders of the second and the third model are practice-oriented philosophers, and the advocates of the last model of rationality are contextualists.

5.   Rationality and Religion

Two of the main issues I shall consider are what rationality
possibly could be or ought to be (the nature of rationality) and under
what conditions something can be said to be rational or irrational (the
standards of rationality). A third major issue will be how rationality
should be applied to religious matters—if it is at all applicable. In
particular, I shall try to develop the consequences of different models of rationality for the rationality of religious belief or for being a
religious believer. But the focus will not only be on what I shall call
religious views of life, but also on *secular views of life*—like ecosophy
and naturalism, since it seems likely that, roughly, the same standards
of rationality should apply to both of these sorts of views of life.

However, my main concern is not to establish whether, for instance, a particular religious belief—like the belief that a God of this
or that kind exists—is rational, nor is the focus on the question of
what exact weight we should give certain proposed evidence for or
against, say, theism. Rather my strategy is to try to go behind this
discussion and investigate what conceptions of rationality are being
used explicitly or implicitly in it, and to discuss which one of them
is the most appropriate to use for religious belief. My perspective is
in this sense a *meta-perspective*. It is not first of all a detailed analysis
of the arguments that have been given for or against the rationality
of religious belief, but an *examination of the conditions for such
discussion*.

To conduct such an examination of the conditions for the rationality debate in philosophy of religion and theology is crucial, because
often when philosophers and theologians have discussed the question
of the rationality of religious belief, the notion of rationality has been
seen as unproblematic, something one could take more or less for
granted when examining the rationality of religion. But especially
during the 1980s it became clearer that the discussion of the rationality
of religious belief is as much a question about the notion of rationality
as about its applicability to religion. It is not only a question of whether
religious belief meets the proposed standards of rationality, but also
a question about *what* standards of rationality are the appropriate
ones to use in this context. In other words, the criticism or defence
of religious beliefs *depends* on particular models of rationality. So if
we ask whether belief in God is rational, we must be aware that

sometimes philosophers or theologians mean very different things by rationality, and, as a consequence, they may be, in fact, trying to answer different questions.

In this discussion, science has frequently functioned as a touchstone of rationality. The reason is that one of the deepest and most widely shared convictions among philosophers and theologians, at least until recently, has been that science is the paradigm example of rationality. Since science is taken to be one of our best examples of a rational enterprise, the debate concerning the rationality of religious belief has often taken its point of departure in the standards of rationality scientific claims or beliefs are supposed to satisfy. And often, what I will call the *scientific challenge to religious belief,* has been raised. It consists of the claim that religious beliefs must fulfill the same, or at least similar, standards of rationality as scientific beliefs in order to be considered rational. The thought has been that all rational beliefs must conform (more or less) to scientific rationality.

The scientific challenge has sometimes been the same as what nowadays is more and more frequently called the *evidentialist challenge to religious belief,* namely, and again roughly, the view that it is rational to accept religious beliefs only if, and to the extent that, there are good reasons to believe that they are true. These two challenges are the same, if the assumed standards and reasons (or evidence) in both cases are identical. However, if one accepts standards other than scientific ones and evidence other than that acceptable in science, then they are two distinct challenges to religious belief. Both these challenges will be discussed so that the explicit and implicit assumptions behind them can be examined.

Often what scientific rationality consists of has been seen as more or less unproblematic and easy to determine, the problem (if any) being to determine whether religious beliefs satisfy these standards. However, as we shall see, before we can determine whether religious beliefs must and can meet the scientific challenge, we have to know: (*a*) what standards of rationality science is in fact supposed to meet, (*b*) whether science actually is able to fulfill these proposed standards itself, and (*c*) what it means to say that science is taken as a paradigm of rationality. Not until we have been able to do this can we adequately consider whether religious beliefs could reasonably be expected to fulfill the same, or at least similar, standards of rationality as science.

Since my approach to rationality in general will be practice-oriented, it will also be my approach to rationality in religious practice. What I shall try to show is that much of the discussion in philosophy of religion has presupposed a formal approach, and, consequently, the discussion of the rationality of religious belief has in general been conducted (more or less) independently of actual religious practice. Instead, I claim that a necessary condition for being able to develop appropriate standards for religious rationality (or irrationality), and for being able to assess to what extent an individual or group of individuals are rationally justified in accepting beliefs of this kind or being involved in a practice of this sort, is that we properly understand the function and nature of religious belief. In short, the formulation of adequate standards for assessing the rationality of religious belief is not independent of the actual practice of religion. An examination of the history of religion and the contemporary practice of it is needed as a basis for a recommendation of appropriate standards for religious rationality. A philosophical discussion of the rationality of religious belief is *religiously relevant* only if it takes into account the ends and function of religious practice and the situation in which it is pursued. (The same is of course also true for science, economy, ethics, and so on.)

Hence I will try to develop an account of what is characteristic of religious practice, of what religious people are aiming at with their actions and beliefs, and of the kinds of situations in which this quest or enterprise is conducted. This must be done before we can determine what the appropriate standards of rationality are and what conclusion an application of them would lead to when applied to religious believers. So a third thesis of mine is that *much of the discussion of the rationality of religious belief has been irrelevant for whether people are rational in being religious believers, and it cannot consequently function as a basis for a recommendation of the appropriate standards for religious rationality.*

When the actual aims and situation of religious practice are taken into account, we will see that the debate on whether people actually are rational in believing in God or the sacred is in fact over! A lot of people are rational in accepting or holding on to their religious beliefs. However, the same will also be shown to be true for adherents of secular views of life; many of them are also rational in believing what they believe. This, of course, is not to deny that many from both of these groups are often irrational in their believings. Nor should I be taken to mean that rationality is an internal affair for the religious community to handle as it pleases. Religion, like science, is too important to be left to the religious believers or the scientists alone. Hence I shall not only argue against a formal philosophy of religion but also against a contextual philosophy of religion. I will affirm what the contextualist denies: that it is possible to criticize what is going on in a practice also from the outside—even if the critic is not directly involved in that kind of activity or believings. Rationality is in this sense not practice-determined, even though it is practice-dependent. This also means that I think it is possible to develop a normative model of rationality that is universally applicable. "Rationality" does not have or should not have, different meanings in different contexts (whether "contexts" means "disciplines," "traditions," "cultures," or the like) just because people of the past and present had or have different sorts of aims in what they were or are doing and used or use different sorts of means to reach these objectives.

So a fourth and last thesis I shall try to defend is that *the demand of rationality is for everyone and everywhere the same, that we ought to do what can reasonably be demanded of us with the limited means at our disposal in the particular situation in which we find ourselves.* I claim that what can reasonably be demanded of us in general (though sometimes maybe more is needed) is that we have a willingness to test our beliefs in situations where something offers resistance. But in the absence of special reasons to the contrary we are rationally entitled to continue to fully accept what we believe. Of course, the ways people fulfill this demand change with time and place, and depend on what means are available to them; but from this it does not follow that they have different rationalities.

6.   The Models of Rationality as Rational Reconstructions

I shall talk about four different models of rationality and try to compare and critically assess them in order to see what consequences they have when applied to religious belief. (An account of what rationality is and under what conditions something is rational I will refer to as a *model.)* However, the models should be understood as rational reconstructions. I do not claim that any existing philosopher or theologian accepts them exactly the way I have formulated them—except of course for the model I myself propose and hence accept. On the other hand, they are not created out of thin air. I think that the models put together are representative and the reader will, I hope, be able to recognize important standpoints in the past and contemporary discussions of rationality in philosophy in general and in philosophy of science and philosophy of religion in particular. This means that the elements these models of rationality are taken to consist of can be combined—at least, to some extent—in ways different from mine, thereby creating new models of rationality different from those discussed here. But to analyze every possible combination is far beyond the intended aim of this study.[5]

Finally, I include a few words about the content of the chapters. In the next chapter I shall discuss different accounts of what rationality is (the nature of rationality), before going on to consider what the standards of rationality are by explicating four models of rationality. The discussion of each model is structured in much the same way: first the model is stated, then its implications for religious belief are developed, and lastly possible criticisms against the model are examined. So in the third chapter the first model, *formal evidentialism,* is developed and its relation to the *formal view of science* is discussed. In the chapter after that, this model's connection to the mainstream discussion of the rationality of religious belief in philosophy of religion is developed. I then go on, in the fifth chapter, to discuss a post-Kuhnian account of science, a *practice-oriented view of science.* After this is done, the account of scientific rationality present in that view of science is, in chapter 6, developed into a general model of rationality, *social evidentialism;* at the same time the former model is critically examined. In chapter 7 the consequences social evidentialism has for religious belief are discussed.

Next, in chapter 8, I develop the model of rationality I myself think is the most appropriate general model of rationality, *presumptionism,* while criticizing the previous two models. Before presumptionism can be applied to religious believing, however, an account of the nature and function of religious belief needs to be developed so that the constraints religious practice puts on rationality can be taken into consideration; this is provided in chapter 9. In the chapter that follows, the implications of presumptionism for the rationality of religious belief are developed and account is taken of the constraints which the constitution, situation, and aims of actual religious believers put on the appropriate standards of religious rationality. However, since my model is practice-oriented and it is located in between formal and contextual accounts of rationality, I need to distinguish my model not only from formal ones, but also contextual models of rationality. This is done in chapter 11 where an explication and a critical assessment of the fourth model of rationality, *contextualism,* and its consequences for the rationality of religious belief and practice is carried out. The last chapter is a short summary of some of the main points of the whole discussion.

2
The Nature of Rationality

The questions we shall address in this chapter have to do with the general characterization of rationality. What *is* rationality? What does it mean to say that something (a belief, a person, an action, and so on) is rational? Many contemporary philosophers have been less interested in this question and instead moved on and tried to explicate under what *conditions* a belief, an action, and the like, is rational. They ask for example: What must a person believe to be considered rational? When is an action rational to perform? But I will try to argue that to focus exclusively on the standards of rationality and not try to give a characterization of the nature of rationality itself is unsatisfying, because without at least a rough idea of the nature of rationality or what rationality is, it is impossible to assess the standards that are proposed. One has to know something about what the different accounts are all about before it is possible to say which is better than the others!

In developing these accounts of the nature of rationality I shall primarily be concerned with theoretical rationality. However, I shall often expand the scope and say things that also apply to practical and axiological rationality—though, the overall focus will always be on rationality of belief. Before we consider this issue, let me first make a short but important terminological remark. In the epistemological discussions we will consider, the terms "rationality" and "justification" are often used interchangeably.[1] No clear distinction is made between these epistemic notions. In what follows I will mainly use the term "rationality" myself, and only occasionally use "justification." However, many philosophers I will discuss and quote from talk as often of justification as of rationality. Unless I say otherwise these notions will be used interchangeably. I shall distinguish between rationality and justification first in chapter 8.

1.   Generic and Normative Rationality

It is of course possible that the different uses of the notion of rationality have nothing in common with each other. The term means a particular thing in one context, and something completely different in another context, and so on. In a similar way as the term "meaning" has more than one sense—a linguistic sense (the meaning of a concept), and an existential one (the meaning of life)—the notion of rationality is then not univocal. On such an account, rationality can mean one thing in science, something completely different in religion, ethics, politics, economics, and so on. This *incommensurability thesis* can consist of not only a descriptive claim—that "rationality" *is* used in incommensurable ways in different contexts, but also of a normative claim—that "rationality" *should* be used in incommensurable ways in different contexts. But I shall try to show that this claim about incommensurable rationalities is often confused because it is not made clear what level of rationality one is talking about. In fact we have to distinguish four levels or aspects of rationality:

a. The questions concerning what rationality is (the *nature of rationality*).
b. The questions concerning what the conditions of rationality are (the *standards of rationality*).
c. The questions concerning what the reasons (or evidence) of rationality are (the *reasons of rationality*).
d. The questions concerning what the aims or goals of rationality are (the *ends of rationality*).

The differences between these aspects of rationality can be explained as follows. It is one thing to claim that what counts as *good reasons* (or evidence) for or against, say, a belief in science, has nothing in common with what counts as good reasons in religion, ethics, or everyday life (aspect c). The reason for this might be that these activities have very different *ends* or *aims* (aspect d). But that does not mean, I will claim, that they cannot share the same kinds of *standards of rationality* (aspect b). An example of a standard is the evidential one: that one has to have good reasons for what one is doing. So it might be that independent of what aims one has (aspect d) one should always have good reasons for what one does. Different beliefs may need different reasons but not necessarily different standards of rationality. Or if the claim is that the standards of rationality are totally different in science, religion, ethics, and everyday life, this does not show that there is more than one *nature of rationality* (aspect a). An example of a conception of the nature of rationality is the deontological one: rationality is an intellectual duty. (What these levels or aspects of rationality can contain and how they are related will become clearer as we proceed in our discussion.)

I will try to defend the thesis that it is possible, at least, to apply one general conception of rationality to all our practices (level a). People of today, of the past, or of other cultures, of course, pursue different sorts of ends by different sorts of means (methods, cognitive tools, beliefs, or the like) but that does not mean that they necessarily have different rationalities.

But in one important sense the term "rational" can have different meanings. Aristotle maintained that "Man is a rational animal." Being rational is a property we have, it is essential for our species. Bennett seems to understand rationality in the same way as Aristotle when he writes:

> I use "rationality" to mean "whatever it is that humans possess which marks them off, in respect of intellectual capacity, sharply and importantly from all other known species." My analysis of rationality, then, will explore the content of the true belief that human beings are on a certain intellectual eminence compared with other terrestrial creatures . . .[2]

Many philosophers have questioned this rationality assumption. According to Føllesdal, for example, we cannot be rational in this Aristotelian sense, since it "goes too strongly against the evidence we get by observing human behavior, our own as well as others.'" It is a mistake because we sometimes, maybe very often, believe or do irrational things. Instead he proposes that "*man has rationality as a norm*. Man is not always rational, nor should we always and at all costs try to regard man as rational."[3]

But is not Føllesdal misunderstanding Aristotle here or, at least, is it not possible to interpret Aristotle in such a way that we can avoid this problem? I think so. Recall the distinction I made in the first chapter between rational, irrational, and a-rational. What Aristotle probably wanted to say was that humans are *not a-rational* beings. That is, they are the kinds of beings that can be either rational or irrational, in contrast to pigs, trees, or stones. It makes no sense to say that an earthquake or a worm is rational (or irrational), but it does when we talk about ourselves! This sense of rationality has sometimes been called "descriptive" or "categorical rationality," but that meaning of the notion will not be our primary concern. Our concern will instead be with what sometimes has been called "normative" or "evaluative rationality," i.e., the questions concerning under what conditions we can and should say that a person is rational in what he or she is doing (believing, evaluating, or acting). The terms I will use to mark this distinction are *generic* and *normative rationality.*

So when we say that human beings are rational, reasonable, or intelligent creatures we can mean two different things. On the one hand, we are the kind of animal that can be either rational or irrational; that is, in contrast to other beings or entities, we have a capacity for reasoning or reason-governed activities. In this sense, rationality, or better *human reason* or *intelligence,* connotes the power, skill, or ability we have to organize and interpret our experiences and to draw conclusions about things that go beyond our immediate experience. "Man is a rational animal" in the sense that we are *capable* of reason. Or more broadly speaking, since there might exist other kinds of beings—fictional or real—that are capable of reason, we define:

> *Generic Rationality:* An agent or a being is rational if
> it has the capacity for reasoning or the resources of
> reason (intelligence or cognition).

But, on the other hand, the fact that we have the resources of reason does not mean that we necessarily use these resources *wisely*— exercise this capacity in a *proper* way. We can use our intelligence unintelligently. However, as de Sousa points out: "The evaluative sense [of rationality] presupposes the categorical sense: to be either rational or irrational (evaluatively) is to be rational (categorically)."[4] Only a creature that has the capacity for rational thinking and acting (reason) can be or act irrationally (unreasonably). So being rational in the generic sense is a necessary condition for being rational (or irrational) in the normative sense. In other words, rationality in this second sense has to do with the *proper exercise of human reason or intelligence.* Or more generally, rationality has to do with the proper exercise of an agent's or being's reason, intelligence, or cognitive resources:

> *Normative Rationality:* An agent or a being is ratio-
> nal if it exercises its reason (intelligence or cognitive
> resources) properly or responsibly.

In the following discussion I will reserve the terms "human reason," "intelligence," and "cognitive resources" for the first sense of rationality and "rationality" for the second one.

2.   Deontological Rationality

How then might rationality—the proper, reasonable, or intelligent exercise of reason—be characterized? First, as we have just noticed, rationality is a normative concept. To say of a belief, action, or evaluation, that it is rational is (at least, to a certain degree) to approve of it, to say that it is proper or acceptable. One has a positive attitude to it. "Rationality" and "justification" are terms of *appraisal.* As Chisholm says about theoretical rationality: "The term 'justify,' in its application to a belief, is used as a term of epistemic appraisal—a term that is used to say something about the reasonableness of belief. The term 'reasonable' itself, therefore, may also be used as a term of epistemic appraisal."[5] Further, rationality is a normative concept in the sense that it tells us how we *ought* to regulate what we are doing. Rationality is not just a matter of doing whatever we want, it is a matter of doing what we ought to do.

One way of characterizing this conception of rationality is to claim that this normative component is *deontological,* that it has to do with duties.[6] So rationality is a kind of duty, responsibility, or obligation. Such an understanding of rationality becomes evident, for example, when theoretical rationality is described as an "ethics of belief." This way of construing rationality can be called a *deontological conception of rationality* (or "deontological rationality"). The basic thought in a deontological conception of rationality is that agents have duties, responsibilities, or obligations with respect to what they do, not only with respect to actions but also with respect to believings and evaluations. Hence deontological rationality for a person is being in

the condition of having satisfied certain duties or obligations in regard
to what he or she is doing:

> *Deontological Rationality:* Rationality consists in the
> fulfillment of certain duties or obligations in respect
> to what one is doing (believing, acting, or evaluating).

Since my main concern is theoretical rationality, let us call these
responsibilities with respect to belief *intellectual* or *epistemic responsibilities.* Theoretical rationality is then a form of intellectual or epistemic
responsibility, and on a deontological account, this responsibility is
a matter of living up to one's obligations and duties. This line of
thought goes at least back to Descartes and Locke. Locke writes for
example:

> faith is nothing but a firm assent of the mind; which if it be regulated,
> as is our duty, cannot be afforded to anything but upon good reason,
> and so cannot be opposite to it. He that believes, without having
> any reason for believing, may be in love with his own fancies; but
> neither seeks truth as he ought, nor pays the obedience due to his
> Maker . . .[7]

Chisholm is perhaps one of the most prominent advocates of the
deontological account today:

> Let us consider the concept of what might be called an "intellectual
> requirement." We may assume that every person is subject to a
> purely intellectual requirement—that of trying his best to bring it
> about that, for every proposition *h* that he considers, he accepts
> *h* if and only if *h* is true. One might say that this is the person's
> responsibility or duty *qua* intellectual being.[8]

Blanshard claims:

> everywhere and always belief has an ethical aspect. There is such
> a thing as a general ethics of the intellect.[9]

Further, BonJour expresses this view when he writes:

> We cannot, in most cases at least, bring it about directly that our
> beliefs are true, but we can presumably bring it about directly
> (though perhaps only in the long run) that they are epistemically

justified. . . . It follows that one's cognitive endeavors are epistemically justified only if and to the extent that they are aimed at this
goal, which means very roughly that one accepts all and only those
beliefs which one has good reason to think are true. To accept a
belief in the absence of such a reason . . . is to neglect the pursuit of
truth; such acceptance is, one might say, *epistemically irresponsible*.
My contention here is that the idea of avoiding such irresponsibility,
of being epistemically responsible in one's believings, is the core of
the notion of epistemic justification.[10]

Lastly, Plantinga says:

there do seem to be duties and obligations with respect to belief, or
at any rate in the general *neighborhood* of belief. One's own welfare
and that of others sometimes depends on what one believes. If we
are descending the Grand Teton and I am setting the anchor for
the 120-foot rappel into the Upper Saddle, I have an obligation
to form such beliefs as *this anchor point is solid* only after careful
scrutiny and testing. One commissioned to gather intelligence—the
spies Joshua sent into Canaan, for example—has an obligation to
get it right.[11]

So for all these philosophers, theoretical rationality (or justification) is a matter of fulfilling an intellectual duty or responsibility.
But *what* this duty consists in is a matter of dispute as we will see.
However, the most common way to spell out people's intellectual duty
is the evidential one. According to the evidentialist a person's duty is,
roughly, to refrain from believing something unless one has a special
reason to believe that it is true. Or as BonJour says above "that one
accepts all and only those beliefs which one has good reason to think
are true." The position I will try to defend claims that people, rather
than needing a special reason for everything they believe, must be
ready to give up their beliefs if special reasons to change or reject
them emerge. But I hold that we also have intellectual permission
to believe something provided we do not have sufficient reason to
believe that it is not true. The proper initial attitude is taken to be
believing, not disbelieving. We will discuss this topic in detail later on;
for now, our concern is with the nature of rationality not the standards
of it. Chisholm and Plantinga suggest that we should—as with moral

duties—not think that these epistemic duties are absolute (*ultima facie*), but only *prima facie* duties. As such they can be overridden by other duties in special circumstances, such as when they conflict with duties that are more important. For instance, Plantinga says:

> in reporting the Grand Teton rappel I neglected to mention the violent electrical storm coming in from the southwest; to escape it we must get off in a hurry, so that I have a *prima facie* obligation to inspect the anchor point carefully, but another to set up the rappel rapidly, which means I cannot spend a lot of time inspecting the anchor point.[12]

Finally, on this account of theoretical rationality, to say that people are *irrational* is to accuse them of having sacrificed their intellectual integrity. (This is done when someone has formed or held on to a belief irresponsibly, by, for example, ignoring easily available counter-evidence.)

3.   Means-End Rationality

A different way of talking about rationality is to see it as the thing that helps us select useful means for the realization of our various goals or preferences. Rationality consists in the efficient pursuit of preferences. This second account of the nature of rationality can be called a *means-end conception of rationality* (or "instrumental" or "means-end rationality"). According to the advocates of means-end rationality, there is no rationality as such, nothing we do can be rational *per se*. Instead, questions of rationality are always goal-related. Foley says: "All claims of rationality are goal-oriented; they are claims about how effectively the individual, via his beliefs or his actions, is pursuing his goals."[13] Therefore, choice of a means (strategy, method, or procedure, and the like) is rational to the extent that it is efficient for achieving a given goal. Scientific rationality is often viewed in this way. Chalmers writes:

> Although much more needs to be said . . . the aim of science can be understood as the production of knowledge of the world. . . . Methods and standards can be argued for from the point of view of the extent to which they serve a practically realizable version of the aim of science.[14]

This understanding of rationality is common in decision theory or rational-choice theory today. Elster writes:

> The theory of rational choice is, before it is anything else, a normative theory. It tells us what we ought to do in order to achieve our aims as well as possible. It does not tell us what our aims ought to be. (At least this is true of the standard version of the theory. . . .) Unlike moral theory, rational-choice theory offers conditional imperatives, pertaining to means rather than to ends.[15]

The basic idea is that a rational individual is someone who asks in situations of choice: "What do I or the group I belong to prefer or want?" and tries to find efficient means to satisfy, implement, or realize those preferences. Hence rationality is the efficient pursuit of personal or group preferences. It is knowing how to get what oneself or one's group wants. A concrete illustration of means-end rationality and the claim that nothing can be rational as such, might be the following one. Suppose that I want to get from one place to another and do this by running. Someone might say that my behavior is irrational because the most effective, that is, the rational, way to get from the first place to the other is by driving a car. But if my goal was not only to get from one place to another but also to get some exercise, my behavior might in fact be completely rational. Hence, before we can assess whether or not something a person does is rational we have to know his or her goals. We have to be clear about what goals or ends are being presupposed. To be able to settle questions of rationality, we always have to ask first: with respect to what goals is this supposed to be a rational or irrational way of proceeding?

Roughly speaking, a decision, action, plan, belief and the like, is rational if it will, or apparently will, satisfy a person's goals. On a means-end conception of rationality, rationality is the establishment of appropriate means-end connections:

> *Means-End Rationality:* Rationality consists in the efficient pursuit of means for achieving certain implicit or explicit ends or goals.

Means-end rationality is then a relative notion, in the sense that the rationality of what an agent is doing is relative to the goals he or she has. However, rationality is also relative in another sense; we not only have to know people's goals to evaluate if what they are doing

is rational; we also have to take into account *people's resources* and
the *reality* they live in. Recall my previous example: even if my only
goal was to get from the first place to the second, it might still not be
irrational for me to run instead of using a car, even though it would
be faster to use a car. This may be so simply because I may not have
access to a car or I might have access to a car but the road might be
blocked. Given my resources and predicament, to run might be the
best I can do.[16]

To what extent must people satisfy their own goals? Or how
effective must one be in pursuing one's goal? One answer is the
objective account of means-end rationality: that the rational thing to do
is, roughly, the one with the highest probability of bringing about the
wanted end. Matters of rationality are objective and can be empirically
determined. But Foley, among others, thinks that this is to demand
too much of a rational person, and that rather "we want to allow the
possibility that things turn out badly for you even if you are rational."[17]
His proposal is instead that what we are doing is rational not if it in fact
will or if it is probable that it will satisfy our goals, but if it apparently
will satisfy our goals. So on the *subjective account* of means-end
rationality, the rational thing to do is, roughly, the one that seems
to the agent at the time to be the one that will bring about the wanted
end. Rescher similarly says that rationality requires us only to do what
appears best. "Reason enjoins us to do what *appears* optimal—what
is optimal relative to the circumstances *as we discernably confront
them,* and so relative to the information *as we have it.*"[18] Matters of
rationality are on a subjective account not objective but circumstantial,
though they can still be empirically determined.

4.   The Connection between Deontological
      and Means-End Rationality

The connection between deontological and means-end rationality is not immediately clear: are they two contradictory ways of
characterizing rationality, two totally unrelated ways, or is there a way
of combining them? I think there is a connection, because the discussion of (theoretical) rationality as an intellectual duty often assumes
a particular goal or end. According to one advocate of deontological
rationality, Chisholm:

Each person, then, is subject to two quite different requirements in connection with any proposition he considers: (1) he should try his best to bring it about that if that proposition is true then he believe it; and (2) he should try his best to bring it about that if that proposition is false then he not believe it.[19]

The goal of deontological rationality is on such an account *epistemic:* it is to try to possess as many true beliefs as possible and try to eliminate as many false beliefs as possible. Roughly speaking, we have an obligation to regulate our beliefs with the epistemic goal in mind of getting more in touch with reality. If this is right, there does not seem to be, in principle, a problem in connecting a means-end conception of rationality with talk about epistemic duties. Individuals can, *given* that they accept an epistemic goal, have an intellectual responsibility to pursue efficient means for satisfying that goal. Or more generally, people can be taken to have a duty to establish appropriate means-end connections with respect to what they are doing.

But there is a problem here. Suppose the goal of our believings is to just increase our peace of mind. The goal is an emotional state, not the goal of holding true beliefs and avoiding false beliefs. A belief could then be rational or irrational in regard to this psychological goal. Here means-end rationality is something very different from deontological rationality, at least, as it is normally understood. However, nothing stops us from saying that people have a responsibility or duty with respect to other ends than truth and the avoidance of falsehood. It might, therefore, be useful to distinguish between epistemic and non-epistemic ends of rationality or between what we can call "epistemic" and "non-epistemic rationality." When rationality is understood as having only values such as truth and the avoidance of falsehood as ends or aims we can refer to it as *epistemic rationality*. And we can use the term *non-epistemic rationality* when rationality is understood as having only values such as well-being, saving the earth, self-interest, happiness, peace of mind, or staying out of trouble with the government as ends or aims. Alternatively, we could say epistemic rationality has only epistemic ends, while the ends of non-epistemic rationality are just non-epistemic ones.

This distinction between epistemic and non-epistemic rationality is not to be confused with the one I made in the introduction between theoretical rationality (concerning what to believe or accept) and practical rationality (concerning how to act or perform). The reason why they should not be confused is that practical rationality may have, and often does have, an epistemic as well as a non-epistemic end, while that is never the case with non-epistemic rationality. For instance, if I want to get from one place to another I might have both the non-epistemic goal of feeling healthy and the epistemic goal of getting a good workout.

Although most philosophers agree that truth is an example of an epistemic end and well-being of a non-epistemic one, there is a group of ends that are more problematic, and there is no consensus on whether they belong to the first or the second class of ends. These include: usefulness, simplicity, predictability, problem-solving effectiveness, and fertility. Are these ends marks of truth? Let me illustrate this problem briefly by focusing on *simplicity*. The first problem with simplicity is that it seems to be hard to characterize. But, very roughly, we might say that simplicity has to do with the character of the entities a theory or hypothesis posits, how many those entities are, and how they are related to one another, and other such considerations. The second problem is that it is difficult to say why we should think that simpler theories, all else being equal, are more likely to be true than more complex theories.[20] Why should we think that reality is more likely to be simple than complex? There does not seem to be any reason to think that there should be, everything else being equal, more simple things in the world than not. Maybe the most successful way of justifying scientists' use of simplicity as a goal is to say that a simpler theory is easier for us to *use* than complex ones; it is, for instance, less difficult to test and control.[21] So if two theories are otherwise on a par, the scientist should prefer the less complex one of the two. On such an account, simplicity is not an epistemic end—something that promotes truth and eliminates falsehood—but a non-epistemic one.

It is of course possible, and common, to *combine* epistemic and non-epistemic ends with one another. And this is exactly what is done in science, on the view proposed above. On such an account the scientific aim is, in general, not only to find truths or produce knowledge as such, but to find truths or produce knowledge that are *useful* for us—at least, in the long run—and that we (the scientists or all of us) can apply in an interesting way. Hence there is, on this account of science, a pragmatic aspect to the scientific enterprise—an interest in finding truths or knowledge that we can use to control and predict events in the world. Science does not, on such a view, have a purely epistemic goal, it has a *complex end,* i.e., an end that consists of both epistemic and non-epistemic goals. More generally, what people are doing most of the time probably has complex ends, as in the example given above concerning practical rationality.

The distinction between epistemic and non-epistemic rationality (or between ends that are and are not epistemic) also shows that what are *good reasons* for or against a belief may nevertheless not be reasons to think that the belief is true or false, since believing what is true and avoiding falsehood is only one among many aims we may have for accepting a belief. For instance, someone could say that "I believe in God not because I think it is true that God exists, but because it gives me peace of mind, and that is all I want" and to the extent that belief in God *gives* this person peace of mind, achieving peace of mind is a good reason for believing in God—if peace of mind is all this person wants. Or consider again the point made above about how one can justify the use of simplicity in science. Scientists have good reasons to take simplicity into account when considering different theories, given the aims of science, but this does not mean that there are necessarily good reasons to think that simplicity is a truth-promoting value. Hence we can have different kinds of reasons for doing (believing, evaluating, and acting) some particular thing. Therefore it is wrong, or at least misleading, to write as Elster does: "While the rationality of an action is ensured by its standing in the right kind of relation to the goals and beliefs of the agent, the rationality of beliefs depends on their having the right kind of relation to the evidence available to him."[22]

But the rationality of a belief also depends on its standing in the right kind of relation to the goals of the agent, for instance, the goal of believing true things, as the examples given above indicate. So both practical and theoretical rationality, contrary to what Elster seems to think, can be construed in terms of means-end rationality, and in both cases good reasons and aims are relevant.

If this is correct it means that there are two basic kinds of reasons, and they correspond to the two classes of ends discussed above. We can call the two kinds of reasons "epistemic" and "non-epistemic" reasons. It is hard to give a satisfying definition of these types of reasons, but we can at least say that a good *epistemic reason* for something one is doing, for example, believing in the existence of electrons, exists only if the reason connects the belief in an appropriate way to the epistemic goals that are presupposed, for instance, believing true things. Correspondingly, we can, at least, say that a good *non-epistemic reason* for something one is doing exists only if the reason connects the doing in an appropriate way to the non-epistemic goals that are presupposed.[23] Of course if the end is a complex one, when evaluating the rationality of choosing a particular means, we have to take into account both epistemic and non-epistemic reasons.

5.   Holistic Rationality

One serious problem with means-end rationality is, however, that it is such a narrow conception of rationality. The function of rationality is *merely* to help us establish sufficient means for our individual or collective ends. The only thing that is possible or permitted is to use rationality to assess the use of particular means. If *all* questions of rationality are goal-related, as, for instance, Foley claims in the quotation given above, then the assessment of appropriate goals or ends is outside the scope of rationality, or at least, in those cases when the ends cannot be explained in terms of means.[24] There exists only a rationality of means not a rationality of ends. To express this limitation in deontological terms: rationality can be construed as a duty, but only in respect to means not ends. If you have *that* goal, then your duty is to find efficient means to reach it.

This means that on a means-end account the only form of rationality that exists is a rationality of means or a *conditional rationality:* If a person holds this, then he or she cannot (to be consistent) fail to hold that. Consequently, ends and values are not (most of the time at least) within the scope of rationality. Means-end rationality is agnostic about proper ends, it allows for the adoption of any end whatsoever. According to Simon: "We see that reason is wholly instrumental. It cannot tell us where to go; at best it can tell us how to get there. It is a gun for hire that can be employed in the service of whatever goals we have, good or bad."[25] Russell writes: " 'Reason' has a perfectly clear and precise meaning. It signifies the choice of the right means to an end that you wish to achieve. It has nothing whatever to do with the choice of ends."[26]

This view of rationality has, according to many intellectuals, had a major impact on the modern Western society. For instance, von Wright says that he agrees with the advocates of "critical theory" that the form of rationality that has been prevailing in our modern society consists in the control of means for the achievement of different aims.[27] But, according to him, the problem with this means-end or technical rationality is that it is unable to legitimate the aims of social activity. Rationality is in this context thought to be exclusively a matter of choosing efficient means for the ends that an individual or a group desires.[28] This way of understanding reason or rationality goes at least back to Hume. For him reason is the slave of the passions. It can help us decide what we must do if we have a certain end, but only passion can give us an end to strive for. He insists:

> It is not contrary to reason to prefer the destruction of the whole world to the scratching of my finger. It is not contrary to reason for me to choose my total ruin. . . . It is as little contrary to reason to refer even my own acknowledged lesser good to my greater, and to have a more ardent affection for the former than the latter.[29]

Here, I think, the problem with this conception of rationality becomes evident. Does it not go strongly against our intuitions about rationality that someone who chooses his or her total ruin would not be irrational in some sense of the term? So why should we accept such a limited conception of the range of rationality? Is it not of utmost importance that we can in some way rationally evaluate what goals we should strive to achieve—that we are able to decide what goals are really worthy to accept? It certainly seems so. Hence only if there exist compelling reasons to doubt that this is possible should we accept a purely means-end rationality. I will claim that we should reject the idea that rationality has to do only with means-end connections or with our intellectual duty (if we express means-end rationality in deontological terms) in regard to means-ends connections. It is possible to defend a conception of rationality that includes both a rationality of means and a rationality of ends. There is on such an account a *categorical* or *axiological* form of rationality (that is, a reasoning about values, preferences, ends, desires, interests, and similar things) not only a conditional form (that is, a theoretical form concerning matters of information and a practical one concerning how people should act given their preferences).

Consider one example given by Berlin.[30] He asks us to imagine a case where an individual possesses a capacity to reason in only a means-end way, and the end he values most of all is sticking pins into surfaces with a particular resiliency. It makes no difference for him what kind of surface it is as long as it has a certain elasticity. So whether it is tennis ball or human skin does not matter to him. And he satisfies this desire or end, via his beliefs and his actions, in a highly efficient way. It follows from the means-end conception of rationality that we cannot say that he has chosen an irrational end. It makes no difference whether he satisfies his desire on a tennis ball or human skin, because questions about appropriate ends for what we are doing fall outside the range of rationality. But can we feel comfortable about calling this man rational? Certainly not. Hence something is seriously lacking in a purely means-end conception of rationality.

Or think of somebody who never takes his or her own self-preservation into account when acting. Is there not something irrational about *never* considering one's own life when considering what to believe and how to act? I certainly think so. We do think in general that people are irrational if for no reason they seek their own death, pain, disablement, deprivation of freedom, and similar things. Notice that people may have reason for trying to achieve these ends, that is, in some circumstances it is rational to prefer one of them to some alternative. For instance, one may sacrifice one's life to save other people or someone might want to die rather than go through pointless suffering, and so on. But what is irrational is to want these ends for themselves, to want them as such. As Nathanson says: "If the choice of an evil is to be rational, it must be a means to avoid some greater evil or to bring about some good."[31]

If these intuitions are correct it does not matter how efficiently people are pursuing their aims, they are *not fully rational* if those aims are meaningless or destructive. Goal-directed action is not automatically rational. If we adopt inappropriate ends then we are not being rational no matter how successfully we cultivate them. As Rescher points out: "Principles of relative [or conditional in my terminology] rationality are pointless in the absence of principles of categorical rationality."[32] Because of this crucial shortcoming of means-end rationality, I will claim that rationality has also to do with choices of appropriate or valuable ends.[33] Such a conception of rationality I will call a *holistic conception of rationality*.

On a holistic conception, people's preferences or desires are not equally rational. Rationality rules out certain ends; some ends are intrinsically irrational to seek. In other words, we must make a distinction between ends or preferences that are and are not in people's best interest. The terms "desire" and "need" might be the concepts we are looking for, because we can say that people do not need everything they desire, and do not desire everything they need. Von Wright defines a *need* as something that is bad for an individual or group not to satisfy. On the other hand, a *desire* or wish that does not correspond to a need can, if it is satisfied, be bad because it can, for example, be harmful for one's health.[34] Nathanson provides us with an illustration. Although one may have no desire to consult a doctor, it may nonetheless be in one's interest, be a need one has, to do so. One may even have no reason to believe that one ought to see the doctor, and yet it could be in one's interest to do so.[35] So to know what one needs is to know what is good or bad for oneself. Everything else being equal, it is always rational to cultivate one's needs (real interests) but not necessarily one's desires. Hence we can say:

> If people know that a means is contrary to their needs
> or best interests, then (everything else being equal) it
> would be irrational for them to perform that action,
> accept that belief, or make that evaluation.

But then what is rationality on a holistic conception? First of all, on such a conception there is both a rationality of means and a rationality of ends. More precisely, rationality is seen as a matter of doing (believing, acting, and evaluating) what we intellectually ought to do and can realistically manage to do, so that in our circumstances we choose appropriate ends and means to achieve these ends:

> *Holistic Rationality:* Rationality consists in the pur-
> suit of appropriate ends and of appropriate means
> to achieve those ends.

On this conception of rationality, a rational person is someone who is able to choose ends that are in his or her best interest and find means that are, or appear to be, sufficient for satisfying those ends. Hence holistic rationality has both a *theoretical-practical* and an *axiological* dimension. On the theoretical-practical (conditional) side, it is concerned with establishing appropriate means-ends connections (beliefs and actions), finding efficient means; while on the axiological (categorical) side it is concerned with the establishment of appropriate ends (values).

In contrast to means-end rationality, holistic rationality is not only concerned with good reasons for whether a *means* is rational to adopt, given one's preferences. Holistic rationality is also concerned with good reasons for whether an *end* is rational. For instance, whether staying out of trouble with the government is reasonable or not, or whether it is rational to believe in God only because it gives one peace of mind. Rationality is a normative notion, and this normative element includes both the cultivation of means and the cultivation of ends. It is not a matter of finding efficient means for whatever we want, it is a matter of doing what we ought to do or prefer. What really counts is not what people prefer, but what people ought to prefer— not what we do want, but what we ought to want. If this is correct, an adequate model of rationality must include both a condition (theoretical-practical) and categorical (axiological) form of rationality.

It is also important to notice that the axiological aspect of rationality does not come in only with respect to the choice of appropriate ends, but also enters in respect to the choices of appropriate means. A particular action may be the most, or one of the most, efficient means for an individual or community to reach their goals but may, nevertheless, be unacceptable from, say, an ethical point of view. Suppose that the most efficient way of reducing the crime rate in a city is to locate the people who commit the most crimes and then kill them all. Supposing that crime rates will be drastically reduced, is this an appropriate or rational means to the end of reducing the crime rate in the city? No, because efficiency is not the only condition for the rationality of means. This means is efficient, but it is not an acceptble solution from an ehtical point of view (or, at least, not according to the one I endorse). The only way this suggestion of how to lower the crime rates can be rational, according to a holistic conception of rationality, is if it can be justified both from a theoretical-practical and an axiological angle. So we could say:

> A means is fully rational to adopt only if it can be shown not only to be *efficient* (that is, practically acceptable) but also *valuable* (that is, axiologically acceptable).

And we could say that a means that is, or appears to be, efficient and valuable is an appropriate means.

The way I have defined holistic rationality it includes a normative, or more precisely, a deontological element. We have a responsibility or duty to do what can be rightly demanded of us in pursuing appropriate ends (truth, well-being, peace of mind, and the like) and appropriate means (beliefs, actions, methods, strategies, standards, and the like) for achieving those ends. And, as long as we understand rationality as a normative concept, it is possible to combine deontological rationality with means-end rationality. However, what can rightly be demanded of us is a matter of dispute; that is, the question as to which *standards* of rationality are reasonable ones to adopt. This is one point where the models of rationality we will discuss differ from each other, and to this discussion we now turn.

3

Science and Formal Evidentialism

The first model of rationality we will examine is an application of the formal approach of philosophy to a specific topic, in this case rationality and science. The advocates of this approach (the *formalists*), as I mentioned in the introduction, claim that philosophical enquiry is only (or almost exclusively) a matter of logic and conceptual analysis; no real survey of the subject matter is therefore necessary. In matters concerning rationality this means, roughly, that philosophers are concerned with investigating which logical properties of propositions or beliefs, and which logical relations among them, suffice for rationality. The general idea or assumption is that the conception of rationality is epistemically independent of any practices to which it can be applied. The contours of this way of understanding rationality will become clearer as we proceed.

1.   The Formal View of Science

The best place to start is with scientific rationality since most of the formalists take it to be the paradigm of rationality. Some early defenders took it to be the only form of rationality, others accept that there are other forms of it, but they all agree that if we can find rationality anywhere, it is in science. I will focus primarily on issues related to scientific rationality and not attempt to give a full account of the formal view of science.

A good place to start is with Frege. He taught that we must distinguish sharply between logic and psychology. Logic is not the study of human thinking but the enquiry into purely logical relationships between abstract entities, like propositions. The formalists took this to heart and stated that philosophy of science is the study of logical

relationships among scientific propositions, hypotheses, or theories:
"Philosophy is to be replaced by the logic of science—that is to say,
by the logical analysis of the concepts and sentences of the sciences,
for the logic of science is nothing other than the logical syntax of the
language of science."[1] Logic is the primary tool for the analysis of
science. So formalists work primarily with logical problems, particularly with the logical structure of theories and the logical relationships
among statements. The assumption is that problems like these can
be solved in a formal and more or less definitive way. "There was
a logic underlying the methods of validation and of explanation in
science, and the task of the philosopher was to disengage this logic
once and for all."[2] This kind of understanding of scientific rationality
is based on the acceptance of what McMullin has called the "logicality
thesis," that the *rationality of science can be assimilated to that of a
logical system*.[3] Scientific methodology has the same structure as the
one logicians found in good arguments, and rational inference is to be
thought of and justified solely in terms of formal or logical categories.
Rationality is essentially, if not completely, a matter of logicality.

There seems to be, according to this, no need to analyze actual
scientific theories. Rather it is assumed, at least by the early formalists
of this century, that simple empirical generalizations like "All swans
are white" or "All sodium salts burn yellow," can adequately represent
the structure of scientific theories or hypotheses. What is needed is
only an analysis of the form of propositions. So a scientific theory
consists of propositions that are structural similar to propositions like
"All swans are white." This means that science, essentially, is a set of
empirically verifiable or falsifiable propositions about reality. Science
could be seen as a fixed set of propositions. In fact since logic is an
a priori discipline and the prime occupation of philosophy of science
is logical analysis, it follows that philosophy of science is also an *a
priori* discipline. Consequently actual scientists and scientific practice
should be of little interest.

According to this view philosophy of science is the study of how
an ideal scientist should proceed, and scientific rationality is what it
is rational for such an agent to accept or believe. The scientist on this
view, as Giere describes him or her, is:

> an ideal type, the ideally rational scientist. The actions of real scien-
> tists, when they are considered at all, are measured and evaluated

by how well they fulfill the ideal. The context of science, whether personal, social, or more broadly cultural, is therefore typically regarded as irrelevant to a proper philosophical understanding of science.[4]

1.1   SCIENTIFIC EVIDENTIALISM

The task of philosophy of science is to make explicit the principles of rationality that (ought to) govern scientific practice. The first requirement of rationality is that proper science demands evidence (i.e. correspondence to empirical data) for all theories (hypotheses or propositions) it accepts. Roughly, the idea is that the ideal scientist first (*a*) collects adequate evidence for and against the theory, then (*b*) examines the relationship between the theory and the evidence so as to determine the probability that the theory is true given the evidence, and finally (*c*) believes or doubts the theory with a firmness proportional to the probability assigned it on the evidence. As Pap puts it:

> The scientific mentality may be roughly characterized as the tendency to suspend belief until evidence of the appropriate kind is produced, and then to believe the proposition in question only to the degree that the available evidence warrants it, without excluding the possibility of a future disconfirmation.[5]

And Rusell writes, "it is not *what* the man of science believes that distinguishes him, but *how* and *why* he believes it. His beliefs are tentative, not dogmatic; they are based on evidence, not on authority or intuition."[6]

So the first part of the formalist account of scientific rationality is an acceptance of evidentialism. By *evidentialism* I will mean, roughly, the view that it is rational to accept a proposition (belief, theory, and the like) only if, and to the extent that, there are good reasons (or evidence) to believe that it is true. If we define evidentialism in this way it is important to notice that it actually contains two different components. I will call them the "evidential principle" and the "proportionality principle." The evidential principle states that one (the scientist in this case) should accept something only if there is good reason to believe that it is true. A classic formulation of this principle is Clifford's claim that: "It is wrong always, everywhere [not only in science, my remark], and for anyone, to believe anything upon insufficient evidence."[7] It is important to notice that this demand implies that a theory one already has, which one has no reason to think is true, but also no reason to reject, must be abandoned. A rational scientist must do without all theories that do not meet this demand. Let us state the principle as follows:

> *The Evidential Principle:* It is rational to accept a proposition or belief only if there are good reasons to believe that it is true.

The evidential principle says nothing about scientists' attitudes to what they accept or reject, how firmly or tentatively they should hold the beliefs they have reasons for. However, evidentialists not only affirm the evidential principle, they also hold that we should believe something only *to the extent that* there is good evidence to believe that it is true. The rational scientist must then have a tentative attitude to the theory he or she has good reasons to believe is true, always being conscious of the requirement that the theory perhaps will have to be given up in the face of new evidence. And that attitude applies independently of what kind of theories the scientist holds. This principle is sometimes called the "proportionality principle," and it can be stated in the following way:

> *The Proportionality Principle:* The firmness with which one accepts a proposition (belief, theory, or the like) ought always to be in proportion to the strength of the evidence for it.

However, the process of giving reasons for theories must start somewhere. But from which propositions or beliefs should a rational scientist start? The evidential principle tells us to start where we are permitted to start, i.e., we should start with propositions we know to be true or reasonably believe to be true. Typically the formalist claims that scientists should start (logically) with the least general propositions that we know, with beliefs that are evident to the senses or propositions about our immediate experience. Let us call these beliefs "observational beliefs" and the propositions that correspond to them "observational statements." Roughly, they are statements about the state of the world, or some part of it, that can be justified or established as true in a direct way by an unprejudiced observer's use of his or her senses. Examples of observation statements are: "At a certain time, and at a certain position in the sky the planet Mars appears," or more down to earth statements like "Jim is jumping into the water," and "There is a tree in front of me." What is characteristic of these examples of observation statements is that they are *singular statements,* statements that refer to a certain state of affairs at a certain place and at a certain time. What is characteristic of the laws and theories in science is that they are not singular statements, but make claims about the properties or behavior of some general aspect of the universe. They make general claims, like "Planets move in ellipses around their sun" and "All copper put in nitric acid dissolves under such-and-such conditions of temperature and pressure." Scientific laws and theories are examples of *universal statements,* statements that refer to all events of a particular kind at all places and at all times.[8]

However, to allow scientists to start with observational beliefs is in fact inconsistent with the evidential principle, because it demands that scientists must have good reasons for *everything* they believe, including observational beliefs. What reasons do the scientists have for accepting these beliefs, and what reasons do they have for accepting the reasons for these beliefs, and so on? This way of arguing seems to lead to an infinite regress. The way formalists have typically tried to avoid being caught in an infinite regress is to give up the general character of the evidential principle and claim that there exist certain beliefs that it is rational to believe without reasons.[9] This strategy of dividing our belief system in two parts: *non-basic* (or derived) *beliefs,* beliefs that need evidential support of other beliefs, and *basic beliefs,* beliefs that do not need evidential support of other beliefs, is normally called *foundationalism.*

Some formalists claim that observational beliefs are examples of basic beliefs. These beliefs are accepted as a result of sense experience and not on the basis of evidence. In fact it seems hard to justify observational beliefs by appeal to evidence. One cannot really give arguments or infer one's belief that there is a tree in front of one from other beliefs, since it is hard to know what would qualify as better grounds for that belief than the fact that one sees and feels it oneself. This means that the formalist, to avoid this apparent inconsistency, must reformulate the evidential principle. Its scope must be limited to cover only non-basic beliefs:

> *The Evidential Principle*:* It is rational to accept a non-basic proposition or belief only if there are good reasons to believe that it is true.

But this means that we also have to reformulate evidentialism. It should be understood as the view that it is rational to accept a non-basic proposition or belief only if, and to the extent that, there are good reasons to believe that it is true.

1.2   EXPLICATING FOUNDATIONALISM

Before we develop the formalist's view of scientific rationality further, let us try to specify the meaning of foundationalism in more detail, since the notion is sometimes used in different and unspecified ways and this has created a lot of confusion concerning its value and strength.[10] The essential thesis of foundationalism is that the relation between the beliefs in our web of beliefs is asymmetrical. There are certain beliefs that are basic and there are others that are non-basic. All of our beliefs fall into either one or the other group of beliefs. The (inferential) justification goes only from basic beliefs to non-basic beliefs, not the reverse. "If my belief that A is based upon my belief that B, then my belief that B must not be based on my belief that A."[11] Hence a belief A could constitute *evidence* (or a reason) for a person to hold another belief B only if it is more basic than B. We can take an example from Wittgenstein to clarify this point. Wittgenstein remarks that philosophers could give hundreds of epistemological justifications of the belief that "cats don't grow on trees," but none of them can start with anything more certain than the fact that cats do not grow on trees.[12] In other words, the beliefs that some philosophers try to give as evidence for the belief that "cats don't grow on trees" are not more basic in people's belief systems than the belief these philosophers are trying to justify, and therefore such beliefs cannot constitute evidence for the belief in question.

However, the foundationalist claims that basic beliefs are not groundless, they can also be justified. But this justification is *non-inferential* or *immediate*. A belief is non-inferentially justified if it is not inferred from other beliefs but rests on an appeal to first-hand experience. (This distinction between inferential and non-inferential justification will become clearer when we consider concrete examples, given by foundationalists, of basic and non-basic beliefs. See also the discussion below of what evidence is.) So we can divide the main thesis of foundationalism into two different parts:[13]

(T1) There are two forms of justification, inferential and non-inferential.

(T2) Basic beliefs are not justified by appeal to non-basic beliefs.

Notice that the asymmetry of foundationalism is strictly speaking *formal*; it says nothing at all about which beliefs are or ought to be basic or non-basic. It is this asymmetry that makes foundationalism different from coherentism. Coherentism is, roughly, the view that the epistemic relation between the beliefs in our belief systems is symmetrical.[14] There is no categorical distinction between basic and non-basic beliefs. All of our beliefs are logically or epistemologically on the same level.[15] However, certain beliefs may sometimes function as basic beliefs, i.e., constitute evidence for other beliefs, and sometimes as non-basic ones. Therefore, there is also an asymmetry in coherentism, but the asymmetry is functional not substantial. The asymmetry of foundationalism is *substantial* because the foundationalist claims that beliefs will always be basic if they have a particular character. The asymmetry of coherentism is *functional* because beliefs function as basic beliefs in a particular context, while in other contexts they function as non-basic beliefs.

To give this formal structure of foundationalism *content* means to specify what type of beliefs count as *properly* basic beliefs, i.e., beliefs that it is rational to accept without accepting them on the basis of any other beliefs.[16] What kinds of beliefs can be properly basic? The three traditional candidates put forward are:

(T3) A belief is properly basic if it is *self-evident*.

(T4) A belief is properly basic if it is *incorrigible*.

(T5) A belief is properly basic if it is *evident to the senses*.

Modern foundationalists, following Descartes, usually claim that only beliefs that are self-evident and incorrigible are properly basic beliefs. Self-evident beliefs are beliefs whose truth is clear to all honest and intelligent persons who properly understand them, like the beliefs that 2 + 2 = 4 and that no one is taller than himself or herself. Incorrigible beliefs are those which are about our immediate experience, like "I am feeling pain" and "I am visually aware of something pink."[17] However, the ancient and medieval foundationalists, like Aquinas (and many contemporary foundationalists), want to add that beliefs that are evident to our senses (what we have previously called observational beliefs) like "There is a table here in front of me" and "I can see the moon," are also properly basic beliefs.

The way most modern foundationalists constructed foundationalism has sometimes been called *strong foundationalism*. Strong foundationalists accept only (T3) and (T4); that is, a belief is properly basic if and only if it is self-evident or incorrigible. The idea behind strong foundationalism is that properly basic beliefs should be beliefs which are immune to doubt. It should be impossible for them to be wrong. By taking as basic only beliefs that are certain or infallible, they hope to build a sufficiently secure epistemic foundation on which our other (derived) beliefs can be rationally grounded. Dancy describes it as:

> a research programme which sets out to show how it is that our beliefs about an external world, about science, about a past and a future, about other minds, etc., can be justified on a base which is restricted to infallible beliefs about our sensory states [and self-evident beliefs, my addition]. It is suggested that if we can do this, the demands of epistemology are satisfied. If not, we relapse into scepticism.[18]

But it is important to see that it is possible to be a *weak foundationalist* instead. A weak foundationalist accepts that a belief is properly basic if it is self-evident, incorrigible, or evident to the senses (T5). Weak foundationalists claim that the definition of proper basicality the strong foundationalist gives is too restricted. Some philosophers want to go further than just adding (T5). Plantinga, for instance, claims that some memory beliefs, like "I had breakfast this morning," are also properly basic beliefs. This belief is not inferred from other beliefs that are taken as evidence for it. I do not infer I had breakfast this morning from the fact that " . . . I have an inclination to believe the proposition that I had breakfast, along with a certain past-tinged experience . . ."[19] So although having the belief in those circumstances (non-inferentially) justifies my acceptance of it, I do not reason (by argument or inference) from those circumstances to my belief, I simply find myself believing it.

However, if we accept a weak foundationalism then properly basic beliefs can be defeasible; they could be wrong. For instance, what I take to be a tree might in fact be an artificial tree. But as Wainwright points out, on this account, if I have no reason to believe that there are any artificial trees in the neighbourhood or for thinking that my visual equipment is defective, just having the belief in those circumstances (non-inferentially) justifies me in holding it.[20]

But what both strong and weak foundationalists have in common is that they claim that our belief system can be divided in two parts and that justification just runs one way, from basic to derived beliefs. In other words, they both accept (T1) and (T2). However, it is important to realize that there is another use of the term "foundationalism" present in the contemporary philosophical discussion. This understanding of foundationalism focuses on the (strong) foundationalist's claim that we must have a secure foundation (that is, a foundation that is infallible, certain, immune to doubt, or the like) for our beliefs to be rational, otherwise irrationality or scepticism follows. On this account someone is a foundationalist if he or she also accepts (T3) and (T4) and maybe also (T5)—Plantinga calls a person a *classical foundationalist* if he or she accepts (T3), (T4) *and* (T5)[21]—and someone who denies this is an anti-foundationalist.

Let me illustrate this use of the notion of foundationalism with two quotations. Stout claims that "Either we are foundationalists, and thus stand within the tradition called Cartesian, or we define ourselves in opposition to all that [as anti-Cartesian or anti-foundationalists]."[22] If one is a foundationalist, one is a Cartesian, i.e., a strong foundationalist; on the other hand, if one is not a Cartesian, one is not a foundationalist. This understanding of foundationalism is also present in much "postmodern" philosophy. Schrag writes:

> One of the dominant features of the postmodern philosophical challenge resides in its reaction against the epistemological paradigm of modernity. The knowledge claims issuing from a Cartesian ego-cogito, the reflections of a Kantian transcendental ego, and the perceptions of the sensorial subject of British empiricism have all become problematized. The quest for *epistemic certainty* and the search for *unimpeachable foundations* for knowledge fall under indictment.[23]

On this understanding, foundationalism is contrasted with *fallibilism* (roughly, the view that we are nowhere entirely immune from the possibility of error), and consequently it is impossible to be a foundationalist and a fallibilist at the same time.[24] The way I have defined foundationalism contrasts it with coherentism, and it is possible to be a foundationalist *and* a fallibilist at the same time, *if* one is not a strong foundationalist. It is of course possible to define foundationalism in the way Stout and Schrag do, but the problem then is to make sense of people who call themselves (at least implicitly) foundationalists but reject strong and classical foundationalism. The contemporary discussion in epistemology then becomes hard to conceptualize, because much of the discussion has been concerned with different versions of weak foundationalism.[25]

So on my account of foundationalism, all foundationalists claim that a rational belief is either supported by evidence or properly basic, even though they disagree about when a belief is properly basic. Further, they typically accept the proportionality principle, that the strength of a non-basic belief should depend upon the degree of support from the foundation (the basic beliefs). According to the foundational evidentialist:

> a belief is *rational* only if that belief is either (*a*) a properly basic belief, or (*b*) it can be shown by acceptable methods of inference to be evidentially supported by properly basic beliefs or other already justified (derived) beliefs; and (*c*) the strength of the non-basic beliefs are proportional to the support from the foundation.

So some beliefs constitute evidence for some other beliefs, but what more precisely is evidence and what could function as evidence?

1.3   EXPLICATING EVIDENCE

Generally speaking, something *A* constitutes evidence or a reason for something else *B* if it supports (though not necessarily establishes) *B* in an appropriate way. In ordinary English something can be evidence for something else in two different ways. On the one hand, we can say that the belief that atoms are made of protons, electrons, and neutrons, or my belief that the train leaves the station in one hour, rests on evidence. On the other hand, we can say that my belief that I have two hands or my belief that there is a tree in front of me now rest on evidence. However, "evidence" is used in two different ways here. In the first cases we believe something on the basis of other beliefs we hold, i.e., inferentially, but in the second we believe something directly or immediately. In the second cases, in contrast to the first, one does not acquire the beliefs by an argument or inference but by a first-hand experience. So we can make a distinction between two classes of evidence:

1. *Inferential* or *Propositional Evidence:* Evidence consisting of accepted propositions or beliefs from which other propositions or beliefs are inferred.
2. *Non-Inferential* or *Experiential Evidence:* Evidence consisting of an appeal to immediate experience.

The philosophical use of the term "evidence" normally includes only (1), and that is the way I will use it. (However, as we will see, not all philosophers are aware of this ambiguity in the ordinary use of the notion of evidence.) Hence a belief (or proposition) can constitute evidence for another belief only if the second one is based on or inferred from the first belief. (Recall Wittgenstein's remark about the philosophical justification of the belief that "cats don't grow on trees.")

We can, following Wolterstorff, call the beliefs that constitute the evidence and thereby the base that supports the inferred belief *databeliefs*.[26] However, since we do not want to tie the notion of evidence to a particular meta-position, foundationalism, the databeliefs could either be *intrinsically* (foundationalism) or just *functionally* (coherentism) more basic than the inferred propositions or beliefs. So we can say:

> A proposition or belief *A* could constitute evidence for another proposition or belief *B* only if it is epistemologically more basic, either intrinsically or functionally, than *B*.

However, if we restrict the term "evidence" to inferential evidence (evidence consisting of other accepted propositions or beliefs that evidentially support a proposition or belief) it is helpful if we have another term which covers the other (ordinary) use of "evidence" (evidence consisting of an appeal to immediate experiences). Let us follow Plantinga and call that use of the word *grounds*.[27] Sense experience or memory are examples of grounds, of *non-inferential justifiers* of our beliefs—one does not get a belief by argument or inference from such experience. Kenny writes: "It is a mistake, I believe, to regard propositions which are evident to the senses as being known by inference from propositions about appearances: my knowledge that it is snowing is not a deduction from propositions about snowlike visual impressions."[28] Rather it is the experience of snowing that non-inferentially justifies Kenny in holding that belief. So we can distinguish between:

3. The *grounds* for a belief, that is, the non-inferential justifiers (like sense experience, memory, etc.) of the belief.
4. The *evidence* for a belief, that is, the inferential justifiers (involving arguments and inference) of the belief.

Let us now turn to the question about what *methods of inference* are, according to the formalists, acceptable in general and in science in particular. This is an important issue because it does not help to have a set of infallible basic beliefs if we cannot connect in a rational (non-arbitrary) way the rest of the beliefs we accept to this secure foundation. If this is not possible most of our beliefs would still, despite the infallible foundation, be rationally unjustified.

1.4   THE RULES OF SCIENTIFIC RATIONALITY

The formal view of science is, typically, a form of either strong or weak foundationalism. It divides the statements of science in two kinds, and justification runs one way from singular observation statement to scientific laws or theories. The observational beliefs are taken as given or, in our terminology, properly basic beliefs. In conformity with the evidential principle science requires evidence for what it accepts. This means that scientific laws or theories must be supported by empirical data. The observation statements provide evidence for the scientific laws or theories in question.

If science is based on observational statements, how can we justify the step from singular statements to the general claims that constitute scientists' theories? The answer is that scientific theories can, with the help of appropriate *rules,* be tested against observation statements. This "logic of science" makes the testing of theories and the choice between competing theories rational and objective.[29] So the standard task of philosophy of science is to try to formulate the rules in accordance with the scientific hypotheses and theories that are to be accepted or rejected. It was Frege's discovery in 1879 of a complete algorithm for the elementary theory of deduction that:

inspired the hope that one might do the same for so called "inductive logic"—that the "scientific method" might turn out to be an algorithm, and that these two algorithms . . . might exhaustively describe or "rationally reconstruct" not just *scientific* rationality, but all rationality worthy of the name.[30]

What type of rules are then appropriate to use in science? On this issue the formalists do not agree, but they do agree that these rules must exist for the assessment of theories in science to be rational. Thus one of the essential theses of the formal model of rationality is that *rationality is rule-governed* or determined by rules. That is, rule-following is a necessary condition for rationality. What follows can be seen as an illustration of that thesis.

The first attempt to specify these rules was, as Putnam noted in the quotation above, made by trying to create an *inductive logic*. Theories can be derived from observational statements by inductive logic. The relation between theory and observation statements can be seen as having the same structure as a good argument: observational statements are the premises and the theory is the conclusion. Since deductive logic functioned as the model for inductive arguments, it was thought that just as there is a necessary connection between premises and conclusion in a deductive argument, there would be a necessary connection in a properly constructed inductive argument too. The only difference is that different rules are used in these two forms of argumentation. If this project proved successful, then a good inductive argument (like a good deductive argument) *proves* its conclusion, if the premises are true. For example, for many philosophers of the past the enormous amount of inductive evidence supporting Newton's mechanics was thought to establish conclusively the truth of the theory. This thought, that for an inductive argument to be successful it must establish its conclusion with necessity, was (and is to some degree still) a widely accepted assumption. But it was that assumption that made it, as Brown points out, so easy for Hume to challenge the rationality of induction:

> Hume, for example, could argue that we have no rational basis for accepting any inductive argument simply by pointing out that in such arguments it is always *possible* for the premises to be true while the conclusion is false. In other words, Hume took the existence of a necessary tie between premises and conclusion, which is the

characteristic stamp of a valid deductive argument, as a requirement for every rational argument, and this criterion was long accepted by those who would defend induction.[31]

However, many formalists, like Carnap and Hempel, acknowledged the impossibility of conclusively verifying any scientific theory. Instead they claimed that acceptable inductive arguments need to show only that the conclusion is probable. A theory must be testable by observation and experiment. The result of the test need not be conclusive, but it must provide a rule for determining the likelihood of the theory. A successful inductive argument need only show its conclusion to be *probable*. For science to be rational it must be possible to develop a set of rules that allow us to decide with certainty how much support the available evidence gives to what is proposed as its conclusion. The required rules are, on this account, provided by *probability theory*. Hempel writes: "it ought to be possible, one feels, to set up purely formal criteria of confirmation in a manner similar to that in which deductive logic provides purely formal criteria for the validity of deductive inference."[32] On this view the inductive evidence that supported Newton's mechanics did not prove that it was true, but merely conferred a high degree of probability to it (so of course it could be false). According to Carnap it is the notion of logical probability that is of special importance for scientific rationality:

> We say to a scientist: "You tell me that I can rely on this law in making a certain prediction. How well established is the law? How trustworthy is the prediction? " . . . I believe that, once inductive logic is sufficiently developed, he could reply: "This hypothesis is confirmed to degree .8 on the basis of the available evidence." A scientist who answers in this way is making a statement about a logical relation between the evidence and the hypothesis in question. . . . His statement that the value of this probability is .8 is, in this context, not a synthetic (empirical) statement, but an analytic one. It is analytic because no empirical investigation is demanded.[33]

Here we can clearly see the *a priori* character of the formal view of science. No real examination of actual scientific practice is needed to determine when a theory is sufficiently supported by evidence for a scientist to be rational in accepting it. What the scientists themselves think or do is, therefore, strictly speaking, irrelevant to formulating an appropriate set of rules for scientific rationality. So it is the philosophical model of rationality that has epistemological authority, not scientific practice itself.

Bayes developed this probabilistic approach to theory-choice. The law that bears his name, which follows by deduction from the axioms of probability theory, provides an algorithm for adjusting our estimates of the probability of a set of rival theories as more evidence becomes available. Some formalists have developed the Bayesian model of inference and decision making even further and applied it to science—assuming that scientists can be or should be seen as what might be called *Bayesian agents*.[34] These formalists claim that Bayes's theorem provides scientists with an appropriate rule for measuring the degree of support the evidence lends a theory or hypothesis under consideration. And rational scientists use this algorithm in their theory-choices; that is, scientists should be Bayesian agents. One version of Bayes's theorem can be stated as follows:

$$P(h/e.k) = P(h/k) \times P(e/h.k)/P(e/k)$$

The claim is that $P(h/e. k)$, that is, the probability of a certain hypothesis h given the relevant evidence e and the background evidence k, depends on three factors $P(h/k)$, $P(e/h.k)$, and $P(e/k)$. $P(h/e.k)$ represents the probability of the evidence given that the hypothesis h is true and given the background evidence k ("." stands for "and"). The background evidence k is the knowledge that scientists take for granted before new evidence turns up, and e represents the new evidence or the latest piece of evidence known by scientists. (This distinction between e and k can be made in different ways.) $P(h/k)$ (read: the probability of h, given k) represents the scientists' initial degree of belief in the theory, or the *prior probability* of the theory, that is, the probability scientists assign to the theory before considering the detailed evidence of observation cited in its support. $P(e/k)$ stands for the probability of the new evidence e, given the background evidence k.

Say that h is Newton's theory of motion and k the background evidence available to Newtonian scientists (like Kepler's law of planetary motion and Galileo's law of fall) and e the new evidence implied by Newton's theory of motion (like the existence of the planet Neptune and the behavior of the tides). Then, with the help of Bayes's thorem, these formalists claim, we can measure the degree of support the evidence gives the theory and determine whether the theory-choices these scientists made were rationally justifiable.

Other philosophers have followed Popper in accepting Hume's criticism of induction. According to Popper it is impossible to develop an inductive logic of any sort, since no appropriate rules can be found to guide induction. All attempts to develop an algorithm for deciding when to accept a theory have failed. However, he agrees with the other formalists that scientific theories have the logical form of universal generalizations like "All swans are white" or "All A are B" and that scientific rationality should be a matter of logic. The inductive formalists run into trouble when they try to *support* such general claims with evidence (observational statements). But we can, according to Popper, avoid these problems if we use evidence only to *refute* such scientific claims, since the falsity of "All swans are white" follows deductively from "This swan is not white." In other words, falsification requires only deductive logic. Therefore, we can have the necessary tie between premises and conclusion that Hume demanded and which guarantees the rationality of the argument.

So for Popper all that science requires to be rational is that scientists have an algorithm or rule for when evidence logically falsifies a theory, and *modus tollens* provides us with that, since it allows us to determine when a theory should be rejected. (*Modus tollens* states that from "If A, then B" and "Not B," we can logically infer "Therefore, not A.") This means that the rationality of a theory does not depend on whether we can support it with evidence, but whether we actively seek evidence that would refute the theory and whether it has survived such tests (that is, been corroborated). In other words, Popper rejects the evidential principle. A consequence of this rejection is that Popper must also reject the proportionality principle since it is based on a measure of evidential support. It states that one's level of acceptance of theory should be proportioned to the evidence supporting it. But this is not possible because we do not have any algorithm that can measure the degree of support a theory has on a particular body of evidence. Popper replaces the proportionality principle with what could be called the "principle of tentativity." According to him, it is not rational for a person to accept any (at least) scientific theory fully, that is, to stop actively trying to falsify it. Generalized, this demand could be stated as follows:

> *The Principle of Tentativity:* All rational propositions
> or beliefs should be only tentatively accepted, that is,

one should never stop actively looking for defeaters (counter-evidence) to them.

Popper also rejects the thought that we must begin from a (more or less) secure foundation (from properly basic beliefs). We can start anywhere we want as long as we treat our starting-point as a conjecture and constantly try to falsify this conjecture. Scientific claims are rational if they can be falsified and have survived some tests. But according to Popper, *modus tollens* could function in the way it should only if scientists can say *beforehand* under what circumstances they are prepared to give up their theory; and if these instances of falsification occur scientists should immediately reject the falsified theory and start to look for a better one.[35] Rationality requires that scientists, so to speak, put their cards on the table in advance. We can summarize Poppers' principle of falsification in this way:

> It is (scientifically) rational for a person to accept a theory (proposition or belief) only if (*a*) it could, by acceptable methods of inference (*modus tollens*), be falsified by an observable situation, and (*b*) what would count as falsifiers have been laid down beforehand, and (*c*) that person actively tries to falsify it, and (*d*) it has survived some previous tests.

All formalists take the rationality of science to be a matter of working out the correct logical relation between different sets of propositions—observational statements and theories. They all accept the logicality thesis. Their account of scientific methods and standards is intended to be universal and ahistorical, because the rules of formal logic are valid everywhere and at all times. According to Lakatos the "central problem in philosophy of science is the problem of stating *universal* conditions under which a theory is scientific."[36] Scientific methods and standards of rationality are universal in the sense that they apply to all scientific theories alike, and ahistorical in that they are supposed to apply to all scientific theories of the past, present, and the future. Scheffler writes:

> Underlying historical changes in theory, there is moreover a constancy of logic and method which unifies each scientific age with that which preceded it and with that which is yet to follow. Such constancy comprises not merely the canons of formal deduction,

but also those criteria by which hypotheses are confronted with the test of experience and subjected to comparative evaluation. We do not, surely, have explicit and general formulations of such criteria at the present time. But they are embodied clearly enough in scientific practice to enable communication and agreement in a wide variety of specific cases. Such communication and consensus indicate that there is a codifiable methodology underlying the conduct of the scientific enterprise.[37]

So the formalists accept, in general, some version of what Zahar has called the "stability thesis.":[38]

> *The Stability Thesis:* Rationality and scientific method
> are invariant over time and domain.

The thesis states that the rationality of science does not change drastically, but stays stable, or at least fairly stable, under the progress of science. The methodological rules of science have not undergone any, or at least not any major, epistemic revolutions.

1.5   EXPLICATING RULE-RATIONALITY

Let us now try to explicate the understanding of rationality that is implicit in the accounts of scientific rationality we have considered.[39] The central claim of the formalist, besides the evidential thesis, is that *all rational beliefs (actions and evaluations) must be arrived at by means of the appropriate rules.* The claim is that rationality is rule-governed or determined by rules. This thesis I will call the "rule principle," and we may define it in the following way:

> *The Rule Principle:* A belief (action or evaluation) is
> rational only if it is obtained by following the appro-
> priate rules.

Alternatively, we could say that a person is rational in accepting a belief only if it is arrived at by following the appropriate rules. The thought is that an ideally rational agent always has a rule available by which he or she can determine whether a belief is rational to accept. Now what we need to know is what it means more exactly to say that rationality is rule-governed and what kinds of rules are involved.

However, before we try to find an answer to these questions let us look at the motivation behind this idea of rationality. The traditional motivation behind the formalist's claim that the rule principle is a necessary condition for rationality has to do with the need to establish a proper connection between the infallible foundation (the properly basic beliefs) and the rest of our (non-basic) beliefs. Somehow we need to be able to transfer the security of the foundation to the rest of what we believe. The principles of inference by which we move from basic to non-basic beliefs must be as secure as possible (according to the strong foundationalist, even infallible) in the sense that they must with the highest degree of probability (or, according to the strong foundationalist, with absolute certainty) take us from true basic beliefs to true derived beliefs. To satisfy this demand, the only acceptable methods of inference by which our non-basic beliefs can be evidentially supported by the properly basic ones seem to be the ones that can function as clearly defined rules, since they can then be free from arbitrariness.

Another motive is of course the great benefit such a set of rules would have. If we have universally applicable rules, then all who begin with the same premises must come up with the same conclusion. There is no room for diverging judgments or opinions regarding what the correct conclusion is. Everyone who applies the rule-governed procedure in a correct way must reach the same conclusion. This is one reason why the formalists take mathematics and logic as paradigms for rationality, since in these fields such a connection between premises and conclusions is possible. In mathematics anyone, anywhere who tries to multiply 320 by 123 will, if using the appropriate rules (that is, proceeding rationally), arrive at the same answer. Or think of a computer program as a set of rules. The only thing we have to do to obtain a rational answer to a problem is to give the computer the relevant information (premises) and of course to know what commands the computer understands. From this information the computer, by using the rules, is able to reach *the* right answer (conclusion)—given of course that the information is correct.

The key idea is, as Brown points out, that there exists both a definite solution and a definite procedure for arriving at that solution, and all who follow that procedure must reach the same result. So if mathematics and logic provide the paradigm for rationality then "rational results must be universal, necessary and determined by rules."[40] The idea is that in matters of rationality:

> Any number of ideal rational thinkers faced with the same situation and suffering through similar throes of reasoning agony will necessarily come up with the same answer eventually, as long as reasoning alone is the ultimate justification for their conclusion. Otherwise reasoning would be subjective, not objective as arithmetic is. A conclusion reached by reasoning would be a matter of preference, not one of necessity. Now *some* people may believe this of reasoning, but rational thinkers understand that a valid argument must be *universally* compelling, otherwise it is simply not a valid argument.[41]

So rational beliefs are those that follow necessarily when universally valid rules are applied to a set of premises. The standards of rationality must be universal and necessary to function as the *appropriate* rules, as the procedure we need for deciding when a belief is rational to accept. Typically, the formalist claims that the rules of rationality must be applicable in any theoretical context or to any set of beliefs, and all rational persons must therefore arrive at the same conclusion in all areas of life. *Universality* is a necessary condition for rationality. Here we can see that it is formal logic that functions as the ideal. In formal logic the validity of an argument is independent of the subject matter, and a valid argument is valid in all possible worlds. So, independently of which practice the beliefs belong to, the logic of assessment allows us to determine to what degree they are supported by a particular body of evidence.

However, it is not enough that the standards of rationality are universal in scope and that all rational people arrive at the same assessment, since, as Brown points out, the universal agreement could just be the result of "a massive coincidence," not a result achieved through reasoning.[42] Again, in logic the conclusion follows necessarily from the premises if the argument is a deductively valid one. Therefore, a conclusion of what belief to accept as rational must follow *necessarily* from the body of evidence that supports it.

What sort of rules is it that the formalists are looking for? They are rules which, when applied to a problem, guarantee a solution in a finite numbers of steps, that is, *algorithms*.[43] Venn diagrams, truth tables in formal logic, and most computer programs are examples of algorithms. Probability theory is another example of an algorithm (Bayes's theorem) to decide how much support a particular theory has on the basis of a particular body of evidence, and according to Popper *modus tollens* is an algorithm that can tell us when a belief is falsified and should be rejected.

It is important to notice that the application of algorithms requires no essential knowledge of the content of any of the theories or beliefs at issue or of the situation in which they arise. Algorithms are *formal* structures. For example, the evaluation of scientific theories against observational beliefs requires no detailed knowledge of the scientific issues involved, no knowledge in detail of the content of those theories or the observational beliefs. From this it is not hard to understand why logic and mathematics are the ideals for the formalists, because this *practice-* or *context-independence* is what is characteristic of formal logic. Evaluating the validity of a well-informed argument demands no real knowledge of the subject matter in question, and no expertise is needed on a topic for the rational enquirer to be able to assess whether a particular belief is rational.

1.6   WHAT SCIENTIFIC RATIONALITY IS

So far we have mainly focused on what the formalists take the scientific standards of rationality to be and their requirements for accepting some standards as appropriate (that is, the satisfaction of the rule principle). Let us now examine what conception of the nature of rationality is used (explicitly or implicitly) by the formalists.

Both a deontological and a means-end conception of rationality can be found among formal philosophers of science. (And this is, as we will see later, not something unique to the formalists but something almost all philosophers of science have in common. I will, therefore, also use material from philosophers of science who cannot be classified as formalists.) Let us start with the deontological conception. On this account rationality is understood broadly speaking as a normative notion, and more specifically this normativity is expressed in terms of obligations and duties with respect to our beliefs. A deontological conception characteristically implies the claim that rationality is a matter of meeting norms or fulfilling duties. This means that scientists have duties or responsibilities with respect to their believing and theory-choices. Lakatos provides us with a good illustration of this understanding of scientific rationality:

> *Sophisticated methodological falsificationism* offers new standards for intellectual honesty. Justificationist honesty demanded the acceptance of only what was proven and the rejection of everything unproven. Neojustificationist honesty demanded the specification of the probability of any hypothesis in the light of the available empirical evidence. The honesty of naive falsificationism demanded the testing of the falsifiable and the rejection of the unfalsifiable and the falsified. Finally, the honesty of sophisticated falsificationism demanded that one should try to look at things from different points of view, to put forward new theories which anticipate novel facts, and to reject theories which have been superseded by more powerful ones.[44]

The advocates of scientific rationality Lakatos refers to do not agree about what this intellectual honesty that scientists should have actually consists in (what the norms of belief or theory-choice are), but they all agree that rationality or justification should be understood normatively, as a matter of being intellectually honest or fulfilling intellectual duties.

On the other hand, scientific rationality is often understood as a kind of means-end rationality. Given the aims of science, science is rational to the extent that its methods or methodological rules helps to satisfy these aims. Hempel writes:

> in so far as a proposed methodological theory of science is to afford an account of scientific inquiry as a rational pursuit, it will have to specify certain goals of scientific inquiry as well as some methodological principles observed in their pursuit; finally, it will have to exhibit the instrumental rationality of the principles in relation to the goals. Only to the extent that this can be done does the conception of science as the exemplar of rationality appear to be viable.[45]

The rationality of science (or more narrowly scientific theory-choice) depends on whether scientific methods and rules are instrumentally efficacious in achieving the aims or ends of science. So scientific rationality requires two things:

1. A specification of the *aims of science*.
2. A specification of the *standards of comparison*.

First, a specification of the aims of science is needed. What should the scientific theories be aiming at? Truth, predictability, increased problem-solving capacity, or what? Here the formalists as well as other philosophers of science give diverse accounts of the proper *goals of science*.[46] Second, a specification of the standards (or the methodology) that can determine what *means* is needed, that is, which theory is most efficient for reaching the goal of science, however it is specified. And also on this issue concerning what the appropriate *standards of comparison* are, philosophers of science we have considered offer different accounts.

Newton-Smith claims that four conditions must be fulfilled for a rational theory-choice to be possible according to a means-end model of scientific rationality:

(1) The scientific community had as its goal the goal posited by the model.

(2) On the evidence then available, the new theory T2 was superior to the old theory T1 (relative to the principle of comparison specified by the model).

(3) The scientific community perceived the superiority of T2 over T1.

(4) This perception motivated the members of the community to abandon T1 in favour of T2.[47]

However, we have to ask ourselves, do these philosophers (illustrated by Lakatos, Hempel, and Newton-Smith) have incompatible conceptions of what scientific rationality is, or can these accounts somehow be combined, and if so, how? I think it is possible to unify them, in the way I did in the second chapter, into one single conception of the nature of scientific rationality. Let us start by noticing that, according to the formalist, scientists' intellectual duty consists, roughly, of accepting a theory only if, and to the extent that, it can be supported by sufficient evidence and of developing a set of rules (or algorithms) that can measure the degree (probability) to which the theory is supported by the evidence. But this can also be expressed in terms of means-end rationality: scientists have an obligation to give good reasons for why they think that a theory is better than rival ones in reaching the goal the production of theories are thought to be aiming at. In fact, often already in the formulation of the evidential principle, which scientists (and the rest of us) have a duty to try to satisfy according to the formal evidentialist, a certain end of theoretical rationality is presupposed, namely truth. Recall the way we explicated the principle: it is rational to accept a proposition only if there are good reasons to believe that it is true.

So as long as deontological rationality can be thought of as goal-directed—as an intellectual duty to satisfy certain epistemic or non-epistemic ends—is it possible to understand it in terms of means-end rationality. Hence the conclusion we should draw is that the deontological and the means-end ways of understanding the nature of scientific rationality present in the discussion in philosophy of science are, at least, compatible with each other.

1.7   THE DEMARCATION STRATEGY: SCIENCE AND NON-SCIENCE

Some of the rules (algorithms) we have considered are intended not only to specify what scientific rationality consists in, but also to function as *criteria of demarcation* separating science from non-science. Typically, but not always, formalists have been very skeptical towards everything that cannot be covered by scientific methods and standards of rationality. In fact some of them have claimed that scientific rationality is the only form of rationality that exists. For them to fail to be scientific is the same as to fail to be rational. On such an account, all theories or beliefs must conform to scientific standards of rationality.

For the positivists the criterion of demarcation is the same as the one that separates meaningful statements from meaningless ones—the *verification principle*. So it has a twofold function (*a*) to demarcate meaningful statements from meaningless ones, and (*b*) to demarcate science from non-science. Ayer writes:

> The criterion which we use to test the genuineness of apparent statements of fact is the criterion of verifiability. We say that a sentence is factually significant to any given person, if, and only if, he knows how to verify the proposition which it purports to express—that is, if he knows what observations would lead him,

under certain conditions, to accept the proposition as being true, or reject it as being false.[48]

According to this principle of verification a statement is not meaningful unless it is (in principle) possible to verify it. Another way of saying the same thing is to say that statements have cognitive meaning if and only if they are (in principle) empirically verifiable. All genuine *synthetic statements* (roughly, statements whose truth depends on how the empirical world is) are thought to be of this kind. However, the positivists also accept another kind of statement as meaningful, *analytic statements* (roughly, statements whose truth depends only on their meaning) like 2 + 2 = 4 and all bachelors are unmarried men. Let us, therefore, define the principle of verification in the following way:

> *The Verification Principle:* A statement has cognitive meaning if and only if it is either analytic or empirically verifiable.

The principle states that every belief must be based on observation or observational statements to have any cognitive meaning, or be an analytic statement. The principle of verification is taken as a rule which can relate all meaningful statements to the empirical foundation of science. It is supposed to function as an algorithm that can tell us what statements are cognitively meaningful in a finite number of steps. And after we have applied this rule to a statement we can use the rules of inductive logic to show its truth or degree of probability.

Popper's and Lakato's criteria of demarcation are not meant to draw a line between meaningful and meaningless statements, but only demarcate science from non-science. Popper writes: "I personally was never interested in the so-called problem of meaning; on the contrary, it appeared to me a verbal problem, a typical pseudo-problem. I was interested only in the problem of demarcation, i.e. in finding a criterion of the scientific character of theories."[49] He explicitly rejects the positivists' view that what is non-scientific is cognitively meaningless. "I thus felt that if a theory is found to be non-scientific, or 'metaphysical' (as we may say), it is not thereby found to be unimportant, or insignificant, or 'meaningless,' or 'nonsensical.' "[50] Nevertheless both Popper and Lakatos claim that the search for a rule that can demarcate science from non-science is of utmost importance, and they are, to say the least, in general skeptical towards theories or claims that they classify as non-science or pseudo-science. Lakatos claims that the demarcation problem is of "vital social and political relevance."[51] And his negative attitude towards what falls outside the scope of science becomes evident when he for example says that "they [Freud's and Marx's theories] do not add up to a genuine research programme and are, on the whole, worthless."[52]

In general one can say that the formalist is quite skeptical towards theories, beliefs, or claims to which the standards of scientific rationality are not applicable. The reason why this is so has to do, I think, with the formalist's conviction that the universality we find in logic should be the ideal for rationality, and therefore the formalist only reluctantly moves to standards of rationality whose scope of application is limited to a particular domain or practice. Therefore it is of great importance for the formalists who want to defend metaphysics, religion, or the like, to show that it is possible to apply the same, or at least very similar, standards of rationality to these practices.

2.   Formal Evidentialism

I will call this formal model of scientific rationality if it is expanded to a general model of rationality, *formal evidentialism,* and the typical representative of it a *formal evidentialist.* What I take to be characteristic for formal evidentialists is that they accept both the evidential principle and the rule principle, and often also the proportionality principle, and they are typically foundationalists. Again, the general idea is that rational people always and everywhere first collect good evidence for and against a particular theory. They then examine the relationship between the theory and the evidence so as to determine the probability that the theory is true on the basis of the evidence. They then believe or doubt the theory with a firmness proportional to the probability that it has based on the evidence. To quote just two philosophers as examples of persons who accept evidentialism as a general model of rationality:

> We advocate evidentialism in epistemology. What we call evidentialism is the view that the epistemic justification of a belief is determined by the quality of the believer's evidence for the belief.[53]

A belief will fail to be rational if it is based on evidence in the wrong way or if it based on the wrong sort of evidence.[54]

However, what I also take as characteristic for formal evidentialists, and as the first part of the name indicates, is that they all adopt a formal approach to rationality. This means that they characteristically understand the issue of rationality as a matter of logic and conceptual analysis only. Standards of rationality can be formulated independently of the subject matter—science, religion, everyday life, and the like. The logic of rationality or the conceptual truths about rationality are applicable universally—everywhere and at all times. Gärdenfors, for example, tends toward such a view when he writes:

> Furthermore, the epistemological theories are *conceptualistic* [or non-empirical] in the sense that they do not presume any account of an "external world" outside of the individuals' epistemic states [i.e., states of belief]. It is true that the epistemic inputs in general have their origin in such a "reality," but I argue that epistemic states and changes of such states as well as the rationality criteria governing epistemic dynamics [i.e., changes of belief] can be, and should be, formulated independent of the factual connections between the epistemic inputs and the outer world.[55]

Formal evidentialists do no think it is necessary to pay any serious attention to the actual agents or to the actual practices of rationality to be able to develop an appropriate model of rationality. And this is exactly what is constantly lacking in their accounts of rationality: a detailed analysis of how people in different practices and cultures actually form and regulate or revise their beliefs. Sociological and historical studies, and the like, can at best provide illustrations of different practices having been pursued as some proposed rules of rationality prescribe. But such studies have no regulative function and put no constraints on a proper model of rationality. Therefore, the standards for rationality are *epistemically independent* of the actual agents and the actual practices the agents are involved in.

2.1 THE LOCUS OF RATIONALITY

What is it that can be rational? According to the formal evidentialist many things can be rational: propositions, beliefs, persons,

decisions, strategies, and the like. But I will claim that their commitment to the logicality thesis, that rationality can be assimilated to
that of a logical system, leads them—as they sometimes admit—to
the view that *rationality is ultimately a question concerning what
logical relation should hold between different sets of propositions.* All
other uses of the notion of rationality can be derived from this. The
locus of rationality is strictly speaking in systems of propositions.
The rules of rationality, as in logic, establish the proper relation between these propositions. What really matters is the logical relation
between evidence and theory or, in the terms of foundationalism,
the logical relation between basic and non-basic propositions. And
a consequence of this, as Brown points out, is that if "a proposition
follows from, say, a body of evidence on the basis of a set of rules
[that] is an *objective feature* of that proposition . . ."[56] And Wolterstorff
writes, commenting on Alvin Goldman's view of justified belief: "The
word 'justified' would pick out a certain merit in beliefs, a desirable
feature of beliefs; 'unjustified' would pick out a demerit in beliefs, a
blemish."[57] So a central assumption of formal evidentialism is that:

> rationality is ultimately a *property* a proposition can
> have or lack.

Formal evidentialists believe that when we speak about a *rational belief* we are concerned with belief in some propositions that
have the property of being rationally justified, and when we speak of
a *rational person* we are talking about an individual who accepts or
believes propositions that are rationally justified. However, typically,
formal evidentialists speak about rational beliefs not rational propositions or statements, and I will do the same when characterizing their
understanding of rationality. But we must keep in mind that this is
strictly speaking not where they take the locus of rationality to be. So
according to the formal evidentialist, the notion of rational belief is
taken as fundamental and the notion of a rational person is derived
from an analysis of the former. This means that a rational person is
someone who accepts or believes only those propositions which are
shown to be rational by appropriate rules, no more and no less. A
rational person is an individual whose beliefs have the (objective)
property of being rational. What a rational person is, is derived out of
a proper analysis of when a belief is rational—he or she is someone
whose beliefs meet those standards.

This explains why there is no need to undertake an analysis of how actual human beings form and regulate or revise their beliefs and why this does not put any constraints on rationality, because rationality is not a relation between an agent of some kind and some of his or her believings, but strictly speaking only a matter of a logical relation between beliefs or propositions. So *what a rational belief is puts constraints on what a rational agent is, but the opposite is not the case.* Therefore it is important to notice that when formal evidentialists talk about a rational person they normally have in mind (explicitly or implicitly) a theoretical construction, an *ideally rational agent,* a being who meets all the demands put on rational beliefs. In this sense we can say that it is rational to believe or act only as the ideal agent would. Such an analysis of rationality and related epistemic notions, seems to be given by, for instance, Hintikka. He writes:

> Our results are not directly applicable to what is true or false in the actual world of ours. They tell us something definite about the truth and falsity of statements only in a world in which everybody follows the consequences of what he knows as far as they lead him. . . . They are applicable to actual statements only in so far as our world approximates one of the "most knowledgeable of possible worlds," as we may call them, or can be made to approximate one of them by calling people's attention to the consequences of what they know.[58]

This is, according to Horwich, the way we should understand the Bayesian account of rationality. "More specifically, the Bayesian approach rests upon the fundamental principle: (B) That the degrees of belief of an ideally rational person conform to the mathematical principles of probability theory."[59]

Hence formal evidentialists work with *idealized models of rationality,* that is, with models that try to give necessary and sufficient conditions for when a belief or an agent is rational, everywhere and at all times—in any possible world. These philosophers strive to establish a conception of rationality which would be appropriate for any reasoning being, which would be good no matter what practice the agent is involved in, and no matter what the world is like. The logic of rationality or the conceptual truths about rationality are applicable universally—everywhere and at all times. These idealized models will later be contrasted with *realistic models of rationality,* models which try to give the necessary and sufficient conditions for when agents of a particular kind and in a particular kind of situation are rational in their believing. On the realistic models, who the actual agent of rationality is puts some constraints on rationality and rational belief, whereas that is not the case with the idealized models. (I will later try to show that these idealized accounts of rationality, when applied to human beings, violate the axiom of reasonable demand.)

According to formal evidentialists, rationality is basically a property a belief may have or lack. This means that their conception of rationality is strictly speaking *person-independent,* if by that we mean that the standards of rationality are not affected by what kind of beings they are supposed to apply to. In other words, since rationality is an objective feature of a belief it does not really matter who holds or rejects it or what kind of situation that individual is in. Rationality is ultimately connected to propositions or beliefs, not persons or agents, and therefore the status of the belief (as rational) does not change.

2.2   EXTERNAL AND INTERNAL RATIONALITY

What standards of rationality then must a proposition or belief satisfy, whether it belongs to the scientific practice or some other practices? Alternatively, how ought an ideally rational agent govern his or her system of beliefs? We have already identified some of these standards, like the evidential and proportionality principle. I shall here introduce a distinction between "external" and "internal" standards of rationality that might be useful for seeing what unites different discussions of rationality with each other and help us pick out further standards of rationality.

Sometimes one wonders if philosophers ever speak about the same thing. "Rationality" seems to be a word with many different meanings. Elster distinguishes more than twenty senses of rationality.[60] (This question will be considered in more detail in chapter 11.) Two common and perhaps quite basic ways of viewing rationality are, on the one hand, to treat it as a matter of *logical consistency,* and on the other hand, to see it as a matter of the *grounds* or *reasons for accepting beliefs.*[61] How could these different ways of discussing rationality be brought together? Is it at all possible?

My proposal is that we can bring many of these different ways of speaking about rationality together under one roof if we focus on the agent (or agents) of rationality—whether the agent is understood as a theoretical construction (i.e., an ideal agent) of some sort or an actual individual—or on systems of beliefs. Then it can be seen that some questions can be raised about the internal relations of a set of beliefs and some about its external relations, between the set of beliefs and other sets of beliefs. If we do this we can see, I think, that rationality as logical consistency deals with one aspect of the proper regulation of the external relation of an agent's belief system.

Roughly the idea is that the internal standards of rationality deal with how an agent ought to govern his or her *internal affairs,* concerning the rational regulation of already accepted beliefs. What we must take into account is only the relations between the beliefs already present in an agent's system, and everything else is bracketed, for example, questions concerning whether the way they were accepted was rationally justifiable. Here the question is what internal standards people must meet when they already have accepted a set of beliefs. External standards, on the other hand, state how an agent ought to govern his or her *external affairs,* concerning the rational regulation of beliefs not yet accepted and the relations between already accepted beliefs and other people's beliefs. What we must take into account here is the relations between an agent's own belief system and things that are at the present outside that system. Here the question is what external standards a belief must satisfy before it is allowed to enter or stay in an agent's belief system. We can explicate internal and external rationality in the following way:

> *Internal Rationality:* The standards of rationality used to determine whether or not agents are rational in the way they regulate the relations between the beliefs in their belief systems.

> *External Rationality:* The standards of rationality used to determine whether or not agents are rational in the way they regulate the relations between the beliefs already in their belief systems and things that are (at present) outside these systems.

Two of the external standards of rationality we have seen that the formal evidentialist advocates are the evidential principle and what we might call the "principle of proper basicality": the principle that specifies what kinds of beliefs qualify as properly basic. And according to the formal evidentialist, an agent is rational in allowing a belief to enter or stay in his or her belief system only if either that belief is properly basic (that is, satisfies the *principle of proper basicality*), or if it can be shown by acceptable methods of inference (that is, the methods meet the demand of the *rule principle*) to be evidentially supported by properly basic beliefs or other already justified derived beliefs (that is, satisfies the *evidential principle*).

2.3   INTERNAL STANDARDS OF RATIONALITY

So far as we have not discussed what formal evidentialists take as acceptable internal standards of rationality. Let us now turn to this subject. As we have seen the formal evidentialist draws an analogy between a person's belief system and a logical system, which is, of course, a consequence of accepting the logicality thesis. Principles of rationality are a kind of logical principle. However, if one views a person's beliefs as a type of logical system then the requirements or principles that apply to a logical system also seem to apply to them. So the answer to what kind of internal standards the formalist accepts is, essentially, the ones that we reasonably can demand that a logical system or a good argument should meet. What, then, are these standards? The standards proposed by Gärdenfors can be taken as typical for the formalist. He writes "if sets of sentences are used as models of epistemic states [i.e., states of belief], then *consistency* is a basic rationality requirement on such a set." And he claims that two standards of internal rationality are: "The set of accepted sentences should be *consistent*" and "*Logical consequences* of what is accepted should also be accepted."[62]

So inconsistency of belief is automatically irrational. Let us call this internal standard, or some other version of it, the *consistency principle*. But why is the maintenance of consistency—the avoidance of self-contradiction—a necessary condition for rationality, according to the formalists? A common answer given by the formalist is that in formal disciplines like mathematics and formal logic it is an absolute disaster if some members of a set are inconsistent. If there is one explicit or implicit inconsistency in a logical system it is impossible to deduce anything from it. Therefore, we cannot allow contradictions in a logical system, and thus the same holds for belief systems. If a logical system consists of the following set of statements $\{p, -p, q, r, s, t\}$, one can, for example, from "q implies p" derive "not-q" because you already have "not-p" in the set, and so end up with another contradiction "q and not-q," and so on for any possible statement. In other words, any absurdity could follow from *one* inconsistency. Analogously, a rational person *must* therefore be someone who eliminates the inconsistencies that exist in his or her belief system. According to the formalist, accepting inconsistent premises commits one to the absurdity of accepting anything whatsoever. Therefore, consistency is an indispensable precondition for rationally acceptable believing.[63]

Further, according to Gärdenfors, the logical consequences of what is believed should also be accepted by a rational agent. This internal standard of rationality, or some other version of it, we might call the *principle of deductive closure*. A person's belief system satisfies the principle of deductive closure if that individual accepts the logical consequences of his or her beliefs.[64] So this principle implies that one's beliefs are closed under entailment. Suppose, for example, that one's belief system consists of only the following set of beliefs: {p, q, r, s, t}, then if p implies q, and not-q is the case, then one can infer not-p. If (p and r) implies q, and not-q is the case, then one can infer not-p or not-r, and so on. A crucial point is that this reasoning holds independently of how many beliefs a person's belief system contains.

Let me illustrate these principles. The principle of deductive closure states that if, for example, an agent has the explicit beliefs that "All swans are white" and that "This bird is a swan," that individual must deduce the implicit belief that "This bird is white" to be internally rational in his or her believing. And the same is the case with the rest of the agent's explicit or implicit beliefs. But to be internally rational means also that the agent must eliminate the inconsistent beliefs present in his or her belief system. The principle of consistency demands that if, for instance, the agent believes that "Everything that happens happens by pure chance," and that "There is a transcendent purpose for my life," then that individual must reject one of these two apparently inconsistent beliefs or modify them so that they become consistent with each other. And the same is the case with the rest of the agent's explicit and implicit beliefs. Let us characterize these two principles in the following way:

> *The Consistency Principle:* It is rational to hold a belief only if it is consistent with everything else one believes.

The Principle of Deductive Closure: It is rational to hold a belief only if one also accepts all the logical consequences of this belief.

Gärdenfors, unlike some formalists, realizes that real human agents cannot meet these standards in their regulation or revision of belief. He writes:

> It is clear, however, that the two criteria are not realistic as descriptions of individuals' actual sets of belief. In particular, this is the case for the requirement of including logical consequences—because of the limitations of our mental powers, we often do not see all the consequences of what we accept. I still believe, however, that the criterion is useful, at least as an ideal of rationality.[65]

But both of these standards are reasonable if we "think of the idealized epistemic states as being *equilibrium states.*" And Gärdenfors gives the following example to explain what this means:

> If a set of beliefs is not consistent or if a probability assignment to a field of beliefs is not coherent, then the individual should, if she is to fulfill the rationality criteria, adjust her state of belief until it reaches an equilibrium that satisfies the criteria. A rational state of belief is one that is in equilibrium under all forces of internal criticism.[66]

So we can distinguish between two groups of formalists. Some formalists claim that only a person who actually satisfies the principle of deductive closure and the consistency principle is rational, that is, someone who accepts all the logical consequences of whatever he or she believes and does not hold any inconsistent beliefs. When human beings actually satisfy these demands they are rational, or better, their beliefs are rational, and otherwise they, or again better their beliefs, are irrational.

However, as we just noted, other formalists like Gärdenfors, acknowledge that human beings can never be rational in this sense. People cannot have infinitely many beliefs, but any set of beliefs has infinitely many consequences; and, further, since "there is no effective procedure for determining inconsistency, there is nothing humans can do to guarantee conformity with . . ." the consistency principle.[67] Hence, neither of the principles understood in this way are *feasible* because it is impossible for people to satisfy them. But instead of understanding these principles of internal rationality as prescribing what a human being must actually achieve to be rational or actually do to hold rational beliefs, these formalists understand these principles as describing the intellectual life of an ideally rational agent; and the principles should only function as *ideal* for us human beings. As Gärdenfors writes above: "I still believe, however, that the criterion is useful, at least as an ideal of rationality." What this means, I think, is not that we are rational only if we *actually* fulfill these demands, but that we are rational only if *we do the best we can* to satisfy these principles. So this second group of formalists can be understood as claming that human beings are only internally rational if they satisfy the following versions of the principles:

> *The Principle of Deductive Closure*: People are rational only if they always try their best to bring it about that they believe (or accept) all the logical consequences of whatever they believe.

> *The Consistency Principle*: People are rational only if they always try their best to bring it about that they eliminate as many inconsistencies as possible in what they believe.

All this means that rational belief-states or beliefs can be understood as idealizations of human cognitive states. I believe that one crucial reason why many philosophers who accept the formal model of rationality make this idealization is that they are trying to connect as closely as possible rationality to truth. To say that a belief is (rationally) justified should be almost the same as saying that the belief is true. Or better, the fact that a belief is rational should be a very strong reason for believing that it is true. This means that it would be hard to accept that a certain belief is rational and at the same time reject it. To admit that a belief is rational is almost the same as to commit oneself to believing it. This is a consequence of the view that rationality is ultimately an objective property a belief can have or lack, irrespective of who actually accepts the belief. There is, of course, nothing wrong with working with idealizations of a subject matter. But the idealization is always relative to what one is trying to achieve. And what the presumptionist will question is the degree of idealization present in the formal model of rationality. According to the presumptionist, not all forms of idealizations are appropriate for evaluating the rationality of belief regulation or revision. But we will come back to this issue later.

Let us see now what consequences the formal evidentialist's claims have when applied to religious belief. I suggest that the acceptance of formal evidentialism has provided the (implicit or explicit) background assumption to much of the discussion of the rationality of religious belief in philosophy of religion and theology during, at least, this century. To this issue we will now turn.

4

The Scientific and the Evidentialist Challenge to Religious Belief

Much of the discussion in philosophy of religion and theology during this century has taken some version of formal evidentialism for granted. In fact, the notion of rationality has been seen as relatively unproblematic, and one is sometimes astonished by how little the notion of rationality was explicated before philosophers and theologians went on quarreling about whether or not religious belief is rational or justifiable. That is, the discussion concerned almost exclusively whether the notion of rationality is at all applicable to religion, and if it is applicable, what consequences it yields. No problematization of rationality was thought to be needed. But in the 1970s and more frequently in the 1980s some philosophers of religion started to realize that the issue of the rationality of religious belief is as much a question about the notion of rationality as its application to religion.

In this chapter I intend to explicate the "unproblematic" notion of rationality used in this discussion and to state some of the consequences it was thought to have. I will also develop some of the criticism directed against this conception of rationality. More will come in the following chapters. Let us start with an early view of the rationality of religious belief, the one which we can find in positivism. No full account will be offered, and my interest will be in the later developments in the philosophy of religion and theology.[1]

1. Positivism and the Meaninglessness of Religious Discourse

Positivism began as an attempt to establish the rationality of science, but it was extended to cover all linguistic assertions and consequently all kinds of beliefs. A basic thesis is that all theories or beliefs must conform to the scientific standards of rationality. To fail to be scientific is the same as to fail being rational. "Reason" and "rationality" are identical with "scientific reason" and "scientific rationality." And verifiable, meaningful, scientific, and rational tend to mean the same thing. So we can say that positivists have a *reductive conception of rationality*. There is a corresponding reduction of knowledge. Positivism, therefore, includes an epistemological reduction. Positivists narrow the scope of knowledge to cover only empirical knowledge. The only genuine claims are empirical claims. This means that human knowledge is in fact equivalent to scientific knowledge. Russell claims "What science cannot discover, mankind cannot know."[2] There exists no common sense knowledge, intuitive knowledge, moral knowledge, or religious knowledge that cannot be reduced to scientific knowledge. Putnam writes:

> Not only was the list or canon that the positivists hoped "logicians of science" (their term for philosophers) would one day succeed in writing down supposed to exhaustively describe the "scientific method"; but, since, according to the logical positivists, the "scientific method" exhausts rationality itself, and testability by that method exhausts meaningfulness ("The meaning of a sentence is its method of verification"), the list or canon would determine what is and what is not a cognitively meaningful statement.[3]

The epistemological reduction generates the view that every belief or thought that is not scientific or closely connected to science is in some important sense unreliable or suspect. And as a consequence fields like religion, philosophy, and ethics have to be transformed into proper science or otherwise be seen as not saying anything about the real world. Traditional philosophy has to be transformed to a scientific philosophy:

> Those who do not see the errors of traditional philosophy do not want to renounce its methods or results and prefer to go along a path which scientific philosophy has abandoned. They reserve the name of philosophy for their fallacious attempts at a superscientific knowledge and refuse to accept as philosophical a method of analysis designed after the pattern of scientific enquiry.[4]

So all non-scientific or metaphysical statements are on this view cognitively meaningless. Whether we say "metaphysical" or "nonscientific" does not matter for the positivists since they define metaphysics or a metaphysical sentence as that which "purports to express a genuine proposition, but does, in fact, express neither a tautology nor an empirical hypothesis."[5] But notice, as Stanesby points out, that the positivists, by defining metaphysics the way they do, rule it out as "nonsense by definition and not by argument."[6]

However, traditional philosophy has mainly consisted of metaphysics, and thus the whole philosophical enterprise must be reoriented. The new task for philosophy would be to investigate whether statements are metaphysical or not. The tool philosophers should use for this is the verification principle. The task is also to try to develop a *logic of science,* to define the appropriate rules of inductive and deductive logic. The central thesis of that philosophical research program is to develop a logical analysis of science.

A consequence of the reductive conception of rationality is that every activity and set of beliefs that falls outside the scope of scientific rationality must be seen as either a-rational or irrational. Now we can see why it would be a failure for philosophical, ethical, or religious beliefs not to be scientific, because it leaves the beliefs without any cognitive content. They do not say anything about the external world. If they say anything meaningful at all it is about the speakers' own attitude or feelings.

1.1   THE VERIFICATION/FALSIFICATION ISSUE

According to positivists, the first standard of rationality every statement or belief must meet is the verification principle. On the basis of this principle they directed what I will call a *verificationist challenge to religious belief* (or maybe better, to religious linguistic expressions):

(1)   A statement has cognitive meaning if and only if it is analytic or empirically verifiable.

(2)   Religious statements are neither analytic nor empirically verifiable.

(3)   Therefore, religious statements are cognitively meaningless.

The crucial question for the positivist is not whether religious belief is true or not, the question is instead, whether it *makes sense to say* "God exists" or "God loves us" or anything similar. The claim is not that religious statements like these are false or irrational but that they do not even express any proper propositions at all: "it can not be significantly asserted that there is a non-empirical world of values, or that men have immortal souls, or that there is a transcendent God."[7] So religious statements are almost on a par with the line in *Alice in Wonderland,* "T'was brillig, and the slithy toves did gyre and gimble in the wabe." They say nothing false, but only because they say nothing at all! Therefore Ayer does not want to call himself an atheist or agnostic since that would be to accept that the question of God's existence has meaning, and this is exactly what he rejects. For the atheist and agnostic it is a genuine question, for Ayer it is a pseudo-question or meaningless question. There cannot be any transcendent truths of religion. "For to say that 'God exists' is to make a metaphysical utterance which cannot be either true or false." Unless the religious believer can "formulate his 'knowledge' in propositions that are empirically verifiable, we may be sure that he is deceiving himself."[8]

So on this account religious belief is, strictly speaking, not irrational but rather a-rational—it falls outside the scope of rationality (or irrationality). Questions of rationality can arise only concerning beliefs that consist of cognitively meaningful statements. Therefore, we must distinguish between: the *semantical question of religious belief,* concerning whether religious belief is cognitively meaningful; and the *epistemological question of religious belief,* concerning whether religious belief is true or rationally acceptable.

Since religious belief does not pass the first test, according to Ayer, the second never arises. A philosopher who, unlike Ayer (who originally refused to argue with religious believers because they were talking nonsense) was ready to engage in a critical dialogue with religious believers, was Flew.[9] He replaced the verification principle with a falsification principle, which grew out of continued attempts to redefine the positivist's view of what is cognitively meaningful. The falsification principle states that it must be possible to falsify a statement empirically, otherwise it lacks cognitive meaning. More exactly:

> *The Falsification Principle*: A statement has cognitive meaning if and only if it is analytic or if it is possible, beforehand, to say in which situation it is empirically falsifiable.

Notice that Flew's falsification principle is not the same one Popper advocates. Popper's principle is not meant as a criterion that should distinguish meaningful from meaningless statements, but only to draw a demarcation line between science and non-science. It says nothing about under what conditions a statement is cognitively meaningful. However, that is exactly the purpose of Flew's principle; it is a criterion of meaning. On the basis of this principle Flew directs a *falsificationist challenge to religious belief*:

(1)   A statement has cognitive meaning if and only if it is analytic or if it is possible, beforehand, to say in which situation it is empirically falsifiable.

(2)   Religious statements are neither analytic nor empirically falsifiable.

(3)   Therefore, religious statements are cognitively meaningless.

It is important to notice that the semantic question here discussed is not the traditional semantic question of religious belief, the one discussed by, for example, the ancient and medieval philosophers and theologians. That is, what meaning *do* religious expressions have? It was by them presupposed that they had a meaning. The question concerned only where to locate it, so to speak. The semantic question of the positivists is, however, much more radical, since they ask whether religious expressions have any meaning *at all*.[10]

Many philosophers and theologians who wanted to hold on to some kind of religion felt the need to try somehow to meet the verificationist/falsificationist challenge. Typically they did not directly challenge the first premise. Rather they tried to reinterpret religious discourse in such a way that it was compatible with the verification or falsification principle. To do that they had to clear religion of metaphysics or all transcendent or supernatural talk. That is, they tried to give religious expressions an interpretation that made them either (*a*) empirically meaningful or showed that (*b*) they are meaningful, but in a different sense from cognitive statements; that they have a non-cognitive function.[11]

However, some philosophers started to realize that it was the verification and falsification principles themselves that were problematic, or even the whole enterprise of trying to formulate principles of cognitive meaningfulness. One serious problem is that these

principles are, according to their own standards, not cognitively meaningful themselves. As Plantinga, for example, has pointed out, they are
self-referentially incoherent.[12] This is so because the only statements
the verification and falsification principles accept as factually meaningful are analytic statements or synthetic statements. But then these principles are self-refuting because they are themselves neither analytic
statements (true by definition) or synthetic statements (empirically verifiable or falsifiable). It is rather a *philosophical* claim about meaning
and the connection between meaning and the empirical world. So the
principles are themselves meaningless statements, and consequently
neither the scientist nor the religious believer (nor anybody else) need
conform to the demands of pseudo-statements.[13]

The objection against these principles of cognitive meaningfulness that perhaps had the most impact was the growing realization
among philosophers of science that not even science, which was taken
to be the paradigm of rationality, is able to satisfy these demands.
The history of science is filled with cases in which scientists were
convinced of the truth (and meaningfulness) of some scientific theory
but were unable to specify exactly the verification or falsification
conditions. The impact of this last objection will become clearer as
we proceed and develop the practice-oriented view of science, and
the model of rationality implicit in that view, in the following chapters.

After intensive discussion the consensus among philosophers
was that religious belief and their linguistic expressions pass the
semantic test. They must be treated as cognitively meaningful statements. Mackie, himself an atheist, expresses this attitude to the
meaning debate among contemporary philosophers of religion when
he writes:

> It is my view that the question whether there is or is not a god can
> and should be discussed rationally and reasonably, and that such
> discussion can be rewarding, in that it can yield definite results.
> This is a genuine, meaningful, question, and an important one—too
> important for us to take sides about it casually or arbitrarily. Neither
> the affirmative nor the negative answer is obviously right, but the
> issue is not so obscure that relevant considerations of argument and
> evidence cannot be brought to bear upon it.[14]

Instead, the really interesting and important question is thought
to be whether religious beliefs pass the *epistemological test,* whether

they are true or rationally acceptable: "If it is agreed that the central assertions of theism are literally meaningful, it must also be admitted that they are not directly verified or directly verifiable. It follows that any rational consideration of whether they are true or not will involve arguments."[15] The epistemic question concerning the truth and rationality of religious belief should be discussed in the context of arguments for or against the existence of God. However, notice that Mackie does not claim that theists have to prove (conclusively or directly verify) the existence of God. The discussion is not concerned with strict proof of God's existence, but with whether good reasons can be given for or against it.

This shows that we should distinguish between two versions of natural theology and atheology, the strong (or classical) and the weak (or contemporary) version. They differ in their levels of ambition. In general we can define *natural theology* and *atheology* as the attempt to argue for or against belief in God (or more broadly the sacred) on the basis of information available only through human reason, that is, through the "natural light of reason" shared alike by all human beings whether they believe in God or not. What the advocates of the *strong version* of natural theology and atheology try to do is to formulate arguments that can prove or disprove the existence of God. Typically, they try to deduce from premises which are universally convincing (that is, statements that all rational people accept) either that God exists or that he does not. The defenders of the *weaker version*, on the other hand, try to give arguments that function as good reasons, arguments whose premises show that it is more or less likely that God exists. And often it is not required that the premises of the arguments be universally convincing.

1.2 THE SCIENTIFIC CHALLENGE TO RELIGIOUS BELIEF

The *assumption* that gave the verificationist/falsificationist challenge its force was that it was taken for granted that science satisfied the verification principle or at least the falsification principle. And since science is normally taken as the paradigm of rationality it seems natural to compare all other putative rational practices with it. A shortcoming of a practice in comparison with science could then be seen as a serious epistemological failure. If the reductive conception of rationality and knowledge is accepted, that activity would simply lose all its supposed cognitive content or become irrational.

However, it is important to realize that the verificationist and the falsificationist challenges are just two versions of a scientifically based challenge. In its most general form such a challenge consists of the claim that all beliefs of whatever kind must meet the same, or very similar, standards of rationality as scientific beliefs do; otherwise they are irrational. Let us call this way of arguing, when it is directed against religious belief, the *scientific challenge to religious belief*:

(1)　Religious beliefs must fulfill the same, or at least similar, standards of rationality as scientific beliefs in order to be considered rational.

(2)　Religious beliefs do not fulfill the same, or at least similar, standards of rationality as scientific beliefs do.

(3)　Therefore, religious beliefs are irrational.

To give the challenge *content* one must specify what standards of rationality one thinks that science satisfies, for instance, by identifying the standards with the verification principle, Flew's falsification principle, Popper's falsification principle, or the like.

There are, I think, in principle three ways this challenge can be met by religious believers, and I will call these the "strong response," the "differentiation response," and the "irrational response." The advocates of the *strong response* accept the first premise but reject the second. Their task is to show that religious beliefs actually fullfill the same, or at least similar, standards of rationality as scientific ones do. The defenders of the *differentiation response* reject instead the first premise, and claim either that (*a*) the notions of rationality and irrationality do not apply to religious beliefs, i.e., they are a-rational; or that (*b*) religious beliefs are rational but in a way different from scientific beliefs, i.e., religious beliefs meet (completely or only partially) different standards of rationality. Religious people who defend the *irrationality response* accept the whole argument, but they claim that this does not count against being religious, since religion has never meant to be rational. Rather religion is absurd, a folly, and it is this that gives it its strength.

1.3　PHILOSOPHY OF RELIGION AND RULE-RATIONALITY

It is clear from the discussion of the verification and (Flew's) falsification principles that it was generally *assumed* that the application of these or some version of them would, if applied correctly, give a definite answer to the questions of the semantical and cognitive status of non-scientific beliefs like metaphysical or religious ones—just as it was assumed that it did in science or in scientific theory-choices. For instance, Flew provides an example of argumentation along these lines. He presents the believer with a dilemma which is intended to give a more or less definite answer: either (*a*) we can apply the criterion of falsification, and then it is clear that religious beliefs are falsified; or (*b*) it is impossible to apply the criterion, then religious beliefs are cognitively meaningless.[16] So a major presupposition in this debate, as well as in philosophy of science, was that rationality is rule-governed or determined by rules. A choice between competing theories (scientific, philosophical, or the like) is rational only if it is possible to specify in advance the appropriate rules in accordance with which the choice is to be made. Or a belief or theory is rational only if it is arrived at by following the appropriate rules.

However, even if the verification and falsification principles fail as appropriate rules—fail to distinguish between meaningful and meaningless sentences and between science and non-science—and the reductive conception of rationality (that rationality is limited to those domains in which scientific rationality or the logic of science is applicable) is rejected, this does *not* mean the end of the formal view of science or formal evidentialism and its implicit or explicit view of what philosophy and the task of philosophy is. In other words, it does not affect the research program of this model of rationality as such, only one attempt to develop it. That *research program* consists in:

> the attempt to find appropriate rules (algorithms) to determine whether beliefs in science, philosophy, religion, etc., are rational, and if this is not possible, to conclude that the beliefs in question are a-rational.

The last part of the program is a consequence of the rule principle, that rule-following is a necessary condition for rationality. Hence even if the verification and falsification principles are rejected, formal evidentialism implies that there *must* exist certain rules which can be used when we examine the meaning and rationality of religious beliefs as well as scientific ones, or any other kind of beliefs. It is only a question of finding the *right* rules. And because the rules that we apply are algorithms we can expect a solution in a finite number of steps. However, if no set of appropriate rules can be found in a field, it means that this area of belief is outside the scope of rationality and any choice there is arbitrary.

So even if the meaning debate as it was construed by the positivists is over, it set out what many philosophers explicitly or implicitly accept as the central task of philosophy of religion, a task that is analogous with the one of philosophy of science, namely, trying to find the appropriate rules in accordance with which religious propositions or beliefs are to be accepted or rejected. If, however, philosophers of religion cannot find any set of appropriate rules, the consequence must be that religious beliefs are either irrational or have no cognitive content (and can thus be seen as a-rational)—not, which of course is a possibility, that the idea that rationality is captured in rules might be wrong.

With this in mind let us now go on and consider the developments in philosophy of religion after the meaning debate initiated by the positivists.

2.   The Evidentialist Challenge to Religious Belief

As we saw, according to Mackie, the rationality of religious belief does not stand or fall with strict proofs or disproofs, but stands or falls with whether an evidentialist case can be made for or against religious belief. And Mackie seems to argue that if the arguments (or evidence) for belief in God are stronger than the arguments against, then belief in God is rational. On the other hand, if the arguments (or evidence) against belief in God are stronger, then it is not rational or even irrational to believe in God. This is typically expressed as a challenge to religious believers: either they provide good reasons for God's existence or they surrender any claim to the truth or rationality of that belief. This challenge has sometimes been called the *evidentialist challenge to religious belief,* and Wolterstorff states it as follows:

> It was insisted, in the first place, that it would be *wrong* for a person to accept Christianity, or any other form of theism [or any form of religion, my addition], unless it was *rational* for him to do so. And it was insisted, secondly, that it is not rational for a person to do so unless he holds his religious convictions on the basis of other beliefs of his which give to those convictions adequate evidentialist

support. No religion is acceptable unless rational, and no religion is rational unless supported by evidence. That is the evidentialist challenge.[17]

The evidentialist challenge consists of an application of evidentialism to religious beliefs: it is rational to accept religious beliefs only if, and to the extent that, there are good reasons (or evidence) to believe that they are true. This challenge has been raised by a number of philosophers. Consider just a few besides Mackie. For instance, Scriven claims:

> Now even belief in something for which there is no evidence, i.e., a belief which goes beyond the evidence, although a lesser sin than belief in something which is contrary to well-established laws, is plainly irrational in that it simply amounts to attaching belief where it is not justified. So the proper alternative, when there is no evidence, is not mere suspension of belief, e.g., about Santa Claus; it is disbelief. It most certainly is not faith.[18]

And according to him the same holds for belief in God. Blanshard writes:

> everywhere and always belief has an ethical aspect. There is such a thing as a general ethics of the intellect. The main principle of that ethic I hold to be the same inside and outside religion. This principle is simple and sweeping: Equate your assent to the evidence.[19]

Flew claims:

> It is by reference to this inescapable demand for grounds that the presumption of atheism is justified. If it is to be established that there is a God, then we have to have good grounds for believing that this is indeed so. Until or unless some such grounds are produced we have literally no reason at all for believing; and in that situation the only reasonable posture must be that of either the negative atheist [someone who is simply not a theist] or the agnostic. . . . It must be up to them [the theists]: first, to give whatever sense they choose to the word "God," . . . and, secondly, to bring forward sufficient reasons to warrant their claim that, in their present sense of the word "God", there is a God.[20]

Let us try to clarify this challenge a bit. Sometimes one gets the impression (as in the quotations above) that the philosophers who

raise the evidentialist challenge to religious belief accept an unqual-
ified evidentialist principle, that is, according to them, it is rational
to accept *any* belief only if there are good reasons to believe that it
is true. They seem to accept, to quote Clifford again, the claim that
"it is wrong *always*, everywhere, and for anyone, to believe anything
upon insufficient evidence."[21] But as I pointed out in the previous
chapter, this leads to an infinite regress. Therefore, they must accept
a stopping place, if any belief is to be rational, a set of properly
basic beliefs that are rationally justified without their justification being
dependent on other beliefs. So I will interpret the advocate of the
evidentialist challenge as accepting the basic thrust of foundationalism: that some of our beliefs need the evidential support of other
beliefs, while some others need not. They should not be understood
as claiming that *no* belief can properly be accepted without evidence
(inferential justifiers). However, since they claim that religious beliefs
need the evidential support of other beliefs, they obviously do not
accept religious beliefs as properly basic. If this is correct it means
that the evidentialist challenge to religious belief should be stated in
the following way:

(1) Religious beliefs are not properly basic beliefs.
(2) Non-basic beliefs without supporting evidence are not
     rationally acceptable.
(3) There is no evidence, or at least not sufficient evi-
     dence, for religious beliefs.
(4) Therefore, religious beliefs are irrational.

The argument consists of, first of all, the claim that religious
beliefs are not properly basic beliefs. In general the evidentialists that
raise the challenge only accept as properly basic beliefs that are self-
evident, incorrigible, or evident to the senses (that is the *standard
principle of proper basicality*), and since religious beliefs are none of
these, they fail to qualify as properly basic. Consequently, religious
beliefs must be non-basic beliefs. However, a non-basic belief without
adequate evidential support from other—basic or already justified—
beliefs is not rationally acceptable. But the problem with religious
beliefs is that there is no good reason, or at least not sufficient reason,
for them. Therefore, religious beliefs are irrational.

So people must, according to the evidentialist challenge, refrain
from accepting religious beliefs until they have collected sufficient

evidence for them, if they want to hold rational (religious) beliefs. To use a phrase from Wolterstorff (who does not share this view), all religious beliefs are intellectually guilty until proven innocent.[22] The only way these beliefs can be classified as rational beliefs is if religious believers can give evidence for them, that is, only if the believers rationally hold other beliefs which support their religious beliefs and the believers accept them on the basis of this supporting group of beliefs.

Both the evidentialist and scientific challenges in their traditional forms presuppose the rule principle—that rule-following is a necessary condition for obtaining rational beliefs. So it is assumed that any attempt to meet these challenges must be able to formulate rules by which the rationality of religious belief can be determined. That is a necessary precondition of formal evidentialism. Let us call the versions of the evidentialist and scientific challenges that presuppose that rationality is rule-governed or determined, the "traditional" or "formal" evidentialist, respectively, scientific challenge to religious belief.

There are, I think, several ways religious believers can respond to the evidentialist challenge. First, and most typically, they can reject the third premise and claim that there is indeed sufficient evidence for religious belief. That is, they accept the evidentialist principle but deny that when it is applied to religious beliefs it has the outcome the advocates of the challenge claim. Second, religious people can argue that religious beliefs are properly basic. They can reject the first premise. Religious believers can do this in two ways. Either they can accept the presupposed principle of proper basicality, but claim that religious beliefs (or some religious beliefs) are either self-evident, incorrigible, or evident to the senses. Or they can reject such a definition of the principle of proper basicality and expand the scope of it, in such a way that religious beliefs (or some religious beliefs) can be taken as properly basic beliefs.

Third, a different model of rationality from evidentialism could be proposed, which would include the rejection of the cornerstone of evidentialism, the evidentialist principle. In other words, the second premise of the challenge could be rejected. However, this third alternative will not be developed here since in this chapter we will discuss only the responses that accept evidentialism and foundationalism as a general framework for rationality. We will come back to this response in chapter 10. Fourth, the whole challenge (all premises) can be rejected. Typically this has been done by claiming that the evidentialist challenge is based on a misunderstanding of the nature of religious belief. I will in this chapter discuss this position in some detail, but the main discussion of it will be in chapter 11, where it is taken to imply an acceptance of a different model of rationality (contextualism). And lastly, an irrational response is possible also to the evidentialist challenge. One could accept the whole argument, but claim that this does not count against being religious, since religion was never meant to be rational. In Wolterstorff's words, these people deny that it would be wrong for a person to accept any form of religion unless it is rational for him or her to do so.

Let us notice a few more things about the evidentialist challenge. First of all, the evidentialist challenge should *not* be confused with the scientific challenge to religious belief, since they are not necessarily the same challenge to religious belief. But they *can* be the same challenge, if rationality is taken to be the same as scientific rationality, and then and only then do these challenges become identical. In such a case the only acceptable reasons that can support religious belief are scientific reasons. Only if religious beliefs fulfill the same standards of rationality as scientific ones do would there be adequate, i.e., scientific, reasons for them. However, this coincidence would not occur if, for example, we allowed other types of acceptable reasons than scientific ones or other acceptable methods of inference than the scientific ones.

Second, we have to ask what the advocates of the challenge mean when they say that a belief is irrational or a believer is irrational in accepting a belief. Scriven talks about "sin"—epistemic sin probably, and Blanshard says that there is a "general ethics of the intellect." It therefore seems reasonable to assume that they construe rationality deontologically. That is, they claim that religious believers fail to meet their intellectual obligations, and so they violate their epistemic responsibilities. The end of rationality they seem to have in mind is purely epistemic. It is a matter of increasing our true or probably true beliefs and, I take it, to eliminate our false ones. Flew says: "The same applies [to bring forward sufficient reasons to warrant their claims], if what is to be made out is, not that theism is known to be true, but only—more modestly—that it can be seen to be at least more or less probable."[23] So according to their conception of rationality the charge against religious believers is that they are not doing what one can rightly demand of them. They are not making sure that their religious beliefs are true or probably true, and therefore their religious beliefs are not rational or, as Scriven says in the quote above, "plainly irrational."

However, there is a problem with this kind of reconstruction of their account of what rationality is. Consider some remarks from Mackie. He seems to think that the argument from evil can establish the irrationality of religious belief. He writes: "Here it can be shown, not that religious beliefs lack rational support, but that they are positively irrational . . ."[24] Or when elsewhere he says: "But my title also echoes Hume's ironic remark that the Christian religion cannot be believed without a miracle by any reasonable person." And: "There is at any rate no easy way of defending religion once it is admitted that the literal, factual, claim that there is a god cannot be rationally sustained."[25]

Here Mackie seems to assume that rationality and irrationality are properties that beliefs can have. If "God is omnipotent; God is wholly good; and yet evil exists," are logically inconsistent beliefs, as Mackie thinks they are, then this set of beliefs has the feature of being irrational. Hence it is not, or not just, some religious believers who are not satisfying their intellectual duties, so that *they* are irrational in their believings, but that some theistic *beliefs* have the property of being irrational. Therefore, rationality is, for Mackie I presume, not strictly speaking a relation between some real agents—actual religious believers—and some of their believings, but a logical relation between beliefs or propositions (recall the logicality thesis). Obviously Mackie can still talk about rational persons, but "any reasonable person" in the quotation above must then be taken to refer to an *ideally rational person*, someone whose *beliefs* have the property of being rational. So when he says that some theistic beliefs are irrational, it is the same as saying that an ideal person would not accept these beliefs. And, of course, it is assumed that the beliefs of real believers can be measured and evaluated by how well they fulfill the ideal. This also means that Mackie, or more broadly the advocates of the formal evidentialist challenge, does not necessarily have to consider the actual situation of real religious people, since that is strictly speaking irrelevant for determining the rationality of religious belief.

Third, we must be clear about what the evidentialist principle demands and permits us to believe. According to this principle, one ought to reject any (non-basic) belief which one does not have good reason to think is true. This means that any belief which one already accepts which one has (*a*) no reason to think is true, but also (*b*) no reason to reject, should be thrown away. It demands that we not only reject any belief which we have no evidence for, but also those which we have no evidence against. The consequence this has for the evidentialist challenge is that people are not only irrational in believing in God when they have no evidence for the belief and when, at the same time, there exists evidence against it, but they are also irrational in those cases in which they have no evidence for belief in God but when, at the same time, they have no evidence against it either. Not having enough evidence for a belief is sufficient for irrationality. Therefore, Scriven can say, as we saw above, that "the proper alternative when there is no evidence is not mere suspension of belief . . . it is disbelief." So, as Plantinga points out: "He [Scriven] holds that if the arguments *for* God's existence fail and the arguments *against* God's existence *also* fail, then atheism is rationally obligatory. If you have no evidence *for* the existence of God, then you are rationally obligated to believe there is no God—whether or not you have any evidence *against* the existence of God."[26]

Plantinga thinks that this view is unique to Scriven, but I think that it is a general consequence of acceptance of the evidentialist principle: only if there is good reason for a (non-basic) belief is one rationally entitled to accept it, and only then. And the same point holds for Flew's presumption of atheism. The presumption should be in favor of atheism if there is not any or at any rate insufficient evidence for theism. So it is strictly speaking sufficient to undermine all arguments supporting religious belief to establish the irrationality of it. Russell is another philosopher who has thought that this strategy (call it *negative natural atheology*) is sufficient against religious belief. Once Russell has shown that the arguments for Christianity fail he concludes not only that he is rational in not being a Christian, but also that no other reasonable person should be a Christian either.[27] As Swinburne correctly observes:

> But, apart from that reason [the argument from evil], the main reasons which atheists have for believing that there is no God have been their claims that there is insufficient evidence, that the theist's arguments do not work, do not make the existence of God probable

to any significant degree. The atheist's arguments, apart from the argument from evil, have been largely in the form of criticisms of the theist's arguments.[28]

However, as Swinburne notes, most of the time the advocates of the challenge have complemented their case against religious belief with arguments which set out the positive evidence against it (call this strategy *positive natural atheology*).[29] The most common argument of this kind has been the argument from evil. But the reason why they engage in positive natural atheology is not clear. Perhaps they think that a positive natural atheology is needed for *them* to be rational in *not* accepting religious belief. This seems to be needed because the belief in God's non-existence is also a non-basic belief so, in all fairness, one is also in this case rational in accepting such belief only if there are good reasons to believe that it is true. And this may be one of the reasons why it is so important to Flew that we not understand the word "atheist" the way we normally do, as one who denies the existence of God, but as someone "who lacks belief in God"; since if atheism involves no belief at all, the evidentialist principle does not apply. So if this is correct it follows from the evidentialist principle that the burden of proof is entirely on the religious believer.[30]

3.   An Evidentialist Case For and Against Religious Belief

So far the most common response to the evidentialist challenge among religious believers is to reject the third premise, that there is no or at least not sufficient evidence for religious beliefs. These objectors to the challenge agree that the burden of proof is on them and try consequently to develop an evidentialist case for religious belief. Note that the third premise is a strong claim, especially if the claim is that there is no evidence for religious belief. Does not any argument proposed by theists throughout the centuries provide evidence? It is a strong claim because the issue is *not* whether the evidence given by theists proves (conclusively verifies) the existence of God, but rather it is *whether the evidence can make the existence of God probable to such an extent that it is rational to believe in God on the basis of this evidence.* I will focus mainly on one discussion here, the one between Swinburne and Mackie. However, I will also bring in material from other philosophers when relevant. The purpose is not to state exactly the positions of Swinburne and Mackie, but to try to identify the central elements in a formal evidentialist case for or against religious belief.

Swinburne tries to overcome the evidentialist challenge to religious belief by questioning the third premise of the challenge. His claim is that religious belief is in fact rational since it is more probable than not on the basis of the available evidence. Mackie claims instead that the balance of probability lies against theism and in favor of atheism. But they both seem to agree that religious belief is irrational if it is not probable with respect to the relevant body of evidence (they accept the first and the second premises). The assumption is, if the evidence favors religious belief, then it is rationally acceptable; if, on the other hand, the evidence favors atheism, then religious belief is not rationally acceptable. As we will see, Swinburne also attempts (at least implicitly) to overcome the scientific challenge to religious belief. However, I shall not examine in great detail the evidence given for and against the existence of God in this debate, rather my interest is in the kind of model of rationality that is (directly or indirectly) presupposed by it.

Swinburne's and Mackie's evidentialist cases for and against religious belief could be reconstructed in the following way. First, we have to isolate the beliefs or propositions whose justification or rationality we are interested in and define them as precisely as possible (let us call this the *simple core approach*). Everything else can be put aside until this core has been justified. So we can reduce religion to a set of abstract and well-defined propositions. In this case it is the proposition "God exists" (theism) that we have to justify and consequently define as carefully as we can. Swinburne takes the proposition "God exists" to be logically equivalent to:

> the existence of a being with one or more of the following properties: being a person without a body (i.e., a spirit), present everywhere, the creator and sustainer of the universe, a free agent, able to do everything (i.e., omnipotent), knowing all things, perfectly good, a source of moral obligation, immutable, eternal, a necessary being, holy, and worthy of worship.[31]

Mackie seems to agree, saying: "The central doctrines of this traditional theism are well summed up by Richard Swinburne." And he goes on to say what is typical for post-positivist philosophers: "It is sometimes doubted whether such descriptions *can* be literally meaningful. But there is really no problem about this."[32]

3.1 FORMAL JUSTIFICATION OF THEISM

Second, we have to develop a *formal justification* of theism, that is, the issue should be decided by the canons of logic or more precisely confirmation theory (i.e., the study of how scientific theories and hypotheses are confirmed).[33] Swinburne explains: "My use of confirmation theory enables me to express my arguments with the rigour appropriate to any detailed presentation of the evidence for or against a large-scale theory of the universe; and also enables me to bring out the close similarities which exist between religious theories and large-scale scientific theories."[34]

Swinburne is a natural theologian, and so he tries to show that it is more probable than not that God exists on the basis of information (premises) that is, in principle, available to all people whether religious or not. However, he does not believe that it is possible to prove God's existence. He attempts to establish that the existence of God is more probable than not—to *confirm* the existence of God. This means that Swinburne does not use the same kind of logic as classical natural theologians, deductive logic, but he instead uses inductive logic or confirmation theory (in particular Bayes's theorem). This means that the arguments he employs are mainly *inductive* or *probabilistic* in character. Mackie agrees with Swinburne also on this point and says that most of the arguments:

> include important non-deductive elements. Each of them starts from various pieces of evidence or considerations about some part of our experience, and in many cases the conclusions clearly go beyond what is contained, even implicitly, in the premises. All such arguments can be seen as resting on one general principle, or as sharing one basic form and purpose: they are arguments to the best explanation. The evidence supports the conclusion, it is suggested, because if we postulate that that conclusion is true—or better, perhaps, that it is at least an approximation to the truth—we get a more adequate overall explanation of that whole body of evidence, in the light of whatever considerations are cited, than would be given by any

available alternative hypothesis. It is well known that it is reasoning of this general form that gives scientific theories and hypotheses whatever support they have, and that makes it reasonable for us to claim truth or verisimilitude for them.[35]

If the evidentialist case for and against theism should be laid out according to the rules of confirmation theory, then it must be possible to *quantify* or *formalize* the arguments. Swinburne and Mackie assume that this can be done in a Bayesian fashion. What kind of probability do they have in mind? Mackie says:

> The probabilities with which we shall be most concerned are epistemic ones: the epistemic probability of a certain statement relative to some body of information is a measure of the degree of support that the information gives to that statement, or, equivalently, of the degree of belief that it is reasonable to give to that statement on the basis of that information.[36]

The epistemic probability of theism is in turn to be measured by an application of Bayes's theorem to it. In measuring the epistemic probability of theism we should proceed in the same way as in science. Swinburne says about the epistemic probability of scientific claims:

> Our grounds for believing a general statement such as "all material bodies attract each other with forces proportional to the product of their masses and inversely proportional to the square of their distance apart" to be a law of nature will be that it belongs to a scientific theory which has high prior probability and great explanatory power.[37]

So Swinburne thinks that the important elements in determining epistemic probability is prior probability and explanatory power. The *prior probability* depends on simplicity (roughly, how few entities or reasons, i.e., laws or intentions, that the theory postulates), fit with background knowledge (roughly, how well the theory fits with what we know about the world in general), and scope (again roughly, how comprehensive the theory is, or how many phenomena it covers). A theory has *explanatory power* in so far as it makes probable the occurrence of many diverse phenomena which are all observed to occur, and it predicts the occurrence of phenomena which are not otherwise to be expected. So what we have to determine is the prior probability and explanatory power of theism.

According to Swinburne, the general form of an evidentialist case for theism is that the theist argues from the world, the facts of its existence and its detailed characteristics, to a God who (intentionally) brought it about. If we apply Bayes's theorem, h will be the hypothesis that God exists and k will be our general background evidence of the world and e will be the various propositions the theist brings forward as evidence for God's existence. For example, if e is "there is a physical universe" then we have the argument from e to h, that is a cosmological argument. $P(h/e.k)$ represents the probability of the hypothesis that there is a God (h) given the evidence (e) that there is a physical universe and also some general background evidence. If we assume that all our empirical data are among the things to be explained, then the background evidence consists in this case only of what logicians call "tautological evidence," such as the truths of logic and mathematics.[38] (Though, generally speaking, background evidence or knowledge is everything we think that relates to the truth of the given hypothesis other than the specific evidence.) $P(h/k)$ represents the probability of h given k, which is the prior probability of the hypothesis. That is the probability people assign to "there is a God" before considering the detailed evidence cited in its support. And the occurrence of certain phenomena will confirm (or disconform)—that is, raise the probability of—theism, if it is more probable that those phenomena will occur if there is a God than if there is not. So the evidentialist case depends on how much more likely God's existence makes the occurrence of those phenomena that are to be explained, than would be the case if we did not assume the existence of God.

These are the general characteristics a formal evidentialist case for theism should have. In other words, theism should (and, according to Swinburne, can) meet the same, or at least similar, standards of rationality as scientific theories. So in the end:

> The probability, on the evidence, of God's existence will depend on how well the hypothesis of God's existence is able to explain the occurrence of phenomena which would otherwise be highly unlikely [i.e., the explanatory power]; and on the prior probability, and for a hypothesis as all-embracing as this one that means merely the simplicity, of the hypothesis that God exists.[39]

Theism has great simplicity because it postulates only one entity, a being with infinite power, knowledge, and freedom. All other properties follow by inference, hence God is also creator of all things, perfectly good, and so on. Further, theism is simple because it ultimately explains all events in terms of the action of personal agents. All explanations (including scientific ones) can be reduced to personal explanations. Therefore: "The intrinsic probability of theism is, relative to other hypotheses about what there is, very high, because of the great simplicity of the hypothesis of theism."[40]

3.2 ACCEPTABLE EVIDENCE FOR OR AGAINST THEISM

The third element of the formal evidentialist case concerns the kind of evidence that is acceptable. The evidence for or against theism should be laid out as carefully and systematically as possible (so the rules of formal logic can be applied to them) to determine the likelihood of the existence of God. But with respect to what should theism be probable or not? What is relevant evidence in this case? With respect to which body of propositions must theism be more probable than not in order to be rationally acceptable? A prior requirement that makes the arguments, evidence, or reasons good is that they are shared by believers and unbelievers alike. Or put differently, the premises of the arguments should be known to be true by those who dispute about the conclusion. Swinburne writes: "I shall discuss only arguments in which the premises report what are (in some very general sense) features of human experience—e.g., evident general truths about the world or features of private human experience."[41]

So good evidence for and against theism are propositions that are *universally convincing,* like some propositions about the world, either common sense or well-established scientific beliefs. Good evidence would also include I take it, a certain body of logic and probability theory, and as we will see some appropriate principles of theory-choice (simplicity, predictability, economy, and the like). So there must be, it seems, an agreed starting-point (a foundation) shared by people of "all theistic and atheistic persuasions" from which the rationality of belief in God can be determined.[42] Here the foundational structure of rationality presupposed becomes evident.

What kind of arguments are discussed in the evidentialist debate? Not only the traditional arguments for belief in God are considered—

the ontological, cosmological, and teleological argument, but also the argument from providence, the arguments from religious experience, and arguments from consciousness and morality, and from history and miracles. But they focus on only one argument against the existence of God—the argument from evil.

However, Mackie and Swinburne differ on one important point from other advocates of an evidentialist case for or against theism—and in this respect they share one characteristic element with the model of rationality we will consider next, social evidentialism—in that they claim that the arguments should not be considered in isolation from one another but that their cumulative effect must be taken into account. Philosophers who have rejected that arguments can be cumulative are, among others, MacIntyre and Flew. MacIntyre writes:

> One occasionally hears teachers of theology aver that although the proofs do not provide conclusive grounds for belief in God, they are at least pointers, indicators. But a fallacious argument points nowhere (except to the lack of logical acumen on the part of those who accept it). And three fallacious arguments are no better than one.[43]

Flew agrees with MacIntyre and says:

> It is occasionally suggested that some candidate proof, although admittedly failing as a proof, may nevertheless do useful service as a pointer. This is a false exercise of the generosity so characteristic of examiners. A failed proof cannot serve as a pointer to anything, save perhaps to the weaknesses of those who have accepted it. Nor, for the same reason, can it be put to work along with other throwouts as part of an accumulation of evidence. If one leaky bucket will not hold water that is no reason to think that ten can.[44]

So we have to distinguish between those philosophers who accept and those who reject cumulative cases for and against religious belief. Let us follow Gutting and call the cumulative arguments "multi-dimensional arguments," and those that are not, "one-dimensional arguments," and define them the way he does. *One-dimensional arguments* are those arguments whose cogency depends on the plausibility of each of the premises taken separately, so that if one of the premises becomes questionable, the argument loses its force. *Multi-dimensional arguments* are those arguments in which the premises overdetermine the conclusion; that is, the conclusion is supported by a large number of different but converging considerations and can remain cogent as a whole even though some of the considerations (premises) are questioned or rejected.[45]

Mackie gives a legal case as an example of a situation where multi-dimensional arguments are used and are valid. A prosecutor may build his or her case on the joint effects of a number of considerations, each of which on its own would be too weak to justify a verdict, but whose combined effect may justify such a decision.[46] Let us also consider an example from Newman, to which Wainwright refers when he writes:

> A historian's conviction that the *Aeneid* couldn't be a thirteenth-century forgery . . . is partly based on his or her knowledge of the capacities of the medieval mind. While this knowledge depends on a lifetime of reading and study, many of the considerations that shaped it have been forgotten and others have merged into a general impression of what the medieval mind could and could not do. "We do not pretend to be able to draw the line between what the medieval intellect could and could not do; but we feel sure that at least it could not write the classics. An instinctive sense of this [as well as] a faith in testimony, are the sufficient, but the undeveloped argument on which to ground our certitude."[47]

In both these cases conclusions are drawn from a variety of different considerations; and none is itself sufficient to establish the conclusion. Nevertheless, when taken together, they justify people in concluding that some hypothesis makes more sense of a range of facts than its alternatives do. Without claiming that the issue is settled, these examples seem to show that multi-dimensional arguments can be valid.

Because Swinburne and Mackie think that this kind of argument is valid, they argue that, when we apply Bayes's theorem to the hypothesis that God exists, it should not be applied to measure only the probability of each argument individually (that is: $P(h/e_1.k)$ and $(P(h/e_2.k)$ etc.), but also the probability of them all taken together (if we suppose, for instance, that these are seven arguments all together, then $(P(h/e_1 \ldots e_7.k))$ is the proper representation of the probability. And the crucial issue is whether all arguments taken together make probable that God exists. Ultimately Swinburne claims that theistic belief is rational since it is more probable than not on the basis of the *total* body of evidence.[48]

3.3 RELIGION AND SCIENCE

The last point I would like to focus on is the parallel drawn between science and religion (theism more precisely). A presupposition of Swinburne's and Mackie's cases is that they take for granted that theism is a *hypothesis,* even a scientific hypothesis, or at least very much like a scientific hypothesis. Swinburne claims that theism should be understood as a hypothesis that explains why the universe exists and why it looks the way it looks. In the same way as science explains phenomena with hypotheses about atoms, genes, forces, and so on, other phenomena can be explained by the hypothesis "God exists":

> The structure of a cumulative case for theism was thus, I claimed [in *The Existence of God*], the same as the structure of a cumulative case for any unobservable entity, such as a quark or a neutrino. Our grounds for believing in its existence are that it is an entity of a simple kind with simple modes of behaviour which leads us to expect the more complex phenomena which we find.[49]

So if we understand theism as Swinburne maintains, it can be confirmed by evidence in much the same way that evidence supports scientific hypotheses. In other words, Swinburne's aim is to propose an evidentialist case for theism that is in all relevant aspects identical, or at least very similar, to scientific reasoning or argumentation. So Swinburne's case for theism can be understood not only as an attempt to meet the evidentialist challenge but also the scientific challenge to religious belief. We can use the same standards of rationality and appeal to the same kind of evidence in religion (or at least theism) as in science, and therefore religious belief (or at least theistic belief) can be rational.

However, another reason why Swinburne maintains a close connection between rationality in science and religion (theism) is that he wants to overcome what might be called the "Hume-Kant objection":

> *The Hume-Kant Objection:* We cannot know or be rationally justified in believing in anything beyond the range of our immediate experience.[50]

We cannot draw justified conclusions about those parts of the world which we are not directly observing. Rational reasoning about nonobserved entities is not possible. So according to them Swinburne's project is doomed from the outset. However, Swinburne writes:

> Those who believe in the ability of modern science to reach justified (and exciting) conclusions about such things far beyond immediate experience, as subatomic particles and nuclear forces, the "big bang" and cosmic evolution, ought to be highly sympathetic to my enterprise; Hume and Kant would not, on their own principles, have had a very sympathetic attitude to the claims of modern theoretical science.[51]

In other words, by showing the close similarities between the assessment of religious beliefs and of scientific theories, he attempts to block the Hume-Kant objection. It is blocked by an appeal to the status of science. In short, *if science is possible, Hume and Kant must be wrong; science is possible, therefore, natural theology is also possible.* So the price for applying the Hume-Kant objection to religious belief is that much of science must go the same way, but that is surely a price too high to be paid, and therefore the Hume-Kant objection should be rejected.[52]

This leads us to a third reason for pointing out the similarities between science and religion. According to the advocates of formal evidentialism science is the paradigm of rationality. Hence if it could be shown that theistic belief is supported by the same methods, logic, and evidence as scientific claims, then the case for theism would be as universally convincing as we could possibly hope for—and, if it did not bring all rational people to theistic belief, it would at least establish clearly the rationality of belief in God.

3.4   THE PROPORTIONALITY PRINCIPLE AND RELIGIOUS ASSENT

But this kind of analysis of religious belief as a scientific hypothesis, or as in all relevant aspects identical with one, seems to create problems for many religious believers, since they tend (so say the least) to accept their religious beliefs in a strong way with full commitment. And according to the formal evidentialist, the firmness of one's believing ought to stand in proportion to the evidence (the proportionality principle). So strictly speaking the believer's assurance ought to rise and fall with the evidence, and never exceed that level. But even if Swinburne is successful (which Mackie does not think) in showing that the probability of theism is closer to 1 than 0 (that is, $P(b) > 1/2$),[53] the evidence seems nevertheless to be *insufficient* to warrant the kind of certainty with which religious believers normally hold on to their convictions.

Swinburne does not directly discuss this problem, but other thinkers have addressed it. And this is one of the main reasons why some philosophers and theologians have questioned an *assumption* behind the evidentialist and scientific challenges: that religious beliefs are, in general, a kind of factual belief—beliefs that state that something is the case. Wittgenstein, for instance, claims that religious beliefs mean something other than what beliefs mean in science and ordinary life. One reason he gives for this is the way religious belief is held. Religious believers do not hold their beliefs with a conviction proportionate to evidence as is the case with scientific beliefs.[54] Consider also MacIntyre's criticism against Ian Crombie's account of religious belief:

> it suggests that religious belief is a hypothesis which will be confirmed or overthrown after death. But, if this is correct, in this present life religious beliefs could never be anything more than as yet unconfirmed hypotheses, warranting nothing more than a provisional and tentative adherence. But such an adherence is completely uncharacteristic of religious belief. A God who could be believed in this way would not be the God of Christian theism. For part of the content of Christian belief is that a decisive adherence has to be given to God. So that to hold Christian belief as a hypothesis would be to render it no longer Christian belief.[55]

Notice, however, that even though both Wittgenstein and MacIntyre question this assumption they seem to take for granted that the proportionality principle is appropriate to apply to religious belief *if* it is factual, and that scientific beliefs are held tentatively and in proportion to the evidence available. This is something they have in common with both the advocates of the evidentialist and the scientific challenge. As we will see, both of these points can be questioned.

So it has been suggested that religious belief does not express propositions about a factual reality, but states something else. What this "else" exactly is, however, these thinkers do not agree on. But

what they all have in common is that they deny that the objects of religious belief exist independently of the experiences (or the linguistic
activities) of the believers. They are what I will call *religious anti-
realists*. And we can define the opposite view as follows:

> *Religious Realism:* The view that the objects of reli-
> gious belief are ontologically independent of the way
> religious believers conceive them.

The proportionality principle does not cause any problems for
the religious believer who desires to be rational, if we understand
religious beliefs the way anti-realists do. The tentative attitude applies
only to propositional beliefs or to propositions, but not to non-factual
beliefs. For many religious anti-realists, belief in God means instead
trusting God, committing one's life to him, having a certain attitude to
him. To believe in God is to have a personal relationship with God.
On this view, the strong personal involvement or commitment of the
believer is taken to stand in sharp contrast to the supposedly detached
and tentative attitude of the scientist.

In other words, such a way of arguing is another way of responding to the evidentialist and scientific challenges, namely by
rejecting all the premises of the challenge. These challenges cannot
be directed against religious belief because they necessarily imply a
misrepresentation of the nature or meaning of religious belief. We will
come back to this response and discuss it more thoroughly in chapter
11, where it is understood as implying an acceptance of a different (a
contextual) model of rationality.

However, other philosophers have questioned whether this anti-
realist view really makes any sense of religious belief. Price has argued
that belief *in* God seems to presuppose belief *that* God exists.[56] To
trust a human person, for example one's doctor, presupposes the
belief in that person's existence. I cannot trust my doctor if I do
not believe that he or she exists. So a necessary condition for a
religion like Christianity seems to be the belief that there is a God.
But this of course does *not* mean that it is a sufficient condition for a
religion like Christianity. Belief in God is much more than accepting
the proposition that God exists, but—and this is the point—it is at
least that. Mackie writes:

> As Swinburne says, there is, particularly in modern Protestant Chris-
> tian theology, a strong tendency to play down credal statements,

assertions of explicit belief in such doctrines, and to locate the centre of religion rather in "a personal relationship to God in Christ." But the latter makes little sense unless the former are at least presupposed. If God is not an objective reality but merely an intentional object, that is, exists only in the believer's mind as do the objects of imagination or events in dreams, then it is misleading to speak of a relationship, and all the more misleading to describe the relationship in terms of "reliance," "trust," "guidance," and "surrender": how could one sensibly rely upon a figment of one's own imagination? Those who are dissatisfied with the old creeds should change them, not try to do without credal statements.[57]

If Price and Mackie are right, it means that *some* beliefs in a religion like Christianity must include a propositional element. But then the proportionality principle causes problems for believers who want to be rational in their religious believing. And here the religious anti-realist seems to be right that religious beliefs function properly only if they are held strongly, with full commitment. This creates a crucial *dilemma* for religious believers: either (*a*) they are rational in their believing, but then their religious beliefs do not seem to function properly, or (*b*) they have the commitment religion seems to demand but are irrational in their believing. We will return to this dilemma again in chapters 10 and 11 when we examine the implications the other models of rationality have for the rational justification of religious beliefs. For now I will assume that Price's and Mackie's arguments are convincing. Let us now go back to the discussion between Swinburne and Mackie and make some concluding remarks.

3.5 THE FORMAL EVIDENTIALIST CASE AND RELIGIOUS PRACTICE

Not surprisingly Swinburne and Mackie do not agree on whether the existence of God is more probable or not given the total body of evidence. According to Swinburne, the evidence makes the existence of God probable to such an extent that it is rational to believe in God and less rational or irrational, or the like, to not believe in God. Mackie, on the other hand, claims that the conclusion should be exactly the opposite: "The balance of probability . . . comes out strongly against the existence of a god." "In the end, therefore, we can agree with what Laplace said about God: we have no need of that hypothesis." And from this it follows he seems to think that theism is not rationally acceptable. "There is at any rate no easy way of defending religion once it is admitted that the literal, factual, claim that there is a god cannot be rationally sustained."[58]

What conclusion does follow concerning the rationality of religious belief if the discussion about the possibility of a successful evidentialist case for it cannot be settled? According to the advocates of the evidentialist challenge what should follow is that it is not rational or even irrational to believe in God. This is a consequence of the evidentialist principle. It demands that we not only reject any (religious) belief which we have no evidence for, but also those (religious) beliefs which we have no evidence against. So if the arguments for and against God's existence take each other out (that is, if $P(b) = 1/2$) or if there is some but insufficient evidence for theism, disbelief is the rational option. Remember that all that is needed is strictly speaking negative natural atheology to show that the arguments for religious belief fail.

The defenders of an evidentialist case for religious belief, or more narrowly theism, can of course reject this version of the evidential principle or claim that they think that *they* have good reasons for belief in God, and that is all that the evidential principle demands. What non-believers think is irrelevant. However, if it is not possible to come to an agreement the formal evidentialist may seriously wonder whether religious belief falls within the scope of rationality. Remember if an appropriate set of rules is found then everyone who (rationally) applies them must, if using the same information (premises), with necessity reach the same conclusion.

Swinburne, however, seems to accept that we have to settle (at least for now) for less than scientific rationality, or scientifically acceptable methods of inference, in religious matters. Some arguments for theism cannot be determined by rules (Bayes's theorem), or at least he has not yet been able to do that, and this is the reason why we cannot reach agreement on the issue:

> My conclusion so far then has been that the probability of theism is none too close to 1 or 0 on the evidence so far considered. However, so far in this chapter I have ignored one crucial piece of evidence, the evidence from religious experience. (I have ignored

this evidence so far, because I had a somewhat different approach to it from the approach to all other evidence, which involved the use of Bayes's theorem.)[59]

So for him, I take it, the rule principle of formal evidentialism is more of a highly desirable ideal that should be satisfied as far as it is possible, than an absolute condition for rational (religious) belief. That is, rationality is *essentially* if *not exhaustively* rule-governed or determined by rules. And his account can be taken as an argument for thinking that the argumentation regarding whether or not one should believe in God can be rationally discussed in the hope that one day we can proceed *fully* rationally (i.e., only use rule-governed methods of inference) in these matters also.

It seems clear that the philosophers we have considered here, who try to develop an evidentialist case for or against religious belief, try to satisfy the demands of formal evidentialism. They accept that rational believers (just as rational scientists) first collect good evidence for and against their hypothesis—that is, that God exists. They then examine the relationship between the hypothesis and the evidence so as to determine the probability of it on the basis of the evidence. They then believe or doubt the existence of God with a firmness proportional to the probability that it has based on the evidence. In short, rational agents are supposed to be Bayesian agents, and theists are rational to the extent that they are Bayesian agents.

They also approach their subject matter (religion) in the same way that the formal evidentialist approaches science. These philosophers of religion lack any detailed analysis of how religious people actually form and regulate or revise their beliefs. The standards for assessing the rationality of religious belief are assumed to be epistemically independent of actual religious agents and actual religious practice. *The actual practice of religion puts no, or at least almost no, constraints on their model of religious rationality (or irrationality).*[60]

So it is, strictly speaking, irrelevant that the actual religious believer's acceptance of the existence of God typically does not rise or fall with the evidence, that they do not treat their religious beliefs as simply more probable than not; that the conception of theism is so abstract and technical that it probably goes far beyond what ordinary religious people understand; or that the assessment of the arguments for or against the theistic hypothesis is so complex that the only reasonable thing ordinary believers can do is to sit down and wait for the verdict of the experts "before filling in their religious coupons."[61]

Such empirical analyses (of how believers actually act) are not needed, it is supposed, because philosophical enquiry—whether in philosophy of science or philosophy of religion—is only, or at least almost exclusively, a matter of logic and conceptual analysis. The philosophy of religion like the philosophy of science, is the study of the logical relationships among propositions, beliefs, theories, and the like. What really matters in determining the rationality of religious belief is the logical relation between the evidence and the hypothesis, in this case that God exists.

4.   Religious Belief as Properly Basic

Another way religious people can respond to the evidentialist challenge is to reject the first premise, that religious beliefs are not properly basic beliefs, and claim instead that all or more likely some religious beliefs are in fact properly basic. Therefore, religious belief is rational. This is what Plantinga and Alston have tried to do in different ways. Here I will just consider Plantinga's argument.[62] To start with he seems to accept the simple core approach to religion. Plantinga, correctly I think, describes the rationality debate in philosophy of religion like this: "the subject under discussion is not really the rational acceptability of belief *in* God, but the rationality of belief that God exists—that there *is* such a person as God." Then he goes on to say:

> So belief in God must be distinguished from the belief that God exists. Having made this distinction, however, I shall ignore it for the most part, using "belief in God" as a synonym for "belief that there is such a person as God." The question I want to address, therefore, is the question whether belief in God—belief in the existence of God—is rationally acceptable.[63]

So he thinks, just as Swinburne and Mackie do, that we can (and should, I presume) discuss the rationality of religion, or the rationality of religious belief, or the rationality of being religious, by exclusively focusing on one particular belief: belief *that* God exists.

Plantinga's thesis is "that it is entirely right, rational, reasonable, and proper to believe in God without any evidence or argument at all."[64] This is possible if we reject, as Plantinga thinks we should, the standard principle of proper basicality which is presupposed by the advocates of the evidentialist challenge, and instead accept a version of the principle that includes some religious beliefs as properly basic. But what is it that is wrong with the standard version of the principle of proper basicality?

Recall first, that this principle states that a belief is properly basic only if it is either self-evident, incorrigible, or evident to the senses. Plantinga calls the foundational evidentialist who accepts this principle of proper basicality a "classical foundationalist." However, one problem with this principle is that it is in fact *false*, because if true "then enormous quantities of what we all in fact believe are irrational."[65] Consider beliefs like: "I had breakfast this morning," "that person is angry," "people sleep," and "the earth existed many hundred years ago." I do not believe any of these beliefs on the basis of other beliefs, and yet they do not satisfy the standard principle of proper basicality. Take, for example, the belief that I had breakfast this morning. I do not believe this proposition on the basis of some propositions about my experience; I take it as basic. And I am entirely rational in taking it as basic, even though it does not satisfy the conditions of classical foundationalism. Therefore the standard version of the principle of proper basicality should be rejected.

If this will not convince the classical foundationalist, Plantinga has another argument available. The standard principle of proper basicality is not only false, it is also *self-referentially incoherent*. This is so because it is not rational for a classical foundationalist to accept the standard principle. It is not rational because the principle fails to satisfy the classical foundationalist's own standards. The principle is not self-evident; many people (among them Plantinga) understand it but consider it false. It is not incorrigible, a report of one's immediate experience; nor is it evident to the senses. So the principle is not properly basic, hence if rational it must be a non-basic belief. But it does not follow from beliefs that are self-evident, incorrigible, or evident to the senses either. So the standard principle of proper basicality is neither properly basic nor supported by evidence. Therefore, it is not rational to accept. If classical foundationalism is true, then no one is rational in accepting classical foundationalism!

So any version of the evidentialist challenge to religious belief that presupposes the standard principle of proper basicality must be rejected. But even if Plantinga is correct on this point it does not follow that belief in God is properly basic, because it must surely be possible to find another principle to put in its place. So how does he reach his conclusion? He simply says that for theists (at least the mature ones) belief in God just is basic. Under the right circumstances theists find themselves believing in God, not reaching that belief by reasoning to it from other beliefs that they take as evidence of it.[66] Agreeing with Calvin he says:

> there is in us a disposition to believe propositions of the sort *this flower was created by God* or *this vast and intricate universe was created by God* when we contemplate the flower or behold the starry heavens or think about the vast reaches of the universe.
>
> . . . Upon reading the Bible, one may be impressed with a deep sense that God is speaking to him. Upon having done what I know is cheap, or wrong, or wicked, I may feel guilty in God's sight and form the belief *God disapproves of what I have done.* Upon confession and repentance I may feel forgiven, forming the belief *God forgives me for what I have done.*[67]

But are these beliefs really *properly* basic, and if they are, cannot just *any* belief be properly basic? Plantinga thinks not. His rejection of the standard version of proper basicality does not commit him to accepting any belief as properly basic. That follows only if one (like the formal evidentialist) endorses the rule principle, that is, if one must have—to be rational in one's choice—a rule available by which properly basic beliefs can be distinguished from not properly basic ones. But Plantinga rejects the idea that we need such a criterion:

> The fact is, I think, that . . . [no] necessary and sufficient condition for proper basicality follows from clearly self-evident premises by clearly acceptable arguments. And hence the proper way to arrive at such a criterion is, broadly speaking, *inductive.* We must assemble examples of beliefs and conditions such that the former are obviously properly basic in the latter, and examples of beliefs and conditions such that the former are obviously *not* properly basic in the latter. We must then frame hypotheses as to the necessary and sufficient conditions of proper basicality and test these hypotheses by reference to those examples.[68]

However, he goes on to say something that seems more problematic:

> But there is no reason to assume, in advance, that everyone will agree on the examples. The Christian will of course suppose that belief in God is entirely proper and rational; if he does not accept this belief on the basis of other propositions, he will conclude that it is basic for him and quite properly so. Followers of Bertrand Russell and Madelyn Murray O'Hare may disagree; but how is that relevant? Must my criteria, or those of the Christian community, conform to their examples? Surely not. The Christian community is responsible to *its* set of examples, not to theirs.[69]

So disagreement exists concerning what beliefs are properly basic. But Plantinga thinks this is not relevant. People disagree about all sorts of things.

4.1   IS BELIEF IN GOD PROPERLY BASIC?

Other philosophers, however, have not taken as lightly as Plantinga seems to have taken the disagreement about whether belief in God, or some related beliefs, are properly basic. Disagreement they claim is relevant. Two of the problems that have been pointed out are the following. The first is that many people in the appropriate circumstances seem to fail spontaneously to form theistic beliefs. The second is that many people seem to accept beliefs that are incompatible with certain theistic beliefs which Plantinga claims are properly basic. Let us start with the former difficulty.

What is characteristic of a basic belief such as "I see a human person before me" or "I had breakfast this morning" is that any normal person, we are inclined to think, will form these basic beliefs in the appropriate circumstances. But this does not seem to be the case with theistic beliefs. As Gutting points out, many of the theists' "epistemic peers"—people who are equal in all relevant aspects, including intelligence, honesty, and the like, do not spontaneously form theistic beliefs when they gaze on the starry heavens, read the Bible, or are overcome with guilt. So these epistemic situations do not, like the first examples I gave, automatically give rise to the same beliefs— theistic beliefs. Gutting concludes, therefore, that theistic beliefs are not properly basic.[70]

The second problem is that it is quite common for people to take beliefs as properly basic that are incompatible with theistic beliefs. For instance this seems to be the case with adherents of non-theistic religions. Wainwright gives the following example, "upon reading the Iśa Upanishad or having a mystical experience, Advaitins may find themselves spontaneously believing that differences are unreal or that the impersonal Brahman is ultimate. If these beliefs are true, theism is false." Then he goes on to say:

> As a Christian or Jewish theist reads the Bible, it may seem immediately obvious that God is addressing him or her through the words of scripture. An Advaitin may find it immediately obvious that the Iśa Upainishad is a revelation of eternal truth. Both think that their beliefs are not only basic but also *properly* basic. Why, then, should theists trust their own "intuitions" rather than those of Advaitins? If both are equally intelligent, informed, and religiously sensitive, it seems arbitrary to privilege one set of intuitions rather than the other.[71]

Therefore, Wainwright claims that since the same type of belief-forming process seems to be involved in both cases, neither process can be reliable because they produce incompatible beliefs. So neither of them is reliable. And consequently belief in God cannot be properly basic.

However, neither of these difficulties seems to be in principle unsolvable. The first problem can be met if theists deny that those who disagree with them are their epistemic peers. Plantinga seems inclined to such a view. We may find ourselves in the right circumstances but fail to form theistic beliefs since the disposition God originally created in us has been weakened by sin.[72] The second difficulty can be met by claiming that the conflicts are not real. Hick seems to adopt this strategy at least when it comes to the conflicts between different sets of religious beliefs. Hick agrees with Plantinga, I think, that belief in God, or as he would say belief in the "Real" or "ultimate Reality," is properly basic, but he claims that there is only an apparent conflict between different religions.[73] They are all ultimately saying the same thing: that human beings need "salvation/liberation," that is, "the transformation of human existence from self-centredness to Reality-centredness."[74] But I think it is unlikely that Plantinga would want to follow this line of argument. Instead, he would probably try to argue that there is some relevant difference in these cases, for example, by denying that Advaitins and theists are epistemic peers.

One could have, and I have, serious doubts whether any argument Plantinga could give along these lines can really be successfully carried out. However, my intention is not to examine in great detail the arguments that have and can be given for or against the first premise of the evidentialist challenge to religious belief, but to focus on the model of rationality that it presupposes.[75] And even if Plantinga challenges the standard principle of proper basicality, a principle that has dominated discussions of religious issues in the West for a very long time, we must remember that he himself is a foundational evidentialist, though the foundationalism he accepts is of a weaker form than classical foundationalism.[76]

Recall that according to the foundational evidentialist, a person is rational in accepting a given belief only if that belief is either (*a*) a properly basic belief, or (*b*) if it can be shown by acceptable methods of inference to be evidentially supported by properly basic beliefs or other already justified (derived) beliefs; and (*c*) the strength of the non-basic beliefs are proportional to their support from the foundation. According to Plantinga:

> a belief is *justified* for a person at a time if (a) he is violating no epistemic duties and is within his epistemic rights in accepting it then and (b) his noetic structure [i.e., the set of propositions he believes, together with certain epistemic relations that hold between him and these propositions] is not defective by virtue of his then accepting it.[77]

A noetic structure is not defective if the belief is either properly basic or based on evidence. He also seems to accept the proportionality principle: "the foundational holds, sensibly enough, that in a rational noetic structure the strength of a nonbasic belief will depend upon the degree of support from foundational beliefs." And he says, and seems to agree, that reformed thinkers (Calvin, Kuyper, and Bavinck) have no objection to the proportionality principle.[78]

But in one crucial aspect Plantinga deviates from formal evidentialism as we have seen, since he rejects the rule principle, at least, when it comes to determining whether a belief is properly basic. It is not clear whether he also rejects the claim that it is necessary to have rules to determine what degree of support the foundation gives to some set of non-basic beliefs, or evidence gives to a theory, for the acceptance of it to be considered rational.

4.2 PLANTINGA AND THE SCIENTIFIC CHALLENGE TO RELIGIOUS BELIEF

Swinburne, as we saw, is probably an advocate of the strong response to the scientific challenge. That is, he seems to accept the first premise: that religious beliefs must fulfill the same, or at least similar, standards of rationality as scientific beliefs in order to be considered rational. He claims that religious beliefs, or rather theistic beliefs, can satisfy this requirement, hence he rejects the second premise of the challenge.

What about Plantinga, how does he respond to the scientific challenge? If by standards of scientific rationality we mean the standards used to assess scientific hypotheses, I think it is pretty clear that he is a defender of the differentiation response. He rejects the first premise of the challenge and claims that belief in God is rational, but the standards of scientific rationality or something similar to them do not apply to it. The same or similar standards of rationality do not apply to belief in God as to scientific beliefs because the former is a basic belief while the latter are non-basic beliefs. For example, the belief in scientific hypotheses like the claims that atoms are made of protons, electrons, and neutrons or that $E = mc^2$ are arrived at by performing certain experiments in a laboratory—they are supported by evidence. However, belief in God is accepted non-inferentially. Therefore, the standards of scientific rationality we have identified so far (the evidential principle, the proportionality principle, the rule principle, and the principles of simplicity, scope, and explanatory power) are inappropriate for assessing the rationality of religious belief, or at least belief in God. Consequently Plantinga objects to and rejects Mackie's application of the principle of simplicity or economy to belief in God:

> . . . Mackie throughout assumes that theism is or is relevantly like a *scientific hypothesis*—something like Special Relativity, for example, or Quantum Mechanics, or the Theory of Evolution. (And when we see this point, it helps to explain the attraction of economy for Mackie; presumably if a pair of scientific hypotheses are otherwise

on a par, the more economical one gets the nod.) Speaking of religious experience, he makes the following characteristic remark: "Here, as elsewhere, the supernaturalist hypothesis fails because there is an adequate and much more economical naturalistic alternative" (198). Clearly this remark is relevant only if we think of belief in God as or as like a sort of scientific hypothesis, a theory designed to explain some body of evidence, and acceptable to the degree that it explains that evidence.[79]

Mackie's remark is not relevant because belief in God is a basic belief while scientific hypotheses are non-basic. Therefore, the analogy between religious belief (at least, belief in God) and scientific hypotheses should be resisted. The scientific challenge to religious belief is not so much false or meaningless as it is *irrelevant* to the problem of the rationality of religious belief.

However, if we think that *all* beliefs, whether they are inferentially or non-inferentially believed, should be rejected if they do not satisfy the demands of the scientific challenge, it means that, for example, belief in other minds is irrational. But no philosopher has, according to Plantinga, ever constructed a cogent argument for the existence of other minds, and it is difficult to see how this task might be accomplished. So belief in God is in the same boat as, among other basic beliefs, belief in other minds. "Hence my tentative conclusion: if my belief in other minds is rational, so is my belief in God. But obviously the former is rational, so, therefore, is the latter."[80] In short, if that is the case, the scientific challenge against basic beliefs should be rejected.

5

The Practice-Oriented View of Science

Thomas Kuhn's book *Structure of Scientific Revolutions* published in 1962 provides an important landmark in philosophy of science, and Giere and others may be right in saying that it is the most influential book in philosophy of science published in this century.[1] Anyway, even though many philosophers of science have rejected many of Kuhn's central theses, most of them have accepted (at least to some extent) perhaps his most fundamental thesis: *that philosophers of science must pay close attention to the history of science and to current scientific practice in developing their theories about science.* This claim provides the basis for much of his criticism of such formalists as the logical positivists, Popper, and Lakatos. (At that time, it was very far from generally accepted that the history of science, something descriptive had anything to with philosophy of science, something normative.)

After Kuhn the main body of work in philosophy of science has become "naturalized." Typically naturalized philosophy of science consists of at least the claim that (*a*) philosophy of science must be true to science as practiced, and maybe also the thesis that (*b*) the methods of science should be applied not only in science but to the methodology of science—to philosophy of science itself. (So "naturalism" in philosophy of science and epistemology means in general something quite different from the meaning of the term in philosophy of religion or metaphysics.) Kitcher in his article, "The Naturalists Return," talks about the *naturalist turn* in philosophy today, away from the previous *linguistic turn,* and he says:

> Epistemological naturalism can be characterized negatively by its rejection of post-Fregean approaches to these investigations [of epistemological issues]. For many Anglo-American philosophers from the

1930s to the present, the epistemological issues I have mentioned reduce to questions of logic, conceptual analysis, or "grammar." . . . Finally, with respect to the improvement of belief, analytic philosophers have yearned for a generalization of Frege's strikingly successful analysis of mathematical proof. An ideal logic of science, encompassing elementary forms of induction as well as appeals to simplicity, explanatory power, and other methodical desiderata, would enable us to emulate Frege's achievement across a broader range. All these enterprises have two important presuppositions: first, following both Frege and the Wittgenstein of the *Tractatus,* they pursue epistemological questions in an apsychologistic way—logic, not psychology, is the proper idiom for epistemological discussion; second, they conceive of the products of philosophical reflection as *a priori*—knowledge is to be given a "logical analysis," skepticism is to be diagnosed as subtly inconsistent, the improvement of methodology consists in formulating the logic of science.[2]

The advocates of naturalized epistemology characteristically reject both of these presuppositions that Kitcher identifies. However, naturalized philosophers of science do not agree on how true one should be to science or how one should explain what is going on in science. Roughly, one could say that two camps have developed, the *sociologists of science* and the *historians of science.* Only the later group can be understood as practice-oriented philosophers, whereas the former group espouses one kind of contextualism, Therefore, in this chapter I will not talk about naturalized philosophy of science in contrast to formal philosophy of science, since the former in fact includes two very different approaches to science.

All practice-oriented philosophers share the claim that any normative account of an aspect of science, such as rationality, must be in *substantial contact* with the actual past and present practice of science. However, they disagree about how close this substantial contact has to be and to what extent it is possible to develop and to criticize an aspect of science, such as scientific rationality, from the outside—by people (typically philosophers) not directly involved in science. Contextual philosophers of science, on the other hand, hold the view that science is good as it is, and we can only describe what is going on there but not criticize it from outside. If they want to talk about rationality (which the contextualists who are sociologists of science do not), the assumption is that the standards and justification of scientific rationality arise solely from science itself.

The post-Kuhnian philosophy of science, in sharp contrast to the pre-Kuhnian, is characterized by a plurality of accounts of science, and no substantial consensus is to be found. However, despite this, I think it is still possible to distinguish between these three general views, formal, practice-oriented, and contextual philosophy of science. But since among practice-oriented philosophers of science there is great diversity, I shall when presenting the *practice-oriented view of science* make a rational reconstruction of it. The focus will be on scientific rationality and no attempt is made to give a full account of this view of science.

In contrast to the formal view, the practice-oriented view is not an *a priori* but an *a posteriori* account of science. According to its advocates this means that if we want to develop a model of scientific rationality we cannot just or mainly focus on conceptual or logical considerations and develop them into a general model of rationality that we then apply to science. Instead we must proceed the other way around: we must first examine actual scientific practice and how scientists form and regulate their beliefs and make theory-choices before we can develop a model of scientific rationality. But neither the actual scientific practice nor the philosophical considerations should automatically have priority. Instead, an adequate model of scientific rationality must acknowledge the epistemic significance of both the actual practices and the philosophical accounts that are proposed independently of such practices.

1.   The Relevance of the History of Science

The most striking difference between the formal view and the practice-oriented view is that the advocates of the latter reject the use of formal logic as the primary tool for the analysis of the scientific practice and instead replace it with a detailed study of the history of science and current scientific practice. The primary way of understanding the scientific enterprise is by studying the history of actual scientific practice. (This is one reason why I have chosen to call this image of science the "practice-oriented view of science.") The assumption behind the emphasis on history of science is that the *actual practice of science puts constraints on normative models of scientific rationality*. A model can be rejected if it does not fit the history of science. Case-studies of actual scientific practice can constitute evidence for or against a proposed scientific methodology. The formal view of science is rejected exactly because of this; it does not fit the history of science.

Let me exemplify this approach to the philosophy of science with what some philosophers of science have written. McMullin says "one must not attempt to prescribe a rationality for an activity as complex as natural science without first examining its actual practice."[3] Giere makes a similar comment:

> For too long philosophers have debated how scientists ought to judge hypotheses in glaring ignorance of how scientists in fact judge hypotheses. Before presuming to give advice on how something ought to be done, one should first find out how it is done. Maybe it is now being done better than one thinks. Indeed, attempting to follow the proffered advice might be detrimental to scientific progress.[4]

A clear expression of this view of science is provided by Moser:

> We could easily formulate a priori standards for scientific justification that either have no direct relevance to the cognitive goals of actual scientists or imply that all past and present scientific goals and assumptions are not scientifically justifiable. So long as these a priori standards need not be constrained by the cognitive goals of actual scientists, but need only to come from one's preferred notion of empirical knowledge, we could have a wide-ranging plethora of such standards that relate at best coincidentally to the cognitive goals of actual scientists. A priori standards for justification are not hard to come by, if they can come, as Carnap suggests, solely from one's preferred notion of empirical knowledge. It seems, however, that our standards for *scientific* justification must have some substantive epistemic connection to actual cognitive goals of scientists; otherwise, these standards will fail to be scientific in any relevant sense.[5]

What consequences does such a practice-oriented view of science yield? Recall that the formal evidentialist claims that theory-choice in science is settled by well-established and appropriate rules (algorithms). One theory follows another in steady progression, and the rules of science show why and how a new theory is to be preferred over the old one. Therefore, scientific theory-choice is objective and rational. If this is not exactly the case at present in science it will be in the near future. All philosophers of science need is some time to make explicit the rules scientists use more or less intuitively. Hence the task of philosophy of science is to formulate the rules in accordance with which theories are to be accepted or rejected. Scientific belief and theory-choices are rule-governed. However, considerations of actual scientific practice have led the practice-oriented philosophers to reject this image of scientific rationality, to reject both the logicality thesis (including the rule principle) and the stability thesis. Scientific theory-choice is not rule-governed. The actual rules of science are not sufficient to determine theory-choice, and the rules of theory-choice change as science develops.

Kuhn's reaction to the formal view of science is (after he has studied in detail out-of-date and contemporary scientific theories and the actual theory-choices made by scientists in the past and in the present) that it "did not at all fit the enterprise that historical study displayed."[6] Scientific decisions neither were nor are governed by some set of pre-established and neutral set of rules that determine which theory it is rational for scientists to accept or reject. Other practice-oriented philosophers have made the same observation and followed Kuhn in claiming that the history of science does not provide any clear evidence for believing that science is more likely to progress if we follow, for instance, a Popperian policy of rapid refutation (by using *modus tollens*) of theories in the face of counter-evidence, than if we follow a policy of protection of apparently refuted theories while we search for supplementary theories or hypotheses that will allow us to protect those theories. The history of science also provides no grounds for believing that we can put a clear limit (provided by a set of rules) concerning how long it is legitimate to seek ways of protecting a theory. Kuhn writes:

We have already noted, for example, that during the sixty years after Newton's original computation, the predicted motion of the moon's perigee remained only half of that observed. As Europe's best mathematical physicists continued to wrestle unsuccessfully with the well-known discrepancy, there were occasional proposals for a modification of Newton's inverse square law. But no one took these proposals very seriously, and in practice this patience with a major anomaly proved justified. Clairaut in 1750 was able to show that only the mathematics of the application had been wrong and that Newtonian theory could stand as before. Even in cases where no mere mistake seems quite possible . . . ,persistent and recognized anomaly does not always induce crisis. No one seriously questioned Newtonian theory because of the long-recognized discrepancies between predictions from that theory and both the speed of sound and the motion of Mercury. . . . They could be recognized as counterinstances and still be set aside for later work.[7]

Kuhn points out that scientists instead of always trying to falsify their theories often are strongly committed to them. Many scientists spend their entire professional lives solving problems within the framework of an accepted theory such as evolutionary theory or quantum theory. They use these theories as a *basis* for their work and do *not* consider themselves obligated to verify, test, or falsify these theories.[8] Kuhn calls these comprehensive theories *paradigms* and the period when scientists work under these circumstances "normal science." "Paradigm" is a complex notion, but basically Kuhn uses it in two related ways, in one narrow and one broad sense. In the broad sense "it stands for the entire constellation of beliefs, values, techniques, and so on shared by the members of a given [scientific] community." In the narrow sense paradigms are "universally recognized scientific achievements that for a time provide model problems and solutions to a community of practitioners."[9] Generally speaking, we could perhaps say that paradigms are standard examples of scientific work that embody a set of conceptual, methodological and metaphysical assumptions. One function of a paradigm is to indicate which aspects of nature are to be studied, what questions are to be asked, and what type of answers are to be sought. Examples of principles that have had or have this kind of paradigmatic function are: the ancient astronomers' agreement that all celestial motions are circular; Newton's laws of mechanics; the idea that biological species are fixed; and the principle that no physical process can take place at a velocity greater than that of light.

It is especially when theories that function as paradigms are abandoned that it becomes most evident that scientific theory-choices are not determined by any set of pre-established rules. (When anomalies accumulate and scientists begin to doubt that the paradigm has the conceptual resources to solve the problems, a research field faces a *crisis*.) In a situation of scientific revolution there exists no set of rules that scientists can use for solving the questions arising. Brown illustrates this kind of problem by asking us to consider a situation of conflict between advocates of Newton's mechanics and advocates of the theory of special relativity. Suppose that:

> you are standing on the ground and, by whatever method, you determine the velocity, v, of a passing jet. As the jet passes over your head it fires a missile in the forward direction, and this missile moves away from the jet at a velocity that the jet's pilot measures to be u. Problem: if you were to measure the velocity of the missile, what velocity would you find? It might seem obvious that the answer is $u + v$, and classical mechanics agrees, but this cannot be the correct answer in the framework of relativity. If, for example, v is half the speed of light, and u is three fourths the speed of light, their sum is greater than the velocity of light, which is forbidden. Of course, relativity does not leave the matter there; the principle of the theory entails a different rule for adding velocities. According to this rule, $u + v$ must be divided by the square root of $1 + (uv/c)$, where c is the velocity for light. Note that this formula will never give a velocity greater than the velocity of light, . . . Note also that the velocity of light is enormous, and we require velocities in the neighborhood of half the velocity of light before we get an easily measurable difference between the relativistic prediction and the results of simple addition.[10]

Brown points out that before the development of the theory of special relativity scientists thought that the velocity addition formula was *external* to all physical theories and that it was obviously true, and thus not subject to any kind of empirical reconsiderations. But what the theory of special relativity shows is that in fact the formula is *internal* to a particular theory and it is indeed subject to empirical reconsiderations. How can we settle this kind of conflict between Newton's mechanics and the theory of special relativity in a rational manner? What kind of rules can we use? To be a part of this sort of debate is to be in a debate that the practice-oriented philosopher claims there exist no clear rules for. It is a debate where we have to consider a proposal on the basis of criteria that opponents of the proposal reject. The opponents argue that the velocity addition formula is intuitively correct, and therefore the proposed theory must be wrong. The proponents of special relativity argue the other way around, that their theory must be right and, therefore, the velocity addition formula must be rejected.

Hence, the practice-oriented philosopher claims that the formalist's view of science simply does not fit the history of science. No set of rules can be found, or even be rationally reconstructed, that can determine the outcome of a change of paradigm in science, say from a Newtonian to an Einsteinian paradigm in physics. So if science is rational, its rationality cannot any longer be seen as located in science (or scientific theory or belief-regulation) being an explicitly or implicitly rule-governed enterprise.

The practice-oriented philosopher, however, rejects not only the rule principle but also the stability thesis (that the rules in science do not drastically change as science develops), because we can give examples from the history of science that show that the rules used by scientists drastically change. The rules with which scientific theory-choices are made change as science develops. Instead they accept what might be called the "revisability thesis":

> *The Revisability Thesis*: The rules or standards according to which theory-choices are made change (gradually or drastically) as science develops.

In response to the claim that there is a "constancy of logic and method" in science, Laudan says: "We need waste little time on this approach. Virtually all the scholarly literature on the history of methodology shows unambiguously that such components of rational appraisal as criteria of explanation, views about scientific testing, beliefs about the methods of inductive inference and the like have undergone enormous transformations."[11] In a collection of essays he illustrates and provides evidence for the revisability thesis.[12] After giving some examples from the history of science of how the rules for what is scientifically acceptable or rational to believe or do change Shapere says:

> A multitude of other examples could (and some will, below) be adduced to indicate that the boundaries between the scientific and the

nonscientific—between, for example, the 'observable' and the 'unobservable', between the scientifically legitimate or possible and the scientifically illegitimate or impossible, between scientific problems and pseudo-problems, between scientific explanations and pseudo-explanations, between science and nonscience or nonsense—are not something given once and for all, but rather shift as our knowledge and understanding accumulate.[13]

So scientific change is not merely an alternation of factual beliefs about the world but goes deeper than that. It also extends to the methods, rules of reasoning, and concepts employed in science. But on reflection, Brown says, this should not surprise us, for there is no more reason to assume that we know *how* to study nature (what methods we should use) than to think that we can know before investigating *what* the world looks like and how things in it work.[14]

Let me also say a few words about the thought that a rational scientist is a Bayesian agent, or the like. The standard task as we have seen in the formal view is to formulate rules in accordance with which scientific theories are to be accepted or rejected. By doing this the formalist tries to show that science conforms to the rule principle and hence is rational. One approach developed to reach this objective is the Bayesian decision model. The aim of the advocates of this model is to explicate an algorithm for rational theory-choice, to find a mathematical function that picks out the rational option for a given agent (or agents) to choose. The claim is that in Bayes's theorem we have the appropriate rule for rational choice and belief.

The question practice-oriented philosophers ask is: do real scientists use (explicitly or implicitly) a probabilistic framework, in particular a Bayesian decision model, in organizing their evaluations of theories and hypotheses involved in their research? To the extent that the answer is "no" they urge us to reject the thought that scientists should be understood as Bayesian agents. The answer they give themselves is "no." Giere says that it is clear that scientists are not, and should not be, Bayesian agents: "there is now overwhelming empirical evidence that no Bayesian model fits the thoughts or actions of real scientists."[15]

The typical scientist is not overtly a Bayesian agent. Nuclear physicists, for example, never publish estimates of the odds of one hypothesis being true relative to others. Nor is this just a result of the enforced style of science journals. Even in their informal moments, nuclear scientists do not talk like Bayesians. The claim of those who would use Bayesian models descriptively must be that scientists are in fact "intuitive Bayesians," whatever they may say, and whatever methodology they might espouse. It is the claim that typical scientists are intuitive Bayesians that is refuted by the empirical studies described above.[16]

The empirical studies to which Giere refers include some studies done to investigate the application of Bayesian models to real people including scientists. All of these studies, he claims, show that the solution real people choose to the problems they are given to solve do not coincide with what a Bayesian agent would prefer.[17] A possible interpretation of this material is of course that these ordinary people and scientists are not rational in their choices and thinking. However, Giere's response, which is typical for practice-oriented philosophers, is instead to reject the Bayesian model of rationality.

2.   The Role of Informed Judgment in Science

Many philosophers have accused Kuhn of being a relativist and of giving an irrationalist account of scientific theory-choice or scientific belief-regulation. For instance, Lakatos writes "it [the growth of science] is non-inductive and irrational according to Kuhn. In Kuhn's view there can be no logic, but only psychology of discovery."[18] Much of this reaction can be understood, I think, only against the background assumption that rationality is, or at least, essentially is, governed or determined by rules. Since Kuhn is saying that such a logic of science does not exist, at least not when fundamental changes occur in the development of science, it follows that if rule-following is a necessary condition for rationality, his account of science is irrational.

But the practice-oriented philosophers understand Kuhn *not* as questioning the rationality of any of these (historical) scientific decisions, but rather as doubting that *if these decision were rational, they must have been governed by some set of rules*. So Kuhn's view of science is best understood as a rejection of the formal view of scientific rationality and not, as some philosophers tend to view it, as a rejection of rationality as such. This is also the way Kuhn claims that one should understand what he is saying. Kuhn says that his project is:

an attempt to show that existing theories of rationality are not quite right and that we must readjust or change them to explain why science works as it does. To suppose, instead, that we possess criteria of rationality which are independent of our understanding of the essentials of the scientific process is to open the door to cloud-cuckoo land.[19]

However, if we accept the practice-oriented philosopher's picture of actual scientific belief-regulation or theory-choice, it seems to leave us basically with three choices. We can (*a*) simply conclude that scientific belief-formation and regulation is either irrational or a-rational. This seems to be the position Feyerabend at least sometimes adopts.[20] Or we can (*b*) continue to search for rules that allow us to accept both the formal model of scientific rationality and the thesis that science is a paradigm example of rationality, as the post-Kuhnian formalists try to do. Or lastly we can (*c*) reject the formal model of scientific rationality and try to develop an alternative model of scientific rationality. It is this last alternative the practice-oriented philosophers choose to explore. They do this because they agree with most formalists that science is a paradigm example of rationality. Kuhn claims: "No process essential to scientific development can be labeled 'irrational' without vast violence to the term."[21] Brown writes: "In the case of rationality, science provides a crucial test case, since science, and particularly physical science, currently stands as our clearest example of a rational enterprise; if a model of rationality were to entail that science is not rational, we would have good reason for questioning the adequacy of that model."[22] And it is the success of science in dealing with theoretical and practical problems that gives it this status. Giere therefore says:

> Before proceeding any further it is worth noting that, apart from some philosophers and sociologists of science, there is practically no knowledge group in the whole of Western (if not world) culture that seriously questions the obvious successes of science. Who would seriously question that Watson and Crick discovered the basic structure of DNA in the early 1950s? Or that geologists in the 1960s discovered that the crust of the earth consists of shifting plates? Or even that the structure of the poliovirus was determined in 1985?[23]

Hence, there is every reason to think that science is a paradigm instance of rationality. But that means that if the choice is between thinking that science is a rational activity and thinking that a particular model of rationality is correct, then the practice-oriented philosophers urge us to reject the model. And the choice we have to make is either to reconsider the rationality of science or to reconsider the formal view. Either the choices scientists make in a scientific revolution are irrational or there is something drastically wrong with the formal model of scientific rationality.

But how are we then to understand scientific rationality? The fact that practice-oriented philosophers reject the claim that the method and rationality of science is essentially rule-governed is clear, but what, positively speaking, they think instead is not always so clear. Often it is said that the standards of rationality do not function any longer as *rules* but as *values*. Kuhn writes:

> What I am denying then is neither the existence of good reasons nor that these reasons are of the sort usually described. I am, however, insisting that such reasons constitute values to be used in making choices rather than rules of choices. Scientists who share them may nevertheless make different choices in the same concrete situation.[24]

So scientific rationality is not governed by rules but by values. But does this mean that science is rational because it is governed by values instead of rules? This could hardly be what Kuhn is trying to say. Before we go on and try to state what Kuhn probably is after, let us see why values cannot be the key. They cannot be the key because the values Kuhn is talking about—"accuracy, scope, simplicity, fruitfulness, and the like"—the formalists also in general accept.[25] Their disagreement is not primarily about these values (or the means, standards, and aims) of science, but whether such values can be specified in some articulated system of rules that can be more or less mechanically applied to a scientific theory-choice in order to determine what is the rational thing to do and believe. So it is somewhat misleading to talk in such a way as Kuhn does. Then what is Kuhn really after? What replaces rules if it is not values? One way of finding an answer is to focus again on the criticism Kuhn's view of science has received. For instance, Lakatos writes:

> For Popper scientific change is rational or at least rationally reconstructible and falls in the realm of the *logic of discovery*. For

> Kuhn scientific change—from one "paradigm" to another—is a mystical conversion which is not and cannot be governed by rules of reason and which falls totally within the realm of the (*social*) *psychology of discovery*. Scientific change is a kind of religious change.[26]

Later on Lakatos writes: "In Kuhn's view there can be no logic, but only psychology of discovery." And he concludes: "Thus in Kuhn's view scientific revolution is irrational, a matter for mob psychology."[27]

Notice that Lakatos's argumentation seems to give Kuhn two possibilities, either scientific change is a matter of logic and rules or it is a matter of psychology. Since it is not a matter of logic and rules, Lakatos argues, it is, therefore, a matter of personal opinion or of psychology. But, as Gutting points out, it is exactly this dichotomy Kuhn is trying to break free from. Gutting expresses this dichotomy and Kuhn's response as follows:

> The authority by which scientific claims are evaluated is either that of impersonal criteria (i.e., methodological rules), in which case science is objective and rational; or that of persons (i.e., the subjective preferences of individuals), in which case science is subjective and irrational. . . . In fact, however, Kuhn is trying to express a third alternative: an account of scientific authority in terms of the informed *judgment* of the community of trained scientists. . . . The judgment is ultimately determined by the carefully nurtured ability of members of the scientific community to assess rationally the overall significance of a wide variety of separately inconclusive lines of argument.[28]

Hence science is rational neither because it is governed by rules nor by values, but because it is *governed by informed judgments*. The practice-oriented philosopher claims that scientific rationality fundamentally consists of professional or informed judgments. So the basic thesis of the practice-oriented view of scientific rationality is:

> Scientific theory or belief-formation and regulation is rational because it is governed by informed judgments.

This thesis, however, does not imply that we can never use rules (or algorithms) in science or that it is inappropriate to use rules in

science. What it implies is that in most of the central theory-choices
scientists make, they do not use algorithms. We should try to use
algorithms whenever it is possible in science but in cases when it
is not possible we can make rational decisions by exercising one of
our skills—judgment. Further, it is by exercising judgment that we
can develop algorithms or rules for certain theory-choices, and hence
judgments are more fundamental in our belief-forming and regulation
processes than rules are.

Before we go on to consider what is characteristic for judgments,
let me comment briefly on the practice-oriented philosophers' attitude
toward the use of logic in philosophy of science. They do not deny
that science can be partly formalized, but the extent to which it cannot
be formalized must not be taken—as they claim that formalists tend
to take it—as a shortcoming of science. It is rather a shortcoming of
the logicality thesis (that the rationality of science can be assimilated
to that of a logical system). For instance, McMullin says:

> Scientists make use of a variety of kinds of inference, and these
> can be at least partially formalized. These formalisms can be (and
> indeed have been) developed as ends in themselves. But the crucial
> question is: do they illuminate what the scientist is actually *doing?*
> And the danger is that to the extent they do not, this will be taken
> by the philosopher to be a deficiency on the part of the scientist
> instead of an inadequacy of his or her own formalism.[29]

So what the practice-oriented philosopher claims is that to the
degree logical formalizations do not illuminate what the scientist is
actually doing, it is to be taken as an inadequacy of the formalization
and not of science.

2.1   EXPLICATING JUDGMENT

Even though we all, I guess, know intuitively what a judgment
is, it is notoriously difficult to define. Some practice-oriented philosophers have tried to explicate this problematic but central notion in the
practice-oriented view of science. Newton-Smith, for instance, writes
that judgment is the ability to make "decisions without being able to
provide an explicit justification at the time . . ." It is a skill a person
can exercise that cannot "be exhaustively described in some explicit
theory."[30]

But the philosopher who has put most effort into this project is probably Brown. Generally speaking, he says that judgments are cognitive acts that involve decisions which are based on information and which are not arbitrary, although they are not arrived at by following rules. A judgment is a skilled (trained) capacity to arrive at rational beliefs or decisions without using explicit or implicit rules. Brown calls judgment "the ability to evaluate a situation, assess evidence, and come to a reasonable decision without following rules."[31]

More specifically, Brown identifies three basic characteristics of judgments.[32] First, judgments are not made by following rules; they are rather presupposed by rule-governed decisions. The ability to exercise a judgment in a particular research field is a *skill*. It is an intellectual skill, and it is a skill that improves with practice. However, it is not possible to reduce these skills to applications of rules. If it were possible we would teach students of science simply the rules and not have them study concrete scientific examples or do problems that will improve their performance. Consider Polanyi's example of how a physician learns to read an X-ray:

> Think of a medical student attending a course in the X-ray diagnosis of pulmonary diseases. He watches in a darkened room shadowy traces on a fluorescent screen placed against a patient's chest, and hears the radiologist commenting to his assistants, in technical language, on the significant features of these shadows. At first the student is completely puzzled. For he can see in the X-ray picture of a chest only the shadows of the heart and the ribs, with a few spidery blotches between them. The experts seem to be romancing about figments of their imagination; he can see nothing that they are talking about. Then as he goes on listening for a few weeks, looking carefully at every new picture of different cases, a tentative understanding will dawn on him; he will gradually forget about the ribs and begin to see the lungs. And eventually, if he perseveres intelligently, a rich panorama of significant details will be revealed to him; of physiological variations and pathological changes, of scars, of chronic infections and signs of acute disease.[33]

The reason why the instructor makes students go through this learning process is that the activity of science cannot simply be explicated in terms of rules. Hence scientists need to learn or develop their *cognitive skills*—their ability to exercise judgments. (One reason why Kuhn introduces the notion "paradigm" is to cover this insight.)[34]

Second, although judgments are *fallible,* they are not arbitrary. According to Brown, the main reason why we jump so easily from "fallible" to "arbitrary" is the impact (strong) foundationalism has had on our thinking. In a sense the (strong) foundationalist and the skeptic share the same view of knowledge, i.e., that properly basic beliefs must be indubitable or incorrigible. In so far as one is optimistic about the program of identifying such beliefs one is a (strong) foundationalist, in so far as one is pessimistic one becomes a skeptic. But Brown thinks that the problem with establishing a proper epistemic foundation is solved not by finding an indubitable foundation, but by making an informed judgment. A judgment that is based on knowledge of the research field in question and which leads to a conclusion that in the present situation is epistemically satisfactory. This leaves scientists with an epistemic foundation but one that is fallible and open to reconsideration when necessary. So to accept the choice of a certain foundation as rationally justified requires only that it is based on an informed judgment. That is, scientists must have reflected long enough to come to a clear understanding of what is involved in the issue and check their understanding of what should count as an appropriate foundation (or reliable information) in the discipline against the views of their epistemic peers, i.e., scientists equal in intelligence, competence and honesty and other epistemic virtues.

The last characteristic of judgment that Brown identifies is that judgments must be exercised by those who are *competent* in the research field—by persons who have adequate knowledge and training. Appropriate judgments are those made by persons who are familiar with the body of relevant information. This information will normally consist of two parts: background knowledge (including techniques), and reliable information relevant to the case at hand. For instance, we would probably not have our medical diagnoses made by someone who has not studied medicine (who lacks the former information) or by someone who has studied medicine but has not studied the facts of this particular case (who lacks the latter information).

This emphasis on competence implies that proper scientific judgments always rest on adequate knowledge of the *content* of the scientific theories at issue. This makes the practice-oriented philosopher's understanding of rationality quite different from that of the advocate of the formal view of science. The formalist tries to capture rationality in terms of rules, and the point is that a formal account of rationality requires no substantial acquaintance with the actual content of the theories under discussion:

> Just as we can check the formal validity of any deductive argument without needing to know its subject matter, or verify a piece of arithmetic without having to know what entities, if any, are associated with the numerals before us, so philosophers have sought means of evaluating scientific theories against the data that did not require that the evaluator know anything about the content of those theories or that data.[35]

But Brown's conclusion is that:

> there are now strong grounds for doubting that scientific decisions can be either made or retrospectively assessed in terms of such formal structures [algorithms], and in their absence we seem to have little choice but to acknowledge that the making of such decisions requires detailed knowledge of the scientific issues involved. In other words, such decisions rest on professional judgment, and judgment is always founded on a grasp of content.[36]

No doubt more needs to be said about the characteristics of judgments. Brown's explication is to a high degree negative, in that it states judgment as the ability to evaluate a situation, assess evidence, and come to a reasonable decision without following rules. But what judgment is positively speaking he has more difficulty saying. However, his analysis is sufficient, I think, for illuminating the difference between the claim that scientific rationality consists of the application of an appropriate set of rules to a situation of theory-choice or belief-choice, and the claim that it consists of the proper exercise of informed judgments.

The practice-oriented philosopher, however, claims that scientific rationality consists of an additional condition beyond the view that a rational scientific decision or belief is arrived at by a person who exercises an informed judgment: it also consists of the fulfillment of a social condition. Let us see what this condition of scientific rationality involves.

2.2   THE SOCIAL CONDITION OF SCIENTIFIC RATIONALITY

Scientists gather evidence for their theories, apply available rules, consider the possible alternatives, and come to informed judgments. However, for scientists' theory-choice to meet the standards of scientific rationality they also have to take into account the judgments of their colleagues (or epistemic peers) and be ready to re-evaluate their position if necessary. Kuhn describes this social aspect of scientific rationality in the following way:

> confronted with the problem of theory-choice, the structure of my response runs roughly as follows: take a *group* of the ablest available people with the most appropriate motivation; train them in some science and in the specialities relevant to the choice at hand; imbue them with the value system, the ideology, current in their discipline (and to a great extent in other scientific fields as well); and, finally, *let them make the choice*. If that technique does not account for scientific development as we know it, then no other will. There can be no set of rules of choice adequate to dictate desired *individual* behaviour in the concrete cases that scientists will meet in the course of their careers. Whatever scientific progress may be, we must account for it by examining the nature of the scientific group, discovering what it values, what it tolerates, and what it disdains.[37]

So the community of scientists is responsible for and guarantees the rationality of science. This is so because scientists are the best equipped (absent appropriate rules) to make an informed judgment on the issue. Hence rational decisions are those made by the scientific community. Its members assess different theories or different solutions to a crisis and eventually arrive at a new consensus which can provide the basis for a new normal science. Brown writes: "In a revolutionary situation different individuals will offer different proposals for a new research consensus. Each of these is offered on the basis of that person's professional judgment, but once a proposal has been made, it becomes a subject for discussion and debate among the members of the professional community."[38] And only those with the relevant expertise are in a position to do this assessment. It is this process of community assessment that makes a scientific decision or theory rational.

So a necessary condition for rationality in science is *peer evaluation*. The individual scientist's beliefs, theories, or proposals must be tested against or exposed to the community of relevant scientific expertise to qualify as rational. It is this social aspect that replaces rules as the basis for scientific theory or belief-regulation and which guarantees the rationality of science. The social requirement functions as an intersubjective test of personal judgments. If, however, a sufficient set of rules is available the practice-oriented philosopher would prefer it, but since that is not normally the case the process of community evaluation is needed in science. Kuhn sometimes seems to think even that scientific rationality requires that the scientific community reach a consensus based on informed judgment about the theory in question. Once the community has arrived at a conclusion on an issue, that is what it is rational to believe or do. It is this ability to reach a consensus that gives science its cognitive authority.

Hence we can say at least that practice-oriented philosophers claim that scientific rationality consists of essentially two demands, the first concerning informed judgment and the second concerning peer evaluation.[39] They think that:

> Scientific theory or belief-formation and regulation is rational because (*a*) it is governed by informed judgments and (*b*) it involves intersubjective testing.

3. Evidence and Commitment in Science

The revisability thesis (that the methods and standards of rationality change as science develops), however, seems to imply that nothing is stable about the methods or rationality of science.[40] But even though many practice-oriented philosophers accept some version of the revisability thesis, their argumentation, I will claim, presupposes that something is stable, namely, that at least the *reliance on evidence* or *good reasons* is a constant feature of scientific rationality. Even though Shapere, Laudan, and Brown all accept the revisability thesis, they write, respectively:

> They [the scientific beliefs about the world] have been arrived at by an increasingly sophisticated and systematic process of investigating nature, a process roughly describable as being, or at least as having

come to be, one of collecting evidence on the basis of observation and experiment . . .[41]

At its core, rationality—whether we are speaking about rational action or rational belief—consists in doing (or believing) things because we have good reasons for doing so.[42]

[A] belief that we arrive at on the basis of an adequate body of appropriate evidence is a rational belief, while a belief that we arrive at without evidence, or against the evidence, or on the basis of irrelevant evidence, is not rational.[43]

Therefore I will argue that practice-oriented philosophers take something as stable in science (and that is something they have in common with the formalists), namely, *evidentialism,* or more correctly the evidential principle. Although it is true that what *counts* as evidence (or good reasons) changes when the scientist's framework changes, the reliance on evidence—whatever it is, and however it is understood—always seems to play a crucial role in science. What happens in a scientific revolution is not that scientists start questioning whether one should support one's theories or proposals of how to solve the crisis with evidence, but what is to count as evidence. They dispute what specific claims can or should support a theory or proposal.[44]

This is also how I think we should understand the thesis about informed judgment. Brown says that "judgments on a topic can only be made by those who have mastered the body of relevant information."[45] To make an informed judgment means that one has reflected long enough to come to a clear understanding of what is involved in the issue, including taking into account what is to count as evidence. Hence to say that a belief is rational only if it is arrived at by an exercise of informed judgment is just another way of saying that a belief is rational only if it is supported by good reasons (the evidential principle).

However, it is not formal but *social* evidentialism the practice-oriented philosopher of science accepts. The rule principle is exchanged for a social condition, what we might call the *social principle:* a scientific theory or belief must be exposed to the community of relevant expertise to qualify as rational. Hence the practice-oriented philosopher I have tried to describe is a *social evidentialist* with respect to scientific rationality. (Let us therefore from now on call him or her a social evidentialist.)

Formal evidentialists like Russell, Pap, and Popper have made a great fuss about the attitude that they think is characteristic of scientists. They say that scientists believe or accept a theory only tentatively. Commitment, a dogmatic attitude, or sometimes even belief is rejected as completely unscientific. Lakatos, a former student of Popper, writes: "*Belief* may be a regrettably unavoidable biological weakness to be kept under the control of criticism: but *commitment* is for Popper an outright crime."[46] Although social evidentialists, like formal evidentialists, accept the evidential principle, they typically reject this celebration of tentativity. More precisely, they reject the proportionality principle (the firmness with which one accepts a belief or a theory ought always to be in proportion to the strength of the evidence for it) and Popper's substitute, the principle of tentativity (all rational beliefs or theories should be only tentatively accepted, that is, one should never stop actively looking for counter-evidence to them). Social evidentialists reject these principles simply because they do not fit the history of science. Therefore, the historical studies of science have made them develop new viewpoints about the *degree of assent* with which a scientist should embrace a belief or theory.

Kuhn has shown the importance of commitment for scientific progress. A theoretical system develops through its capacity to deal with counter-evidence or anomalies. According to him, there are pragmatic reasons—if scientists believed in their theories only in a tentative way the scientific activity would degenerate—for discarding these principles. If scientists are going to be successful they should not follow the proportionality principle or the principle of tentativity. It is a historical fact that all new theories are, strictly speaking, falsified in their initial phase, and they are almost never rejected because they do not survive a test. No theory solves all problems it is confronted by, nor are the solutions the theory gives perfect. There is always a discrepancy between theory and evidence, and this requires that the scientist *believe* in his or her theory. Kuhn writes:

> there are pressing practical reasons for commitment. Every research
> problem confronts the scientist with anomalies whose sources he

cannot quite identify. His theories and observations never quite agree; successive observations never yield quite the same results; his experiments have both theoretical and phenomenological by-products which it would take another research project to unravel. Each of these anomalies or incompletely understood phenomena could conceivably be the clue to a fundamental innovation in sci-entific theory or technique, but the man who pauses to examine them one by one never completes his first project. . . . The men who make these reports find most discrepancies trivial or uninteresting, an evaluation that they can ordinarily base only upon their *faith* in current theory. Without that *faith* their work would be wasteful of time and talent.[47]

So the scientist's belief that a theory is correct is necessary for progress in science. A new theory must have the chance to develop its potential and this is possible only if scientists have a right to believe in their theories to a higher degree than the evidence warrants. The sci-entist's commitment must sometimes reach further than the evidence, and sometimes even against evidence (when rejecting anomalies).

Kuhn also points out that much of the training of students in natural science puts no emphasis on the problematization of the sci-entific tradition they are to inherit or the way of stating and solv-ing problems in their own discipline. They learn their profession by reading specially designed textbooks, and there is no collection of "readings" in natural science. "Nor are science students encouraged to read the historical classics of their fields—works in which they might discover other ways of regarding the problems discussed in their textbooks . . ."[48] In fact they are taught to take the paradigm of their discipline for granted and put their energy into developing its consequences even further. Kuhn, however, sees no irrationality inherent in natural science because of this. Instead, he thinks it might be necessary for the rapid progress for successful scientific work. But this does not mean that Kuhn does not think that tentativity is important in science:

I do not at all doubt that this description of "divergent thinking" [crit-ical thinking, tentativity, breaking established research traditions, etc.] and the concomitant search for those able to do it are entirely proper. Some divergence characterizes all scientific work, and gi-gantic divergences lie at the core of the most significant episodes in scientific development. But both my own experience in scientific research and my reading of the history of sciences lead me to wonder whether flexibility and open-mindedness have not been too exclusively emphasized as the characteristics requisite for basic research. I shall therefore suggest below that something like "convergent thinking" is just as essential to scientific advance as is divergent. Since these two modes of thought are inevitably in conflict, it will follow that the ability to support a tension that can occasionally become almost unbearable is one of the prime requisites for the very best sort of scientific research.[49]

What he wants to emphasize is that the basic mentality or attitude in science is characterized by tentativeness *as well as* commitment. However, there seems to exist a certain tension or dialectic between them in the progress of science. In science proper the scientist must live with this tension between the attitude of tentativeness and the attitude of commitment. And the most fruitful attitude to adopt in science cannot be decided—as the formalist tries to do—in an *a priori* manner, but must be the subject of historical case-studies. But both attitudes, Kuhn thinks, have to be present if scientists are going to be successful in their work.

If Kuhn's arguments for the importance of commitment (or full acceptance in contrast to mere tentative acceptance) in science are basically correct, it will imply at least two important things: that (*a*) the proportionality principle and the principle of tentativity must be rejected if we want to continue to see scientific practice as rational; and that (*b*) we cannot use these principles as a necessary element in our model of rationality. A more reasonable view might instead be that a scientist is at least *prima facie* rationally justified to act and believe as if his or her beliefs or theories are right against anomalies or counterevidence. All else equal, a scientist is rationally entitled to hold his or her beliefs with a commitment that exceeds the strength of the evidence for or against them. When this is no longer rationally justified cannot be established by a rule-governed procedures, but must be the subject of an informed judgment of the scientific community.

This discussion of tentativity and commitment in science leads naturally to the discussion of science and non-science (and pseudoscience), since advocates of the formal view have typically seen tentativeness as an essential component of a proper criterion of demarcation. According to Popper, as we have seen, the intellectual dishonesty, irrationality, or unscientific character of committed Marxists and Freudians consists in that they refuse to specify precisely the conditions under which they are willing to give up their positions. The defenders of the practice-oriented view, on the other hand, claim that we must take a close look at actual scientific practice before we can say what is unscientific or irrational. Newton-Smith says, concerning Popper's view:

> One's first response to this claim is to ask rhetorically whether physicists ever lay down in advance what would lead them to reject either physics itself or a particular theory. Even if we set aside the Popperian hostility to psychoanalysis, do physicists ever lay down in advance what would lead them to give up, say, Quantum Mechanics? Of course not. Has anyone ever encountered a paper in the *Review of Physics* that begins with an explicit statement or an implicit acknowledgment of what anomalies would lead the author to reject his theory? I doubt it.[50]

In fact, it is not clear that the institution of science could survive if all or most members of the community made it their aim to falsify theories. For that is too easy, and it also involves neglecting the need for the sympathetic development of *prima facie* plausible theories. Popper gives, therefore, a distorted picture of actual practice of science. Instead Newton-Smith thinks that: "Progress requires that most scientists get themselves in the grip of a theory which they aim to develop and defend, and without simply trying to dispose of it as fast as possible."[51] Hence successful scientific work requires commitment and Popper's criterion of demarcation must be rejected, otherwise science itself might end up being unscientific!

And typically, since social evidentialists accept a practice-oriented approach, they make no claims—without further investigation—about whether their conclusions apply outside the practice they investigate. Chalmers writes:

> If some area of knowledge, such as Freudian psychology or Marx's historical materialism, to take two favourite targets of philosophers of science, were to be criticized on the grounds that they do not conform to my characterization of physical science, then it would be implied that all genuine knowledge must conform to the methods

and standards of physical science. This is not an assumption I am prepared to make, and is one that I think would be very difficult to defend.[52]

However, if one wants to consider whether a practice is scientific (is rational, makes justified knowledge claims, or the like), one cannot do that by claiming that the practice does or does not conform to some ready-made and once-and-for-all conception of science and scientific method. Rather, Chalmers's suggestion is that we must investigate what the aims of the practice under investigation are and to what extent those have been attained. We would then be in a position to evaluate the practice "in terms of the desirability of what it aims for, the extent to which its methods enable the aims to be attained, and the interests that it serves."[53]

6

Social Evidentialism

Brown in particular has tried to develop the practice-oriented model of scientific rationality into a general model of rationality. Let us call this model *social evidentialism*. By "general" model of rationality I mean simply that the advocates of the model claim that it can be applied to more than one practice, and maybe even to all the practices we (or some other agents) participate in. In this case, social evidentialists claim that their model of rationality can be properly used also outside scientific practice.

Before we go on developing social evidentialism let us first think a little about the benefits of a general model of rationality. Do we really need any general models of rationality? What are these models good for? I shall claim that all things being equal, a model that can be applied to as many human practices (such as science, religion, everyday life, ethics, economy, or the like) as possible is to be preferred over a less widely applicable model. An integration of our cognitive world is to be preferred over a separation or division of it. It is hard, I think, to disagree with Jeffner, when he says that such an integration should be a "primary philosophical goal."[1]

However, though Jeffner and others have been optimistic (perhaps too optimistic) about the likelihood of reaching such a goal, my claim at this stage is not that it is likely, but that such integration of our world of thoughts is more valuable than a fragmentation or sectorization of it. Hence it is worth exploring whether we can develop a general model of rationality and, therefore, a limited model of rationality will always be a fallback position, to be accepted only if the former project fails. If it seems to be the case that what is reasonable to do (what to believe, how to act, and how to make evaluations) completely changes as soon as we move from one practice or area of life to another, this is not something we should be too happy about or

141

desire. This means that if my argument is correct on this point, we have here a meta-criterion, an appropriate standard for assessing different models of rationality: *All things else being equal, the broader the scope or the field of application a model of rationality has the better it is.*

1.   The Appropriate Standards of Rationality

As we have seen, the social evidentialist does not view rationality as an essentially rule-guided process, but rather as a process that is first of all guided by the exercise of informed judgments. A rational decision or belief is obtained by a person who performs an informed judgment. This is one version of the evidential principle. It is just another way of saying that we need good reasons for what we do, but it is one which emphasizes that the assessment of how well a belief is supported by evidence is typically not a rule-governed process, but is a result of a judgment. (I will focus on beliefs, but as Brown points out the outcome of a judgment does not have to be a belief, it can also be a decision.)[2] So the term "informed" in the phrase "informed judgment" signifies the evidential principle, and "judgment" indicates the main method of evaluation. The social evidentialist claims that the main method of evaluation open to us is a judgment-based method of reasoning. However, an individual's informed judgment concerning what to believe must also be exposed to the community of competent others before what is believed can be said to the rational. Rationality requires peer evaluation.

So the advocates of social evidentialism, who accept it as a general model of rationality, claim that these two standards of rationality ought to be applicable to *all* practices we participate in or to *all* areas of life where the question of rationality arises. According to them, the two individually necessary and jointly sufficient conditions of rationality are:

> *The Evidential Principle:* A belief is rationally acceptable only if it is arrived at by a person who exercises informed judgment.

> *The Social Principle:* A belief is rationally acceptable only if it has been exposed to or tested against the judgments of a community of relevant expertise.

Hence the *thesis* is that people's actual belief formation and regulation processes are rationally governed only if what they deliver (beliefs) is arrived at by an exercise of informed judgment and exposed to peer evaluation. Let us take a closer look at these two principles.

Rationality requires people to have the ability to make informed judgments. First, this means that if we are to be rational we must believe on the basis of evidence: to believe something without evidence or against evidence or on the basis of irrelevant evidence is not rational. Second, judgment is required especially in those situations in which we lack sufficient rules to determine what to believe on a topic. Such situations the formal evidentialist thinks are outside the scope of rationality, since what to believe is in those cases arbitrary and cannot be rationally determined. However, Brown thinks that exactly the opposite is true. A rational person—which Brown also thinks is in accordance with our pre-analytical conception of rationality—is one who is able to come to a reasonable conclusion particularly in such situations, cases in which we lack clear guiding principles. He writes:

> We expect a rational person to be amenable to new ideas, and even to be capable of making new proposals in a sticky situation. . . . newspaper editorials do not issue calls for rationality in balancing checkbooks or differentiating algebraic functions, but they do call for rationality in moral and political situations, and in doing so they are not urging people to follow well known rules.[3]

Third, our ability to be rational in what we believe is limited by our expertise. This is the reason why judgments need not be arbitrary even though they are fallible. They are not arbitrary because to be able to arrive at an informed judgment requires a certain degree of cognitive competence in the particular field in question. Even if we do not have the cognitive resources to be an expert in every field, this does not mean, according to the social evidentialist, that we are irrational in accepting beliefs in those domains. This is so because it is possible for us to make a rational decision in such situations— to seek expert advice, to rely on authority. People can often make informed judgments about which authorities to accept and can also seek advice on this issue from their epistemic peers or from what we might call their *epistemic superiors,* individuals who on this issue have more relevant knowledge, more competence, and better access to the relevant facts.

The idea that rational believing is governed by informed judgments also seems to satisfy our intuitive idea that rational beliefs should be more *reliable* than irrational beliefs. Social evidentialists claim that their model of rationality meets this requirement because informed judgments are based on appropriate evidence. To conform to this idea, it seems that our models of rationality have to do better than chance in the long run. But on the other hand, they do not have to work perfectly—as sometimes formal evidentialists (in particular strong foundationalists) have demanded. In this common sense intuition, I think, we have a second meta-criterion, an appropriate standard for evaluating different models of rationality: *A model of rationality must do better than chance in the long run.*

So what Chemiak calls "null rationality" would not qualify.[4] A *null model of rationality* does not put any rationality restrictions at all on people or beliefs. One is allowed to believe anything one likes and take any way one find suitable to reach that belief. One can flip a coin, look in a hexagram or do whatever one likes. The answer to the question: "How stupid can you be and still be rational?" is, according to the advocates of this model: "As stupid as you like."

But as we saw in the last chapter, the social evidentialist rejects the second element of evidentialism as it is traditionally understood, namely, the proportionality principle (the firmness with which one accepts a belief or a theory ought always to be in proportion to the strength of the evidence for it). According to the social evidentialist, one is not obligated to proportion one's beliefs to the strength of the evidence for them, as one has instead an epistemic permission to be committed to what one believes. The restriction on rational believers is that they must in principle be ready to re-evaluate their beliefs if the amount of counter-evidence increases or if their competent others disagree. And a certain dialectic must remain in their believing between an attitude of commitment and tentativeness. The thought is that people must, at least sometimes, have a right to accept their beliefs with a firmness that exceeds the strength of the evidence for or against them. When this right is suspended cannot be decided in an *a priori* fashion—as the formal evidentialist tries to do—by formulating and following some rule-governed procedure. Instead, this must be decided on the basis of empirical case studies, where the verdict is subject to an informed judgment of the community of relevant expertise.

Let us now take a closer look at the second standard of rationality which is proposed by the social evidentialist. According to the social principle, a rational belief must be submitted to a community of relevant expertise for evaluation. Here the social evidentialist introduces a social constraint on rationality by claiming that beliefs based on judgments are rational only if they are tested against a community of the believer's competent others.

The reason why social evidentialists introduce this social requirement is that they think that we need some kind of *intersubjective test* that can replace rules as the decision procedure for testing personal judgments. We would not need the social requirement if formal evidentialism had been successful, because a central idea of that model is that an impersonal and a rule-governed decision procedure is available to us. Once we have these rules, no person other than the believer need exist to apply them correctly. But the problem with the formal model of rationality is that we are not able to develop a rule-governed decision procedure that we can actually use, all or most of the time, in the practice of science or in any other cognitive enterprise. Therefore we are forced to try to find some other non-arbitrary way of testing individual beliefs based on judgments that are in fact available to us. This way is provided for us by introducing a social constraint on personal judgments. Brown expresses the social requirement by saying: "for a belief based on judgment to be a rational one, it must be submitted to the community of those who share the relevant expertise for evaluation against their own judgments."[5] And Gutting writes:

> Now it is surely true that the mere fact of some disagreement about a proposition need not lead us to question its truth or proper basicality [or its rationality, my remark]. I can, for example, rightly disregard the dissent of the lunatic or the eccentric philosopher who thinks that he or she is the only person in the world. But the disagreement of substantial numbers of those who, as far as I can tell, are my *epistemic peers* . . . is surely another matter.[6]

Let me make three observations here. First, it is not enough that just one competent other disagrees with me, there must be a substantial number of them. There is no need to say exactly how many there must be; the important point is that it is not enough that just one or two disagree with me. Second, the persons who disagree with me must have a certain *quality,* so not just anyone's disagreement counts. They have to be experts or competent others in the relevant field. Lastly, it must be possible for me to see that these persons are my competent others. The fact that I have competent others who disagree with me is not enough to challenge the rationality of my belief, since I must have the cognitive ability and be in circumstances where I can *recognize* my competent others, so I can submit the belief to the "right" community for evaluation.

Brown is quite serious about this social constraint on rationality. What a person believes is not rational if it is not subjected to critical evaluation:

> In these terms, Robinson Crusoe alone on his island could exercise judgment, but he would not be able to achieve rationality. This is not because of some failing in his faculties, but rather for a reason akin to the reason why he could not play baseball, even though he could throw balls in the air, hit them with a bat, and run bases. On the model I am proposing, rationality requires other people—and not just any people, but other people who have the skills needed to exercise judgment in the case at hand.[7]

Even if this conception of rationality conflicts with our common sense intuitions, Brown does not think that constitutes an argument against his proposal. He is trying, he says, to construct a model of rationality, not trying to analyze the (pre-analytical) concept, and therefore some improvements are quite in order.

Neither of these two principles is in itself sufficient for rationality. The evidential principle is not sufficient. It is not enough that a belief is arrived at by an exercise of informed judgment to qualify as rational. Since no set of appropriate rules is available, the belief must also be submitted to critical evaluation by members of a relevant community. On the other hand, a belief that has been exposed to and even been accepted by a community is not automatically rational. It is also necessary that the belief is arrived at in an appropriate way—by the exercise of an informed judgment:

> Thus a consensus that is imposed on the members of a community by external political authority, or by force, or by manipulation of

data, or by any of a number of other familiar, unsavory techniques, will not generate rational beliefs on this model. Moreover, the point of requiring expertise is that individuals must actually make decisions on the basis of that expertise. If, to take a wild example, all of the physicists in the world were to agree that, beginning today, data would be communally fudged, and results announced would be those they had agreed to announce, we would have communal decisions by the relevant experts, and no qualified dissenters, but these decisions would not result from the exercise of expertise, and would not be rational.[8]

So the social principle is also not in itself sufficient for rationality. Expertise is clearly important according to the social evidentialist, but then two crucial questions are: "Who has expertise?" and "Who is to choose the experts?" In science the answer seems natural, since it is the existing scientists who recognize the new scientists. But is this a sufficient answer in general? Is it true that in every field or on every topic the persons who are currently seen as experts choose the new experts? But what if they just want to preserve their own position, and therefore they accept as new experts only people who conform to their own views? Brown's response to this question is to say, look at how we actually proceed, and normally we do quite well proceeding in this manner. Therefore this process is reliable. He writes:

> How are new physicists trained and certified? They are trained and certified. by present physicists, and who else could we expect to be in a position to do the job? . . . What about pilots, engineers. welders, mechanics, etc? Who else would we expect to train and evaluate these people other than those who already have the necessary expertise? Is the process fallible? Of course it is, but note that many of these fields involve continual interaction with the populace at large who are capable of recognizing when airplanes crash and bridges fail, even though they could not select a competent pilot or engineer on their own.[9]

What is crucial then is that there is a continual interaction between the public and the experts. This interaction requires that we (the non-experts) be able to recognize when these activities cease to be reliable and to question indirectly the experts' choices, but until that happens there is no reason to not trust the normal procedure.

2.   The Locus of Rationality

To sum up, the social evidentialist claims that a *rational person* is someone whose beliefs are based on informed judgments and intersubjectively tested. From this it is possible to derive what a *rational belief* is. It is a belief a rational person arrives at by performing an informed judgment, one which has been tested against the informed judgments of other well informed persons.

Notice the order: first the notion of rational person then the notion of rational belief. Here is another difference between formal evidentialism and social evidentialism. According to the formal evidentialist, the locus of rationality is primarily a person's beliefs (actions and evaluations). A central assumption of formal evidentialism is that rationality is ultimately a property a belief can have or lack. Rationality is a question concerning what logical relation should hold between different sets of beliefs. Hence the system of beliefs, not the agent (or agents), is taken to be the basic category for the question of rationality. The notion of a rational belief is primary and the notion of a rational person is derived from the outcome of a logical analysis of the former. But Brown says that the model of rationality he proposes instead:

> will take the agent to be basic, and the way in which an agent deals with evidence in arriving at a belief to be determinative of the rationality of that belief for her. We will see that this involves considerable relativization of rational belief to individuals, but that this is not the same as a relativization of the notion of rationality.[10]

So social evidentialists, on the other hand, revise the order and take the locus of rationality to be primarily the *person* holding the beliefs. Instead of seeing the belief system as the central category of rationality, they take the believer to be the category. Hence the notion of a rational person is primary and the notion of a rational belief is derived from an analysis of what a rational person could possibly be. This implies that the constraints we put on a rational person will determine the constraints we can reasonably put on a rational belief, but the opposite is not the case. Hence rationality is in the end a question concerning *under what circumstances a person is rational in accepting a belief* (performing an action or doing an evaluation), and all other uses of the notion of rationality can be derived out of this. It is not the case—contrary to what is presupposed by the formal evidentialist—that the conception of a rational person is arrived at by describing what meets the standards of a rational belief. A rational belief is rather one that a rational person can hold or arrive at. "Rational" is a predicate primarily applying to persons. So a central assumption of social evidentialism is that:

> Rationality is ultimately an *ability* that a person (or persons) exercises or fails to exercise.

Notice, however, that an individual cannot (because of the social requirement on rationality) exercise this ability alone; he or she needs also other people—and not just any kind of people, but those who have the relevant competence. But if the locus of rationality is persons and not beliefs, this means that we cannot talk about the rationality of belief systems *per se,* that is, without relating rationality to a person of some sort. Rationality is in this sense *person-dependent.* As Brown says in the quotation above, this involves a relativization of rational belief to individuals. But that is not the same as a relativization of rationality because rationality is the same for all these individuals. However, even though social evidentialists identify persons as the locus of rationality, this does not mean that we always have to talk about rational persons and never about rational beliefs. What it implies is that our conception of rational belief must be based on our prior understanding of a rational person and not the other way around.

3.   The Majoritarian Objection

Let us consider one possible objection to social evidentialism. (Some other problems will be discussed after I develop the third model of rationality in chapter 8.) Putnam is sympathetic to the idea that rationality is captured somehow in judgments, but he thinks that a model of rationality which includes a consensus requirement has some serious problems. Typically he takes such a version of rationality to rely on a *majoritarian argument*: that the agreement of educated or intelligent people is a necessary condition for a belief to be rational. He claims that this is by no means a necessary condition for rationality:

> people have lived for centuries with the uncomfortable knowledge that on some matters one has to rely on one's judgment even when

it differs from the judgment of the majority. . . . And it is plausible
that one of the highest manifestations of rationality should be the
ability to judge correctly in precisely those cases where one cannot
hope to 'prove' things to the satisfaction of the majority. It seems
strange indeed that the fact that some things should be impossible
to prove to everyone's satisfaction should become an argument for
the irrationality of beliefs about those things.[11]

The question I would like to address is whether Putnam's objection applies to the version of social evidentialism we have developed
here. Is social evidentialism a consensus model of rationality? First
a minor point: the social evidentialist as I have characterized him
or her does not claim that one has to *prove* things to be rationally
justified in accepting them—if by "proof" we mean that the premises
in an argument must be convincing to any reasonable person and
that the conclusion must follow from the premises by an application of
universally accepted rules of inference. Instead, the sort of justification
that is proposed by social evidentialists is one where the justification involves informed judgment, rather than by following universally
accepted rules of inference. In fact, they think that judgment is the
primary mode of justification. For example, Gutting claims:

> There is no doubt that this sort of justification by "judgment" rather
> than "proof" is a legitimate way of drawing conclusions that plays a
> central role in many areas of human life. Indeed, I think that a strong
> case can be made for the view that it represents the primary mode
> of justification in *every* area. Certainly, recent work on the nature
> of scientific rationality—especially that of Kuhn and Toulmin—has
> supported the conclusion that scientific justification fits the "judg-
> ment" rather than the "proof" model.[12]

Hence the social evidentialist does not contradict Putnam's claim
that judgment must be used in cases where we cannot prove things to
the satisfaction of the majority. A second and related point is that the
social evidentialist does not insist that a belief that cannot be proved
to *everyone's* satisfaction is irrational. Strictly speaking, not everyone's
view is important when we evaluate the rationality of a belief, since it
is only the judgment of people who are competent on this particular
topic we have to take into account.

But still the last objection remains, that it seems reasonable to
assume that sometimes one is perfectly justified to rely on one's own

judgment even when the experts disagree. So a natural question to ask is: to what *degree* does the social evidentialist think that a rational person must be ready to re-evaluate his or her beliefs when competent others disagree? As we noted in the last chapter, Kuhn seems sometimes to believe that once the relevant experts of the scientific community arrive at a communally informed judgment on a topic this communal judgment is the only rationally acceptable one. Kuhn also thinks that if a scientist does not agree with the community he or she at a certain point ceases to be a member of it.[13] If we generalize his view, the answer to Putnam's question seems to be that a rational person is obligated to *totally* re-evaluate his or her beliefs if the experts in the field in question come to that conclusion.

Gutting is not totally clear on what the consequences are when competent others disagree with me, except that in that situation I must *try* to justify my belief. He claims that the reason why we should accept the social requirement as something that our beliefs have to meet to be rational is that the denial of the requirement leads to *epistemic egoism*. That is the view that a person is entitled to give preference to one of his own beliefs just because it is his. There is no reason to think that my judgment is more correct than that of the competent others who disagree with me. Gutting asks: "Isn't it just common sense to admit that, when there is widespread [dis]agreement (sic!) about a claim, with apparently competent judges on both sides, those who assert or deny the claim need to justify their positions?"[14]

Those who do not justify their beliefs are guilty of epistemic egoism. And epistemic egoism is "just as arbitrary and unjustifiable as ethical egoism is generally regarded to be."[15] But if I try to justify my beliefs and the competent others still disagree with me, what then? Am I irrational in continuing to hold my beliefs? It seems as if Gutting's position is that if people try to justify their beliefs and still fail, then they must try to give up those beliefs or they are unjustified in believing them and hence irrational. If this interpretation of Gutting is right it means that his conclusion is the same as Kuhn's and that rational people are obligated to totally re-evaluate their beliefs if the competent others in the field in question come to that informed conclusion.

But is Kuhn's and Gutting's answer satisfying? It does not meet Putnam's objection that it sometimes seems (at least afterwards) completely rational to rely on my own judgment even when my competent others disagree. Thus a total re-evaluation of one's beliefs seems not to be a necessary condition for rationality.[16] Therefore, I think Brown's more modest position is more reasonable than the one Kuhn and Gutting take. He writes:

> the model of rationality that I am proposing only requires that individuals submit their judgments for evaluation by their peers, and that they take this evaluation seriously. The model does not require that each member of the community agree with the majority, and indeed, agreement with the majority view is neither necessary nor sufficient for rationality.[17]

It is not necessary because in the test case of science rational disagreement is a common feature. For example, the conflict initiated by Copernicus and his Aristotelian contemporaries went on for 200 years, and not until the time of Newton was a real informed consensus reached among scientists.[18] (See also the examples given in the previous chapter.) Nor is it sufficient because even if the majority agree with your beliefs, the beliefs are not rational if you have not obtained them by performing an informed judgment. Perhaps the conclusion to draw is rather that in general (or *prima facie*) an informed communal judgment carries more epistemic weight than an informed personal judgment, so we should be a little less certain if our personal judgment goes against our competent others' judgment or we should be more suspicious about a personal than a communal judgment. But the conclusion should not be that if people's individual judgments contradict a communal judgment and they still continue to hold their individual judgment, then they are necessarily irrational in doing so.

This gives us the following general characterization of social evidentialism as a general model of rationality. People are rational in their acceptance of a belief only if:

1. they arrive at the belief by exercising an informed judgment (the *evidential principle*), and;
2. they submit the belief to evaluation by the competent others who are well-informed in the field in question and their evaluation is taken seriously (the *social principle*).

A social evidentialist would add a third condition if he or she instead wanted to hold the position Kuhn and Gutting seem to take on this issue, namely:

3. they reject or totally re-evaluate the belief if a sufficient number of competent others demand so (what we could call the
   conformity principle).

Let us call the former view just *social evidentialism* and the
latter *strong social evidentialism*. So the social evidential account of
(external) rationality runs as follows:[19] A person is rational in allowing
a belief to enter in his or her belief system only if that belief can be
supported by good reason; the assessment of how well a belief is
supported by evidence is typically not a result of a rule-governed
process but a result of a judgment-based method of reasoning; the
belief is exposed to critical evaluation by the members of an appropriate community; and, the strong social evidentialist also wants to
add, if this community of competent others approve of the belief.

Formal evidentialists typically accept a standard of rationality
that states what beliefs qualify as properly basic ones. Do social evidentialists have a similar standard? So far we have not discussed
social evidentialism in relation to *foundationalism*. Let us now consider whether foundationalism is compatible with social evidentialism. Clearly strong foundationalism (only beliefs that are certain or
infallible can be properly basic) is not. This is so because social evidentialism is a form of fallibilism. Informed judgments are fallible but
nevertheless not arbitrary since they require a certain degree of expertise. Brown seems inclined to think that foundationalism requires self-
evident premises and therefore his view of rationality must be a form
of non-foundationalism.[20] But as we have seen this does not follow.
Foundationalism does not typically require self-evident or absolute
secure foundations, rather the foundationalist claims that (*a*) there are
two forms of justification, inferential and non-inferential, and (*b*) basic
beliefs are not justified by appeal to non-basic beliefs. Foundationalists
disagree about what kind of beliefs qualify as properly basic beliefs—
whether they must be self-evident, evident to the senses, and the like.

But is there no immediate justification of our belief in social
evidentialism? Brown does not discuss this issue. However, I think we
can still find an answer. Consider my beliefs that I see a tree in front of
me and that I had breakfast this morning. Do I arrive at these beliefs
by exercising an informed judgment? It surely does not look that way;
I do not reason my way to these beliefs—whether the process of
reasoning is rule-governed or judgment-based. Nor do I believe these

things on the basis of other beliefs I have that constitute evidence for them. If this is correct, then the social evidentialist accepts (or, at least, can accept) that some beliefs are properly basic, that is, that we are rationally entitled to believe them even though we do not believe them on the basis of evidence.

However, the social principle still applies even if the beliefs in question are basic beliefs.[21] A rational person must be ready to re-evaluate the status of what he or she takes to be properly basic beliefs if competent others in the field in question disagree. Therefore, if competent others disagree with me, I am obligated to try to justify my beliefs irrespective of whether they are non-basic or basic beliefs. The formal evidentialist does not demand this and that is because no additional testing is necessary if one applies the appropriate rules correctly. But the social evidentialist, as we have seen, takes the social requirement as a replacement of rules, for checking individual judgments.

To sum up, social evidentialism is compatible with weaker forms of foundationalism, but social evidentialists do not explicitly discuss when a belief should be considered to be a properly basic belief.

4.   Rationality and Truth

Let us now turn to a subject we have not yet discussed in detail, that of how rationality is related to truth and how questions of rationality are connected with questions about realism and anti-realism. Brown makes the following comment concerning the relation between truth and rationality:

> We only want to accept those claims that we have reasons to accept, and if the foundationalist project had been successful, we would know that rationally founded claims are true. The failure of this project leaves us in a genuine quandary. We are still in a position in which the only basis we have for accepting a claim is that we have reasons for it, but on our new model of rationality, having reasons does not assure us of achieving truth. Our reasons rest on the best available judgment, but those judgments are tied to the evidence available at a particular time. The significance of this evidence is never beyond question, and further evidence may show any judgment to be wrong.[22]

However, Brown's remark about a successful foundational project is true only if we are talking about strong foundationalism. Given that we have a self-evident or absolutely certain foundation and that we have rules which connect our non-basic beliefs in an appropriate way to this foundation, then we would know that rationally founded claims are true (or at least, that they have a very high degree of probability). So some formal evidentialists have thought that truth or at least high probability is a necessary condition for rationality. On such an account to say that a belief is rational is a strong reason—maybe even a conclusive reason—to believe that it is true. Hence it would be strange or irrational to accept that a belief is rational and at the same time reject the belief itself, or to accept that a person is rational in believing something and at the same time not believe it oneself. But as soon as a formal evidentialist rejects strong foundationalism, this close connection between rationality and truth disappear. All that is left is the thought that rationality requires that *if* one's premises are true then the conclusion must be true or at least have a high degree of (measurable) probability.

This tie between truth and rationality is even weaker in social evidentialism. This is so not only because, as Brown says, informed judgments are always based on evidence which is available at a particular time, which might later be shown to be wrong. In addition, even if two persons start with the same evidence and if there is no available rule-governed procedure to follow (as the social evidentialist typically thinks is the case), they might reach different informed judgments of what to believe and submit their views to criticism and still both be rational. Such a situation is not possible on a weaker version of formal evidentialism. If two people start with the same information (though fallible) they must reach the same conclusion. So clearly the social evidentialist does not think that truth is a necessary condition for rationality. On this model of rationality it is more likely than on the formal one that false beliefs could be rationally acceptable. But Brown maintains:

> Nevertheless, there is a weaker but vital tie between rationality and truth. We proceed rationally in attempting to discover truth, and we take those conclusions that are rationally acceptable as our best estimate of the truth. In other words, while a rationally supported claim need not be true, and a claim chosen at random need not be

false, it does not follow that either choice is as good as the other. We need not only truth, but reasons for believing that we have the truth, and it is through the process of assessing evidence and submitting our views to criticism that we develop those reasons.[23]

According to Brown, this is the function of rationality. And he refers to Putnam's writing, thinking that Putnam argues for the same relation between rationality and truth when he says "that there is an extremely close connection between the notions of *truth* and *rationality;* that . . . the only criterion for what is a fact is what it is *rational* to accept."[24] But Putnam, nevertheless, claims that truth and rationality are two related but distinct notions. This leads us to the related issue of what relation the social evidentialist thinks there is between rationality and realism (or anti-realism). Putnam writes at another place:

> Truth cannot simply *be* rational acceptability for one fundamental reason; truth is supposed to be a property of a statement that cannot be lost, whereas justification can be lost. The statement "The earth is flat" was, very likely, rationally acceptable 3,000 years ago; but is not rationally acceptable today. Yet it would be wrong to say that "the earth is flat" was *true* 3,000 years ago; for that would mean that the earth has changed its shape.[25]

This sounds like a typical expression of realism, and Brown apparently interprets Putnam in such a way. But it is not clear that this is the way Putnam himself understands it. What it shows, in Putnam's opinion, is that "truth is an *idealization* of rational acceptability. We speak as if there were such things as epistemically ideal conditions, and we call a statement 'true' if it would be justified under such conditions."[26] But this is presumably not what Brown has in mind. Rather rationality for him has to do with how we proceed in our attempts to discover truth, but truth is what it is regardless of how we think of it. A belief is true not if it is justified under epistemically ideal conditions, but if it tracks what there is regardless of what we think of it or whether it meets these ideal conditions or not. Consider the following lines from Brown:

> First, what exactly do we mean by "truth," i.e., what is the proper analysis of this concept? This is much too large a topic to be tackled here, but a rough correspondence approach will do for our

purposes. On this analysis, when we make a claim about some domain, we are asserting that there is a feature of that domain that holds independently of this claim. If I assert that there are three chairs in my study I am making a claim about my study *that is correct or incorrect independently of what anyone may believe* . . . . Nothing has been said here about how we decide whether a claim is true or false. This is a different question from the question of what we mean by "true", and the detailed answer to this question may be different in different domains.[27]

A question that we have to answer, to be able to say whether Putnam's and Brown's view of the connection between rationality and truth is of a realist or anti-realist kind, is what we should mean by the terms "realism" and "anti-realism" in this context. Brown gives us a clue when he says that truth is "independent of what anyone may believe." Putnam, on the other hand, seems to think that truth has something to do with us and our cognition, and therefore it depends on what we may believe. So for Brown there exists what we might call *evidence-transcendent truths,* truths that lie beyond our powers of recognition. In fact truth does not at all depend on our cognitive powers, what is true is true regardless of what we think of it. This I take to be the core of realism. But for anti-realists there exist only *evidence-immanent truths;* the only truths are the ones we are able to recognize, discover, or state the conditions for. In other words, anti-realists define truth in terms of whatever they take to be the appropriate or ideal standards for accepting a belief. Consider for instance the examples Alston gives of anti-realist attempts to define truth:

> the truth of a statement, S, will be identified with S's cohering with the rest of one's beliefs, with S's leading, or having the capacity to lead, to fruitful consequences, with S's satisfying the standards of the particular language-game in which it is a move, with S's being one of the survivors at the ideal limit of scientific inquiry, or whatever.[28]

With this in mind let us try to define realism and anti-realism. The difference I have ascribed to these views is in terms of *truth,* but the more common way of understanding them is in terms of *what exists* and how the things that exist are related to us. However, as we will see, "normally" when we speak of these views we mean something other than what Putnam seems to have in mind. The traditional way of speaking about realism and anti-realism is with respect to a given domain of objects, whether the objects in that domain exist or not, for example, whether there really are such things as numbers, electrons, or other minds. Plantinga calls this kind of realism *existential realism*.[29] An existential anti-realist is, correspondingly, a person who denies that there really are such things as, for instance, numbers, electrons, or other minds. Hence we can give the following characterization of existential anti-realism:

> *Existential Anti-Realism:* The view that some (or all) domains of phenomena or objects do not have ontological status, i.e., they do not exist.

Existential realism as well as existential anti-realism can be *limited* or *universal* in scope. Typically people are existential anti-realists with respect to some kinds of things. For instance, one can be an existential anti-realist with respect to such theoretical or unobservable entities as electrons or quarks, but be an existential realist when it comes to ordinary objects like trees, chairs, and planets.[30] But if Putnam is an anti-realist he is not an anti-realist of this sort. Putnam does not deny the existence of the world or the ontological status of the objects in it in general, rather he denies that "the world consists of some fixed totality of mind-independent objects." And our beliefs, or truth as such, are "not correspondence with mind-independent or discourse-independent 'states of affairs.'"[31] How are we supposed to understand this?

Let us distinguish three ways of understanding the term "dependent" in this context. It is one thing to say that (1) what we experience is always to some extent shaped by our concepts, by our language. Reality is *semantically dependent* on the way we think and believe. It is another thing to say that (2) the only reality we can know anything about is the reality we encounter through the framework of our language. Reality is *epistemologically dependent* on the way we think and believe. It is yet another thing to say that (3) the only reality that exists is the reality we encounter through the framework of our language. Reality is *ontologically dependent* on the way we think and believe.

Plantinga calls somebody who holds the last thesis, that reality is ontologically dependent on the way we think and believe, a *creative anti-realist*. The creative anti-realist does not deny the existence of objects like electrons, physical objects, values, god(s), and so on.

He or she "holds instead that objects of the sort in question are not ontologically independent of persons and their ways of thinking and behaving."[32] (Religious anti-realism, the way I characterized it in chapter 4, would then be a species of creative anti-realism. I said that what religious anti-realists all have in common is that they deny that the objects of religious belief exist independently of the experiences of the believers.)

Creative anti-realism can in the same way as existential realism be of a limited or universal sort. Further, a person could be either an existential or a creative anti-realist with respect to a particular domain, but not both. For instance, one can be an existential anti-realist with respect to theoretical entities but a creative anti-realist with respect to ordinary or everyday objects. Let us follow Plantinga's suggestion and characterize creative anti-realism in this way:

> *Creative Anti-Realism:* The view that some (or all) domains of objects are ontologically dependent on the way human beings think and believe.[33]

It is hard to tell, but if Putnam is an anti-realist he is a creative anti-realist of the universal sort, and that is how we should understand, I think, his claim that the world does not consist of mind-independent or discourse-independent objects. However, for our purpose here it does not really matter what exactly his view is. What is important, and what confuses the whole issue to a certain degree is that (creative) anti-realism could be expressed either in *terms of truth* or in *terms of existence*. So it would be helpful if we could define creative anti-realism in terms of truth as well.

First of all, we must try to see where the connection is between truth and existence, and again Plantinga can give us some help. The statement: "It is true that dinosaurs once roamed the earth" seems to entail and seems to be entailed by the statement that "Dinosaurs have existed on the earth." But then (as the existential anti-realist seems to claim) if the former statement owes its truth to our cognitive and linguistic activities, the same goes for the latter. Hence a consequence of this seems to be that the existence of dinosaurs is somehow dependent upon us.[34] What is true (or exists) for us is the same as what is true (or exists) as such, or rather truth as such does not exist, or is a meaningless concept, there exist only evidence-immanent or mind-dependent truths. The realist, on the other hand, denies this. There exist such things as truth (or existence) as such, there exist evidence-transcendent or mind-independent truths. If we try to characterize creative anti-realism in terms of truth instead of existence we might do it in the following way:

> *Creative Anti-Realism*:* The view that there exist only evidence-immanent truths, or the view that there exist only (human) mind-dependent truths.[35]

Now back to the connection between rationality and realism. It seems reasonable to think that whether we hold a realist or an anti-realist position it is going to affect the relationship we see between rationality and truth. But the way we view the connection also depends on whether we are existential or creative anti-realists. On a realist account of social evidentialism, rationality is, as we have seen, taken to be person-dependent, and truth is understood as person-independent or evidence-transcendent. "Rationality" is a person-dependent notion because it is always related to a person of some sort. And if the persons are human beings then the only rationality that really matters is the one that we as human beings with our limited cognitive resources are able to recognize or, more important, can reasonably meet.

However, on a creative anti-realist account of social-evidentialism, *both* notions would be person-dependent. The rationality and truth that exist are only the ones we are *able* to recognize or discover. The two concepts could on this account be connected in two different ways: (*a*) either rationality and truth are identical, or (*b*) we make a distinction between some kind of standard rationality and some kind of ideal rationality—which is identical with truth. Putnam could be interpreted as holding the latter position. Truth is for him something more "stable or convergent" than rationality or rational acceptability. He writes that "truth is independent of justification here and now, but not independent of *all* justification."[36] Exactly what Putnam means by rationality is not totally clear, but nothing would stop him or someone who holds a similar view from taking social evidentialism as representing a reasonable account of it.

What complicates the picture profoundly is that according to Putnam it is possible to talk about more than one truth. "Many 'internalist' [in the terminology developed here, creative anti-realist] philosophers, though not all, hold further that there is more than one 'true' theory or description of the world."[37] I will not try to develop here what consequences this possibility of pluralities of truth have, but one important consequence worth mentioning is that it seems to imply that it is possible to talk about more than one rationality; each rationality is then connected to each (different) truth.

Consequently, it is possible to view social evidentialism either from a realist or an anti-realist perspective. (The same holds, I think, for any model of rationality we might propose.) And as I have briefly mentioned, this will have certain implications for how we see the connection between rationality and truth. The social evidentialist who is a realist claims that "truth" is a person-independent notion, whereas "rationality" is person-dependent. The social evidentialist who is, on the other hand, a creative anti-realist takes both "truth" and "rationality" to be person-dependent notions. However, I will in general assume that the social evidentialist is a realist since that seems to be the position both Brown and Gutting adopt.[38]

5.   The Scope of Social Evidentialism

The basic argument that social evidentialists give for why we should accept their model of rationality is that it makes sense out of scientific theory and belief-formation and regulation. Therefore, this model is to be preferred over formal evidentialism since given a choice between rejecting a model of rationality and rejecting the view that science provides a paradigm example of rationality in action, they urge us to reject the model. We should reject the model because the choice of science as a paradigmatically rational enterprise is more reliable than any view we may have as to what it is that makes science rational. Hence every adequate model of rationality we develop must make sense out of scientific believing, and social evidentialism, they claim, satisfies this requirement.

A further reason the social evidentialist gives is that the scope of rationality is considerably greater in social evidentialism than in formal evidentialism. And as I argued in the beginning of this chapter, all else being equal, the broader the scope or the field of application a model of rationality has the better it is. One advantage of accepting social evidentialism is that we can talk of rationality in science in both the context of justification and the context of discovery—and, of course, the same is true for any other human practice where we can use this distinction.

A central idea of formal evidentialism is that we have to distinguish between these two contexts in science. The context of discovery is the process by which scientists come up with new ideas, develop new theories, whereas the context of justification is the process in which these new ideas and theories are tested. According to the formal evidentialist only activities to which it is possible to apply a rule-governed method can be rational. This is the reason why the advocates of the formal view of science have stopped seeing the context of discovery as within the scope of rationality. They realized that there is no set of rules that makes it possible for scientists to generate mechanically new discoveries from data.[39] From this it follows that the concept of rationality (the way they understand it) cannot apply to the domain of scientific discovery. In other words, different research strategies cannot in themselves be more or less rational.

However, in social evidentialism the context of discovery falls within the scope of rationality. This, Brown claims, is really in accordance with our intuitions on the matter:

> Note particularly that we expect a rational person to be capable of functioning well in the context of discovery; the distinction between discovery and justification, along with the limitation of rationality to the latter, is not an idea that commonly leaps to the mind when we think of a rational human being. Instead, I think that most of us, at first blush, take the scientist or the physician who is struggling to solve a problem without benefit of clear rules as paradigms of a person involved in a task that requires rationality.[40]

It is not, on this view, hard to understand why a rational person functions better than an irrational person in developing a theory. A scientist trying to solve problems where there exist no or insufficient rules is exactly a person who needs to exercise informed judgments, i.e., is doing a task that requires rationality. The scientist must be able to consider what is worth believing, what hypotheses seem fruitful to develop, and so on. If rationality does not figure in this context then on what should scientists base their choices? By flipping a coin? No, but by making informed, though fallible, judgments. An essential part of what it means to be a scientist is to be able to exercise informed judgment *both* in the context of discovery and in the context of justification. Again, this is true for all practices in which we can distinguish between a context of discovery and one of justification, and I think the distinction can be applied to almost any practice that involves at least some cognitive elements. If this is correct the scope of rationality is not only expanded in science, but also in many other practices in which we are involved.

Social evidentialists claim that their model of rationality is also applicable to, and makes sense out of, belief-formation and regulation in *everyday life*. Just as in science, people in everyday life have the ability to perform judgments and to come to reasonable conclusions about what to believe and how to act in particular situations. It might be the case that the evidence for a belief or a decision in everyday life is not as good or as carefully scrutinized as in science, but social evidentialism makes it possible to understand what is going on and why people after all seem to be fairly rational beings. The model also takes into account what Brown thinks to be a central part of our everyday concept of rationality, namely, that rationality has to do with reasons, that we must have reasons for our rational beliefs, and that we can provide those reasons on request.[41]

Hence social evidentialism also makes better sense than formal evidentialism of our intuitive understanding of how we normally proceed in our everyday lives and why we can rely on the conclusions we reach. Think of everyday beliefs like: "My name is Mikael," "My wife loves me," "My friend John does not normally lie to me," "I have a brain," "People should see a doctor when they are badly wounded," "Drivers normally do not drive when the stoplight is red," and so on. We normally think or believe that we can make a rational (or trustworthy) evaluation of the reliability of these kinds of beliefs, and we assume that other people can also do this. In fact, to function properly as human beings we seem to be *required* to make these assumptions. We believe that we should go to a doctor when we are seriously ill, and when we travel in an airplane we believe that normally the pilot is sufficiently trained to do this type of job. We base these beliefs on judgments that take certain facts, our experiences, and other people's experiences into account, and we think—or take more or less for granted—that both the process and the outcome is fairly rational or reliable. And all this makes sense on a social evidentialist account of rationality, at least, so its advocates claim.

But formal evidentialism, on the other hand, implies that for us to be rational in holding these everyday beliefs we must formulate rules for when it is justified to believe them and that we must be able to apply these rules to the beliefs in question. (At least it must be possible to reconstruct the rules we intuitively follow.) In other words, for us to be justified in holding and acting on everyday beliefs like the above, we must find appropriate rules for evaluating the trustworthiness of a doctor or an airplane pilot. But it seems that we would never even get out of bed in the morning if we took formal evidentialism so literally! Almost all of the choices we *must* make everyday to function appropriately as human beings turn out on such an analysis to be either a-rational or irrational.

So according to the social evidentialist, in addition to activities in which it is possible to apply a rule-governed reasoning, *all* activities where we can exercise some kind of informed judgment and which have some competent others to whom we can submit our beliefs fall within the scope of rationality—which is a considerable extension of the domain of rationality (and irrationality) compared to formal evidentialism. Hence it is likely that also religious activities fall within the scope of rationality, and to this subject we will turn in the next chapter.

Brown and Gutting do not address the question of the nature of rationality explicitly, at least not in the way I have done (in chapter 2). But it is clear that they think that rationality is normative. It states what we *ought* to do to be considered rational in our believing. However, they do not directly talk about intellectual duties or responsibilities, but despite this I think it involves no violation of social evidentialism if we understand it in deontological terms—if we interpret the evidential and the social principle (and the conformity principle) as obligations we humans ought to fulfill.Therefore, though the social evidentialists we have considered do not explicitly address this question, I shall assume that they accept a deontological conception of rationality. But this understanding of rationality is often combined with a means-end conception of rationality, as for instance in the writing of Newton-Smith. He says: "A rational model involves two ingredients. First, one specifies something as the goal of science. . . . Second, some principle or set of principles are specified for comparing rival theories against a given evidential background."[42] (See also the discussion in chapter 3 of means-end rationality.) So in this respect there is no essential difference between social and formal evidentialism.

Brown concludes that the standards of rationality the social evidentialist claims that we must fulfill to be rational in our believing are within our grasp, given our cognitive abilities. "To require that we only accept those claims which are rationally grounded is to demand something that is within our grasp."[43] To ask for truth would be to ask for too much, but the demands of social evidentialism Brown takes to be in our power to satisfy. Not only in science can we fulfill these demands but in all other areas of life as well. However, we will see that there are reasons to doubt that the demands of social evidentialism really are within our grasp, but before we do that we have to develop what consequences the acceptance of social evidentialism has for philosophy of religion and the question of the rationality of religious belief.

7

Social Evidentialism and Religious Belief

Let us now turn our attention to the consequences of social evidentialism for philosophy of religion. In particular, let us address the question of the rationality of religious belief, or more basically according to the social evidentialist, whether or not a person can be rational in his or her religious believing. But at the same time we must consider whether this model of rationality is applicable at all to religious practice and whether these standards are appropriate for evaluating religious rationality (or irrationality). Social evidentialism is applicable to religious practice if it is reasonable to assume that in religious matters we can also exercise (or fail to exercise) informed judgments and expose (or fail to expose) our beliefs to peer evaluation—and this seems, at least, *prima facie,* to be a reasonable assumption.

1.   The Initial Presumption of Philosophy of Religion

A first project a social evidentialist working in philosophy of religion would undertake is probably *to set philosophy of religion on a par with philosophy of science* (the same holds of course for any other "philosophy of" besides philosophy of religion). The general idea is that the same, or roughly the same, relation between philosophical inquiry and its subject matter should hold in both disciplines. Recall that practice-oriented philosophers of science characteristically never see the task of philosophy of science as only a matter of discovering the subject matter's logical structure, where the analysis is not based on an investigation of the actual practice of science. Proper philosophy of science must be a discipline that takes into account the history and the actual practice of science. Scientific rationality, or any other dimension of science under investigation, cannot be studied in the abstract but must be related to the activities of the people involved in the enterprise themselves. The formulation of adequate standards of rationality for assessing an activity such as science cannot be done independently—as the formal evidentialist assumes—of the actual practices of scientists. The actual practice of science put constraints on normative models of scientific rationality. A model can be rejected if it does not fit the history of science. Case-studies of actual scientific practice can constitute evidence for or against a proposed scientific methodology.

I characterized the advocates of the practice-oriented view of science as claiming that neither actual scientific practice nor philosophical considerations should automatically have priority. The point was that an adequate model of scientific rationality must acknowledge the epistemic significance of both the actual practices and the philosophical accounts that are proposed independently of such practices. However, practice-oriented philosophers all seem to assume that we should have an initial presumption in favor of science: until anything else is proven we should assume that science is correct as it is—that scientific decisions are normally rational, that scientific explanations are normally properly stated, and so on.

Now, according to the social evidentialist, these points should also hold for the work done in philosophy of religion and, in particular, when formulating the adequate standards of rationality for evaluating religious practice and belief. This means, among other things, that to be able to do proper philosophy of religion one must have a certain acquaintance with actual (past and present) religious practice and that the philosopher of religion must acknowledge the epistemic significance not only of philosophical accounts of rationality but also of the actual practice of religion. However, this has typically not been the case in philosophy of religion. On the contrary, not only have philosophers often completely ignored actual religious practice, but they have also treated religion with strong distrust. The *central issues* have been whether religion is at all worthy of pursuing, whether religious statements have any meaning at all, whether any religious believer can be rational, and so on. Questions of this extremely critical kind have almost exclusively been the focus of philosophy of religion. So the initial presumption in philosophy of religion has typically been against its subject matter, against religion. Let us call such a point of departure for a philosophical discipline a (methodologically) *negative presumption* in contrast to the *positive presumption* the practice-oriented philosopher adopts in philosophy of science.

The social evidentialist would claim that the philosopher of religion should reject such a negative presumption. In fact this is exactly what Gutting is arguing for. Gutting points out that among the philosophical disciplines "philosophy of religion is peculiar in the suspicion with which it regards its subject matter." He asks us to think about "how odd it would be if the central question of the philosophy of science were whether science is at all worth pursuing, or if a major preoccupation of aesthetics were the propriety of writing poetry."[1] Would there not be something seriously wrong if the basic issue in philosophy of history were whether it is rational to write history at all, or whether all historical claims are unjustified? And yet this is exactly the way that traditional philosophy of religion has focused on religious phenomena most of the time. What Gutting wants to say is not, I take it, that philosophers have no right to ask such questions, since they do; his claim is rather that questions like these should not be taken as the basic issues or the point of departure for the research work done by the community of philosophers working in philosophy of religion.

He says that if we accept the tendency in contemporary philosophy of science (a central thesis of the practice-oriented view) to take science as primary in relation to different views of science or models of rationality, then it would seem reasonable to do philosophy of religion in a similar fashion. According to such a view, there would be something profoundly wrong if philosophers took as their point of departure claims like "all scientific knowledge claims are unjustified." As Gutting points out, to take this as a serious challenge against science is to adopt far too extreme a methodological skepticism as a reasonable starting-point for philosophy of science. Such skepticism ought not, he says, to be a challenge against science itself but rather a challenge against the models of science philosophers use.

Gutting goes on to argue that the initial presumption of philosophy of religion should be in favor of religious practice instead of against it, just as the parallel presumption is in philosophy of science. This does *not* mean that religion is protected from philosophical criticism. But, as is the case with science, our *initial* confidence should be in favor of so central and comprehensive a practice, not in our philosophical models:

Here I am saying no more on behalf of religion than might be said, in the face of radical skeptical questioning, on behalf of science, art, morality, or any other pervasive achievement of human existence: that every presumption must be in favor of so central an element of our culture and that, lacking strong evidence for a contrary construal of human life, we should continue to assume its essential validity.[2]

In other words, an important argument for why we should treat the subject matter of philosophy of religion the same way we treat the subject matter of philosophy of science is that reflective activities central to the history and contemporary life of the human race cannot be—from the very beginning—assumed to be imbued with irrationality: "To say that something that has such deep roots and that has been sustained for so long in such diverse contexts is nothing but credulity and hypocrisy is as extraordinary a claim as any made by religious believers."[3] The only thing this shows, Gutting thinks, is a profound arrogance and ignorance. Of course the claim *might* be true, but to be able to show that requires the development of a secular alternative that is well confirmed. And as Gutting goes on to argue, since secular alternatives have meager support in the history of the human race, the proper initial attitude philosophers of religion should have towards its subject matter is a positive presumption.

The aim of arguing for a positive presumption in philosophy of religion, Gutting says, is not to eliminate the criticism against religion but rather to *refocus* it. We should start out thinking that there must be something essentially "right" about religion. This does not of course mean that what a religious believer does or believes is taken at face value. The initial presumption could turn out to be false *after* investigation and the development of a secular alternative; or it could turn out that religious believers have profoundly misunderstood themselves. But Gutting claims that we should start with a positive presumption in philosophy of religion. Hence we must try to understand what religion is all about with at least an initially sympathetic mind, before we are in an appropriate position to evaluate its rationality or truth.

A reason Gutting gives to explain why so many contemporary philosophers have had an initial presumption against religious belief is that they base much of their thinking on an inadequate analysis of the relationship between believer and non-believer. We might call the central thesis of this traditional analysis the "thesis of the presumed asymmetry between believers and non-believers" (or just the *asymmetry thesis*). The advocates of the asymmetry thesis claim that there is an essential difference between the commitment of the believer and that of the non-believer. In fact the choice of the terms "believer" (somebody who accepts something, *p,* as true) and "*non*-believer" (somebody that does not commit him or herself to, or suspends belief in *p*) reflects this difference. The thought is that the believer is committed to a position, for example, belief in God, whereas the non-believer simply withholds judgment on the issue, since he or she makes no positive commitment at all. If philosophers of religion accept the asymmetry thesis, it is natural for them to find belief rather than non-belief puzzling, and therefore to see its subject matter with suspicion, if not with outright skepticism. Gutting thinks that this picture is unrealistic. He argues that:

> Nonbelif in religion is in fact always the reverse side of some set of positive beliefs that regulate the nonbeliever's life. Not believing in God is just one aspect of believing in Marxism, liberalism, humanistic existentialism, materialism or some other guiding set of secular beliefs. . . . My point is just that any disagreement between believers and nonbelievers involves substantial positive claims on both sides, so that the portrayal of nonbelief as mere withholding of assent is inaccurate.[4]

So on Gutting's analysis, to be a non-believer always involves positive claims like: man is the measure of all things, reality is fundamentally impersonal in character, human beings are only a complex form of matter, and the like. Or put in another way, nonbelief involves beliefs about the nature of human beings, the nature of the nonhuman world, the fate of individuals, what a good life consists in, and so on. Hence, if Gutting's view is correct, it would be less misleading, I take it, to call the "believer" a *religious believer* and the "non-believer" a *secular believer.* Correspondingly we can make a distinction between *religious* and *secular beliefs.* And in what follows I will use these terms instead. Of course, the degree or character of the commitment might be different, but that does not change the fact that both parties are believers. (I will develop these thoughts in more detail in chapter 9.)

Gutting's remarks seem to be in line with a practice-oriented approach to philosophy (of religion). This is so because it looks as

if one cannot *acknowledge the epistemic significance* of religion if
one thinks that the basic issue in philosophy of religion is whether
religion is at all worth of pursuing or whether religious believers say
anything meaningful at all, or the like. It would seem unlikely that
the actual practice of religion could then put any, or any significant,
constraints on normative models of religious rationality, that a model
could be rejected if it did not fit the history of religion, or that case-
studies of actual religious practice could constitute evidence for or
against a proposed philosophical account of religious rationality. But
it is not clear how far Gutting is ready to go along this line, that is, to
what extent his view is practice-oriented. However, it should be clear
that he tends towards such a position and that in this case he rejects
or is critical of a formal approach to philosophy of religion. In fact,
when I develop my alternative model I will claim that he and other
social evidentialists do not go as far as they should in this regard.
On the other hand, Gutting does not adopt a contextual approach to
philosophy (of religion) either, because his emphasis on the epistemic
significance of religion does not lead him to the claim that religious
believers have epistemic authority on these questions. According to
him, religion can be criticized from the outside, and the religion can
even be totally rejected—after a close examination.

However, is not Gutting overlooking one alternative? It might be
true that a negative presumption is inadequate, but does it follow from
that fact that the right initial attitude should be a positive presumption?
Why not try to be neutral? Why not conclude that a *methodological
neutrality* is the right initial attitude of philosophy of religion? If by
methodological neutrality we mean the position of eschewing both a
negative and a positive (initial) preference to the activity under investigation, is not this approach possible and preferable over the others?

Gutting does not consider these questions. However, I think that
one serious problem with such an approach has to do with the fact
that philosophers have to start *somewhere,* since they cannot question
everything. They must make some assumptions if they are going to
be able to get their project going. Philosophers must take some things
as initially given. Therefore, a general methodological neutrality is not
possible. So the question is really *what* should philosophers take as
initially given? What is problematic about a methodological neutrality
in our context here becomes evident, because if we try to be neutral
and to assume neither the validity nor the invalidity of an activity

like science, religion, or aesthetics, what positive assumptions may we then make? Such a methodological neutrality seems to leave us without any starting point in which we can have confidence because we might wonder whether we have anything that is more reasonable to start from than the central elements in the life of human beings, such as science, religion, and art. Our epistemological models are certainly not more reliable.

So we have to begin with a confidence in some pre-philosophical opinions, to use Plantinga's phrase, and therefore a general methodological neutrality seems to be an unreasonable, if not an impossible position to adopt.[5] Of course, not just any opinion is worthy of our initial confidence, but that is not the claim. The *claim* is rather that central elements of our cultures like science, religion, and art, are worth our initial confidence. Therefore, a methodological neutrality should not be adopted in philosophy of science, philosophy of religion, aesthetics, or the like.

2.   The Exercise of Informed Judgments in Religion

Let us now turn our attention to the consequences the adoption of social evidentialism as a general model of rationality has for the question of the rationality of religious belief. Social evidentialists share with formal evidentialists the assumption that science is the best example of a rational enterprise we have at present, but they deny that actual scientific practice conforms to the formal view. Social evidentialists take their own account to be much closer to what is actually going on in science. Therefore, if someone wants to raise the scientific challenge to religious belief, it should be based on the best available account of science we have, i.e., on the practice-oriented view (or its superiors).

The scientific challenge to religious belief in its traditional form consists of the claim that if religious beliefs are to be seen as rational they must fulfill the same, or at least similar, standards of rationality that scientific beliefs fulfill—tacitly understood, as they are specified by the formal view of science. This is not the case. Therefore, religious beliefs are irrational. (The standards proposed by formalists that we have considered are the verification principle, Flew's falsification principle, Popper's falsification principle, the evidential principle, the proportionality principle, the rule principle, and the principles of simplicity, scope, and explanatory power.) The claim is that by the standards of rationality which govern the acceptance of belief in science, religious belief is irrational. However, if we adopt social evidentialism, the content of the challenge changes. That is, the view of science presupposed is no longer the formal view but the practice-oriented view, and therefore the appropriate standards of rationality have changed. For the sake of simplicity let us refer to the challenge in its former sense as the *traditional scientific challenge to religious belief,* and call this latter version the *contemporary scientific challenge to religious belief.*

Let us now consider what the change of standards of rationality means more precisely and what implications this change has for the question of the rationality of religious belief. Note that by accepting social evidentialism as a general model of rationality, a philosopher is committed to being either an advocate of the scientific challenge or a defender of the *strong response,* that is, someone who accepts the first premise (religious beliefs must fulfill the same, or at least similar, standards of rationality as scientific beliefs in order to be considered rational) but rejects the second premise of the challenge (religious beliefs do not fulfill the same, or at least similar, standards of rationality as scientific beliefs do).[6]

To start with, if the social evidentialist's account of rationality is correct, it is not surprising that philosophers of religion have not found clearly defined rules that can be applied to determine the rationality of religious belief. In fact, if this were possible we could exchange science for religion as the paradigm example of rationality, because, as we have seen, science could not itself satisfy the demands of the rule principle. (What this shows is probably that searching after a rule-governed decision procedure in philosophy of religion is a waste of time.) So one difference between the traditional and the contemporary scientific challenge is that according to the advocate of the latter, rule-following is not taken as a necessary condition for obtaining rational religious beliefs. On such an account is not the case that only if religious beliefs can be assessed by an application of the appropriate rules, the choice of accepting or rejecting them can be rational (or irrational).

The fact that religious belief-regulation does not satisfy the rule principle is, therefore, not a good reason for thinking that religion falls outside the scope of rationality. Instead, if it is possible to make informed judgments and expose one's beliefs to peer evaluation in religion then we have good reason to suppose that the question of rationality can properly be raised also in this context or area of life. Hence the crucial question philosophers of religion should be occupied with is not whether we can find appropriate rules that can determine the rationality of religious belief, but *whether people can (and do properly) exercise informed judgments in their religious believing*. So our questions for now will be: is the evidential principle (as it is understood by the social evidentialist) applicable to religious belief, and if it is, what consequences does it have for the rationality of being a religious believer? Applied to religious belief this means that *a religious belief is rationally acceptable by someone only if it is arrived at by an exercise of an informed judgment*.

Are religious believers people who exercise informed judgment in their believing? Before we can answer this question we need to know the answer to another question, namely, what does it mean to claim that rational people must exercise informed judgments in their believing? Because science is taken to be the best example of a rational activity we have at present, it is probably the manner in which scientists arrive at their beliefs that the social evidentialist has in mind. The idea is that scientists try to evaluate the evidence in favor of a theory. They try to decide what to believe by weighing the evidence and coming to a conclusion about which theory seems to be the best supported one. But this weighing of evidence is not determined by rules alone. It is done primarily by exercising judgment. More generally speaking, it implies that a person should have a certain degree of cognitive competence on a topic. It also means that a person must reflect long enough to acquire a clear understanding of what is involved in a particular issue and investigate the relevant evidence for and against before he or she takes a stand on what to believe. Can religious people fulfill this demand? Clearly a social evidentialist like Gutting does not think that religious people can satisfy the evidential principle the way formal evidentialists explicate it:

Those interested in weighting the epistemic propriety of religious belief frequently take upon themselves the impressive burden of constructing (though often for imminent destruction at their own hands) elaborate philosophical arguments for the believer's fundamental assertions. Even if such constructions were successful, they would have no importance for the vast majority of believers, since in their elaborateness and subtlety, they are utterly implausible as explications of most believers' reasons for belief. My view, however, suggests that the philosophers of religion can look, with some expectation of success, at ordinary believers' actual, operative reasons for belief. If, as I presume, belief is not just credulity or irresponsibility, we should be able to find in the experience and thoughts of typical believers grounds that entitle them to their belief.[7]

Further down the page he writes: "If we think that the traditional arguments for God's existence, as they are ordinarily construed, are paradigms of the way religious belief must be founded, then it is obvious that hardly any believers are epistemically entitled to their faith."

Gutting, however, thinks that if rule-governed reasoning is exchanged for judgment-based reasoning, and multi-dimensional arguments and not only one-dimensional arguments are allowed, the situation would change.[8] Before we go into this, note that Gutting is here concerned with *real* religious believers. He obviously seems to think that what they can and cannot do has some relevance for the question of the rationality of religious belief. The actual practice of religion puts at least some constraints on a proper model of religious rationality.

The social evidentialist's *assumption* seems to be that we could reasonably demand of religious people that they should, by using judgment-based reasoning, be able to give good reasons for their religious beliefs in the form of multi-dimensional arguments. Mitchell suggests how such a cumulative case for Christian theism might look:

> *Prima facie* the elements of the theistic scheme do tend to reinforce one another. . . . Thus, although the cosmological and teleological arguments do not . . . prove that there must be a transcendent creator of the world, they do make explicit one way (arguably the best way) in which the existence and nature of the universe can be explained, if indeed they can be explained at all. The atheist is entitled . . . to deny that the universe requires explanation, and so long as the matter is left there, the theist's far-ranging claims can rest on nothing more than the abstract consideration that explanation is

to be sought wherever possible. But when there is brought into the reckoning the claim of some men to be aware of the presence of God, and of others to have witnessed the action of God in the world or to have been addressed by him, the case is altered. . . . if there were a God who had created a universe in which there could develop rational beings capable of responding to him and to one another with love and understanding, it is to be anticipated that he would in some way communicate with them. The existence, then, of what purport to be such 'revelations' is something which tends to support the belief in a God who has in these ways revealed himself.[9]

Gutting identifies two parts of such a cumulative case: "the apparent power of a theistic framework to explain diverse features of our world and lives" and "the claim of being many to have experienced the immediate presence of a divine being."[10]

As I pointed out in chapter 4, not all formal evidentialists deny that multi-dimensional arguments are well-formed arguments. Both Swinburne and Mackie use this kind of argument in their evidentialist cases regarding theism. However, the social evidentialist's point is that religious people do not need to be able to formulate or use a probability calculus, or some other set of sophisticated rules (or to rely on the authority of those who can), in order to evaluate the force of this evidence. What they must be able to do is only something which we all master, to assess these arguments by exercising judgments. Gutting says, "evaluating these arguments does not require the resolution of any esoteric philosophical disputes, but only the sort of judgment that we all employ in countless everyday matters. Here we should expect to find whatever justification there may be for religious belief."[11]

Let me point out another difference between a formal and a social evidentialist case for (or against) religious belief. Formal evidentialists typically accept what I have called the "simple core approach." We have to isolate the belief or beliefs whose rationality we are interested in and define them as precisely as possible. Everything else can be put aside until this core has been rationally justified. In this particular case, the formal evidentialist claims that it is on the rationality of the proposition "God exists" that we should focus. The social evidentialist, on the other hand, rejects in general the simple core approach and claims that it is on religious belief as a whole, as a complex and large-scale system of belief that we should focus.[12] To draw a parallel to science we could say that it is not a single low-level hypothesis, but a complex high-level theory, or maybe even better a paradigm, with which we should make the comparison. Mitchell suggests that it is the "intellectual aspect" of religion on which we should focus and it can "be regarded as a world-view or metaphysical system," that is, a comprehensive picture that attempts to make sense of human experience as a whole.[13] Before I raise up one problem with this view of proper rational justification in religion, let me say a few words about reducing one phenomenon to another that is of relevance for this issue.

Both formal evidentialism and social evidentialism involve a reduction of religion to propositions or beliefs, even though the social evidentialist does not think that religion can be reduced to one core belief, as the formal evidentialist seems to think. However, this reduction is not, I think, meant as a claim that this is all religion is or even that it is all that is of relevance to the rationality of being a religious believer. Let me therefore say a few words about proper and improper forms of reduction in this context.

In many cases philosophers (and others of course) have to reduce religion to sets of statements or beliefs in order to be able to apply their philosophical tools to them. It is perfectly appropriate for a philosopher to make a *methodological reduction* of this sort. That is, for a particular purpose one may reduce a phenomenon x to a phenomenon y without claiming or presupposing that y gives an exhaustive account of x.[14] And at least some philosophers seem to acknowledge that they are performing a methodological reduction when they start their inquiry, for example, of the rationality of religious beliefs. But sometimes when they draw their conclusion in the end this methodological reduction somehow seems to have changed into an *epistemic reduction*. That happens when someone claims or assumes that only one element, z, of a phenomenon x is of importance or relevance for determining particular epistemological questions (concerning rationality, knowledge, truth, and so on). In this case this is done when someone claims (or assumes) that the only thing we have to take into account when we evaluate the rationality of religion is the core proposition "God exists," or the set of beliefs that constitutes a religious theory of life as a whole. The reduction consists not of the claim that religion is nothing but beliefs (that is an *ontological reduction:* phenomenon *x* is nothing but phenomenon *y*), but of the claim that only a religious belief, or a set of them, is relevant to the question of rationality (i.e., an epistemic reduction).

However, formal evidentialism seems to imply an epistemic reduction of religion to a core proposition or at best to a set of core propositions. This is so because according to them, only an object to which we can apply a rule-governed method of reasoning can by evaluated rationally. Hence the only thing that is relevant to rationality is what can be assessed by a rule-governed method of reasoning; nothing else is of any importance. So to the extent that other aspects of religion or complex sets of religious beliefs cannot be a proper object for such a method, they are consequently irrelevant to questions of religious rationality. In other words, the problem with the traditional scientific challenge is that in so far as it is not possible to determine the rationality of religious belief with the help of a set of appropriate rules, it is taken as a criticism against religion and not as a limitation of the model (or the formalization) the philosophers work with. Social evidentialism, on the other hand, seems not to imply such a reduction of religion. It is clear that social evidentialists focus on sets of religious beliefs. But nothing seems to preclude them from bringing in elements of religion other than beliefs, if we assume that a judgment-based reasoning can include an evaluation of elements other than propositions or beliefs. Hence the social evidentialist's reduction need be only methodological.

With this in mind let us consider a difficulty with a social evidentialist account of religious rationality. According to the social evidentialist, a necessary condition for rationality is that people arrive at their religious belief by making an informed judgment, which implies that they must have good reasons for their religious beliefs before they accept them and that they evaluate these reasons by performing a judgment. But a problem with this view of rational belief-formation is that many, maybe most, religious believers typically do not arrive at their faith in this way. This is so because religious beliefs are often a natural part of the cultural environment in which people grow up and are in a more or less unreflective way integrated into their belief systems. Religious beliefs are in this sense "culturally produced beliefs" (and so epistemically unassessed). One significant feature of this group of religious believers is that they are asked when and how they became religious, they are normally unable to give a precise answer. There are, of course, religious believers who acquire their religious beliefs in a manner similar to that by which scientists seem to acquire their scientific beliefs, but they are clearly exceptions. What are we supposed to conclude from these observations about *actual* religious belief-formation? Does this mean that most religious believers are unable to meet the demands of the evidential principle, and that they are therefore irrational according to the social evidentialist?

Before we try to answer this question we should notice that even though both the practice of science and religion can be described as *activities* of some kind, science is more than an activity, since it is an intellectual *enterprise* or a set of *disciplines*. Religion is an intellectual enterprise or a discipline only in forms like theology or philosophical theology. In this sense there is a crucial disanology between the practice of science and the practice of religion, one we may have to take into account. To be able to take part in an enterprise like biology, physics, or philosophical theology requires a special training and a much higher degree of cognitive competence than is required for taking part in an activity like religion. In fact some religions, like Christianity (at least in some forms), proudly claim that to be a part of their activity requires no special cognitive competence at all. To become a Christian is taken to be an act of faith alone. So science is a highly theoretical or intellectual enterprise for the cognitively well trained, whereas religion, on the other hand, is an activity in which anyone can, if they like, participate. This means probably that if we want to make a parallel between religious and scientific believing, the *relevant* comparison should be, first of all, between scientists and religious people involved in enterprises like philosophical theology or philosophy of religion. If so we must distinguish two question: Can and should religious believers involved in fields like philosophical theology arrive at their religious beliefs by making an informed judgment? Can and should "ordinary" religious believers arrive at their religious beliefs by making an informed judgment?

Suppose for the moment we claim that only religious people of the former group must satisfy the evidential principle. However, this does not seem to help these religious believers a lot, because it is very likely that the majority of them have also acquired their religious beliefs through the cultural environment in which they found themselves. This seems to be true even though the percentage of religious believers who have acquired their religious beliefs in a way similar to that of scientists is probably much higher in this group than in a group of ordinary religious believers. If this is correct, it would mean that not even this group of cognitively well-trained religious believers can meet the demands of the evidential principle.

But there are clearly problems here. For one thing, the picture of how scientists form their beliefs seems to be inadequate. This is because many of their scientific beliefs were formed before they became scientists, and many of them were learned by authority in their education. In other words, a great number of their scientific beliefs were not arrived at in a rational way according to this model but were simply taken for granted. And further, it is not just religious beliefs that are culturally produced beliefs, probably many of people's beliefs are of this sort. These include, Yandell says, beliefs which people in a certain culture:

> find it entirely easy and natural to accept, which enjoy widespread acceptance within the culture, which there is subtle pressure or influence to accept (not necessarily by anyone's intention that this be so), and which are false, or at least which most of those who accept them have not subjected to any sort of epistemic assessment. Yet it may not dawn on anyone to question them, and likely will be beyond the powers of many to ferret them out and investigate them on their own . . .[15]

It would seem unduly harsh to claim that people are irrational or failing to do their intellectual duty because they arrive at or form beliefs in such a way. (This point will be developed in detail in chapter 8.)

However, the social evidentialist could get, at least partly, around these problems about how we *arrive* at our beliefs by saying that no matter how one comes up with one's beliefs there is, at least, a certain intellectual duty in *sustaining* them:

> People must try to give good reasons for all beliefs they find themselves believing, or else give up the beliefs.

As soon as you find yourself believing something, you have to give good reasons for what you believe. On this account people's beliefs are still intellectually guilty until they are proven innocent, but the way people arrive at them is not the crucial question to ask if we want to be to able to evaluate their rationality. This account still meets the requirement that a rational person exercise informed judgment in his or her believing, though it is given a different interpretation. On this interpretation, the evidential principle is understood as a principle regulating primarily the maintenance, not the formation, of belief. The requirement on rational religious people is then, at least, that *they must be able to give good reasons for their religious beliefs no matter how they arrived at them in the first place.* The intellectual obligation is that the beliefs people already have must be critically evaluated and those that they have insufficient evidence for must be rejected.

Our concern here is not to develop or examine a cumulative case for religious beliefs as such, or for a particular set of religious beliefs like Christian theism, but rather to evaluate whether it is possible in principle for religious believers to meet the demands of social evidentialism. Or, to put it another way, our concern is to determine whether religious people can and should fulfill one of the same standards of rationality (the evidential principle) that the social evidentialists claim that scientists can and should satisfy. It is clear that it is possible for many more religious believers to be rational in their religious believing on this model in comparison to the former. However, one can, of course, still seriously doubt whether religious believing can be rational. But this sensitivity to what one reasonably can expect of real religious believers, and this attempt to take real religious practice seriously, seems to open up new possibilities not only for finding appropriate standards for evaluating rationality in this area of life, but also for *actual* religious belief-formation and regulation to put some constraints on normative models of religious rationality (or irrationality).

Without getting into any detailed examination the conclusion we can probably draw, with the modification and qualification given, about the first standard of rationality of social evidentialism (that rational people must exercise informed judgments in their believing) seems to be that it is likely that *some* religious believers are in principle able to satisfy this standard when it comes to their religious beliefs. But in the following chapters I will try to argue that it is highly questionable whether ordinary religious believers are able to—the same is, however, also true of ordinary secular believers. I shall claim that this is not primarily a problem for ordinary religious or secular believers, but it is in fact a problem for social evidentialism. Before we go into that in the following chapters, let us consider what implications the second standard of rationality proposed by the social evidentialist, the social principle, has for the question of the rationality of religious belief.

3. The Social Requirement and Religious Judgments

Many philosophers, and theologians too, have noted the changing view of science in contemporary philosophy of science that in previous chapters I have been trying to sketch. They claim that according to this new conception of scientific rationality religious belief can be shown to be rationally acceptable.[16] Gutting describes this change in philosophy of religion in the following way:

> Both believers and their critics have traditionally invoked the authority of science, its methods as well as its results. In recent years, the sword of science has been mainly wielded by critics of religion; philosophical discussions, in particular, have been dominated by challenges to religious belief based on standards of meaning and justification derived from analyses of scientific methodology. It has, for example, been argued that, if religious beliefs, like scientific ones, express factual claims about the world, then they must in principle be falsifiable by experience. . . . However, some recent defenders of religious belief have noted that the standard challenges are based on empiricist views of science that postpositivist philosophy of science has severely criticized. They have further suggested that these criticisms lead to new conceptions of scientific justification that can be successfully applied to a defense of religious belief.[17]

Gutting goes on critically evaluating an evidentialist case for religious belief based on this new (basically Kuhnian) conception of scientific rationality by trying to determine whether religious belief satisfies these new standards of scientific rationality. He thinks—and here he agrees with Barbour and Mitchell, whom he takes as defenders of this view—that it is possible to develop some interesting epistemic parallels between science and religion, but he claims (and here he goes against them) that the most crucial element in scientific justification is lacking in religion, namely:

its ultimate foundation in a *consensus* of judgment among scientists. Because religion has been incapable of generating the relevant sort of consensus, Kuhn's concept of a paradigm and the attendant notion of rational authority based on consensus cannot be extended to religious belief. The most that can be salvaged from the parallel with Kuhnian science is the idea . . . of a justification of religious belief by a cumulative case, rather than a single master argument.[18]

Because of the lack of consensus in religion "the Kuhnian account of scientific cognitive authority cannot be extended to religion, where there are a wide variety of competing paradigms, without the consensus needed for a cognitively authoritative judgment."[19]

So Gutting's claim is that the lack of informed consensus in religion casts doubt on the possibility of our proceeding in a rational manner in a religious context. Here it is clear that Gutting advocates a strong version of social evidentialism because he is not satisfied with just the social requirement (that religious beliefs must be submitted to evaluation by competent others for the beliefs to qualify as rational). But, as we saw in the last chapter, Gutting also demands that they must be rejected or (totally) re-evaluated if a sufficient number of competent others disagree (the conformity principle), and in this context he seems to add one more condition for achieving scientific rationality: that it is possible for the experts to come to an informed consensus on what to believe (what we could call the *consensus principle*). A necessary condition for the rationality of not just scientific practice, but of *any* practice, is that the experts in the field can come to a consensus based on informed judgments. We could explicate this standard of rationality in the following way:

> *The Consensus Principle:* A belief (or a set of beliefs)
> is rational for a person to accept only if the experts in
> the field can reach an informed consensus about it.

Wolterstorff thinks that it is the social situation of religious diversity that is the reason why Gutting claims that religious beliefs must meet this condition.[20] But as we have seen this is not entirely right. First of all, it is the comparison with science that is the reason why Gutting claims that also in religion must it be possible to reach an informed consensus. Roughly, the argument seems to be that: Science is the paradigm example of a rational practice. In science people are able to satisfy the demands of the consensus principle. Therefore, the same principle should be met by all other participants of rational practices (including religion).

But one problem with taking informed consensus as a necessary condition for rationality is that it would mean that periods of scientific revolutions must be seen as not totally rational, if not irrational. Large parts of the history of science seem to be threatened by this demand. For instance, in the dispute initiated by Copernicus and his Aristotelian contemporaries which went on for about 200 years, not until the time of Newton was a real informed consensus reached by the scientists. Does this mean that something was lacking in regards to rationality during this period? And it seems also to be the case that, at best, natural science is able to meet this demand. But what about human science? There seems to be a fairly limited degree of informed consensus in human science. Is it therefore lacking rationality? That does not seem obviously right. And what about philosophical disagreements—can they be rational? Philosophers are notorious for disagreeing with one another. Hence if the consensus principle is true, it is not possible to proceed fully rationally in philosophy until informed consensus has been reached to a degree that is comparable with natural science. If we take all this into account, it seems to be highly questionable whether this is a reasonable standard for rationality—it seems to be too demanding.

Maybe what Gutting really wants to say is something else. Natural scientists have a remarkable ability to reach informed consensus on what to believe. And this surely is an important epistemic merit. So what he might have in mind is that informed consensus is not a necessary condition for rationality but it rather is a necessary condition for reaching the *same level of cognitive authority* as science has. Hence informed consensus is an important epistemic virtue, but failing to reach it is not an epistemic vice. If religion wants to have the *same* cognitive status as (natural) science *then* it must be possible for the experts in that field to come, at least sometimes, to informed consensus about important aspects of religion. But remember that our project in this chapter is to try to determine what is required for a religious belief to qualify as rational, or better, to determine what is required for people to be rational in their religious believing. It is not an attempt to develop an account of when a person's beliefs are true, or when they constitute knowledge, or the like. The scientific challenge as I have defined it is a challenge about rationality, not about whether one in religion can reach the same level of cognitive authority as in science.

Suppose, even though this is unlikely, that the experts of religion (whoever they are) *can* reach an informed consensus. Does this mean that a religious believer must agree with the experts' consensus in order to be rational? Let us further suppose that it consists in the rejection of theism. Does it follow from this that theists must give up their theistic beliefs if they want to be rational or intellectually responsible in their believing? As we have noted, Gutting's answer seems to be "yes." This must be his answer because, according to strong social evidentialism, a rational person should reject or totally re-evaluate the belief at issue if a sufficient number of competent others demand it. Hence, all theists would be irrational in holding on to their theistic beliefs under those circumstances.

In the previous chapter, however, we saw that there are reasons for being skeptical about this claim. In particular, Putnam's objection is that sometimes one seems completely justified in relying on one's own judgment even though competent others disagree. It is also possible to give examples from the history of science in which scientists have relied on their own judgment in this way. This second remark is an objection because the advocate of the strong version of social evidentialism takes science to be the paradigm case of rationality. Again, the right conclusion to draw seems to be not that these persons are necessarily irrational (or intellectually irresponsible in some way), but that *prima facie,* communal judgments carry more epistemic weight than personal judgments.

So these objections delivered by Gutting do not seem to stop someone who tries to overcome the contemporary scientific challenge to religious belief. Let us, therefore, instead, focus on the social principle, which is less demanding than either the conformity or the consensus principle. Can religion satisfy the social requirement of social evidentialism? This is necessary if people want to be rational in their religious believing. It is not sufficient that people exercise informed judgment in their religious believing, their informed judgment concerning what to believe must also be exposed to a community of relevant expertise before what is believed can be said to be rational. Rationality requires peer evaluation. A belief must go through a process of community evaluation to qualify as rational in science, and, therefore, it is also required in any other domain claimed to be rational. This standard of rationality is what the social evidentialist thinks we should accept as a reasonable replacement for the formal evidentialist's rule principle. The *social principle* requires that a person should accept a religious belief only if it has been exposed to or tested against the judgments of a community of relevant experts. But it does not follow that if the "religious experts" agree that theism is irrational, then a person who continues to hold his or her theistic beliefs is necessarily irrational. There is no doubt that *some* theists would end up being intellectually irresponsible in their believing, but it does not follow that it would be the case for *all* theists.

However, the fulfillment of the social requirement is possible only if we suppose that there are people who are experts in religion; but are there and who are they? If there are no relevant experts in a field it is not possible to proceed rationally in it. My ability to act as a rational agent is limited not only by my expertise, but also by others' expertise or lack of it. Rationality requires other people but not just any group of people: it requires those who have a particular competence. Brown says: "on investigation we might discover grounds for doubting that the Azande poison oracle leads to rational beliefs. And this failure of rationality could occur for either (or both) of two reasons: because witch doctors refuse to submit their results for evaluation; or because there just is no relevant expertise."[21]

Is there any expertise on religious questions, and if, who possesses it? Brown does not think that this is really a problem. He says, "various groups of theologians who belong to different religions may all be engaged in a fully rational endeavor, and the same may hold for, say, Azande witch doctors." So the existence of theologians or, I take it, well-informed religious believers in general, is sufficient for peer evaluation on religious issues. But Brown does not think that the possibility that "questions of denominational theology may be capable of a rational resolution" need cause us any problem about choosing between scientific and religious claims if we have to. This is so for two reasons: "to claim that a belief is rational is not the same as claiming that it is true, and while rational acceptance of a claim depends on assessing evidence, some forms of evidence provide a stronger warrant for belief than other forms of evidence."[22] And the more reliable or better supported evidence is clearly the scientific evidence. Hence if scientific and religious beliefs come in conflict it is rational to stick to the former ones. This implies that not only religious believers but also other people can function as competent others on religious issues; and, therefore, it is possible to critically evaluate what is going on in religious practice also by people who are not themselves religious believers.

4.   The Social Evidentialist Challenge to Religious Belief

The main reason why I do not identify the scientific challenge with the evidentialist challenge to religious belief is, as I have previously pointed out, that they can be , but need not be, the same challenge to religious belief. They are not necessarily the same challenges because, for instance, it is possible that one can accept other kinds of evidence than strictly scientific (however it is specified), but still claim that religious people must give evidence for their religious beliefs. Hence someone can be an advocate of the evidentialist challenge to religious belief without being a defender of the scientific challenge. Wykstra, for example, claims that the evidential principle should apply both to scientific and religious claims, but he rejects the claim that religious beliefs need to be supported by scientific evidence: "Many who reject the demand for evidence for religious belief are, it seems to me, right in rejecting the demand for *scientific* evidence. Their mistake is to see scientific evidence, as defined by the inferential policies of science, as the only sort of evidence."[23] The same kind of position seems to be defended by Jeffner. He claims that one should believe something only if there are good reasons to think that it is true. In other words, Jeffner accepts an unrestricted version of the evidential principle, but he thinks that when arguing about the epistemic status of belief in God we should accept "that there are more kinds of rational reasons than those one typically uses in science."[24]

However, here the two challenges coincide because an account of scientific rationality is expanded into a general model of rationality, and none of the standards of rationality identified puts any restriction on possible kinds of evidence. Despite this coincidence, it could be illuminating to try to see the problem about the rationality of religious belief from the perspective of the evidentialist challenge. Recall that the traditional evidentialist challenge consists of the following set of claims: Religious beliefs are not properly basic beliefs. Non-basic beliefs without supporting evidence are not rationally acceptable. There is no evidence, or at least not sufficient evidence for religous beliefs. Therefore, religious beliefs are irrational. There are some significant differences between this traditional version of the challenge and one based on social evidentialism. A *social evidentialist challenge to religious belief* can, I think, be stated in the following way:

(1)   A belief is rationally acceptable only if it is arrived at by an exercise of informed judgment (the *evidential premise*).

(2)   A belief is rationally acceptable only if it is submitted to evaluation by a community of relevant expertise (the *social premise*).

(3)   All or some religious beliefs are not arrived at by an exercise of informed judgment and/or submitted to evaluation by a community of relevant expertise (the *factual premise*).

(4)   Therefore, all or some religious beliefs are irrational.

If the social evidentialist wants to avoid taking a stand on the issue of how we arrive at our beliefs (the issue of belief-formation), and hence accepts that religious beliefs are often culturally produced, premise (1) might be formulated in the following way:

(1*) A belief is rationally acceptable only if it is arrived at by an exercise of informed judgment, or if it is, at least, continuously held on to only after it has been evaluated by an exercise of informed judgment.

And if the stronger version of social evidentialism is advocated the second premise could be changed to:

(2*) A belief is rationally acceptable only if it is submitted to evaluation by a community of relevant expertise, and if it is rejected or totally re-evaluated if a sufficient number of experts demand so.[25]

Note first that the traditional version of the evidentialist challenge presupposes the acceptance of the rule principle. But in the social version this implicit demand is replaced with an explicit demand stated in the social premise. Rationality always requires peer evaluation. The reason for introducing this social requirement, as we have seen, is that the social evidentialist tries to avoid arbitrariness by finding a substitute for the demand that rational beliefs must necessarily be acquired by following rules. Second, this version, in contrast to the traditional one, omits in one sense the distinction between basic and non-basic beliefs. *All* beliefs, whether basic or not, are subject to justification, *if* a sufficient number of competent others questions them. Hence, if all or some religious beliefs are supposed to be properly basic, then they must still satisfy the requirement of the social principle (and, according to Gutting, also the conformity principle).

One element missing from the social version of the evidentialist challenge, but presupposed in the formal version, is the proportionality principle (the firmness with which one accepts a belief ought always to be in proportion to the strength of the evidence for it). This issue concerning how strongly committed one should be to what one believes has also been a central part of the traditional scientific challenge to religious belief. Let us focus on what consequences the social evidentialist's rejection of this principle might have when it comes to religious beliefs.

Often the distinction between the attitude of tentativeness and the attitude of commitment has been thought to constitute a crucial watershed between science and religion. The claim is that scientists have a tentative attitude toward their beliefs or theories, whereas religious believers have a dogmatic, unchanging attitude to their beliefs. This, as I pointed out in chapter 4, seems to create a *dilemma* for religious people: either they hold on to their beliefs with the strong commitment religion seems to require in which case they will be seen as intellectually irresponsible persons; *or* they hold on to their religious beliefs in a tentative and hence responsible way, in which case they will not have the degree of commitment religion seems to demand.

This dilemma is not necessarily solved by rejecting formal evidentialism and accepting social evidentialism instead. But the thought that these categories are totally exclusive ones or that commitment is essentially connected with irrationality does not follow. As we have seen (in chapter 5) a scientist's faith in his or her theory is a necessary presupposition for progress in science. The scientist's commitment must reach further than the evidence, and even sometimes go against evidence. Therefore, it seems reasonable to reject the proportionality principle and also the Popperian substitute, the principle of tentativity (all rational beliefs or theories should only be tentatively accepted, that is, one should never stop actively looking for counter-evidence to them), and instead try to find a reasonable alternative.

If the argument above is correct, we are more likely to understand why religious believers embrace their beliefs very strongly without therefore being necessarily irrational in doing so. All else being equal, people are rationally justified in holding their religious beliefs with a commitment that exceeds the strength the evidence for or against them. And when this is not rationally justified it cannot, according the social evidentialist, be established by rule-governed procedures, but must be the subject of an informed judgment of a community of relevant experts.

However, there might still be something suspicious or epistemically problematic about religious believing, but it is not necessarily or obviously irrational. One problem might be that the *dialectical relation* (or the "essential tension" as Kuhn says)[26] between the two attitudes is not as apparent in religion as it is in science. Therefore, a reasonable demand might be that rationality requires that a tentative attitude must be more emphasized in religion than what is typically the case. I will take a closer look at the purported dilemma, this demand, and what it implies for religious believers in chapter 10, when the nature of religious assent will be more carefully discussed.[27]

To sum up, the paradigm case of a rational practice is taken by the social evidentialist to be science and hence the paradigm example of a rational person is a scientist. Therefore, religious believers must regulate their beliefs in the same, or at least a similar, way as scientists do in order to be rational. More precisely, the demand is that religious people must be able to make informed judgments and submit their religious beliefs for evaluation by competent others. Brown, as we noted in the last chapter, thinks that these demands of rationality are within people's grasp to fulfill. However, I will try to show that, in fact, scientists themselves are not even able to meet these standards of rationality when it comes to domains of beliefs *other* than the scientific. As soon as scientists leave their laboratory they will most certainly fall short of these standards. (For example when it comes to the domain of everyday beliefs.) Further, the time and resources scientists invest in working with scientific beliefs or theories cannot be invested in other areas of their life. The reason for this is simply that scientists are human beings and they have *limited* cognitive resources. Therefore, it is reasonable to think that scientists do not have the capacity to reach the same standard in all other areas of life as they are able to reach in science. If this is correct, it has important consequences for the question of what the appropriate standards of (general) rationality are. In the following chapters I will try to develop this criticism against the social evidentialist's account of rationality. I shall argue that we need a more realistic model of rationality after all.

Before we turn to this project let me make some general comments. First, it should by now be clear that *criticism against religion is always relative to a particular model of rationality.* The discussion is as much about the notion of rationality as its application to religion. We cannot take the meaning of "rationality" as something unproblematic, as something we can take for granted when we try to investigate the rationality of religious believers or religious beliefs. The different consequences formal evidentialism and social evidentialism have for the question of the rationality of religious believing shows this clearly. Second, we have also gained some insight into the *order of priority* between our philosophical models and the reality they try to depict or evaluate. As we have seen, the danger is that philosophers sometimes tend to be more critical about the subject matter under investigation than they are of their own models. And that is, at least, according to the practice-oriented philosopher, to get things the wrong way around. Philosophers should always be more skeptical about their accounts of a phenomenon—especially if it is of central importance in human life—than about the phenomenon itself. So critical challenges against, for example, religion, science, or the rationality of ordinary people, are first of all challenges against the models of these phenomena philosophers elaborate with and not challenges against the actual practices of religion, science, or everyday living.

8

Presumptionism

I think that there is reason to believe that social evidentialism gives a good, maybe even the best, account of scientific rationality we have at present. It might give an adequate account of what we can reasonably be expected to do in regard to rationality in one area of life, the scientific domain. Despite this, I have deep doubts about its adequacy as a *general* model of rationality. In this regard I think it has some serious defects. These defects should become clear when we consider everyday belief-formation and regulation. In relation to this, two questions will be addressed: First, is social evidentialism after all applicable to everyday beliefs and ordinary people? Second, if it is not applicable to everyday beliefs can it then be an appropriate model for evaluating religious beliefs and religious believers? My answer to these questions will be "no." Because of these shortcomings of social evidentialism I shall argue that it is necessary that we construct an alternative model of rationality.

I will call my own proposal for such a new model, for lack of any better term, the *presumption model of rationality,* or just *pre-sumptionism.* (The reasons for using this term as a name for the model will become clear as we proceed.) My claim is that this model takes into account, better than social evidentialism (and, of course, also formal evidentialism), human beings' actual predicament, which includes, among other things, that humans are finite beings with limited cognitive resources.

1.   A Realistic Model of Rationality

Rationality is, as we have seen, a normative notion. It has to do with how agents ought to regulate their believings (actions and evaluations). Rationality is an intellectual duty or responsibility in regard to what one does. So rationality consists in satisfying one's intellectual obligations, and correspondingly irrationality consists in failing to meet these obligations. But this means that someone must have this obligation, that is, someone must be the *agent of rationality* (or irrationality). So rationality is in this sense always related to somebody. Typically, the agent of rationality is an *actual being* of some sort. Almost exclusively, the agents are then human beings, like religious believers or scientists, but they can of course also be real beings of other kinds with less cognitive resources than ours, like certain highly developed animals, or beings with greater resources than ours, like god(s) or angels—if one thinks that they exist. However, as we have seen, the explicit or implicit agent of rationality discussed by philosophers is, in fact, often a *fictive being* of some sort, a theoretical construction of some kind, like a purely epistemic being, an ideal cognizer, or a being with only ten beliefs in its belief system. This is common among formal evidentialists, who focus on beliefs rather than on agents, and therefore, the agent of rationality must often be derived from an analysis of rational belief. A rational agent is here an individual whose beliefs have the property of being rational.

Now, according to the presumptionist, rationality should be *realistic,* in the sense that it cannot reasonably require more than what the agent of rationality (whoever that is) can possibly do. But, of course, what reasonably can be expected of someone depends on that person's resources and situation. This means that a proper model of rationality must take into account the constitution and the actual predicament of the agent. This thesis, that rationality is realistic, relies on the truth of what we could call the *axiom of reasonable demand,* the truth of which the presumptionist takes to be self-evident. This principle can be specified in the following way:

> *The Axiom of Reasonable Demand:* One cannot reasonably demand of a person what that person cannot possibly do.[1]

Given this characterization of a realistic model of rationality, we shall say that an *idealized model* of rationality (or better: a *too-idealized* model of rationality, since rationality always involves a degree of idealization) is a model which violates the axiom of reasonable demand. That is, the model demands of the agent more than what that creature can reasonably be demanded to do.

If this is correct, it means that rationality is always *agent* or *person-related* and it is, I will claim, also *agent* or *person-relative* because, at least on the level of standards, rationality is not (or ought not to be) the same for all possible agents. In particular, I will argue in this chapter that the demands of the evidential principle are beyond the capacity of humans to satisfy in their life, though some other kind of being might be able to satisfy it—beings with, for instance, greater cognitive resources. Rationality is person-relative or more specifically *kind-relative,* if what is outside our cognitive grasp may be within some other kinds of beings' grasp, beings with greater intellects than ours. Hence we can say:

> Rationality is *kind-relative* if it (on some level) varies
> to some extent from species to species or from kind
> to kind.

Consequently, the presumptionist disputes the fruitfulness of asking the question of theoretical rationality in the traditional unspecified or abstract way: as in "What is it rational to believe?" or "What are the appropriate standards of rationality?" or even the more problematic "Is belief *p* a rational belief?" The presumptionist disputes this because it leaves out *whose* rationality or rational beliefs it is that we are talking about. Only when we know who the agent of rationality is can we give an answer to these questions. We must first ask "Who is the being that is supposed to be rational (or irrational) in his or her believing?" before we are able to answer "What is it rational to believe?" or "What are the appropriate standards of rationality?" For instance, we can ask what it is rational to believe *for* beings of the kind often stipulated in decision theory, that is, agents with a very limited set of beliefs and of possible choices. Only after such a specification has been done can the issues of rationality be properly discussed.

Our concern, however, is human rationality. We are interested in questions concerning what it is rational to believe *for* a human being. If, however, rationality is realistic, this means that a proper model of human rationality must take into account the actual constitution and predicament of the human agent. This does not mean that presumptionism is not a *general* model of rationality, as some might infer from its advocates' claim that rationality is kind-relative. This is not so because the demands of rationality can be the same for everyone of *us* (of the human-kind)—to fulfill the same intellectual duty with respect to our believing. In this respect rationality can be universal for every being of a particular kind. If they are in the same situation they should accept the same belief; if not they are irrational. But presumptionism is not universal in the sense that formal evidentialists typically hope that their model of rationality is, that is, that the "logic of rationality" should apply to all reasonable beings whoever they are and wherever they are.

So the presumptionist takes our actual predicament as a framework, or limits, within which the question of (human) rationality has to be addressed. I call this constraint, the *human constraint on rationality*. (In what follows I will mean by "rationality" "human rationality" if I do not say otherwise.) The thought is that it makes no sense to define the standards of rationality in such a way that it is not possible for real people to be rational in their believing. Such standards violate the axiom of reasonable demand, they require of people more than they are able to do. People cannot have an intellectual duty to regulate their beliefs in a way that is practically impossible because of their constitution or the circumstances they find themselves in. This realistic thesis in respect of human rationality can be expressed in the following way:

> In matters concerning our rationality we have to take into account who and where we are (and anything else is irrational for us to do).

It follows that the search for an adequate model of rationality has to be based on certain facts about human beings. We have to try to find an answer to questions like: What cognitive resources do humans have? How do they use them? How successful are they in using them in everyday life, science, religion, and the like? The first element of the "human condition" that the presumptionist thinks is relevant to rationality is that our cognitive resources are limited, and this in its turn is related to the fact that we are finite beings. *We are finite beings with limited cognitive resources.* As a consequence, every application of our cognitive resources has a certain cost. This means that if we want to proceed rationally no time should be spent on valueless or unimportant justifications, inferences, eliminations of inconsistencies, and the like. Time, memory, and so on, are precious, and any waste of these resources must be avoided.

An adequate model of rationality must take into account not only our physical constitution, but also the inescapable historical and social context of our lives. Where a person lives and what people a person meets daily put constraints on rational belief. Therefore, an adequate model of rationality must be sensitive not only to the constraint that the human nature sets on rationality, it must also be *socially sensitive*. We are not cognitive islands, we are not living in a cognitive vacuum; rather we are beings who grow up in a particular community, in a particular culture, and this social situation always affects who we become and what we think is reasonable to do and believe. The social situation always puts some constraint on rational belief, on what a person could reasonably be required to believe.

All this means that the presumptionist understands rationality as dealing with *people's proper exercise of their reason (intelligence or cognitive resources) in the particular physical, historical, and social situation in which they find themselves*. If this is what rationality is, we could say that we are rational when we use our cognitive equipment in a wise or intelligent way. When we use our reason in such a way, we are, in general, able to live successfully and function appropriately in the environment that nature and culture provide us with. However, to achieve these objectives not just any belief (action or evaluation) goes. The reason why not anything goes is that although people have created different conceptual schemes or belief systems and with them have organized different items in different ways, this freedom is not unlimited if we want to do it in a successful way. There exist what Herrmann has called *experiences of resistance*. Features in the world in which we live exercise a considerable constraint on the amount of beliefs we can successfully hold and the amount of actions we can successfully perform. We can fail to cope with the world we live in because the beliefs we have do not help us in the situations of resistance we meet. Herrmann gives the following example of experiences of resistance:

> There is a table in front of me. If I am fairly normal, it will hurt if I rush headlong into it. I want to maintain that in an analogical way the same applies to our relations with other people. If I am normally sensitive, I will probably not realize without pain that I cannot treat people in just any way I like. In one way or another my actions will produce a counter effect. I am forced to meet with the resistances with which the reality of human intercourse will confront me.[2]

If this is the situation of rationality, then the demands of rationality must be related to (*a*) who we are and (*b*) where we are, and (*c*) what we are (or should) try to achieve. The standards of rationality must be shaped in a way that takes into account our human abilities and our situation. And probably not only our cognitive resources must be taken into account, but also all other abilities we have that together make us function as whole and integrated beings. With this in mind, let us investigate more closely what implications this realistic approach to rationality has by once again reflecting on what light scientific practice can shed on these questions.

1.1   THE STATUS OF SCIENCE IN CONSTRUCTING A MODEL OF RATIONALITY

We have accepted the claim that science is probably the best example of a rational enterprise we have so far developed. It is, at least, one of the clearest instances of rationality in action we have at present. The social evidentialist's suggestion is that this means that in science we have a *test case* for examining models of rationality. If it follows from a proposed model of rationality that science is irrational, then we have good reason for being highly skeptical about that particular account of rationality. Hence we have here one more meta-criterion for evaluating a model of rationality:

> An adequate model of rationality must not entail (without a very good reason) that science is irrational.[3]

As we have seen, this is one of the major reasons why social evidentialists urge us to reject (or at least be highly suspicious of) the formal view of science. An unfortunate consequence of this view is that actual scientific practice turns out to be mainly irrational. And this is one of the reasons why formal evidentialism should be seen as an inadequate model of rationality. The presumptionist accepts this meta-criterion but rejects another one that seems, at least sometimes, to be assumed by both the formal and the social evidentialist. It is one thing to claim that (*a*) if a proposed model of rationality entails that science is irrational, we have good reasons, in general, for rejecting the model. It is, however, quite another thing to assume (*b*) that if a practice does not meet the same standards of rationality as science does, then the practice is irrational. Formal and social evidentialism seem to imply the acceptance of both (a) and (b), but the presumptionist accepts only the former. If this is correct, the formal and the social evidentialist, in fact, accept a stronger claim than the one specified above, namely:

> An adequate model of rationality must not entail (without a very good reason) that science is irrational, and for *any* practice to be considered rational, it must meet the same standards of rationality as science does.

But the presumptionist rejects this as a reasonable criterion for an appropriate model of rationality. Another way of expressing this difference between the models of rationality is to say that the claim that science is, at present, our best or clearest instance of rationality can be interpreted in two different ways. One could mean that science is *the* (one and only) paradigm case of rationality, or one could have in mind something else, namely, that science is *a* (one among several) paradigm case of rationality. From the fact that science is *the* paradigm case of rationality it necessarily follows that scientific rationality must be extrapolated as a general model over all domains of beliefs, or that rationality is limited to the scientific domain.

I will argue that one reason for rejecting the claim that science is *the* paradigm case is that it would mean that we take as the lowest level what in fact might be the highest level of rationality which we finite human beings with our limited cognitive resources are currently able to reach. An unfortunate consequence of doing this is that— because of our finite predicament—in almost all other areas in life, people almost always will be irrational. In short, my claim is that this kind of conceptualization of rationality is still too idealized to apply in an interesting way to the *whole* of human life. In particular, the social evidentialist's conception of rationality does not make enough sense out of everyday belief-regulation.

I think the mistake the social evidentialist makes is analogous to a common mistake in philosophy of science. Philosophers of science have a tendency to focus almost exclusively on the most "developed" forms of science, in particular physics, and they have concluded that what counts as justification, explanation, and so on, are the same or rather should be the same in all other scientific disciplines. What this tendency overlooks is that we cannot settle these kinds of questions without taking into account the *nature of the subject matter* under consideration. In a similar way we cannot solve the question of what rationality is by exclusively focusing on the best we humans are able to do. Brown seems to make this mistake when he writes:

> We can now return to the question of why science provides an especially important test case for a model of rationality. Rationality requires the assessment of evidence, and we should be able to get our best examples of rationality by looking at cases in which the most varied and reliable evidence is systematically gathered and deployed. If we were to look at fields in which decisions must be made on the basis of minimal evidence, or dubious evidence, and in which decisions could not be checked by gathering further evidence, we would likely get a very distorted view of the significance of evidence in arriving at beliefs.[4]

But it is equally important to emphasize that if we focus *only* on the best example of rationality, science, or only on what is often conceived of as the best of the scientific disciplines, we can get a very distorted view of what rationality *in general* is all about. We also have to ask: "What is the least we can and have to do?" Furberg writes in another context that: "Meaning in life must be found most in everyday living. Over the scrub bucket we learn a great deal about the conditions of life."[5] This, I think, is also true about the conditions of rationality.[6] I will try to argue that just as belief-formation and regulation in science is an important control case of rationality so is belief-formation and regulation in everyday life. "Real life" situations also provide a test case for appropriate models of rationality.

1.2   EVERYDAY BELIEVING: A CONTROL CASE OF RATIONALITY

In my view everyday believing is a paradigm case of rationality not in the sense that it is the *best* we humans can do, but in the sense that it is the *most* we do. With this cryptic sentence I mean that everyday beliefs are by far the largest domain of beliefs we human beings have, and everyone must be able to form, sustain, and evaluate them to be able to function appropriately in the kinds of situations one encounters every day in life. Everyday beliefs are about: other people, what one's own name is, living, driving, how to buy things, how to know when to trust someone, what love means, what good relations are, and so on. Because these beliefs normally amount for the vast majority of the beliefs in our belief system, an adequate model of rationality must be able to make sense out of them and the processes that are used to arrive at and regulate them. It is in this way that everyday beliefs are a paradigm or control case of rationality. In fact they are in a way more *fundamental* than scientific beliefs in our belief system, because we *cannot* avoid believing them and at the same time function appropriately as human beings. They are practically necessary beliefs for us to have, but the same is not true of scientific beliefs. It seems perfectly possible to function appropriately as a person and not accept any scientific beliefs at all. Therefore I think that an additional meta-criterion for evaluating models of rationality should be the ability to take into account everyday believing:

> An adequate general model of rationality must be able
> to make sense out of everyday belief-formation and
> regulation.

I think that we have to *assume* that people have an ability to be rational—at least to some extent. The reason why we have to do this is that without this assumption, it would be impossible to understand or make sense out of people's actions and beliefs. In order to understand and explain beliefs and actions we must presuppose rationality. We normally presuppose that people have a purpose in what they are doing. I remember how as a kid I stood and looked at the sky and fooled other people to look up even though there was nothing there to see. And there was nothing irrational in these people's way of behaving. Or think about communication, and try to imagine what language would be if people did not follow grammatical rules at all and changed the meaning of their concepts all the time. It would be impossible to communicate with them or learn their language. Meaningful human communication requires that people normally proceed rationally. So the crucial question is not whether we proceed rationally in everyday life or not, but to what extent we do so. The presumptionist claims that in everyday understanding of human beliefs we require only minimal rationality. If instead we required ideal or maximal rationality most people's behavior would be unintelligible to us.

The *thesis* I shall try to defend is that when we evaluate people's rationality in ordinary life we do not, and should not, use the standards of either formal or social evidentialism. They are not, and ought not be, a part of our everyday understanding of rationality or of what being reasonable is. Or to put it differently, my claim is that the conception of rationality in both these models is too idealized to apply in an interesting way to the whole of human life, and in particular to everyday believing. In everyday practice we distinguish "good enough" (presumptionism) from "perfect" (formal evidentialism) or from "very good" (social evidentialism) ability to proceed rationally, and if we did not do that it would be difficult to understand what was going on in everyday life. So one important argument for the presumption model of rationality is that it takes into account better than the other models the actual predicament of human beings.

What support is there for these claims? Is there a price to pay? Before we try to answer these questions let us start with another one: what cognitive resources do we have, how are they structured, and do they affect the question of rationality?

2.   Internal Rationality and the Structure of Human Memory

If we want to take into account a human being's cognitive capacity, a reasonable starting-point might be the structure of human memory—the forum or basis for our choices and beliefs. It is widely held among psychologists that human memory consists of two basic units: a small, active short-term memory, and a large, largely passive, long-term memory. The storage capacity of the short-term memory is thought to be very limited, while the long-term memory is regarded to have almost no practical limits. Maybe a good way to understand these two subsystems of the memory is to see them as having different degrees of activation and not to think that only the short-term memory is active and the long-term memory is totally passive. It is more a falling scale of activity than a case of either/or.

This *duplex model,* as Cherniak calls it, seems reasonable if we take into account the enormous number of beliefs a normal adult human possesses.[7] Because of the tremendously large size of a person's belief system, it is obvious that a person cannot, at one moment, think about all of his or her beliefs. What an individual can think about at a moment is only what is in his or her small short-term memory. Hence the vast majority of someone's beliefs are in the long-term memory. But a person can always recall beliefs from the long-term memory by, so to speak, copying them into the short-term memory. The picture of human memory that emerges is of an entity that is divided into two or more subsystems, where some subsystems are more limited than others, and where some subsystems are more active than others at a given time. A good analogy may be to see memory as a kind of filing system, where a file can in turn consist of subfiles.

With this information in mind let us consider whether such an account of human memory has any implications for our understanding of a rational regulation of the internal relation of people's belief systems. (Recall that the *internal standards of rationality* deal with how an agent ought to govern his or her internal affairs, concerning the rational regulation of already accepted beliefs. An individual's beliefs are taken as a closed system.)

From the account the formal evidentialist gives of a rational belief we can, as I pointed out, deduce a conception of what a rational person is. It is, among other things, an individual who believes or accepts the logical consequences of the beliefs he or she already holds (the principle of deductive closure). Put differently: if a belief implies another belief and a person accepts the first one, then the person ought to accept the second one as well. If p implies q and A accepts p, then A must accept q. On this account there is something irrational or intellectually irresponsible in not accepting the second belief if one already holds the first belief. And seen as a formalization there seems to be something intuitively right about it.

The basic problem, however, with these types of formalizations is that they tend to isolate beliefs in the sense that the content of the beliefs, the situation in which the beliefs arise, and the believers and their cognitive resources are not taken into consideration. What is problematic with this kind of formalism, when applied to human beings, is that it does not take into account the size of people's belief systems or the structure of their memory. To start with, a normal person's belief system is enormously large. It contains all the beliefs an individual has acquired during his or her life time, and there is practically no limit to it. A person is not in any way able to explicate all of his or her beliefs on request. Therefore it is impossible for human beings to consider all, or even a majority, of the implications of their beliefs. Second, people's webs of beliefs are not only enormously large and complex, but they are also structured in such a way that large parts of them are inactive. If human memory consists of two major subsystems, then it matters whether or not an implication between two beliefs is in the short-term memory, in the long-term memory, or between one belief in the short-term memory and one in the long-term memory. From the perspective of the duplex model of human memory, people are at best likely to notice the implications of their belief systems when the beliefs have been retrieved from long-term memory and activated in short-term memory. If an implication is between a belief in the short-term memory and one in the long-term memory, it is less likely that a person will realize it than if both beliefs are simultaneously activated in the short-term memory. Since the capacity of the short-term memory is limited, the detection of consequences or implications of the belief system will usually be incomplete.

Hence people do not have the ability to deduce consequences as the formal evidentialist's account of rational belief presupposes. But if we take this fact about the structure of human beings' cognitive equipment into account, that seems like an unreasonable demand to make of the rational regulation of one's beliefs. Whether a belief is internally rational or not depends not only on whether an individual who accepts belief p, which implies q, accepts q, but also on the size of the system this inference is a part of and on its location in the system.

The situation is not much better when it comes to the opportunities real people have to reduce inconsistencies in their belief systems. Many accounts of rationality see inconsistency as a cardinal sin. According to the conception of a rational person implied by formal evidentialism, a rational individual eliminates the inconsistent beliefs in his or her belief system (the consistency principle). If a belief is inconsistent with the beliefs already held then a rational individual has to eliminate the inconsistency. If q implies not-p and A believes p then A must either reject q or p or both. But again if the structure of human memory is taken into account real people are likely to notice inconsistencies among their beliefs only if they are at the same time activated in the short-term memory. The enormous size of people's webs of beliefs makes it *practically impossible* to detect all inconsistencies among their beliefs.

Cherniak discusses what ability to detect consequences and eliminate inconsistencies we can reasonably expect of a rational human being by bringing in some results from a branch of mathematics called "complexity theory." To summarize his account, he claims that complexity theory shows that decision procedures in many areas are computationally intractable and hence practically impossible. Cherniak considers, for example, the question of how large a set of beliefs an ideal computer can check for consistency using the truth table method:

> Suppose that each line of the truth table for the conjunction of [a set of] beliefs could be checked [by an ideal computer] in the time a light ray takes to traverse the diameter of a proton . . . and suppose that the computer was permitted to run for twenty billion years, the estimated time from the "big bang" dawn of the universe to the present. A belief system containing only 138 logically independent propositions would overwhelm the time resources of this super-machine.[8]

Cherniak claims that these results throw entirely new light on recent psychological experiments that seem to show that people "use . . . prima facie suboptimal 'heuristic strategies,' rather than formally correct procedures, in everyday intuitive reasoning."[9] Psychologists typically take themselves to be studying human irrationality,[10] but since people—as the results from complexity theory indicate—cannot possibly use only algorithms in their belief-regulation the use of "formally incorrect heuristics need not in fact be irrational at all. They are not just unintelligible or inadvisable sloppiness, because they are a means of avoiding computational paralysis while still doing better than guessing."[11]

It is held among psychologists not only that human memory is divided into a short and a long-term memory, but also that the long-term memory itself is divided into different subfiles or compartments. This means that: "Logical relations between beliefs in different 'compartments' are less likely to be recognized than relations among beliefs within one compartment, because in the former case the relevant beliefs are less likely to be contemporaneously activated, and . . . it is only when they are activated together that such relations can be determined."[12]

The price of structuring memory in this way is that inconsistencies and inferences that involve beliefs in different subsets are likely to be overlooked. But the compartmentalization of memory cannot, because of this price, be seen as a serious flaw of our ability to proceed rationally, for there would be intractable problems in searching a memory as large as the one human beings have. Therefore, it

seems reasonable—given our limited cognitive and time resources—
to restrict the searching of our memory to a few subfiles:

> prima facie, the resulting behavior can be characterized as depar-
> tures from rationality, but on the assumption that exhaustive
> memory search is not feasible, such memory organization is ad-
> visable overall, in the long run, despite its costs. Correspondingly, a
> person's action [or belief] may seem irrational when considered in
> isolation, but it may be rational when it is more globally considered
> as part of the price of good memory management.[13]

Let us return to the question of appropriate standards for internal
rationality. It should by now be clear *why* it is impossible for people
to meet the demands of the principle of deductive closure and the
consistency principle, as they are specified by the formal evidentialist.
This is so because of the size of the belief system humans have and
the structure of their memory. People seem to be able at the most
to make all *feasible* inferences from a particular belief or from their
belief systems as a whole.

However, some formalists, as we have seen, claim that these
principles should be understood as only an *ideal* we should strive to
reach, not as something we actually must fulfill. Their claim is merely
that people are rational only if they always *try their best* to bring it
about that they believe all the logical consequences of whatever they
believe (the *modified principle of deductive closure*), and that they
eliminate as many inconsistencies as possible from what they believe
(the *modified consistency principle*). Formulated in this way these
principles seem to be feasible, and human beings can actually satisfy
these demands. But should they?

The presumptionist claims that people should not try to conform
to these principles, despite the fact that they are feasible, because it is
still to require too much. This is so because inferences that are feasible
might, nevertheless, not be directly *useful* for people to make at a
given time. Even though an inference may be sound and feasible, it
is not necessarily reasonable to make it because it may be of no clear
value at the time and it may prevent the person from using his or her
limited cognitive resources to do other things that are more urgent.
To perform some of these inferences would be a waste of a person's
time and might in some cases even be insane. Someone could waste

his or her entire lifetime making only useless but feasible inferences. For example, in a situation where my own existence is in danger it would be irrational to deduce some feasible consequences of my belief in planets. Or in a situation when somebody else is drowning, my thinking about some feasible consequences of my belief in other minds could prevent me from helping the person. Goldman argues in a similar way for a rejection of these principles, because a person who tries to satisfy them:

> would expend all his conscious energy tracing the logical conse-
> quences of his beliefs and worrying about their possible incon-
> sistency. This would be an all-consuming mental occupation. Is
> that a reasonable allocation of limited cognitive resources? Surely
> not. Someone who uses all his information-processing time and
> equipment in these tasks will acquire little or no "new" information,
> e.g., information about dangers in his current environment.[14]

So even if they are feasible they should not necessarily be accept-able because of our limited cognitive capacity and our predicament. Not trying to make the vast majority of feasible inferences and not trying to check all feasible inconsistencies among one's beliefs is not irrational, it is rather rational. In fact, people who do not take into account the limitations of their cognitive resources are acting irrationally, and standards of rationality that do not take this into account are inadequate and should be rejected.

Again, the mistake made by many formal evidentialists is that they see the question of internal rationality as too much of a logical problem, without any real empirical input or constraints. The rational-ity of an inference is taken to be only a matter of its intrinsic character, and the conditions under which it is performed and the reasoning and psychology of the believer are (most of the time) bracketed. This way of proceeding is a consequence of some important features of formal evidentialism, namely, that its advocates accept a formal approach to philosophy and that the locus of rationality is taken to be beliefs, not persons. Therefore, formal evidentialists have a strong tendency to discuss the logical structure of a belief system *per se,* without relating it directly to agents, in this case real people—with their limitations—who actually have webs of belief. The appropriate way of proceeding must instead be to focus on people's cognitive abilities and situations, which means that we have to take into account facts about how human cognitive equipment functions. Logic alone cannot generate appropriate standards of rationality.[15]

The presumptionist claims that we can arrive at an adequate understanding of internal rationality only if in our analysis we take our starting point as the fact that humans are finite beings with limited cognitive resources. As a consequence, we must, when trying to give a reasonable content to a principle of deductive closure, take into account not only the logical validity, but also the feasibility and usefulness of an inference for people at a given time. In general we could say that to be considered internally rational people must do what can be *reasonably demanded* of them in matters concerning the reduction of inconsistencies and accepting the logical consequences of their beliefs. More specifically this might mean that a reasonable way of stating the principle of deductive closure is to argue that it should consist of the demand that to be internally rational people must make all inferences of their belief systems that are sound and useful for them at a given time and in a particular context—given that the inferences are derivable from beliefs that are located relatively close to the activated beliefs in the short-term memory. And a reasonable understanding of the consistency principle might be that to be internally rational people must eliminate all inconsistent beliefs in their belief systems when the elimination is feasible and of appropriate usefulness for them at a given time and in a particular context—given that the inconsistencies are among beliefs that are in reasonable search distance from the activated beliefs in the short-term memory.

The conclusion of this discussion must be that the issue of internal rationality cannot be settled by focusing only on the logical features of sets of beliefs. It is simply not true that the question concerning the rational internal regulation of belief can be settled independently of a conception of the kind of being whose set of beliefs we are investigating. If we are talking about human beings, then we have to take into account their actual cognitive resources and situation. If this is the case, it follows that the only rational way of governing the internal relation among our beliefs is one that takes into account that we are finite beings with limited cognitive resources that are structured in a certain way. That is, we must construe rationality *realistically*. Because of the structure and the limitations of our cognitive equipment every application has a cost. A human being who wants to proceed rationally cannot, therefore, spend time on valueless inferences or the elimination of unimportant inconsistencies. So the goal people should strive to reach cannot be to ensure that their beliefs meet the internal standards of formal evidentialism, since that would be for them to proceed irrationally.

3. External Rationality and the Rejection
   of the Evidential Principle

Let us now turn our attention to what consequences the acceptance of presumptionism has for external rationality (the standards of rationality that state how people ought to govern their external affairs, concerning what conditions a belief must satisfy before it is allowed to enter or stay in their belief systems). The formal evidentialist tells us, among other things, that to be rational we must formulate and follow rules that tell us when it is rationally justified to accept scientific, religious, or everyday beliefs. The social evidentialist, on the other hand, denies this and claims instead that we are rationally justified in accepting them if we arrive at them by exercising informed judgments and if we submit our beliefs to evaluation by competent others. But the social evidentialist agrees with the formal evidentialist that rational people must have good reasons for their scientific beliefs, as well as their everyday and religious ones. The advocates of these models agree that we have an intellectual duty or obligation to regulate our believing in such a way that we accept or hold beliefs for which we have sufficient evidence only.

Suppose we accept that this is the case in science, that scientists meet the requirement of the evidential principle. But can scientists— or is it reasonable to demand that they must—meet the demands of the evidential principle in regard to *all* their beliefs? What about, for example, the scientists' (or other people's) everyday beliefs? Do scientists have good reasons for their certainty that they exist, are human beings, have brains, know their names, know that suffering is evil, and so on? Or do scientists have sufficient evidence for the number of assurances that they (and we all) rely on more or less unconsciously? Convictions like: that everything has a cause, or is a part of a connected whole? The answer we and the scientists must give to the question: "How many of our actual beliefs do we have good reasons for?" must be, I think, not so many. I would guess that the majority of any adult person's beliefs and actions would, according to the evidential principle, in fact be more or less irrational. If that is the case, is it reasonable to conclude that so many adult human beings' beliefs and actions are in fact irrational? In practice, as Andersson and Furberg point out, the evidential principle seems to prohibit our believing in almost everything we have been certain of before—except maybe for our area of specialization, if we have one.[16] But this prohibition does not seem obviously reasonable. Hence if we took the evidential principle seriously enough it would simply make us *incapable of acting and functioning properly as human beings*. How could we, in our short lifetime, have time to think through and give good reasons on request for all the beliefs we accept or hold more or less unconsciously? There is not time enough. Someone could waste his or her entire lifetime searching for evidence for all kinds of beliefs. If this is correct, then the evidentialist's demand is unrealistic, and it violates the axiom of reasonable demand.

So the presumptionist thinks there are strong pragmatic reasons for rejecting the evidential principle. If, for example, our ancestors had tried hard to follow the demands of this principle, would we be alive today? To survive our ancestors had to act out of habit, without hesitation or paralyzing doubt, and without always asking what reasons do I have for believing this, doing that, and so on. On the other hand, of course, if our ancestors never asked for evidence, never questioned anything, we would not be where we are now either. So a sound balance between living on "automatic pilot" and living a deeply reflective life was what was needed then, and I think the same is true today. But the point is that *a constant questioning of our beliefs, a constant search for evidence or reasons is not a rational way of governing one's believing, it is rather highly irrational.* The reason why it is highly irrational is that it seems to waste too much of our limited cognitive resources and the limited time that are at our disposal. It we take the evidential principle literally in real life situations, the principle would create only chaos in our thoughts and actions.

Another reason for questioning the evidential principle has to do with the fact that not all beliefs are of equal importance in our lives. Certain beliefs, for example, "I am starting to go bald" or "there are more leaves on the trees in southern Sweden than in the northern part on the 15th of October," can be very unimportant in my life. Therefore

I could hardly have an intellectual responsibility to seriously consider what good reasons I have to support these beliefs.[17]

One way formal and social evidentialists can respond to at least the second objection is to restrict the application of the evidential principle to only important beliefs. Sure they might say, it is not necessary to have good reasons for unimportant beliefs, what we really had in mind were beliefs that are of essential value for us human beings and our society, either intrinsically or depending on the situation. Hence we should instead define the evidential principle in the following way:

> It is rational to accept an important non-basic belief only if there are good or sufficient reasons to believe that it is true.

Though it is certainly true that we should try to get more evidence for important beliefs than trivial ones, it is still doubtful whether it is within our cognitive resources to meet the evidentialist's demand on a general level. Think about beliefs and actions where our lives are at stake. I take it they qualify as intrinsically important beliefs. For example, beliefs about driving. Sometimes when I drive I think about the people driving the cars I meet on the road. Often we pass each other at a speed of say 110 km/h and there is, perhaps, 2 meters between the cars, sometimes less. Do I have good or sufficient reasons for trusting the drivers I meet to a degree that it is reasonable or rational for me to drive on the road? Certainly not. I do not know anything about them except that they are driving the cars I pass and perhaps what kind of car they are driving. I think I know some things about car drivers in general, but I have never checked the facts myself, except for the facts that are directly connected with my own experience of car driving. Still you and I "risk" our lives almost everyday in situations similar to the one I have described. Or think about every time you and I step onto a crosswalk. We risk our lives on expectations about a motorist's behavior without having sufficient evidence regarding his or her intentions; and the same goes for flying in airplanes, and so on. Now according to the standards of the modified evidential principle, must we not be seen as acting irrationally? It certainly seems that way. We hold important beliefs without having good or sufficient evidence for them. But what else can we do? We would never get around in life if we were afflicted with this sort of evidential doubts.

4.   The Principle of Presumption

It is not impossible that the evidentialist might qualify the evidential principle in such a way that these difficulties would be avoided,
but I think that is unlikely. However, because of all these problems
presumptionists reject the evidential principle instead of trying to
modify it. Presumptionists claim that evidentialists get things the
wrong way already from the start. According to evidentialists we
should *start* by questioning all of our beliefs. (All beliefs because
we also have to give good reasons for why we take certain beliefs
to be basic beliefs.) Hence what we believe should always be met
with a high degree of suspicion. Instead of allowing us to hold beliefs
until reason to criticize them has emerged, we are supposed to have
a hyper-critical attitude towards them already from the start and not
accept beliefs until we have good reasons for them—which shows
either that they are properly basic beliefs or that they can be derived
from these by acceptable methods of inference. Evidentialism, taken
literally, seems to drive us to a destructive form of skepticism. A
constant questioning of our beliefs is not rational, it is rather highly
irrational, since it wastes too much of our limited cognitive resources.

The presumptionist claims instead that the only rational or
proper attitude towards our beliefs must be one of (at least, initial)
trust—not of distrust. This means that our beliefs should be taken to
be intellectually innocent until proven guilty, not guilty until proven
innocent. One is not forbidden to believe something unless one has
sufficient evidence for it. One is *permitted* to believe something without having special reasons, but one has to give up what one believes
when sufficient counter-evidence has emerged. I call this model of rationality "presumptionism" because its advocates claim that our belief-
forming processes and their deliverances (beliefs) should be *presumed*
to be intellectually innocent until proven guilty.[18] These processes
and their deliverances do not first need to be justified (given good
reasons for) before it is rational for us to believe in them. Instead, our
beliefs are initially justified through the force of a presumption. And
we can call the key element of this model of rationality the "principle
of presumption." It can be stated as follows:

> *The Principle of Presumption:* It is rational to accept
> a belief unless there are good reasons to cease from
> thinking that it is true.

Andersson and Furberg seem to accept this principle when they write: "one should not believe something if there exist good reasons to believe that it is untrue."[19] So does Harman when he says that "one's present beliefs are justified just as they are in the absence of special reasons to change them."[20] And lastly, Wolterstorff says: "A person is rationally justified in believing a certain proposition which he does believe unless he has adequate reason to cease from believing it. Our beliefs are rational unless we have reason for refraining; they are not nonrational unless we have reason *for* believing."[21]

Note that the evidential principle and the principle of presumption are not identical. This is so because the principle of presumption allows that it is rational to keep beliefs which are included among those one already accepts, even if one has no reason to think they are true, provided there is also no reason to reject them. The evidential principle demands that we abandon those beliefs we do not find any special reason to think are true but also no special reason to reject. According to the evidentialist, we ought to reject any belief which we have no good reason to think is true. The presumptionist claims instead that we ought to reject any belief which we come to know or have good reasons to think is false. So the presumptionist denies that having no evidence for a belief is an acceptable reason for rejecting a belief.

The basic problem with the extremely critical attitude towards our beliefs that evidentialism seems to imply is that we cannot have this attitude and at the same time function appropriately as human beings in all areas of life. Again, the reasons for this are that we have limited cognitive resources, a limited amount of time, and a need to have beliefs in our lives. In this respect the principle of presumption is much more *economical* and therefore is more *realistic* than the evidential principle. It is a more economical principle because we have to begin somewhere in our believing, and this principle allows us to start with any belief we do not know or reasonably think is false. Hence if followed, the principle of presumption does not waste as much of our limited cognitive resources as the evidential principle does, and this is a major advantage because we must (if we want to use our cognitive resources wisely) spend as little time as possible on valueless or unimportant justifications, inferences, eliminations of inconsistences, and the like. Therefore, a crucial and decisive argument for presumptionism is that it is better than the other models at taking into account the actual resources and predicament of human beings.

Having reasons, then, plays a different role in the presumption model of rationality than in the two other models. But evidence still has an important function. To use Wolterstorff's terminology, evidence plays primarily a *rationality-removing* role.[22] This shows that presumptionism, though it is a form of anti-evidentialism, it is not a form of fideism, if by *fideism* we mean the position that evidence does not play an essential role in the regulation of beliefs, or more exactly, the view that beliefs cannot be subject to rational evaluation.[23] Presumptionism is not a form of fideism because its advocates do not deny that there might be good evidence for a belief, or that evidence can count against a belief.

Presumptionists claim only that having good reasons is not a necessary condition for being rational in one's believing. They deny that it is rational to accept a belief only if, and to the extent that, there is sufficient evidence for it. People have permission to accept what they believe without evidence (not only basic but also non-basic beliefs), but not contrary to evidence. (Presumptionism also includes the rejection of the proportionality principle, and this is something it has in common with social evidentialism. This topic is discussed in chapter 10.) So the evidentialist and the presumptionist disagree on *which* role reasons play in questions of rationality, but neither accepts the fideist's claim that reasons play *no* role at all or at least no critical role. The difference is that the evidentialist claims that evidence plays a *positive* role (a rationality-establishing role), whereas the presumptionist claims that it plays primarily a *negative* role (a rationality-removing role), in regard to whether or not a person is rational in believing something.

One *basic intuition* behind the principle of presumption is that we must—because of the human condition—have an epistemic right, at least initially, to rely on our own cognitive equipment or belief-formation and regulation processes. If this is not the rational way of governing one's beliefs it seems difficult to avoid a destructive form of skepticism. The conclusion that we should draw from this is that, in general, it is first in situations of resistance that the demands of rationality come in, and only there. However, as Herrmann points out, experiences of resistance can be of different kinds.[24] They can take, for example, a physical, cultural, or an existential form. We experience these resistances in the form of physical objects like walls, but also in the form of language and human relations; and situations of suffering or death could be examples of existential experiences of resistance. Now the thought is that it is first when we experience situations of resistance that we have to justify our believing. In these situations of resistance special reasons could emerge that make it necessary for us to revise or even totally reject what we previously believed. It is how we react to these anomalies or defeaters that determines whether we are rational or not in our belief-regulation.

But is there not a price somewhere to pay for the presumptionist? Consider a possible objection to presumptionism. It could be argued that surely, it might be true that the evidential principle allows far too little to be rational, but does not the principle of presumption allow far too much? Do we not end up with classifying far more as rational than what seems reasonable? For example, suppose an individual just decides to believe something stupid, say that cats grow on trees, and that he or she has no good reasons to give up the belief. Is this person rational in believing this? Certainly not. But does the principle of presumption imply that this person is rational? I do not think so. This is the case because this person *knows* that the way he or she arrived at the belief is unreliable. And if the person knows this he or she in fact *has* good reasons for giving up or at least being suspicious of that belief. Counter-evidence is not something that other people must produce; that is something one can imagine or come up with oneself. Therefore, this objection does not seem to count against presumptionism. (Other objections will be considered later on.)

Presumptionists have certain things in common with social evidentialists. However, the main differences between them is, of course, that the presumptionist rejects the evidential principle. But presumptionists also reject the social principle as a necessary standard of rationality. (The reason why they reject the social requirement will be discussed at the end of this chapter.) Presumptionists accept, on the other hand, the thought that *judgment* is the primary mode of evaluation open to us. In other words, they reject the rule principle. This means that determining when sufficient evidence against a belief has arisen is primarily a matter of a personal or a communal judgment, so it is not necessarily a rule-governed process—as Popper thinks, though of course presumptionists use rules or algorithms whenever they are available. (Since we always have to act and believe on incomplete information, judgment also comes in when deciding to stop looking for evidence for or against one's beliefs.) And as we have already seen, the presumptionist also accepts the social evidentialist's claims that the locus of rationality is persons, not beliefs. The central category of rationality is a rational person not a rational belief.

5.   Rationality, Knowledge, and Truth

Let us now try to see how the presumptionist understands the connections between rationality, knowledge, and truth. We start by considering the relation between rationality and knowledge, and then we go on to discuss the relation between rationality and truth.

5.1   RATIONALITY, JUSTIFICATION, AND KNOWLEDGE

Rationality, as we have seen, has to do with what one can reasonably demand of people when it comes to regulating their believing processes or their accepting and holding on to beliefs. And according to the axiom of reasonable demand, people are irrational only to the extent that they fail to do what can be rightly demanded of them, that is, their intellectual duty (a duty which of course can be spelled out in different ways). So whether what one believes fails or succeeds in reaching the status of knowledge is nothing that counts against the rationality of those beliefs. We could say that:

> Rationality has to do *exclusively* with the knowing subject or the subjective dimension of belief-regu-lation—with things an agent can reasonably be ex-pected to believe.

Knowledge, on the other hand, has to do with whether a certain kind of relationship holds between the knowing subject and the known object. A belief is not considered knowledge if this relationship between the knowing subject and the known object is not established. According to the traditional view of knowledge, this relationship between the knowing subject and the known object is provided by justified belief, which together with true belief constitutes knowledge. Knowledge is *justified true belief*. (Someone S knows that something is the case p if and only if: (1) S believes p, (2) p is true, and (3) S has good reasons for p.) Being justified is, together with having a true belief, what turns something into knowledge.

With respect to this connection between the knowing subject and the known object two positions, *internalism* and *externalism,* have emerged in contemporary epistemology. Both the traditional account of knowledge and the models of rationality we have been working with are examples of internalism. The internalist claims that rationality and justification have to do with a person being capable of recognizing the evidence or counterevidence with respect to a belief. What makes a belief knowledge or rationally acceptable must be something available within a person's perspective, something to which he or she has "privileged access." Whether a true belief is rationally acceptable or constitutes knowledge depends on factors (justifiers and defeaters) to which the agent has internal access. The basic idea with respect to knowledge is that one has to know that one knows to know.

But one crucial and well-known problem with the traditional account of knowledge as justified true belief is that no matter how much we do from the subjective point of view (checking the evidence really carefully, etc.) we might still fail to gain knowledge. (Gettier was the first to give a generally convincing example of a situation in which the three traditional conditions of knowledge were satisfied but we would still not admit that *S* knows *p.*)[25] The conclusion some philosophers draw from this is that justification understood in internalist (and therefore deontological)[26] terms does not seem to be sufficient for knowledge, and externalist accounts have been given instead.[27]

The main difference between internalism and externalism is that the internalist claims that the knowing subject must him or herself be aware of the connection between him or herself and the known object, but the externalist denies this. For the internalist this relationship is one to which the knowing subject must have access. For the externalist it is a relationship to which the knowing subject need not have access. But, and this is my point, it is important to recognize that even if we reject an internalist (and hence a deontological) account of knowledge it does *not* imply that we have to reject an internalist (and hence a deontological) account of rationality. The reason why is that rationality, as specified above, and in contrast to knowledge, *has to do only with the knowing subject, with things a person can be expected to believe.* Rationality has to do with what you and I can and ought to believe. The externalist's point is that no matter how much we do at the subjective pole (we could have a very high degree of justification) things could still go wrong at the objective pole. But since rationality has to do only with the subjective pole, the acceptance of externalism does not necessarily lead to a rejection of a deontological conception of rationality. This means that for the externalist the difference between rationality and knowledge is not just a matter of degree of justification (which internalists seem to think);[28] there is also something else that must be *included* in an adequate account of knowledge, but that can be *excluded* from an adequate account of rationality. What this something else is exactly, is something about which externalists disagree. However, my intention is not to discuss whether externalism is a more reasonable position to take than internalism with regard to what knowledge is, it is only to make it clear that if one accepts an externalist account of knowledge this does not imply that one has to do the same when it comes to rationality.

How then is rational believing related to justified believing, and what is the connection between rationality and justification? We have seen in the previous chapters that philosophers often do not make any clear distinction between them, they use them interchangeably. However, it is important to distinguish them, because it is reasonable to think that what should be required for rational belief should be weaker than what is required for justified belief. We can see this by focusing on how the notion of justification is used in discussions of knowledge. To show that knowledge is possible and even likely for us to achieve, philosophers have in general thought that they must overcome the skeptical challenge. The skeptical challenge consists, roughly, of the claim that knowledge is impossible. To overcome the challenge these philosophers think that they must justify our belief or conviction that we can know certain things. And they have tried not only to defend their own belief in knowledge but also to provide grounds that would satisfy the skeptic.

My suggestion is that in this context we must distinguish between the question of the philosophers' being rationally entitled to their belief in the possibility of knowledge and the question of whether these philosophers have succeeded in justifying the belief, that is, given an account that should convince the skeptics that they are wrong. The presumptionist claims that the philosophers need not convince the skeptics that they are wrong, to be themselves rationally entitled to their belief. This point holds more generally. We do not have to convince other people to accept our beliefs to be rationally entitled to them ourselves; at most we need to convince other people that we ourselves are rationally entitled to them—whether they are equally rational is another question.

The standards that a belief must satisfy to convince the skeptics are typically high. Most of the time, however, people are satisfied with far less. But the general idea seems to be that a belief is *justified* only when people who are neutral or of other opinions could accept the belief themselves. If this is correct, then rationality has to do with what is required of us to be entitled to believe what we believe, and justification has to do with what is required for someone's believing or a belief to be generally acceptable. What is required for a belief to be generally acceptable is, of course, an open question. It could mean when every or a sufficient number of reasonable persons should accept it, when the skeptic or an ideal observer is convinced, or the like.

Let me suggest some other examples to illustrate the differences between rationality and justification. Hanson says, in a famous passage, that he is willing to believe that God exists if he is confronted with the right kind of evidence:

> Suppose . . . that on next Tuesday morning, just after our breakfast, all of us in this one world are knocked to our knees by a percussive and ear-shattering thunderclap. Snow swirls; leaves drop from trees; the earth heaves and buckles; buildings topple and towers tumble; the sky is ablaze with an eerie, silvery light. Just then, as all the people of this world look up, the heavens open—the clouds pull apart—revealing an unbelievably immense and radiant Zeus-like figure, towering up above us like a hundred Everests. He frowns darkly as lightning plays across the features of his Michaelangeloid face. He then points down—*at me!*—and exclaims, for every man, woman and child to hear: "I have had quite enough of your too-clever-logic-chopping and word-watching in matters of theology. Be assured, N.R. Hanson, that I do most certainly exist."[29]

This is what Hanson says would convince him of the existence of God. So to convince Hanson that God exists theists have to be able to provide quite a powerful case. And as long as theists are not able to provide such grounds for their belief in God, it is not a justified belief, at least, not to people like Hanson. However, despite this, it seems reasonable to think that theists might be quite rational themselves in believing in God.[30]

Or we can see the difference between rationality and justification if we take a situation from everyday life. Imagine that somebody I ask tells me that the train to Stockholm leaves in 10 minutes. I may then be rational in believing that the train to Stockholm leaves in 10 minutes, but to be able to say that I know this surely requires more. To be rationally entitled to believe what one believes, one need not know that what one believes is true.

If this is correct we have to distinguish between what is required for me to be entitled to believe what I believe, that is, the question of rationality, and what is required for my believing to be acceptable to other people, that is, the question of justification. (Either we reserve, as I have just done, the notion of rationality for the former aspect and the notion of justification for the latter, or we call the former *rational justification* and the latter *epistemic justification*.) We can say that what is characteristic for rationality and justification is the following:

> *Rationality* has to do with when (under what circumstances) a person or a group of persons are entitled to believe what they believe.

> *Justification* has to do with when (under what circumstances) a person or a group of persons have provided sufficient grounds for a belief to render it generally acceptable.

A consequence of the distinction between justification and rationality is that if I claim that my belief is justified (everyone ought to accept it or it should be considered a part of our body of knowledge) my argumentation for the belief must be much stronger than if I claim only that my belief is rational (I have an intellectual right to accept it).

If the demands of justification are put so high as to provide sufficient grounds for the skeptic to be convinced that knowledge is possible, then justification (together with true belief) may be a necessary and sufficient condition for knowledge. However, we sometimes think that a belief satisfies the demands for justification, even though it later turns out to be false. For example, in the nineteenth century scientists thought that Newtonain mechanics was justified, since scientists had provided sufficient grounds for it to be rendered generally acceptable or an element of scientific knowledge. But today we do not consider Newtonian mechanics a part of the scientific body of knowledge. Scientists have overwhelming evidence that it is false, if taken as a description of the world. It gives incorrect results when applied to objects moving at high velocities, to objects of atomic and subatomic dimensions, and so on.[31] The same point can be made concerning Aristotle's physics or the phlogiston theory.

If it is the case that a belief can satisfy the demands for justification and yet be false, then justification is not always sufficient for knowledge (given, of course, that true belief is a necessary condition for knowledge) and more is needed. If one uses justification in this weaker sense then we might want to reserve the notion of warrant for the quality that turns true belief into knowledge.[32] And this would fit nicely with externalism, because the externalist claims that justification (at least, as it is traditionally construed) is not sufficient for knowledge. So we could say:

> *Warrant* has to do with when (under what circumstances) a person's true believing constitutes knowledge.

If this is right then sometimes justification and warrant mean the same thing, and other times they do not.

To sum up, *questions of rationality* deal with when a person (or a group of persons) should be entitled to believe what he or she believes. *Questions of justification* deal with when a belief should be generally acceptable or be considered a part of our body of knowledge. And *questions of warrant* deal with what quality it is that turns true belief into knowledge. Let us now move from the discussion of what relationship there is between the presumptional account of rationality and justification and knowledge, to a discussion of what implications presumptionism has for the connection between rationality and truth.

5.2 RATIONALITY AND TRUTH

One important consequence of the presumptionist's person-relative understanding of rationality is that rationality must be clearly disconnected from truth. Since rationality has to do exclusively with the subjective dimension of belief-regulation, the fact that someone is rational in his or her believing does not imply that what he or she believes is also true or even likely to be true. Because this is so, many of us want something more with our believing than merely being rationally justified, we also want to believe *true* things. Therefore, it might be fruitful, as Mavrodes suggests, to distinguish between having a rationality ambition and having a knowledge or truth ambition when we make judgments about beliefs or theories.[33] This means that we can make a distinction between two different questions:

1.   When we are within our intellectual rights in accepting what we believe (the *rationality ambition*)?
2.   When is a particular belief true or when does it constitute knowledge (the *truth* or *knowledge ambition*)?

A complete answer to (1) does not automatically give a complete answer to (2). To see why this is so, another related consequence of presumptionism must be taken into consideration. Namely, someone might *not* violate his or her intellectual duties by believing that a particular person is rationally entitled in accepting a belief, and yet believe that someone else is equally rational in believing the very opposite. According to formal evidentialists, in general, it would be strange or irrational to accept that a person is rational in accepting a belief and at the same time reject it oneself. This is so because the model closely connects rationality to truth. Social evidentialists, on the other hand, have pointed out, as we have seen, that the truth of a belief is not a necessary condition for a person's being rational in accepting that belief. An example taken from Rowe can well illustrate this point:

> Suppose your friends see you off on a flight to Hawaii. Hours after take-off they learn that your plane has gone down at sea. After a twenty-four hour search, no survivors have been found. Under these circumstances they are rationally justified in believing that you have perished. But it is hardly rational for you to believe this, as you bob up and down in your life vest, wondering why the search planes have failed to spot you. Indeed, to amuse yourself while awaiting your fate, you might very well reflect on the fact that your friends are rationally justified in believing that you are now dead, a proposition you disbelieve and are rationally justified in disbelieving.[34]

In a similar fashion there need be nothing paradoxical about the claim that, for instance, it is rational for you to believe in God but rational for me to believe the very opposite.

The presumptionist, on the other hand, goes one step further and claims that the fact that a particular belief is very likely untrue is not a sufficient condition for a person to be irrational in accepting that belief. Contrary to what the social evidentialist claims, a belief does not have to rest on the best available judgment and on the best available evidence at a time to be rational.[35] Does this mean that the presumptionist's construal of rationality is a very weak form of rationality? The answer to this question must be both yes and no, or rather it depends. The answer depends on *whose* rational believing we are taking about, in what *social context* these persons live, and on *which* of their beliefs we investigate. That is, it depends on whether it is people living on the street or successful scientists we are talking about, it depends on which area of these persons' beliefs (scientific, religious, legal ones, etc.) we are talking about, and lastly, it depends on what social circumstances these individuals are living under.

I suggest that presumptionism is *weak* in the sense that, for example, some ordinary religious or secular believers might be rationally entitled to believe something that we as trained philosophers know to be totally wrong. But we philosophers are of course *not* rationally justified in accepting these beliefs because we know that there exist strong reasons that count against them. On the other hand, the presumptionist's account of rationality is *strong* in the sense that the connection between rationality and truth could be fairly close in some cases, for instance, in case where a group of successful scientists is rationally entitled to believe that their scientific theory is right because the theory takes into account all the relevant counter-evidence they know.

Whether presumptionism is weak or strong depends, therefore, broadly speaking, on the context. The presumptionist takes seriously the fact that rationality has to do with the subjective dimension of belief-regulation—with things a person can reasonably be *expected* to believe. This means that how close the connection between the rationality and the truth of a belief is, will *vary* from person to person depending on cognitive skills, access to relevant facts, social circumstances, and the like. The question: "Is it the case that if a belief is rational, this gives much support to the claim that the belief is in fact also true?" is not possible to answer in this unspecified way. It makes real sense only when we have clarified *whose* rational beliefs we are talking about. Now the really interesting question for *philosophers* might be: "What is rational to believe with respect to a particular domain of beliefs for well-educated men and women who are well-informed on the matter in question?" But to ask this kind of question is to do something different from asking questions of rationality in an unspecified, totally situation and person-unrelated way.

But presumptionism is, of course, in another sense weaker than both formal and social evidentialism, in that the presumptionst rejects evidentialism, or more precisely the claim that we need to have positive evidence to be rationally justified in accepting a belief. This is so because, everything else equal, if there is evidence in favor of a belief this makes that belief more likely to be true than if there is merely no evidence that counts against it. If a belief meets the demands of the evidential principle then there is evidence that *supports* it, which everything else unchanged, makes the belief more likely to be true than if it simply meets the demands of the principle of presumption, which implies that there exists no counter-evidence that *refutes* the belief in question. Is this a reason to modify presumptionism?

Andersson and Furberg have argued that we have to qualify the principle of presumption in order to prevent it from becoming absurdly generous. They may have something like the following situation in mind. Suppose that it is not something necessarily stupid we believe (as was the case in the first objection), but it is rather something that is quite normal to believe. But our strategy is to avoid all possible counter-evidence or objections, by, for example, never meeting people that we know or could imagine having reasons or objections against our belief. These people are surely not behaving rationally, nevertheless they seem to meet the demands of the principle of presumption. Must we not, therefore, modify the principle? I think the same response is possible to this objection as to the one we considered earlier. These persons *know* that they are deliberately avoiding all objections. They know that objections exist, but they do not want to find out their content. There exists counter-evidence, and these people know this but choose to ignore it. But if this is the case, they are not in fact satisfying the demands of the principle of presumption, and, therefore, there is no need to revise it for this reason.

But Andersson and Furberg think that something more is needed than the principle of presumption, at least in certain cases. Must we

not demand, at least when it comes to the really important questions
in life, that people *actively* search for counter-evidence? The more
important a belief is the more important is it that we know that we are
justified in believing it. Hence if we want to take their objection into
account, it seems as if we have to revise the principle of presumption
in the following way:

> It is rational to accept an important belief only if one
> actively tries to find good reasons to think otherwise,
> but is in fact unable to find any.

So we have to actively put ourselves in situations where we
can experience resistance; we have to actively test our important
beliefs. If we do not do this we are, according to Andersson and
Furber, intellectually irresponsible. Rational people pitch their important beliefs against the world as much as possible. "You should . . .
search for your political or religious (and so on) opponents, listen
to their argumentation, take on their best arguments against your
own belief and try to make these arguments as crushing as possible,
preferably harder and smarter than what the opponents themselves
have succeeded in doing."[36]

The force behind Andersson's and Furberg's argumentation depends on the claim that if we want to know that what we believe
is true it seems like a reasonable demand that we should actively
test our beliefs. But is it really necessary to qualify the principle of
presumption in this way? Are they not confusing here the rationality
ambition with the truth ambition? Surely we want what we believe on
important topics to be true and constitute knowledge, and to be able
to establish *that* we might need to do more than what the principle
of presumption requires; but that is a different matter. This does not
constitute an argument against a person being rational in believing
what he or she believes, it is only an argument for the claim that we
have to require more if we want to know that what we believe is true
and constitutes knowledge (questions concerning justification and
warrant)—but that is something the presumptionists and Andersson
and Furberg could all agree on.

5.3. A QUALIFICATION OF THE PRINCIPLE OF PRESUMPTION

The principle of presumption is a principle that is supposed to
guide our belief-regulation *in general*; everything else being equal,

we are rational in believing what we believe unless there are good reasons to do otherwise. The main reason why I claim we should accept the principle of presumption is that it is more economical than the evidential principle, since it does not waste our limited cognitive resources. If this is why we should accept the principle, however, it can be overthrown for at least two reasons: in cases where it is worth spending more of our cognitive resources than usual, and in easy cases where the cognitive cost is relatively low. In such situations we could either demand that people give good reasons for what they believe or that they must actively search for good reasons against what they believe, or something else.

An evidentialist could claim, as we have seen, that when it comes to important beliefs at least, we must ask for more than what the principle of presumption demands of us. But I pointed out that even this is in fact beyond our cognitive capacity, since it is not possible for us to test all our important beliefs. Some examples I gave to support this claim were cases in which our life is at stake—beliefs about driving. So my conclusion was that the evidential principle violates the axiom of reasonable demand even when its scope is limited to the class of important beliefs.

However, even if it is not reasonable to demand that we should test *all* our important beliefs, it would clearly be irrational not to give good reasons for *some* important beliefs, for instance, when the cognitive cost is low. Suppose that I hear on the radio that I have won 1,000,000 dollars in a lottery, and the only requirement is that I show my ticket and answer a telephone call within an hour. Normally I believe that the receiver is in place and, according to the principle of presumption, I am rational in doing this unless there are good reasons to believe otherwise. However, in this particular situation, given that I want the money, it would be irrational of me to not check out this belief of mine (even if I have no good reasons to believe otherwise), to go to the kitchen and actually look if the receiver is in place. The principle of presumption is not in this case sufficient for rationality: it is an important belief and the cognitive cost is low, therefore, evidence is needed. Or take a more realistic example, and suppose that we are mountain climbing and I am setting the anchor for our life line, and I form the belief that this anchor point is solid. In such a situation I have an intellectual obligation to test this belief, to convince myself that the anchor point is really solid. I have to provide some evidence for this belief to be rationally entitled to accept it.

But these examples do not count against that the principle of presumption should be our *general* principle for rational belief-regulation—how we should normally proceed. The examples show only that in *some* cases it is rational to spend more of our cognitive resources than usual, and this is in particular true of cases where the beliefs are important and the cognitive cost is, at the same time, low.

6. The Person-Relativity of Rationality

Another interesting and related question about the relation between rationality, knowledge, and truth, is to what degree rationality is, according to the presumptionist, person and situation-relative. What is general or universal about rationality, what is stable and what is changing? Is rationality totally person-relative or context dependent? The presumptionist claims that in *all* contexts and for *all* beings rationality is a normative notion. Rationality is a matter of fulfilling one's intellectual obligations. At the level of the *nature of rationality,* rationality is unrestrictedly universal. However, on the level of the *standards of rationality,* the claim is that rationality is in one sense person-relative, more specifically, rationality is kind-relative. Although rationality is a matter of satisfying one's intellectual obligations, these obligations are not the same for every possible agent, they are the same only for everyone of the same kind or species. For us human beings it means that we should, at least, satisfy the demands of the principle of presumption. So rationality is person-relative only in the sense that the standards of rationality must be sensitive to the actual constitution and predicament of the agent; otherwise they will become utopian. Rationality cannot ask for more than what it is reasonable to demand of the agent given his or her kind-capacity. Someone who claims something else violates the axiom of reasonable demand.

But, to complicate the issue, note that by "agent-relative" or "person-relative" we can refer to two different things. Rationality is (more or less) relative either to: (1) a *kind of being* in general, like humans or some sort of fictive beings, or to (2) a *particular individual of a kind,* like Mikael Stenmark. In the first case the notion signifies that rationality in some way depends on, or is restricted by, the kind of being somebody is; in the second case, rationality is constrained by the kind of individual someone (of a particular kind) is. So when we say that rationality is person-relative we can mean either that it is "kind-relative" or that it is "individual-relative." I said in the beginning of this chapter that rationality is *kind-relative* if it (at some level) varies to some extent from species to species or from kind to kind. Now we can say that:

> Rationality is *individual-relative* if it (at some level)
> varies to some extent from individual to individual of
> a particular kind.

Does the presumptionist also claim that rationality is individual-relative? The answer is "no," since the claim is that rationality is the same for everyone of its kind, hence for all individual of the same species. However, we need to add one qualification. Strictly speaking, rationality is not the same for all human beings, since what rationality requires is not the same for adults and children. As Wolterstorff notes:

> a person is rationally justified in all his beliefs until such time as he has acquired certain conceptual equipment and the ability to make use of that equipment. Before that time his system of beliefs may lack a variety of merits, but until, for example, he has grasped (or ought to have grasped) the concept of a reason, he is doing as well in governing his believings as can rightly be demanded of him. According, there is probably a time in the life of each child when he is rationally justified in all his beliefs. Increase in knowledge makes noetic sin possible.[37]

Despite this qualification of presumptionism, I think it is most appropriate to say that the presumptionist does not claim that rationality is individual-relative, because being a child is just a phase we *all* have to go through before we reach adulthood. But what about people who are insane or whose cognitive equipment malfunctions? Are they rational—if they are doing what reasonably can be demanded of them in their situation? Consider, for example, Mort, who is inclined to believe that all women who do not constantly smile at him in fact hate him. The reason he is inclined to believe this involves certain psychological traumas in his childhood which make his belief-formation and regulation on this matter unreliable.[38] Given the acceptance of presumptionism and the axiom of reasonable demand, is Mort rational in believing that when women do not constantly smile towards him they hate him?

I do not think so for the following reason. In this context we do not mean by "irrational" falling short of meeting certain deontological standards, rather we think that he is not functioning normally or properly—his cognitive equipment is malfunctioning. Being irrational in this way is more like a kind of *sickness* than an *intellectual irresponsibility*. What is characteristic of Mort is that even if it were not the case that women who do not constantly smile towards him do not hate him, he would not be able to discover or perceive this, not because of the natural limitation of human cognitive resources (as in the case of children) but because—in this area at least—*his* cognitive equipment is unreliable. The term "rationality" here means absence of malfunction with respect to cognitive equipment (and this is probably the way the term is used in psychiatric discussions). But such a use of the notion of rationality is related to what in chapter 2 I called *generic rationality* (an agent is rational if it has the capacity for reasoning or the resources of reason) not what we have been discussing as *normative rationality* (an agent is rational if it exercises its reason properly or responsibly).

Recall also that I said that being rational in the generic sense is a necessary condition for being rational (or irrational) in the normative sense. So normative rationality (to which the axiom of reasonable demand applies) presupposes that there is nothing wrong with the agent's belief-forming and regulating processes, and that they are functioning properly or as they typically function among normal human beings.[39] Sanity or normality is a precondition for normative rationality. Therefore, the axiom of reasonable demand does not apply to Mort or to persons who are insane or suffer from pathological confusion or the like. These people are irrational in a generic sense and, therefore, they cannot be irrational (or rational) in a normative sense.

With this clarification in mind let us go back to the distinction between the kind-relativity and individual-relativity of rationality. This distinction makes it clear that to be able to answer the traditional, unspecified, question of theoretical rationality: "What is it rational to believe?" we have to ask two sub-questions. The first, and more general question is: "What is it rational for beings of kind B to believe in situation S?" (the question concerning the kind-relativity). We might ask this question about human beings, about beings with a limited set of beliefs and of possible choices, or about beings whose only interest is to maximize the number of true beliefs. The second question is "What is it rational for a particular human being N to believe in situation S?" (the question concerning individual-relativity). We might ask this question about a peasant living in a small village in Iran today.

To sum up, to say that we should develop a realistic account of rationality means that we cannot reasonably demand of an agent something which is completely beyond his or her ability because of constitution or situation. This means at least, I think, that rationality is person-relative in such a way that the standards a rational agent can reasonably be demanded to satisfy must be restricted by that agent's *kind-ability,* but not by his of her *individual-ability.* In this context, however, we must not forget the crucial distinction between the *relativity of rationality* and the *relativity of rational beliefs* or between rationality and what it is rational to believe. By the phrase "What is it rational for a person to believe?" we can mean two different things. On the one hand, it can be interpreted as a question concerning what particular *beliefs* it is rational for a person to accept. On the other hand, it can also be a question about what *standards* it is rational for this person to use to govern his or her believing.

The presumptionist claims that what is rational to believe is always relative to a particular situation, and hence there exist strictly speaking no rational beliefs as such. What is rational for you need not be rational for me. What is the rational thing to believe or do always depends on the situation. But what rationality is or what the appropriate standards of rationality are do not. This means that whatever considerations make it rational for a group of people to accept a particular belief will automatically render it rational for anyone to accept this belief, and irrational to not accept it, that is placed in circumstances sufficiently like theirs. So it does not follow from the fact that what particular beliefs it is rational to accept is completely person-relative (the *relativity of rational beliefs*) that the same must also be the case with the standards for what it is rational to believe (the *relativity of rationality*).

Let me say a few words about the relativity of rational beliefs. Strictly speaking, as I said, there exist no rational beliefs as such, or beliefs that are rational in the sense that there exist beliefs that are true. What is rational to believe is in this sense completely dependent on the circumstances. The rationality of a particular person's beliefs is relative to the reasons available to that person. So to be able to determine whether people are rational in their believings, we have to know whether or not there are any special reasons available that count against their beliefs, reasons that they ought to be aware of. What is rational for you need not be rational for me. For example, is it rational to believe that God exists, that all Swedes are blond, or that all swans are white? The answer can only be: it depends. It depends on whom we are talking about. For instance, is it an individual or group of individuals who have never heard of anything other than white swans or is it someone who sees black swans everyday? So to believe that God exists, that all Swedes are blond, and that all swans are white, might be rational for you, but not for me. The fact that we are individuals with changing bodies of information or experiences means that we must, to be rational, resolve the issues concerning what to believe differently—if we resolved them in the same way we would be behaving irrationally. This also means that different individuals can have beliefs in common and yet differ in the rationality of their believings.

So we must not confuse the claim, on the one hand, that what particular beliefs it is rational for us to believe is totally context dependent, with the claim, on the other hand, that human rationality is totally context dependent. The presumptionist accepts the first claim but rejects the second. It is easy to overlook this distinction between the relativity of rationality and the relativity of rational beliefs. For example, Wolterstorff seems not to be fully aware of this distinction when he writes:

> It must be clearly noted that rationality . . . is in good measure person specific and situation specific. When I was young, there were things which it was rational for me to believe which now, when I am older, it is no longer rational for me to believe . . . Rationality of belief can only be determined in context . . . The proper question is always and only whether it is rational for this or that particular person in this or that situation, or for a person of this or that particular type in this or that type of situation, to believe so-and-so. Rationality is always *situated* rationality.[40]

It is not that rationality is in this sense always person and situation-relative. Rather what is relative is what it is rational to believe, which particular belief it is rational to accept. It is not rationality—as

Wolterstorff writes—but rational beliefs, that are "always *situated* rationality." What is rational to believe is completely context dependent, but that is not the case with rationality.[41] Rationality is *universal* in the sense that what is rational for one human being to believe should be equally rational for anyone else in the same situation. The standards of rationality are general because what is rational for one person is also rational for anyone else in this or her shoes. So a belief is rational only if one can say that, although I myself do not believe this, I can understand that it is reasonable for someone in its person's situation to believe it, and therefore it is rational for him or her to believe in such a way.

7.   Science and Presumptionism

At the beginning of this chapter I said that social evidentialism gives perhaps the best account of scientific rationality we have at present. My only complaint concerned its adequacy as a general model of rationality, when it is supposed to state the conditions for rational believing in other domain besides science, such as everyday life and religion. And my thesis has been that presumptionism is a better, a more adequate, model of general rationality than social evidentialism. In this section I will raise some doubts about the adequacy of using social evidentialism as a model for even scientific rationality and give some reasons for thinking that presumptionism might after all be the appropriate model of rationality also in the scientific domain.

Recall that according to the social evidentialist, scientific theory or belief-formation and regulation is rational because (1) it is governed by informed judgments and (2) it involves intersubjective testing. Claim (1) is just another way of saying that scientists need to have good reasons for what they believe, but this emphasizes that the evaluation of how well what is believed is supported by good reasons is typically not rule-governed. So (1) is a version of the evidential principle. And claim (2) is the social principle; the demand is that a scientific theory or belief must be exposed to or tested against a community of relevant scientific expertise to qualify as rational.

I suggest that these demands of social evidentialism seem reasonable when our concern is *scientific justification* but that they need not be so when it comes to *scientific rationality*. For a belief to qualify as scientifically justified it probably needs to satisfy the evidential and the social principles, but for the belief to be scientifically rational the fulfillment of the principle of presumption seems to me sufficient. Why should we think that a scientist (or a group of them) must be able to give a belief adequate evidential support and submit it to a community of relevant expertise in order to be rational in accepting it? It seems like a waste of valuable time and limited cognitive resources. Why should we not allow that scientists are, in general, entitled to continue to believe something as long as they have no special reasons to believe otherwise? As long as nothing decisively counts against a theory a scientist is using, why could it not be rational for the scientist to accept it (and continue to use it)?

Of course, if a group of scientists want their theory to be considered a component of scientific knowledge, or if they want what they believe to be generally accepted by the scientific community, more is certainly needed. So scientific rationality is not sufficient for scientific justification. And when stating standards for scientific justification, then clearly the social principle makes sense. A belief must be at least intersubjectively tested before it is generally acceptable in science. We could characterize scientific rationality and scientific justification in the following way:

> *Scientific rationality* has to do with when a scientist or a group of scientists are entitled to believe what they believe on a particular scientific topic.

> *Scientific justification* has to do with when a scientist or a group of scientists have provided sufficient grounds for a belief or theory to be generally accepted by the scientific community or to be considered a part of the body of scientific knowledge.[42]

If this distinction makes sense it is not clear or obvious that the principle of presumption is not sufficient for rationality also in science. But, of course, more careful and detailed argumentation is needed than what I have provided here before we can say that for sure. However, what I have said is I think, sufficient to raise some doubt about the adequacy of the social evidentialist's account of scientific rationality.

In connection to this topic we can also see why the presumptionist thinks that we should reject the social principle as a necessary condition for rationality in general. Brown anticipates an objection against his claim that what a person believes is not rational if it is not subjected to critical evaluation by other people, when he says that the social requirement implies that people like Robinson Crusoe could not be rational (or irrational).[43] This he thinks goes against our common sense intuitions, but since he is developing a normative model of rationality and not analyzing the concept of rationality, he thinks some improvement is in order. But is this really improvement, to propose a model of rationality that entails that I could not be rational even if I were the sole survivor of a nuclear attack? Or suppose I am out travelling. As long as I meet and submit my beliefs to people I encounter I can be rational in my believings, but as soon as I travel through non-populated areas I suddenly cannot be rational any longer! To me this does not seem like an improvement of rationality, quite the opposite. However, the social principle makes perfect sense if we take it to be a standard of justification. As in science, if one believes certain things in everyday life or in religion and wants one's beliefs to be generally accepted or accepted by a particular group of people, then certainly the beliefs must be exposed to or submitted to a community of competent others.

There is also another problem with claiming that the social principle is a standard of rationality. It seems like the principle would waste far too much of our limited time and limited cognitive resources. Must I test or submit every one of my beliefs to be rationally entitled to accept them? What about my belief that I now have a mild pain in my left knee, or that Anna loves me, or that the train leaves in ten minutes, do I have to ask other people their opinion before I am rationally justified in believing these things? Hardly.

Let us now turn to religious believing and see if presumptionism is applicable to this area of life, and, if that is the case, what implications it has for questions concerning religious rationality (or irrationality).

9

The Nature and Function of Religious Belief

Let me start by summarizing some of the main points I have made so far. First of all, I have tried to show that the question of the rationality of religion is as much a question about rationality as religion. That is, we cannot proceed anymore in philosophy of religion as if what rationality is and what it is to be rational is perfectly clear, and then ask whether religious believing is rationally acceptable. In order to be in a position to ask and try to answer the question whether religious believing is rational we need instead to first state *our* account of rationality. Second, I have defended the thesis that we should understand rationality *realistically*. Rationality has to do only with what an agent can reasonably be expected to do, given his or her resources. This means that in matters concerning human rationality our actual predicament—who we are, in what world we live, and the like—is something which an adequate model of rationality has to take into account. Hence rationality is to some extent relative to the agent who accepts the beliefs and the situation he or she is in; rationality is *person-relative*.

In this and the following chapter I will try to defend a third point, namely, that in order to be able to formulate a proper model of rationality and to be able to evaluate, in an appropriate way, the possibility of applying this model to a particular domain of beliefs or a certain practice, one has to take into account the character of the beliefs or the practice the beliefs belong to. So an important question for us to ask is: what function does a particular kind of beliefs fulfill? If we take scientific beliefs as our example, we have to ask: is this type of beliefs of a kind different from say religious or ordinary life beliefs? I will claim that we have to know the function and the content of a domain of beliefs before we can evaluate what conception of rationality, if any, is appropriate to use. If this is correct, rationality is also to some degree relative to the kinds of belief or practice we are investigating; rationality is, what I will call, *domain* or *practice-relative*. It might matter then whether the beliefs or practices in question are scientific, religious, legal, and so on.

I do not think, however, that the crucial question is really whether or not rational believing is practice-relative, since that is not hard to show, as we will see. Rather we need to ask *why* this is so and to what *degree*, and what implications this in its turn has for the question of the rationality of religious believing. We will see in the following chapters that it is possible to answer these questions in more than one way. But our primary concern in this chapter is something else, because if we want to know whether the rationality of some kind of believing in general, or religious believing in particular, is practice-relative, we need to know what is *characteristic* of this kind of believing. To be able to compare practices and see if they have or rather should have (since the question of rationality is normative) different conceptions of rationality, we have to know what they are all about—their characteristics. So if our concern is what conception of rationality is applicable to religious believing, we need to know what is distinctive of religious practices. The purpose of this chapter will therefore be to try to give an account of the nature and function of religious believing. When this is done—and only then—we will be in a position to try to find an answer to the question of the rationality of religious believing.

This is also in accordance with the general view of philosophy I have tried to develop. I have previously tried to argue for a practice-oriented approach to philosophy in general, and we have seen some of its implications when it is used in philosophy of science. Now I will argue that we have to do the same in philosophy of religion. The basic thought behind the practice-oriented approach is that the actual practice of something, religion, science, and the like, is relevant for settling the appropriate conception of rationality, explanation, and the like. This means that we have to focus as I highlighted in the last chapter, not only on the actual *agents of rationality,* but also on what kinds of beliefs the agents are accepting or committed to, or the activities their beliefs belong to—the *practices of rationality*. The full importance of this perspective on philosophy will become clear in the following chapter. With these preliminary thoughts in mind let us take a closer look at what might reasonably be taken as characteristic of religious believing.

1.   The Function of Religious Believing

One way of trying to find out what is characteristic of religious believing, is to ask questions like: What is religion or religious belief all about? Why do people engage in religious activity? What good does religion do? What kind of job does religion do for the religious believer? Note that these questions are not concerned with what religion *is*, but with what religion *does*—the function of religion. Maybe we can find a clue to these questions if we rephrase them in the following way: What kind of questions are religious beliefs thought to answer? One opinion is that religious beliefs try to answer questions concerning who we are, why we exist, what the meaning of our life is, and what stance we should take towards experiences of death, suffering, guilt, and the like. According to this perspective religion can be seen as an answer to one kind of experience of resistance—what previously I have referred to as *existential experiences of resistance*—that human beings encounter in their lives. We could say that religion is an answer or a response to existential questions.

Correspondingly, we can call the beliefs that are formulated as a response to existential experiences or questions "existential beliefs." I prefer, however, to call these beliefs "life-orienting beliefs" to avoid the connotation existential assertions have for logicians, as purely a claim about what exists. Life-orienting beliefs can be characterized, roughly, as beliefs that are formulated as *a response to existential experiences or constraints and that, if we accept them, would in general deeply affect how we live and understand our lives*. They are the kind of beliefs that determines to a high degree the general direction of our lives.

On the account of religion we have considered, one could say that the human search for meaning as such is religion. Religion characteristically deals with existential concerns and not, for example, scientific or technical ones. This kind of understanding of religion becomes manifest when, for example, Batson and Ventis claim that we can "define religion as *whatever we as individuals do to come to grips personally with the questions that confront us because we are aware that we and others like us are alive and that we will die. Such questions we shall call existential questions*."[1]

Does this mean that *every* human being is religious? It certainly seems that way if we accept this account of religion: we cannot avoid sometimes raising existential questions and answering them, perhaps not always theoretically, but always in the way we choose to live.

So if it is true that we should call every belief that determines the meaning of the cosmos and the place of human beings within it a religious belief, then it seems to be *impossible* for people to function in their personal and social lives without such beliefs—without being religious! On such an account we have to doubt the possibility of there being a choice between raising or responding to the religious quest and not raising or responding to it.[2] To be a human being includes asking the question of the grounds and goals of one's own existence and giving a response. Therefore, all humans are religious believers of some kind or another.

We can of course claim that everyone is religious in *that* way. But it seems to me that there is a fundamental difference that this understanding of religion overlooks between being, for example, a Christian, a Muslim, or a Hindu or say being merely a Marxist, a Feminist, or a Humanist. It is not so easy to state exactly what the difference between them consists in, but I think most of us are aware that there is a difference here. (We will come back to this question later.) Because of this it may be better to find another concept for the human activity that is concerned with existential matters and instead claim that religion deals with the existential concern *plus* something else—whatever that is. If this is correct it means that religious beliefs are not identical with life-orienting beliefs, but can be seen as a proper subset of them.

What should we call this view people develop as a response to existential experiences of resistance? Some common suggestions are "world view," "life world," ideology," "metaphysics," and the like. In Swedish we use the term "livsåskådning." In English, I think, the closest equivalent is "life-philosophy," "theory of life," or "view of life." The term "view of life" is maybe the most appropriate one. To see why this might be the most appropriate notion, we have to remember what we are looking for, First, we need a concept that is more comprehensive than "religion" in the sense that it must be possible to formulate a response to existential experiences and not be religious, but, on the other hand, if one is religious then one must have given such a response. Such a conceptualization, I think, goes better with our ordinary intuitions than the one that we discussed earlier, proposed by—among others—Batson and Ventis.

Second, because all human beings raise existential questions we want a concept that includes not only the existential concerns of theologians or philosophers, but also the concerns of ordinary people. We must try to find a concept that does not exclude "popular" interpretations of life. An individual can formulate a response to the existential quest even though it is not explicitly or systematically formulated. This is why I want to avoid the term "life-philosophy" in this context since philosophy, at least in the academy, normally connotes a systematization and explication, together with a high degree of theoretical consciousness. (This connotation can of course be avoided to some extent by using the phrase "popular life-philosophy.")[3]

This leads to the third point I want to make. Many ordinary men and women are not systematic thinkers, that is, they do not have an intellectually worked out view of life. Their existential response often consists of different fragments that are put together into less than comprehensive and coherent whole or systems.[4] Therefore, it is better to talk about a view of life than a "world view" since the latter concept leads one's thought to an all inclusive picture of the world. This means that a view of life can either be fragmentary or unified and comprehensive. We can be either what I call *globalists* or *fragmentists* with respect to our views of life. The choice to be a fragmentist can be made either unconsciously or consciously: either we are not aware of the fact that the fragments of our views of life do not fit together or we have deliberately chosen not to structure our life-orienting beliefs into a system.[5]

All this means that every properly functioning human being has a view of life though not all have a world view; but, on the other hand, if one has a world view one necessarily possesses a view of life. Further, one can have a world view without being religious, and it also seems possible that one can be religious without having a world view. (The latter is possible if one can be religious and at the same time be a fragmentist.) If my analysis is correct then something follows that is of importance for the question of the rationality of religious believing, that is, that our only *real existential choice* is between (*a*) having a religious or secular view of life, that is, being a religious or secular believer, and (*b*) between having a fragmentary or non-fragmentary view of life—the choice cannot be between having a view of life or not.[6]

2.   A View of Life

Let us now ask the question about what a view of life is or contains—about the *nature* of views of life. Normally we have something like the following in mind when we talk about views of life: they are ways of thinking about life and the world as a totality, which are connected with certain values. But what is it in more detail? Exactly what is this thinking about and what values are involved? Jeffner has made an interesting attempt to define a view of life (*livsåkådning*): "A view of life consists of the theoretical and evaluative assumptions (1) that constitute or have a decisive importance for a comprehensive picture of human beings and the world and (2) that form a central system of values and (3) that express a basic mood."[7] According to him a view of life consists of three elements:

(1) *A Cognitive Element:* A person's comprehensive view about human beings, the world, and their inter-relation.

(2) *An Evaluative Element:* A person's central values.

(3) *An Affective Element:* A person's basic mood.

Not all *cognitive elements* belong to a person's view of life, only those elements that contribute to the formulation of a more comprehensive view of reality. Basically, it consists of theories about the nature of human beings and the nature of reality in general and their interrelation. These theoretical assertions must also have an influence on the second component in a view of life—the central value system—and the individual in question must accept this influence. The *evaluative element* consists of "those values most important to someone which are retained for a long period of time."[8] Not all values a person accepts are a part of his or her view of life, only the central values that have a high degree of internal saliency and ego-involvement. The third factor a view of life consists of, according to Jeffner, is what he calls the basic mood. These *affective elements* are those feelings toward life which express a certain disposition or tone that gives an emotional color to our experience. This can be an attitude of trust or fear, despair or hope, and the like. But an attitude qualifies as a basic mood only if it has a certain degree of stability: it must stay the same in the same type of situations for a long time.[9]

Jeffner's definition is illuminating, but there are, I think, some problems with it. The first problem concerns his characterization of the cognitive element of views of life. According to Jeffner, it consists of those beliefs that contribute to the formulation of a more comprehensive view of reality. But the difficulty is that if this is right then fragmentists do not seem to have a view of life because their existential response consists of different fragments that consciously or unconsciously are not put together into a comprehensive picture of reality. Therefore, it might be better to say that the cognitive element consists of any belief that is crucial for a person's understanding of his or her life which is also of great importance for what it means to exist in the world as a human being—whether or not these beliefs are put together into a comprehensive picture. Further, Jeffner uses the term "cognitive" to describe the first element of a view of life. The term might, however, be misleading because on some accounts values are supposed to be cognitive. It might, therefore, be better to talk about a *doxastic element* instead of a cognitive element. This is possible if we understand "doxa" as "opinion" or "belief." If we take into account these suggestions the first element of a view of life could be characterized as follows:

(1*) *The Doxastic Element*: A person's beliefs that are of crucial importance for what it means to exist in the world as a human being.

A third problem with Jeffner's definition is that it is a rather theoretical or intellectual conception of a view of life. Roughly, on his account, a view of life is certain comprehensive beliefs and central values that are connected with and colored by a basic mood. A view of life is essentially a conceptual system. So philosophers' or theologians' theoretical constructions or systems seem to qualify as views of life. But can this be right? I do not think so, because a view of life is not merely a vision *of* life, it is always a vision *for* life. That is to say, a view of life must actually lead an individual or a community in a particular way, actually regulate the way the adherents of it live their lives. A view of life does not only guide the way we *think* but must also concretely guide what we actually *do*. To be counted as an adherent to a view of life one's assent cannot be only an act of intellect but must also be an act of will. Every view of life is practical in the sense of being one to be actually lived.

In fact, I think that the ultimate life-view issue concerns what *way of life* a person should adopt, not what theories of life one should accept. It is at bottom a matter of ordering one's life in one way or another, not of making up a theoretical map over reality. It is a matter of choosing what strategies for living one should adopt or reject. So views of life must not be confused with theologies or philosophies. They are always to a degree conceptual systems, that is true, but views of life are never exhausted in them. Philosophical and theological systems are rather derived from a view of life. Theoretical systems are second level expressions of the intellectual dimension of a view of life. This is crucial, and we have to somehow take it into account when we define a view of life. I think one way to proceed is to add a fourth element to Jeffner's definition. This element has to capture the *life-directing character* of a view of life, which a merely theoretical system cannot convey. The component lacking must therefore be conative. Something like the following might qualify:

> (4) *A Conative or Regulative Element*: A person's volitional affirmation of the practical consequences of elements (1*), (2), and (3).

On this account a system of thought that satisfies (1*), (2), and (3) cannot qualify as a view of life if it does not have a *regulative function* in people's lives, that is, if it lacks a conative element. On such an account, a person who merely assents to a view of life intellectually shows that he or she in one important sense does not believe (lacks faith), since the view does not receive expression in action. In fact, I think, one could say that a view of life is "dead" if it no longer regulates people's lives. It no longer functions as a view of life, and it is only a conceptual system. As I think Malcolm rightly observes:

> If a man did not ever pray for help or forgiveness, or have any inclination toward it; nor ever felt that it is "a good and joyful thing" to thank God for the blessings of this life; nor was ever concerned about his failure to comply with divine commandments—then, it seems clear to me, he could not be said to believe in God. Belief in God is not an all or none thing; it can be more or less; it can wax and wane. But belief in God in any degree does require, as I understand the words, some religious action, some commitment, or if not, at least a bad conscience.[10]

If we want to include the life-directing character of a view of life and that it need not be comprehensive, the following modified definition might be more appropriate than Jeffner's original one:

> A *view of life* consists of the assumptions that (1) constitute or have a decisive importance for a picture of human beings and the world, that (2) form a central system of values, that (3) express a basic mood, and that (4) have a regulative function in people's lives.

A view of life contains a certain kind of beliefs and values, a basic mood, and a disposition to act in accordance with those beliefs and values. If my argument is correct, it follows that every view of life has a twofold function:

(A) *A Theoretical or Perceptual Function:* A view of life structures and makes reality intelligible.

(B) *A Practical or Regulative Function:* A view of life actually guides the adherents in their concrete lives.

First, a view of life gives the world a more or less developed structure, pattern, or gestalt. To some degree it makes the world a cosmos and determines the place of human beings in it. A view of life also states what is of value or worthwhile in life. Second, a view of life actually leads people in how they should live their lives, how to get through the obstacles that block the road toward ultimate well-being. (Or if the view of life denies the possibility of ultimate well-being, to give guidance about what else to do.) Now I hope it is clear why I think the term "a theory of life" is also inadequate, since what we seek to conceptualize cannot be reduced to a theory of some kind. This also shows the difference between metaphysics on the one hand and views of life on the other hand. Metaphysical claims can be about the same objects as life view claims, but the interest of views of life, in contrast to metaphysics, is practical rather than purely theoretical. A life-view claim is a life-orienting or directing claim. A view of life is supposed to give concrete guidance on how to overcome existential constraints, and this concern is lacking in metaphysics. So views of life cannot be reduced to a metaphysics of some sort.

In sum, a view of life is an answer or response to existential experiences of resistance, but the answer is not merely *intellectual*. It is also—and perhaps most of all—*a practical* answer, and this is one thing that distinguishes a view of life from philosophical or metaphysical systems. Hence only a response to an existential question that contains *both* aspects or functions of a view of life can be a (possible) answer, otherwise the question is misunderstood.

3.   The Conception of Religion

Now we have at least some understanding of what a view of life is and why it is reasonable to think that everyone has such a view. We have seen one function (in my view the essential one) that a view of life tries to fulfill. But what is the main difference between a secular and a religious view of life? So far I have said only that religion is a response to existential constraints plus something else, but what is this "else"?

Jeffner follows Holte, who suggests that we should define religion as a view of life whose three components (cognitive, evaluative, and affective) are all marked by a confidence or trust in one or more divine power(s) that is connected with a ritual behavior.[11] The problem with this definition is, however, that there seem to be religions without any gods, spirits, or divine powers. For example, in some versions of Buddhism this element is entirely missing. Is it possible to give a general characterization at all of such a complex phenomenon as religion? It might be.[12] Recall that the crucial concern of religious and secular believers is to find a way of solving or responding to existential experiences of resistance. Now what I think is characteristic of religious believers is that *they are convinced that the sacred provides a way of solving our existential problems,* whereas that is something secular believers deny. Religious people believe that without taking into account the sacred a radical transformation of our present defective situation is not possible. This suggests that if we add the following element to a view of life we have a religion:

> (5)   *A Transcendent Element*: A person's consciousness of and trust in the sacred.

The term "transcendent" does not in this context refer merely to what goes beyond us and the universe. It can also be used to mean behind or in the depth of human beings and the world. This transcendent object is experienced as sacred or holy, as distinct from all profane or ordinary reality. But the conceptualization of the sacred varies from religion to religion, since it can be conceived as a unity or diversity, personal or impersonal, divine or not, and so on.[13] So what all religious believers have in common in contrast to secular ones is a consciousness of and trust in a reality beyond the ordinary world, a belief in the existence of a transcendent dimension of reality. The presence of the holy is felt by religious participants "behind, beyond or in the depths of ordinary things, persons and events."[14] This reality is viewed as a *mystery*, as something that goes beyond what we can really understand or comprehend. No matter how much one knows about it, it eludes one's grasp. So the sacred is a mystery not because it is a problem or a puzzle to be solved, but because it is something out of the ordinary, so to speak. It is the presence of the sacred that gives the lives of religious believers their substance and meaning—the holy gives the strength or wisdom to deal with or get through existential constraints.

According to the classical account given by Rudolf Otto in *The Idea of the Holy*, the religious believer's reaction to the sacred is characterized by an ambivalence before it that is grounded in a consciousness of creaturehood. In religious experiences people claim that they become aware of the presence of something that is more real than they or the world around them. Religious believers experience themselves as less real than what they encounter, as having less ontological reality. At the same time the sacred evokes feelings of awe and fascination. On the one hand, when religious participants experience the majesty of the holy, they tremble. For example, the Bible depicts the wrath of God, and the Greeks talk about the jealousy of the gods. But on the other hand, the sacred is also overwhelmingly attractive. In their encounter with the holy, religious people experience a profound love, mercy, grace, and joy.[15] This conception of religion is not as specific as the one given by, for example, Holte, but it is preferable because it seems to have the strength of including views of life that we intuitively classify as religious, but at the same time it seems to be narrow enough to exclude what we would regard as secular views of life. Westphal expresses a similar opinion:

> Much of the strength and appeal of Otto's concept lies in just this ability to understand religion in terms of whatever it is which evokes the consciousness of creaturehood and the ambivalence which is an inevitable part of such a sense. Whether this "whatever" is God or gods or spirits or the impersonal power called *mana* or an absolute so far beyond the finite categories of being and non-being as to

be nothing at all, the religious nature of the life built around such experience need not be questioned. God in the monotheistic sense associated with Judaism, Christianity, and Islam would be a special case of the numinous, the holy, the sacred, the divine.[16]

Thus we can say that religion is constituted by *those modes of thinking, speaking, feeling, and acting that express a consciousness of and a trust in the sacred.* Or to relate the definition of religion to the one given above of a view of life, we could say:

> A *religion* consist of the assumptions that (1) consti-
> tute or have a decisive importance for a picture of
> human beings and the world, that (2) form a central
> system of values, that (3) express a basic mood, that
> (4) have a regulative function in people's lives, and
> that (5) express a consciousness of and a trust in the
> sacred.

So we have to add only one extra element to a view of life to arrive at a rough but adequate account of religion—the experience of the sacred or the holy. On this account the conclusion we should draw is not that everyone is religious, but that everyone has a view of life. Hence we cannot avoid having a view of life and at the same time function as human beings. It is a *practical necessity* that we have beliefs of this sort. Another conclusion is that religion cannot be reduced to a set of abstract propositions or a conceptual system. It is more than just that, and this more is important, I will claim, for giving an appropriate account of religion and, further, for the question of religious rationality. It consists of the life-directing character religion has. Religion is to be *lived*, and a focus merely on the theoretical func-tion of religion cannot convey that. Religion is ultimately concerned with what way of life people should adopt, not what theories of life they should accept.

4.   Existential Questions and Religious Belief

Let us focus on the sort of questions our beliefs can be thought to answer before we take a closer look at what is characteristic of religious belief (if religion is characterized in the way I proposed above). I think that we can ask at least five different sorts of questions: practical, factual, conceptual, existential, and evaluative questions. A *practical* question is a question one asks to solve practical problems—how does one do this or that? For example, "How can we construct shelters that protect us during the winter season?" or "How can I find my way to the railroad station?" A second kind is the *factual* type, which includes questions about what is the case, what exists, and the like. They can be said to be of roughly two classes. The first class contains empirical questions, like "How many planets exist in our solar system?" or "Do electrons exist?" The second includes metaphysical questions, like "Are other people robots or do they possess minds?" or "What are the basic constituents of reality?" (In my opinion it is not possible to make a clear demarcation between empirical and metaphysical issues, rather they are two opposite poles on the same factual scale.)[17] Another kind of question concerns what, among other things, a good and meaningful life consists in or what is morally right or wrong. Let us call this type *evaluative* questions or questions of value. A fourth kind, *conceptual* questions, are about the function and meaning of the concepts we employ in our thinking and speaking. For example, how do evaluative questions differ from factual ones? What is the difference between a concept and a conception?[18] But it is the fifth type that we are primarily interested in, that is, *existential* questions. They are—as Gyllensten points out—questions:

> about the meaning of life, about how we should be able to cope with suffering and death, about our responsibility towards others and ourselves, about the limits of our own ability and about our dependence on forces outside what is solely within the reach of humans, about guilt and non-guilt, about weariness and despair and the instinct to reject oneself and life and about devotion and trust, about compulsion and degradation in this world and about its greatness and glory.[19]

We are interested in these questions because if life-view beliefs should be understood as answers to existential questions, it is important to know what is characteristic of *that* kind of questions. Otherwise it might be hard to judge whether a particular belief was an answer to an existential question and not to some other type of question. If we do not know what is asked for, we cannot know whether the response is a proper answer to the question.

What is characteristic of existential questions? In what follows I will try to specify some of the things that characterize existential questions without claiming that it is an exhaustive characterization. First, they are the sort of questions that arise because of the kind of beings we are or the kind of existence we enjoy. Here, "existence" is used in the way existentialists use the notion; that is, it refers to the distinctive being of humans, the aspects of their being that make them different from "mere" physical objects, for instance. Above all, what they have in mind is a human being's capacity to be self-reflective. Humans are able to reflect on their existence, take a stance towards it, and base their choice of direction in life on their reflections.

Further, I will argue that an existential question is by definition a question of an agent. It is raised by someone who is prepared to act. This kind of question is asked with the purpose in mind of getting information that is relevant to what one should be doing to respond in a proper way to the existential constraints one encounters in one's life. Existential questions are an "agent's questions." They are asked by somebody whose intention is to participate in what is happening. But the questions are probably more than an agent's questions. A person who is asking them does not only want to know "What *can* I do to overcome existential constraints" but also wants to know "What *should* I do to overcome existential constraints?" The quest is not only for an answer concerning actually possibilities, but for which one of these possibilities one should choose. The existential question includes a normative as well as a practical component. For example, experience of evil or death makes urgent what sort of (cognitive, emotional, and volitional) posture an individual *ought* to, not only can, adopt to the basic conditions of human existence. Let us call this kind of question that demands an answer to what the agent *should* do "agent-questions." And as long as an answer to what the agent should do is not given they are unanswered. On the other hand, let us call the questions that do not demand a response or answer regarding what should be done "spectator-questions."

Furberg claims that questions about meaning in life are agent-questions which demand an *urgent* answer.[20] By "urgent questions" he means the ones that are acting-obligatory, time-bound, and irrevocable. Questions of meaning are acting-obligatory because they are concerned with problems from which people cannot withdraw. They have to do something. Their reply must imply that something gets done or is neglected—which is also a kind of act. The question is also time-bound. If the response to the question is not given within a certain time, the point of it is lost. For instance, a couple's marriage might crack before they made up their minds of what to do to solve the problems in their marriage—then the delay is negligent. And what is done is irrevocable. So we could say roughly that urgent questions are those we ask that demand an immediate resolution from us, from which it is impossible for us to withhold judgment or withdraw.

I think this is true not only for questions about the meaning of life, it is also characteristic of existential questions in general and of questions concerning views of life in particular. These questions are typically urgent questions, and they require acting-obligatory, time-bound, and irrevocable answers. Further, what is also characteristic for existential questions is that they are, in general, of utmost importance for us. They are examples of what we could call "important questions"—the ones we ask whose resolution, if we accept them, would deeply affect how we understand ourselves and how we live our lives. Existential questions are important questions because they are crucial for what it means to exist in the world as a human being. So existential questions, or questions concerning choice of view of life, are important agent-questions which demand an urgent answer or response. They are normative questions, concerning the basic conditions of human existence, asked by a reflective agent who *must* make choices, accept beliefs, and act on the basis of these choices and beliefs.

Now if this understanding of existential questions is correct, it means that a belief that is formulated as an answer or response to existential questions must include advice about what one should actually do. So typically, only a life-orienting belief can answer an existential question. A purely theoretical response which does not include a normative and practical element cannot be a proper answer. Someone who gives that kind of answer to questions like "What is the meaning of life?" or "Who am I?" or "Does God exist?" has misunderstood not only the purpose of the question but also its primary semantical meaning. As Gutting rightly points out concerning religious beliefs, "a belief is religious not only in virtue of its content (e.g.., the fact that it is about God [or the sacred]) but also in virtue of the way it functions in the life of one who holds it."[21] However, that does not mean that an existential question is necessarily expressive or non-factual. It means only that an answer must contain a practical and normative as well as a theoretical dimension. It remains true, however, that views of life are first of all (but not only) responses to existential questions, not to purely factual ones. So existential questions can be about the same "thing" as factual or evaluative ones, but the former requires an answer that includes what the agent should actually do, whereas that is not necessarily true of the latter kinds of questions.

What is the agent asking for in this context? What people want to know is *how* they can solve, get through, or respond to the existential experiences of resistance that they encounter in their life—theoretically as well as practically. What is the *religious* answer to these questions? As we have seen it is essentially the claim that the only way to solve our existential problems is to let the sacred transform our lives. The picture of religious belief that emerges is then something like the following. Religious beliefs are a subset of life-view beliefs and are, therefore, life-orienting or existential in character. That means that they are beliefs that are formulated as a response to existential experiences, and if we accept them they would typically deeply affect how we live and think about our lives. To a great degree, therefore, they would determine the general direction of our lives. Religious beliefs are supposed to be about or refer to a transcendent dimension in reality. They are beliefs about the sacred and about the relationship between the sacred, us, and the world.

Existential concerns, however, are not all on a par for religious believers. Some concerns are of much greater importance than others. For them only the sacred is, in Tillich's terminology, of *ultimate concern*—roughly, what you care most about—every other concern becomes secondary.[22] And as we have already seen the object of their ultimate concern is experienced as holy, as a mystery, as a reality that is more real and of more value than everything else. But as Wainwright points out religious believers' ultimate concerns take different forms:

> It often takes the form of worship and then involves praise, love, gratitude, supplication, confession, petition, and so on. It can also take the form of a quest for the ultimate good. The object of this quest is a knowledge of the ultimate good or a union with it that transfigures us and overcomes our wrongness. These forms of ultimate concern may be combined or they may exist separately. Christianity, for example, combines both. In Buddhism, however, ultimate concern usually takes the second form but not the first.[23]

Wainwright goes on and wonders whether something can be a completely worthy object of the religious believer's ultimate concern unless—in an Anselmian vocabulary—it is so great that we can conceive of nothing greater. Only the sacred conceived as the greatest of all beings, or better conceived as the greatest of all reality, seems to be an appropriate object for the religious believers' experiences. This is so since it cannot be reasonable to characterize the sacred in such way that there might exist, or come into existence, other realities equal or even more worthy of the religious attitude. Hence a fully appropriate object of ultimate concern must be not only the most perfect existing reality but the *most perfect possible reality*.[24] Whether this is completely right is not so important in this context. What is crucial is that if the purported object of religious belief is supposed to have something like or similar to these properties, then the religious "object" is very different from the objects of scientific or everyday belief, and this might be relevant to what it should mean to be rational in one's believing concerning that kind of belief.

To sum up, the thesis I propose is that we need to ask not only *whose* believing it is that we are talking about to settle the question of rationality, we also have to ask what *kind* of belief is involved. On such an account, we first have to know what is characteristic of religious beliefs to be able to evaluate the rationality of religious believing. Therefore, what I have been trying to do in this chapter is to give a rough account of what the function and nature of religious belief might be. We have seen that religious beliefs are primarily answers to existential questions and that answers to existential questions in general must include both a practical and theoretical dimension. But they must say not only what can be done, but what actually should be done. They must include a normative element. This kind of belief is also life-directing, that is, if we accept religious beliefs they would in general, deeply affect how we live our lives. Religious beliefs are concerned with a special object, namely the scared; and the sacred is, for many religions but not for all, experienced as the most perfect possible reality. It is primarily this that distinguishes religious views of life from secular ones.

If this analysis of life-view beliefs is correct it implies that the choice of a view of life (secular or religious) is primarily an *existential choice* and not a purely theoretical one, but it is nevertheless a cognitive choice. It is a choice of what to live for, not only a choice of a vision of life (the theoretical function of views of life) but a vision for life (the regulative function of views of life). And it is the *rationality of that kind of choice or that kind of believing we should be investigating*. But we have also seen that properly functioning human beings cannot be without a view of life—that choice is a practical necessity. Questions concerning views of life cannot be left open. They are urgent existential questions, and they are always answered. The question we have to raise in the next chapter is how this information about the nature and function of views of life (in particular religious ones) affects the conception of rationality, and thus what we can and should rightly demand of people concerning their choice of and commitment to views of life, or what the rationality of life-view believing should consist in.

For now it is sufficient to say that if this characterization of religious and secular believing is correct, it has three important consequences for the question of rationality. First, human beings cannot live without a view of life. This means that the choice is never between having a view of life and not having one. From this it follows, I will claim, that it can never be irrational for humans in general or for an individual in particular to have *a* view of life. The question of rationality concerns only *which* view of life one should accept and in what *way* one holds it. Second, the choice of a view of life is primarily an existential choice. If we are interested in saying anything exhaustive or essential about the rationality of a human being's religious and secular believing it is the rationality of *that* kind of choice or *that* kind of believing we should focus on. And concerning religious belief, if the standards of rationality are going to be *religiously relevant* they have to take into account the nature of religious believing and the ends religious practice has (given, of course, that these ends are themselves rationally acceptable). Lastly, the object of religious belief—the sacred—is different from the objects of scientific belief—electrons, genes, and the like—and this must be taken into account when one proposes standards for what it should mean to be rational in one's believing concerning *that* kind of object.

10

Religious Rationality

In the last chapter I tried to give an account of the believings that are involved in the practice of religion. The reason for doing this is that it seems likely, at least to me, that the particular kind of belief that is held has an impact on the demands of rationality. Roughly, the thought is that what and how it is rational to believe might depend on what it is that is believed and, in particular, on what kind of practice the belief in question belongs to. In fact, this way of proceeding is a consequence of my acceptance of a practice-oriented approach to philosophy (of religion). On such an account, an examination of the history of religion and the contemporary practice of religion is needed as a basis for a recommendation of appropriate standards for religious rationality (or irrationality).

I will try to show that a philosophical discussion of the rationality of religious belief is *religiously relevant* only if it takes into account the aim and function of religious practice and the situation in which it is pursued. My claim is that a necessary condition for being able to develop appropriate standards for religious rationality, and for being able to assess the extent to which an individual or group of individuals is rationally justified in accepting beliefs of this kind or being involved in a practice of this sort, is that we properly understand the function and nature of religious belief. In short, the formulation of adequate standards for assessing the rationality of religious belief is *not* independent of the actual practice of religion. I hope to be able to show that much of the discussion of the rationality of religious belief has been conducted in such way that it is, in fact, irrelevant to whether real people are rational in being religious believers and consequently cannot function as a basis for a recommendation of the appropriate standards for religious rationality.

1.   Rationality and Human Practices

We have previously seen that questions of rationality cannot be asked in the traditional unspecified way. Instead we always have to determine whose rationality we are talking about. Rationality is person-dependent. I claimed in the last chapter that we also have to add another dimension to our discussion of rationality if we want to get things right. It is the question concerning the type of practices to which the beliefs of the believer belong. In other words, to be able to settle the question of human rationality we have to take into account not only (*a*) the *kind of beings* we are, but also (*b*) the *kind of activities* we are involved in. If this is correct it means that the question of theoretical rationality should be: "What is it rational to believe for a particular person *N*, or a particular group of persons *G*, in situation *S*, in field or practice *F*?" This is the appropriate question to ask if it is the case that rationality is not only person-relative but also practice-relative. Roughly, we can say that:

> Rationality is *domain* or *practice-relative* if it (on some level) varies to some extent from practice to practice.

Rationality is practice-relative if, for instance, the standards of rationality in science are different from those in ethics. The term "practice" will be used in this context as an umbrella concept. It is meant to cover some of the more general concepts we can use to divide up our life in separate or different parts or activities. So by a "practice" we can mean a mode of life, a discipline, a language-game, a discourse, a paradigm, a conceptual scheme, a tradition, a culture, a religion, a form of life, and the like.

One way of proceeding when we want to know how and to what degree rationality is practice-relative, and what consequences this in its turn has for the demands of rationality in general and for religious believing in particular, is to *compare the aims* of different practices with each other. If we proceed in this way some questions we should try to answer are: (1) what is the aim of religion or religious believing, and does this aim differ from the aim of science, everyday believing, ethics, and so on? In fact, I think that philosophical, scientific, every-day and religious reasoning sometimes, maybe often, have different goals or aims. An important question will therefore also be: (2) if the practices have different aims what consequences does this have for rationality? But we also have to ask ourselves: (3) what kind of ends is it rational to try to satisfy in our life? That is, we have to develop standards for axiological rationality (the ones concerning what we should value or prefer). The basic thought is that if we compare the aims of different practices with each other we might then be able to see whether rationality is practice-relative and if so why and to what degree. Now, practices (and beliefs) are always *some* agent's practices (and beliefs). If that is so, then who we are and the situation we are in affects what aims we have or should have and, correspondingly, also what practices we are or should be involved in. There is an essential connection between the aims of our activities and beliefs and our predicament.

So in this study I have emphasized one aspect of the human predicament: that *we are finite beings with limited cognitive resources,* and this we have seen is of great importance for rationality. Now we have to add another dimension of our situation to the discussion. It sounds trivial but its implications for rationality are often over-looked. It is that *we are situated in an already existing world, with a certain natural and social structure.* Since we are living in the world we cannot completely avoid formulating explicit or implicit beliefs about that reality, and we do not formulate these beliefs just for fun .We need them for our orientation and flourishing. We want them to do certain jobs for us. We have needs of different kinds and our beliefs help us satisfy those needs. We experience resistance of different sorts and our beliefs help us overcome these constraints.

In this context it is important again to make the distinction I introduced in chapter 2, between a *desire* and a *need.* People do not need everything they desire, and do not desire everything they need. A need is, roughly, what is in one's best interest, what is of importance for one's flourishing. To know what one needs is to know what is good for one. What needs do we have then? Among other things, we need nourishment and protection for the maintenance of our well-being, information, freedom of action, love, friendship, and much more. If these needs are unsatisfied we cannot attain the condition of human well-being or flourishing. These are things worth striving towards, to have as one's aims or ends. But are these really good ends? In a sense the question is trivial. We can see this if we rephrase the question in the following way: is human well-being a good end? Of course, *for us* it must be good; if this is not good for us—then what can be good for us? In other words, the kind of being we are determines some of the ends which are appropriate or good for us. Rescher makes a similar point:

> The universally appropriate ends at issue in our human condition are not somehow freely *chosen* by us; they are fixed by the (for us) inescapable ontological circumstance that—like it or not—we find ourselves to exist as human beings, and thus as free rational agents. Their ultimate inherence in (generic) human needs determines the appropriateness of our particular, individual ends.[1]

Now, the presumptionist claims that a truly rational person is one who takes into account his or her own situation (and that includes his or her needs or real interests). In fact, according to the holistic conception of the nature of rationality which the presumptionist accepts, someone who does not do this is not fully rational. For example, an individual can live irrationally in the sense that he or she is satisfying desires or preferences that are harmful for his or her well-being in the long run. And a standard of axiological rationality I previously proposed is that if people know that a means is contrary to their needs or best interests, then (everything else being equal) it would be irrational for them to perform that action, accept that belief, or make that evaluation.[2] (Recall that on the holistic account, rationality is seen as a matter of doing—believing, acting, evaluating—what we ought, and realistically can manage, to do in our circumstances to choose appropriate ends and to choose appropriate means to achieve these ends.)[3]

If what I said above is correct, our constitution and situation put constraints not only on what *means* we ought to use, but also on what *ends* we ought to adopt, and correspondingly on what beliefs we hold and what practices we are involved in. So a thesis I want to defend is:

> *Who* and *where* we are affects (*a*) what ends are rationally justified for us to adopt for our believing and (*b*) under what circumstances we are rationally justified in accepting our beliefs and getting involved in a practice.

To see why this is so, we need only take into account our actual predicament, that we are beings *who-live-in-the-world*. We are the kind of creatures who live in a world that has dangerous surprises from which our well-being must be secured. In *that* kind of situation we need, and therefore value, beliefs and activities that do certain jobs for us: in *science* to make (among other things) predictions and to manipulate or control our environment, in *views of life* to express (among other things) a way of getting through the barriers of suffering and death, guilt and meaninglessness, and the like, in *everyday life,* to put into words (among other things) possible ways of how to live in peace and co-operate with our neighbours, and so on.[4] Thus activities like science, religion, and everyday living are not going on in an epistemic vacuum; rather they are practiced by human beings who are finite beings with limited resources, and because of their constitution and the environment in which they live they have certain needs. Hence our constitution and predicament affect what appropriate ends we should (rationally) have in our believing and when we are rationally justified in accepting what we believe or in taking part in a practice.

So we hold beliefs, in general, because we have certain needs and because we want certain jobs done. However, if this is the case, it is highly problematic to propose or rather presuppose, as many philosophers seem to do, that the appropriate end of rational believing should be purely epistemic, that is, to view epistemic rationality (when rationality is understood as having only such values as truth and the avoidance of falsehood as ends) as the only relevant form of theoretical rationality. Such an assumption is problematic because it *neglects* what kind of beings we actually are, that we have certain needs to satisfy besides, and perhaps more urgent than, epistemic ones. For instance, the primary aim of our ancestors, and rationally so, was probably survival and not trying to come into possession of as many true beliefs as possible and to eliminate as many false beliefs as possible. And further, if we are (or ought to be) interested in truth we are, I will claim, normally and rationally not interested in just any truth, rather we are interested in the kind of truths that are *useful,* broadly speaking, for us in our actual predicament. For instance, we do not care about the precise number of grains of sand on the beaches of the world. So trying to acquire a lot of true but trivial beliefs would be irrational if it excluded (which—because of our limited cognitive resources—is very likely) the possibility of our acquiring important true beliefs, that is, beliefs that are relevant for us in our situation. Therefore, the epistemic goal could not reasonably be to strive to hold as many true beliefs as possible and avoid as many false beliefs as possible. We must use our cognitive resources much more wisely than that.

This kind of reduction of rationality to epistemic rationality is sometimes made in philosophy of science when it is claimed that the use of principles of induction or simplicity in science must be justified solely by their truth-promoting function.[5] But these principles that scientists employ cannot (and need not) be given a justification which is purely epistemic. Their use in science cannot be justified if the only proper end of science is to increase our true beliefs about the world and to eliminate our false ones. According to a practice-oriented approach to philosophy of science, however, the conclusion we should draw from this is not that science is irrational, but that these characterizations of scientific rationality are inadequate; they do not give an appropriate account of scientific rationality. What then justifies scientists in using, for example, principles of induction? Well, why do they use them in the actual practice of science? For one thing, these principles help scientists make predictions, which they need to be able to manipulate and control the physical world. Roughly, it is this that justifies the use of these principles in science. But that means that the end or aim of science is not purely epistemic. Science has a complex aim, including both epistemic and non-epistemic ends. And the end of scientific rationality ought not to be entirely epistemic simply because we are who we are, and have certain needs that must be fulfilled.

2.   The Rationality Debate in Contemporary Philosophy of Religion

The same type of reduction of rationality that has been made in philosophy of science has often also been made in regard to religious or existential matters. This happens when philosophers of religion assume that the only *proper* or *essential end* of these practices should be to increase true beliefs and to eliminate false beliefs. And correspondingly, religious believing—or for that matter any believing—is rational only if it can be justified with respect to *that* end. In much contemporary philosophy of religion the discussion of the rationality of religious belief has taken this form. That is, philosophers not only adopt, as we have previously seen, a formal approach to the philosophy of religion, they also construe the question of the rationality of religious believing as a question only of epistemic rationality. The only relevant aims of religious practice, when assessing its rationality or the rationality of participating in a religious practice, are epistemic ones.

A religion such as Christianity is pictured as a conceptual or theoretical system, "theism," where the core proposition is "God exists." Hence a theist is an individual who accepts this system or the core proposition as true. These philosophers then ask whether belief that God exists or theistic beliefs are rational or whether it is rational to be religious, that is, to be a theist in this limited sense. By a rationally acceptable belief they mean (among other things) a belief that is justified with respect to its truth-promoting function. Typically this assumption is expressed in the way the evidentialist challenge to religious belief is stated. Roughly, it is rational to hold a religious belief only if there are good reasons to think that it is *true*.

Since the end of religious believing ought to be purely epistemic, the theist must be a purely epistemic being (a being whose sole concern is believing as many truths and as few falsehoods as possible), which means—if my account is right—that the theist is not an actual religious believer. So these philosophers tend to discuss the rationality of this conceptual system or the proposition "God exists" without relating it directly to actual religious people—with their abilities and their needs—who actually have these beliefs. *The presupposed agent of religious rationality (or irrationality) is not a human but a fictive being!* Of course there is nothing wrong with working with a theoretical or idealized construction, but if the philosopher wants to say anything substantial about the *real* world, *real* science, and *real* religion, and so on, then this will not do. In particular, if we want to make claims about the intelligibility or rationality of *human beings'* religious believing then we run the risk of getting a distorted picture if we proceed in such a way. It would probably take us as far from the truth of the matter as when the logical positivists were stating the appropriate standards for scientific rationality without taking into account the actual practice of science.

Why philosophers of religion have in general been much more interested in the so called proofs of God's existence and divine attributes like simplicity or omnipotence than in real religion in the life of actual people can probably be explained, at least partly, by their

understanding of what philosophy is, by their formal approach to it
and their understanding of theoretical rationality. But as Alston writes:

> The most general point is that the conceptions, the beliefs, and
> the talk that set our problems are rooted in the life of theistic
> [and non-theistic] religions. We only have this thought and talk to
> philosophize about because these religions have existed as ongoing
> communities. This should be too obvious for notice, but I'm afraid
> that it is often ignored by philosophy of religion like the "problem
> of foreknowledge and freedom" are purely theoretical philosophical
> problems that have their ultimate roots in the course of philosoph-
> ical thinking about the world and would still pose the questions
> they pose for philosophical reflection if there were no such thing
> as religion. But this historical mode of dependence on the actual
> practice of religion is one that, if I am right, attaches, willy nilly, to
> all philosophy that is concerned with religious issues.[6]

If Alston is right, and I think he is, it is crucial to see that such
understanding of philosophy of religion has a direct impact not only
on what issues, problems, or questions philosophers should work
with, but also on how they are characterized. In particular, if we want
to know whether it is rational to be a religious believer we have to
ask this question in a way that takes into account both the *situation*
in which a religious believer actually finds him or herself and the *aim*
and *function* of religious practice.

What I am saying here is not that it is wrong to say that theism, in
this case Christianity, is at least a conceptual system,[7] or that belief in
God at least implies the proposition "God exists."[8] But what is wrong
is then to go on as if we did not have to take into consideration *other*
ends of religious believing than epistemic ones or the *situation* in
which the religious quest actually arises. It is in fact to presuppose that
the "rest" is of little importance for the question about the rationality
of being a religious believer—in this case a theist or a Christian. These
philosophers, however, do not necessarily deny that the religious
practice has other than epistemic aims, but they tacitly assume, or
they proceed as if, the other aims were *irrelevant* to the question
about the rationality of religious believing.

So my criticism is not against the assumption that religious believing includes a cognitive element or has an epistemic end. It is
against the assumption that what really matters when evaluating the

rationality (or irrationality) of religious life-view believing, or when stating the standards of rationality for the religious or secular practices, is only the epistemic ends, and the thought that the situations in which life-view believing occur is irrelevant for the issue.

2.1 THE QUESTIONS OF LIFE-VIEW RATIONALITY

Another effect of this approach to rationality and religious practice is that it gives the impression that the choice of religion is essentially if not purely a *theoretical choice* (concerning what conclusions we should draw in regard to certain arguments for or against religious belief). The theist and his or her opponents are not only purely epistemic beings, they are also thought of as having almost unlimited time resources, and the issue concerns only the epistemic force of certain arguments. Again, there is nothing wrong as such in employing this approach to rationality and religion, but if we want to say anything substantial about our actual world and our actual predicament and, therefore, the actual issue, we have to adopt a more practice-oriented view of philosophy of religion—at least, if we want to discuss the rationality and religious practice of real humans.

Now, if we do that, we can see that the *acceptance of religion for the actual religious believer is, ultimately, an existential choice.* This is so because religious life-view beliefs are essentially answers to existential questions, and existential questions are, as we saw in chapter 9, agent-questions not spectator-questions. For the believer (and if I am right we are all believers) the questions concerning the choice of a view of life are agent-questions. They are asked with the purpose in mind of choosing or continuing to hold a particular view of life. On what foundation should I build my life, my existence? So the choice of accepting or holding on to religious beliefs is an existential choice, not a purely theoretical one—but, so I will claim, nevertheless a cognitive choice. This means that what is at stake is not only whether some beliefs are true or what conclusions we should draw regarding certain arguments, but *how we actually should live our lives.* It is not just a matter of making up one's mind, it is also a matter of choosing a *way of living*—changing one's life. It is a choice of not only a vision of life (the theoretical function of views of life) but a vision for life (the regulative function of views of life). And this choice cannot be postponed for real human agents. We must live right now, one way or another.

Our questions—which are really The Questions Of Life-View Rationality—are, first, *whether real concrete believers can be rational in their life-view believings or their existential choices, in the kind of reality they find themselves,* and, second, *what standards of rationality it is appropriate to apply to that kind of believing or practice.* Hence an evaluation of rationality that does not take into account that the agent must *do* something, choose a way of living, that treats the matter as a purely theoretical matter (as if a response or resolution need not be more or less immediately practically implemented into the agent's life) is inadequate or is in fact assessing something else than what here is at issue.

It is not only that existential questions (and therefore also their answers) are semantically misunderstood, as I tried to show in the last chapter, if one does not take into account the notion of agent, but they and their answers are also epistemologically misunderstood. To see this, compare what it is rational to believe for a purely epistemic being or an ideal spectator in contrast to an actual human agent. We could say that an ideal spectator is a person who, among other things, has no interest in the question, has all the time needed at his or her disposal, has no need to take a stand on the issue, has nothing to lose or gain, and who wants to believe as many true things as possible and as few false things as possible. Now, under what conditions is it rational for *such a being* to accept life-view beliefs? For one thing, since the ideal spectator need not make a choice, he or she can postpone the choice until sufficient evidence has emerged. In fact, it would not be rational for this being to do otherwise. But this is not the situation of human beings, they *must* make a choice, choose a way of living, and they have much to lose or gain since their lives are at stake. Therefore, a human being is not rational in postponing the choice as the ideal spectator is. Hence people are rationally justified in taking risks, because of their predicament, that an ideal spectator (or the agent of philosophical rationality) would not be justified in taking. So what it is rational for such a being to believe on religious or secular matters cannot help us, since we are in a radically different situation. Rationality is kind-relative. A somewhat different way of stating the same point is to say that we cannot equate *agent-rationality* (when somebody has to make a choice) with *spectator-rationality* (when somebody need not make a choice).

So the problem in this context is not, first of all, how a religious believer can be rational, but how this kind of philosophical discussion can be *religiously relevant*. That is, how can it be a discussion which is relevant for religious, or for that matter secular, believers, for *their* questions and the rationality of *their* believing?[9] As I pointed out in chapter 1, the problem with the formal approach is that it risks divorcing epistemology (in this case the theory of rationality) from the actual practice of views of life (or science, everyday living, morality, and the like). If the conception of rationality (standards, appropriate ends, and the like) is derived from considerations that ignore or are unconstrained by the ends and functions of life-view practice and the situation in which it is pursued, then how can such understanding of rationality be relevant for this kind of practice?[10]

2.2 THE RELEVANCE OF THE ACTUAL AIMS OF RELIGIOUS PRACTICE

What then is the aim of religious practice and how does it differ, say, from the aims of science and metaphysics? Roughly, both science and metaphysics aim to make the world *theoretically intelligible*, but science also aims to make it *predictively intelligible*. Views of life, however, aim not only to make our lives theoretically intelligible but, and primarily, also *existentially intelligible*.[11] We formulate life-view beliefs to come to grips with our existential experiences of resistance. In our lives we encounter experiences of suffering, death, guilt, meaninglessness, and the like. In that situation or context we value (and rationally so, I would claim) a practice that *makes sense out of these experiences, diagnoses them, and helps us find a way through these existential constraints*—and this is the actual end of life-view believing and practice. This end is something that both religious and secular views of life have in common. What is distinctively religious is to claim that it is possible for us to overcome existential constraints in a more profound way only if we let our lives be transformed by the sacred or if we enter into a right relation with the sacred. The specific *aim of a religious life-view practice* is to help people theoretically understand and practically implement the sacred dimension of reality into their lives and thereby release its capacity or value for their lives and for their existential concerns.

How then does this understanding of religion and the actual context in which it arises affect the question of the rational acceptability of religious believing? In what way is this relevant to the rationality debate in philosophy of religion? This question can be answered on two levels, and it is the first one of these that is our major concern here. The first level concerns how the religious practice affects the *standards* of life-view rationality. The second level deals with the *outcome* of the application of these standards to a particular religious believer or a particular group of them.

A first consequence of this practice-oriented approach to religion is that if the end of religious believing is rationally acceptable, it is with respect to *that* end that religious practice should be rationally evaluated and nothing else, or for which good reasons should be given (evidentialism) or for which good reasons against must be taken into consideration (presumptionism). This means in its turn that it is wrong to assume that only epistemic ends are relevant when we characterize the evidential principle and the principle of presumption. We defined the first principle as the claim that it is rational to accept an important non-basic belief only if there are good reasons to believe that it is true. We defined the second one as the claim that it is rational to accept a belief unless there are good (or special) reasons to cease from thinking that it is true. But formulated in this way they presuppose a purely epistemic end. To avoid this unnecessary restriction we can instead define the principles in the following way:

> *The Evidential Principle**: It is rational to accept a (important) non-basic belief only if there are good reasons for holding it.

> *The Principle of Presumption**: It is rational to accept a belief unless there are good (or special) reasons to cease from holding it.

(Or, if we want to apply the principles not only to theoretical rationality but also to practical and axiological rationality, we could say that according to the evidential principle, rationality calls for pro-ceeding on the basis of good reasons in whatever we do (believe, act, or evaluate); and according to the principle of presumption, rationality calls for not proceeding against good reasons in whatever we do.)

What we gain by formulating the evidential principle and the principle of presumption in this way if that we then leave the ends of theoretical (practical and axiological) rationality open. Formulated as above they are open to goals other than truth. As I pointed out in the second chapter, what counts as a good reason always depends on what it is supposed to be a reason for. So a reason which is adequate for a particular belief an individual holds may nevertheless not be a reason to think that what is believed is true, since the individual's aim might be non-epistemic, for example, to have peace of mind or to be happy. This is why earlier I made a distinction between epistemic ends (including values such as truth and the avoidance of falsehood) and non-epistemic ends (including values such as well-being, saving the earth, self-interest, happiness, peace of mind), and another distinction between epistemic reasons (the ones that connect a belief in an appropriate way to an epistemic end) and non-epistemic reasons (the ones that connect a belief in an appropriate way to a non-epistemic end).

Let us now go back to our question concerning what relevance the actual religious practice has for religious rationality. It is obviously not enough to say that the aims of religious practice must be taken into account if they are rational. We also have to ask if these ends really are appropriate ends for rationality, that is, do they meet the standards of axiological rationality (concerning what it is rational to value or prefer). We have to ask this question because if these ends are not rational ones then there is no need for philosophers or theologians to take them into account when discussing the rationality of religious believing, since a rational person ought not to adopt those ends. Which then are these standards of axiological rationality? This is of course a very complex question indeed, but as I pointed out earlier in this chapter, what ends it ought to be rational to adopt must be resolved from our vantage point. Our very constitution and our predicament determines to a very high degree what ends it is rational for *us* to have in what we are doing. So at least we could say that one of the *standards of axiological rationality* is that it is rational to accept an end if it is based on intrinsic human needs.[12]

Do the actual ends of life-view practice satisfy this demand? Is, for example, Bowker conforming to this axiological standard when he claims that the function of religions is to fortify our trust that there is some way through the barriers that block the road toward ultimate fulfillment, and that their *plausibility* (in my words rationality) depends (at least partly, my qualification) upon the *effectiveness* of the paths they make through the most difficult obstacles?[13] Certainly, it is difficult to see how religious or secular believers can do something axiologically irrational or irresponsible when they take into account the capacity a view of life has, to overcome existential constraints. They could be irrational in doing this only if existential concerns are not among human beings' intrinsic needs. But trying to overcome or deal with experiences of grief, anxiety, alienation, meaninglessness, suffering, and so on, cannot plausibly be treated as not an essential part of our true interests. To come back again to the parallel discussion in philosophy of science, just as the end of scientific practice ought not to be entirely epistemic, simply because we are who we are, and have certain needs that must be fulfilled, the end of religious practice ought not to be either; in this context also it is rational to take into account one's real interests.

However, a typical objection against regarding existential concerns as rational ends of acting and believing is that these concerns are thought to be non-epistemic. For example, believing in God may help people to feel a meaning with their lives; but despite this it might be true that there is no meaning in life, and these people are just fooling themselves. But this objection does not count against what I am saying, since on my account existential concerns have *complex ends.* What these believers do is that they reject a purely epistemic goal, not an epistemic end altogether. In fact if they did not do this they would no longer be religious or secular believers because of the second element in a view of life. A view of life not only (successfully or not) structures and makes reality intelligible, it also (successfully or not) actually guides the adherents in their concrete lives, which includes dealing with existential experiences of resistance. Therefore, they have to take into account non-epistemic aspects such as the "liveability" of a view of life too.

This twofold function of views of life might also explain the way "truth" is typically used in religion. The religious understanding of truth differs in some important ways from the understanding of it in science and philosophy. Consider, for instance, what Gandhi says: "Nothing is or exists in reality except Truth. That is why *Sat* or Truth is perhaps the most important name of God."[14] And St. John writes: "But he who practices the truth comes to the light, that his deed may be manifested as having been wrought in God."[15] According to St. John, only those who *do* the truth will be enlightened by it. Dupré claims that this way of thinking about truth is common to all religions: "Despite their substantial differences, all religious traditions agree in stressing the ontological and moral qualities of truth over the purely cognitive ones. Truth refers to *being*, rather than to knowledge."[16]

Now if this is an accurate characterization of the use of the notion of truth in religion, we can see why truth is understood in such a way. It is in concordance with what a religion is all about. Religious believers stress the ontological and moral qualities of truth over the purely cognitive ones because of the aims of religious practice. The aim of religious practice is not only to structure and make reality intelligible but also—and primarily—to regulate or guide people's actual way of living. So only a view of life that can also successfully guide believers in their lives can be really true, satisfying both the theoretical and regulative function of a view of life.

However, despite these differences I think that the religious, scientific and philosophical uses of the notion of truth are compatible. The difference is mainly that "truth" in religion is a richer notion since it includes more than the cognitive dimension. Religious truth is not reducible to correct beliefs because truth is also something to be done, to be lived. Therefore, cognitive truth might be a necessary condition for religious truth, but it is clearly not a sufficient condition. This also gives us a clue to why persons like Jesus, Buddha, and Mohammed are considered to be of such importance for religious people. MacIntyre, when discussing the modern society, expresses a certain indignation when he notes that people "put their trust in persons rather than in arguments."[17] But this is understandable and even a rational way of behaving, at least in a life-view context, when we take into account that what is asked for is first of all how we should live our lives and how we should overcome existential constraints. This is nothing that can be solved just in theory (by argumentation), the solution must prove itself in practice. Therefore, persons like Jesus, Buddha, and Mohammed are of the utmost importance when it comes to holding on to or accepting a religious view of life, since they embody the religious way of living and dealing with existential constraints. People look at not only what they said but also how they lived, because they exemplify what it is to *be* a Christian, a Buddhist, or a Muslim and show how to *live* a Christian, a Buddhist, or a Muslim life.[18]

So only standards of life-view rationality that take into account the twofold function of views of life can be adequate. In order to assess and weigh properly the rationality of what the adherents of a view of life tell us, we have to assess and weigh not only what they *say* (the *theoretical adequacy*), but also what they *are*—how they live (the *existential adequacy*). The existential adequacy of a view of life can be determined only by focusing on how successful it is in actually guiding its adherents in their concrete lives, in overcoming existential constraints. Rolston is on to this aspect of life-view rationality when he tries to point out the differences and similarities between science and religion:

> Religion does [like science] use the if-then mode of deriving consequences from its creeds and testing them in experience. In this, however, religious convictions cannot usually be cast into empirically testable frameworks. Simple events, such as planetary motions or chemical reactions, adapt well to watching with objective instruments, but more complex events, such as guilt and forgiveness, quantify poorly and are difficult to make operational. The instruments for their recording are *subjective selves*, and the hunting down of those experiences that are found when armed with religious creeds is a matter indeed of experience, of "*going through*," and not merely of observation, "looking on." In physics and chemistry, material things instantiate laws in a rather tight way, but living things, even in biology, often show only generalizations or statistical trends, hardly rejected by occasional counterexamples. Personal beings, as unique, rational, affective agents, can test religious convictions only *experientially*, not experimentally; *existentially*, not operationally.[19]

So the rationality of religious believing can be evaluated properly only if we take into account how it *does* things, overcomes guilt and alienation, creates forgiveness and meaning, and so on.

2.3   DO SCIENCE AND RELIGION HAVE DIFFERENT RATIONALITIES?

The aim of life-view believing is a rational end, and therefore it is relevant, both when it comes to establishing the appropriate standards and when making the assessment of what the application of those standards to concrete believers actually would lead to. However, does it follow from the fact that scientific and religious practices have different ends that they also have different rationalities? Is the *incommensurability thesis* applicable, at least to the rationality in science and views of life? (Recall that this thesis is, roughly, the claim that there exist different uses of the notion of rationality that have nothing in common with each other. It means a particular thing in one context and something completely different in another context.)

If the end of religious believing is only to overcome guilt, mean-inglessness, alienation, and the like, and the ends of science are only prediction and control, then their rationalities seem to be, at least in this sense, significantly different. As Wykstra points out:

> If we approach the claims of a theistic complex like Christianity—claims having to do with Creation, Covenant, Sin, Judgment, Grace, Incarnation, and the like—as if they must embody the values of scientific theorizing, *we will not assess them by appropriate criteria;* indeed, we will probably not even understand them. Their point is not to help us predict, control, and contrive the world.[20]

Wykstra makes an important remark here, which it is true not only of scientific but also of philosophical theorizing. If we pay no attention to what is characteristic of the practices we investigate and compare with each other, we might not only apply *inappropriate standards* and ask for the *wrong kind of evidence,* we might also totally *misrepresent the beliefs* in question (their function and nature). But again, does this mean that the rationalities of science and religion (in Wykstra's case only Christianity) are so significantly different that they are incommensurable? To be able to answer this we need to take into account the distinction between the levels or aspects of rationality introduced in the second chapter. The questions concern: (*a*) what rationality is (the nature of rationality), (*b*) what the conditions of rationality are (the standards of rationality), (*c*) what the reasons (or evidence) of rationality are (the reasons of rationality), and (*d*) what the aims or goals of rationality are (the ends of rationality).

First, the fact that religion and science have different aims (the *ends of rationality*) does not imply that they have different conceptions of what rationality is (the *nature of rationality*). Rationality in both cases can be seen as a matter of fulfilling one's intellectual duty with respect to what one believes. And people are irrational when they fail to meet these obligations. Second, the evidential principle or the principle of presumption might apply in both science and religion even if they have very different aims (the *standards of rationality*). For example, it might be rational to hold both a scientific and a religious belief unless there are good reasons to cease from believing them. But, and here the difference in aim matters, what counts as a good reason depends on what it is supposed to be a reason *for,* what the end or aim in question are (the *reasons of rationality*). Since the aims, or some of the aims, are not the same in these two practices, what can count as good reasons (or evidence) is probably not exactly the same. For instance, it is probably not a good reason against the acceptance of religious or secular life-view beliefs that they cannot predict new phenomena, though that might be a good reason against the acceptance of a theory in physics; and it is not a good argument against a theory in astronomy that it cannot help us become morally better persons; however, if the moral fruits of a view of life are bad this is a serious objection against it.

But does this not mean that *some* scientific standards and reasons are not applicable to religious practice? The answer is, I think, yes. The principle of predictability (roughly, a good theory should generate new predictions) is probably not a principle that can or should be used in religious or secular life-view practices. In other words, some standards of rationality are directly related to the particular aims of different practices. What this shows, I think, is not that *all* standards of rationality are practice-relative, but that these standards can be divided in two groups: the basic and the derived. The basic standards are independent of, and the derived standards are dependent on, the distinctive ends of a practice.

Basic standards of rationality are the ones that state what function good reasons (or evidence) should have in what an agent does. In theoretical rationality basic questions are: "What is the proper function of reasons (or evidence) in belief-formation and regulation?" and "With what firmness ought one to hold on to what one believes?" The answer to the first question seems either to be one form or another of the evidential principle or the principle of presumption. (As we have seen for most philosophers this is not even thought to be an issue, since they take evidentialism simply for granted.[21] The second has not been thoroughly discussed either, except maybe by philosophers working in philosophy of religion, and here the basic choice seems to be either to accept the proportionality principle or to reject it and try to find some proper substitute.[22] We will come back to this latter question in the end of this chapter.)

The other standards of rationality can be seen as derived from this first group of standards in the following way. A good reason for (or against) the rational acceptance of a set of beliefs, a hypothesis, a theory, and the like, might be that:

(1) it is logically consistent, that is, it avoids self-contradiction (the *principle of internal consistency*);

(2) it is consistent with other theories (the *principle of external consistency*);

(3) it is coherent, that is, its components hang together (the *principle of internal coherence*);

(4) it is coherent with other theories (the *principle of external coherence*),

(5) it is less complex than rival theories (the *principle of simplicity*),

(6) it makes possible the prediction of new phenomena (the *principle of predictability*);

(7) it provides illuminating explanations of puzzling phenomena (the *principle of explanatory power*);

(8) it is more comprehensive than other rival theories (the *principle of scope*);

(9) it is easier to apply than its rivals, that is, in a given situation it is practically more useful (the *principle of practical applicability*), and so on.

In other words, the derived standards of rationality specify what should count as good reasons in general, and a good reason for accepting a set of beliefs will meet, or at least in principle can meet, the demands of a particular standard. But by a good reason we can also mean the concrete instantiation of a standard. For example, theory T predicts the new phenomena p and q; this means that p and q constitute evidence for theory T; by "evidence" we then have in mind p and q.

So by "reason" (or "evidence") we can mean that a set of beliefs or propositions conforms to the demands of a standard of rationality, for example, "Scientific theories make predictions possible" or "Religious beliefs give life a meaning," and so on. Or we can indicate by "reason" the particular item (an argument, proposition, fact, belief, or the like) that is the evidence, for instance, "John killed his brother," "The litmus paper turned red when immersed in the liquid," "There exist evil in the world," or "Alice says that she is now free from her anxiety," and so on.

However, when we are dealing with life-view rationality we have to add some other standards and good reasons that are of importance to *this* kind of practice. For example a good reason for (or against) the rationality of accepting a view of life, might be that:

(10) it helps satisfy intrinsic human needs (the *principle of human adequacy*);

(11) it answers or helps deal with existential matters better than other accounts, or the like (the *principle of existential adequacy*);

(12) it helps people better than its rivals actually to live a morally good life (the *principle of moral adequacy*), or the like.[23]

If my argument is correct then rationality is practice-relative in at least two ways: (*a*) all or some of the *derived standards* of rationality are (more or less) relative to a particular practice, and (*b*) what counts as *good reasons* are (more or less) relative to a particular practice. So the fact that science and religion (or any other practice) have different ends or aims does not necessarily mean that they also have different rationalities. What follows is only that at most some of the derived standards and what is concretely taken to be a good reason is different in science and religion (or in different practices).

2.4   THE SCIENTIFIC CHALLENGE RECONSIDERED

Let us once again take a look at the scientific challenge to religious believing. The claim is that religious beliefs must meet the same, or at least similar, standards of rationality as scientific beliefs in order to considered rational. They do not meet the standards of scientific rationality. Therefore, religious beliefs are irrational beliefs. Russell writes, for instance:

God and immortality, the central dogmas of the Christian religion, *find no support in science.* . . . No doubt people will continue to entertain these beliefs, because they are pleasant, just as it is pleasant to think ourselves virtuous and our enemies wicked. But for my part I cannot see any ground for either. I do not pretend to be able to prove that there is no God. I equally cannot prove that Satan is a fiction. The Christian God may exist; so may the Gods of Olympus, or of ancient Egypt, or of Babylon. But no one of these hypotheses is more probable than any other: they lie outside the region of even probable knowledge, and therefore there is no reason to consider any of them.[24]

More recently, Provine writes: "Show me a person who says that science and religion are compatible, and I will show you a person who (1) is an effective atheist, or (2) believes things demonstrably unscientific, or (3) asserts the existence of entities or processes for which no shred of evidence exists."[25]

Now suppose that it is true that religious beliefs cannot be justified by scientific standards of rationality. What follows from this fact? The answer the advocate of the scientific challenge seems to give is that we (rational people) should not accept any religious beliefs at all. According to Russell there is no reason even to consider any of them! But the problem with such an answer is that if being scientific is supposed to be the criterion for rejecting religious beliefs, it seems likely that the very same argument rules out *any* life-view belief whatsoever, or at least so many of them that it is not possible to have a view of life in all its essential aspects. So if we treat equal cases alike, the challenge should instead be stated as follows:

(1)   Life-view beliefs (religious and secular) must fulfill the same, or at least similar, standards of rationality as scientific beliefs in order to be considered rational.

(2)   Life-view beliefs do not fulfill the same, or at least similar, standards of rationality as scientific beliefs do.

(3)   Therefore, life-view beliefs are irrational.

Where does this leave us? The first choice we have is, of course, to stick to the challenge and claim that every view of life should be rejected and classified as irrational, because there is, for example, no or at least insufficient scientifically acceptable evidence for life-view believing. The problem with this position, as I pointed out in chapter 9, is that it seems impossible for us not to have some kind of life view. We cannot avoid having life-view beliefs and at the same time function properly as human beings. It is a practical necessity that we have beliefs of this sort. But more than that, the advocates of the scientific challenge also run the risk of becoming irrational in the axiological sense, since they are not taking into account one of our best interests or true needs—to come to grips with our existential concerns. The reason they give for withholding judgment in this area of life is that there is not sufficient scientific evidence for the answers that can be given to our existential questions, or that this type of belief cannot be evaluated by scientific standards. However, the fact that there is no scientific evidence, or at any rate not sufficient scientific evidence, for religious beliefs is not as such an argument against the rationality of holding such a view. The fact is that even if one is a strict evidentialist, like Russell, one cannot avoid having a view of life, which means that one has to reject one's scientific evidentialism in this area of life or see all human beings (*including* oneself) as irrational.

But there is another possibility open to strict evidentialists. They can say that this kind of choice or believing can be neither rational *nor* irrational. Certainly it might be necessary for us to choose a view of life, but that has nothing to do with rationality or reason. (On this point many religious believers would be in agreement with the strict evidnetialist.) Since it is not possible for us to be without a view of life we have, unfortunately, to classify the domain as *a-rational,* and say that it is merely a matter of taste: just as some people like pizza, blondes, or ice-cream, and other people do not, some of us prefer to be Christians, Buddhists, or existentialists, and others do not. So then the conclusion of the challenge (3) is replaced with:

(3*)   therefore, life-view beliefs are a-rational.

But there is, I think, a third and more satisfying alternative. What I have tried to show is that we can find *sufficient similarities* between scientific (and philosophical) and life-view belief regulations— and certainly everyday belief regulation—to be justified in claiming that the life-view practice falls within the scope of rationality (and irrationality). My claim is that we can make a rational choice between different views of life, but the standards and the reasons are somewhat different from the ones used in science. If this is correct then it is not as disturbing as some philosophers have thought that religious claims cannot meet the same standards as scientific claims, because we can still proceed in a rational manner in this field. What follows from this fact alone is at most that the choice of a religious view of life seems to be a more subjective matter than scientific theory choices, which might, of course, not be surprising considering what is at stake.

This means that at bottom the *crucial question* is not why religious beliefs are not, or cannot be, treated like scientific beliefs (or ordinary factual beliefs for that matter), but rather whether they are or are not treated in the same or similar way as *other* life-view beliefs. The issue is not "Shall we have a view of life?" but "Which view of life should we choose?" because we have to make a choice (consciously or unconsciously) no matter what. If we do not vote with our head, we vote with our feet. So the really important question is whether it is irrational to accept religious beliefs instead of secular beliefs, not whether religious believing is scientifically acceptable or not. If this is correct it means that the choice in question is not really between science and religion (as the advocate of the scientific challenge seems to tacitly assume).

2.5   THE EVIDENTIALIST CHALLENGE RECONSIDERED

The choice is not even, as some of the defenders of the evidentialist challenge seem to assume, a choice between evidence (whether scientific or not) and religion. Recall the criticism Kuhn and Lakatos deliver against Popper. Lakatos says that Popper pictures scientific rationality as a two-way confrontation between a theory and evidence, in such a way that: "(1) *a test is—or must be made—a two-cornered fight between theory and experiment so that in the final confrontation only these two face each other*; . . . However, history of science suggests that (1') test are—at least—three-cornered fights between rival theories and experiment . . ."[26] In a similar fashion life-view rationality is not a two-way confrontation between a view of life and evidence, but is—at least—a *three-way confrontation* between rival views of life and evidence (or existential experiences of resistance). But this means that we might have to modify the principle of presumption by adding one important qualification, namely that what is believed, for example, a theory or view of life, should not be abandoned, *even if* there exists evidence that goes against it, *except* in favor of a better theory or view of life. This qualification would give us the following version of the principle of presumption:

> It is rational to accept a belief only if there are no good reasons not to do so and there is no rival belief one would be better off believing.[27]

The need for this qualification becomes more clear when we define the principle with respect to a purely epistemic end (as the

evidential principle is typically defined):[28] "It is rational to accept a belief unless there are good reasons to cease thinking that it is true." The point is that even if there exists adequate counter-evidence that makes it likely that the belief is untrue, we should not abandon it *until* we have something better, a rival belief, to put in its place, given of course that we cannot withhold judgment. For example, if it were the case that Christianity was the only view of life around, or more likely,
· that we had no other view of life that was better to put in its place, and suppose that it was also the case that the evidential version of the problem of evil was successful, it would nevertheless not be irrational for a person in that situation to hold on to Christianity. This is so not because there is other evidence in favor of Christianity that outweighs the counter-evidence, but, in this case, simply because *a* view of life is better than none. Or take a more realistic example, and suppose that an individual who is Muslim and lives in a small village in Iraq finds adequate counter-evidence against Islam. Nevertheless, as long as there are no other life options for him or her, this person is rational to be—despite the counter-evidence—a Muslim.

We have seen that according to the presumptionist, rationality is first of all a function of the proper relationship between an individual, his or her believing, acting, and evaluating, and the circumstances he or she is in. It is a quality someone's doing *ought* to have. This means that the primary focus for rationality is not beliefs as such but rather the believers and their situations; and the proper question is basically what it is for a particular individual or a particular group of individuals to be rational in their believing—*given* their abilities and situations. In respect of religion, we can express this thought by saying that we are concerned not with:

(1)   arguments for or against the *existence of the sacred* (the truth or knowledge ambition),

but rather:

(2)   arguments for or against the *rationality of believing* in the existence of the sacred (the rationality ambition).

More fundamentally, we try to:

(3)   establish *appropriate standards* for evaluating the rationality of life-view believing in general and religious believing in particular.

If this is the focus of rationality, it means that we can no longer ask in an abstract fashion whether religious beliefs are rational or whether the belief that God or the sacred exists is rational. Instead we have to rephrase the question so that we are asking whether or not *believing* in God or the sacred is rational, so that we emphasize that it is always someone's believing that is rational or irrational, not the belief or proposition as such. But that is not enough, since we also have to ask *who* this somebody is who is supposed to be rational in believing in God or the sacred, or more generally, in having religious beliefs. In other words, the question we should try to answer is: *Is it rational for a particular human agent or a particular group of them to have—in their predicament—religious beliefs, or especially to believe in God or the sacred?* The question of rationality in this context is concerned with whether or not people are rationally justified in accepting or holding on to their life-view beliefs—which has as its primary aim to make possible ways of dealing with existential concerns. But that question must be distinguished from whether it is rational for human beings in our situation or predicament to have or hold a view of life. This last question is about whether we have an intellectual right to hold *any* view of life—religious or secular. The former one, on the other hand, is concerned with whether it is rational for us (or some of us) in our situation to have or hold religious rather than secular views of life. And if we accept that to try to overcome existential constraints is a rational end, then basically our question is whether or not the religious way is a rational means for a human being to adopt to reach this goal.

What I have tried to argue is that if this is the context of life-view rationality, then the human condition becomes relevant. As we have seen, what (among other things) is characteristic of our predicament is that we are finite beings with *limited cognitive resources,* and because of our predicament we have *certain needs* that we must try to fulfill. We encounter certain experiences of resistance we have to try to overcome. Because we are finite beings, every use of our cognitive resources has a certain cost. So a rational person wants to spend as little time as possible on unimportant and useless justification of beliefs, and the like. Waste of one's resources must be avoided. We do not want to clutter up our minds drawing implications or conclusions willy-nilly. Therefore, to be sane or rational must be to take into account one's situation (including one's needs) and cognitive (as well as other) resources. That is, it is rational to put forward aims that are valuable and achievable (which must at least include the satisfaction of basic human needs) and to try to find appropriate and feasible means for reaching them. So our limited cognitive resources and our location in this world are two crucial aspects of the predicament of actual human beings. This means that the question concerning our rationality in general must be: "What should a rational person or a group of them do or believe in *that* kind of situation?" and with respect to life-view rationality: "What should a rational secular or religious believer do in *that* kind of situation about life-view beliefs?" With these questions in mind let us consider the answers the evidentialist and the presumptionist give.

If we follow the *evidential policy* the proper initial attitude we should have towards our beliefs and thereby also to our belief-forming and regulating processes is one of skepticism. According to this policy, one is intellectually forbidden to believe in the sacred, or some other life-view belief, unless one has sufficient evidence to think that what one believes is true. So we should *start* by questioning our beliefs, actions, and evaluations. In matters concerning religious believing this means that rational people must be critical about their religious beliefs and investigate whether there are good reasons for believing in God or the sacred before they accept or continue to hold on to these beliefs. One needs a special reason to be rationally entitled to believe in the sacred. So rational people should first collect adequate evidence (or arguments) for or against the existence of the sacred, then estimate the combined strength of the evidence, and the result of this estimation determines whether it is rational for them to believe in the sacred or hold any religious beliefs.

The problem is, as I pointed out, that most religious people do not proceed in this way at all—as the evidentialist sadly acknowledges. Most of them have never given much thought to the arguments for or against religious beliefs. However, some evidential philosophers have thought about these matters. For example, Klemke has considered this issue, and his assessment is this:

> Thus in the usual sense of the term "evidence," there seems to be no evidence for the existence of a transcendent ultimate. Why, then, should I accept such a claim? After all, throughout the rest of my philosophical activity *and* throughout my normal, everyday activities, I constantly rely upon criteria of evidence before accepting a

cognitive claim. I emphasize that this holds for my *everyday* life and not merely for any philosophical or scientific beliefs which I may entertain.[29]

What conclusion should we draw from this? According to many evidentialists (including Klemke) the answer is that most religious people are far from being rational in their religious believing, since they do not take into account the philosopher's informed judgment on this issue. But is this really a problem for these people or is it not rather a problem for the evidential policy? What I have tried to argue is that it is first of all a problem for the latter. One way of seeing this is to focus on ordinary *secular* believers and ask, are they any better off? Probably not, since they have neither gathered and assessed the relevant arguments (they might not even know what these arguments are) nor based their rejection of religious beliefs or their acceptance of claims like "man is the measure of all things" and "reality is impersonal in character" on that assessment.

This is not only true in questions concerning views of life but is also the case in everyday believing. People in general and philosophers in particular, *pace* Klemke, do not estimate the strength of various arguments for or against every thing they do, not even all the important things. They do not do this simply because they do not have the time or cognitive resources needed. In fact they would be irrational if they took the evidentialist seriously, as the examples I gave in chapter 8 show. What I have been trying to point out is that in "real-life" situations such a way of regulating what one does is counter-productive or even destructive, since it wastes too much of our limited resources. Rather we have to act more economically. To be able to do that, according to the presumptionist, the best thing we can do is to turn the tables. That is, an individual must instead have the intellectual right to rely, at least initially, on his or her own cognitive resources and their deliverances. Our initial attitude to what we believe should not be one of skepticism but of *trust*—besides, what else can we reasonably do? If we do not rely on our cognitive equipment how can we survive or function as human beings? So, according to the *presumption policy,* religious people are intellectually permitted to accept what they believe without evidence that supports it, as long as they do not know, or should know, that sufficient counter-evidence against what they believe has emerged.

2.6   EVIDENCE, GROUNDS, AND SKEPTICISM

To say that one needs no evidential support or evidence (or arguments) for one's beliefs does not mean, as it might seem, that the beliefs are groundless, because our beliefs are grounded in the *source* or *disposition* from which they arise. This requires a bit of explanation. The presumptionist is saying first of all that we have a right to take *all* things that we find ourselves believing at face value unless we believe (or ought to believe) we have a special reason not to do so. Fundamentally, he or she claims that:

> We ought to trust our cognitive faculties and their deliverances unless reason (or experience) provides us with substantial grounds for questioning that belief.

What does this mean? Normally we suppose that our experience is a reliable guide to the external world, to those parts we can observe and to those parts we cannot directly observe. In other words, we form beliefs about the world directly and indirectly from sense experiences. We also form beliefs from the testimony of other people, from memory, from inferential processes like induction, from introspection, and so on, and in the absence of special reasons we trust them. These ways of forming beliefs have been called many different things, "sources of belief," "belief-producing mechanisms," "belief-forming dispositions," or "belief-forming processes." They are, we could say, the ways or channels through which our cognitive faculties (or human reason) deliver beliefs.

Now according to the unrestricted evidentialist or the evidential skeptic, we have no intellectual right to trust our belief-forming processes. We first have to have good reasons to think that the deliverance of our cognitive faculties is reliable, otherwise we are behaving irrationally. This means that a rational person (someone who is justified in his or her believing) must have good reasons to believe that it is true that:

(a) if I seem to remember doing an action, then I did the action (*memory beliefs*);

(b) if other people tell me that they observed an event, then the event occurred (*testimony beliefs*);

(c) if it seems to me that a certain object is before me,
     then it is before me *(perceptual beliefs);*

(d) if it seems to me that I am in a particular internal state,
     for example, I have a mild headache, then I am in that
     state (*introspective beliefs*);

(e) if it seems to me that something happens, like a tree
     is not growing well without water, then it will happen
     again (*inductive beliefs*);

(f) if it seems to me upon understanding the meaning of
     beliefs like, if John is taller than Bill, and Bill is taller
     than Sara, then John is taller than Sara, that they are
     true, then that is so (*a priori beliefs*), and so on.

Otherwise, he or she is not rationally justified in accepting these beliefs
or trusting the processes which delivered them.

But the problem (for both the skeptic and the non-skeptic) is that
we have to use reason to criticize or defend reason. We have to rely
on our belief-formation processes to be able to criticize or defend
them. Therefore, we always beg the question in our argumentation
because we assume already the truth of what we are trying to justify
or criticize. So we cannot give any adequate evidence for or against the
reliability of our belief-forming processes. The presumptionist, on the
other hand, claims that one does not need to justify these processes
to be rational in believing in them and the good they deliver. They
and what they deliver are presumed to be innocent until proven guilty.
These processes and their deliverences do not first need to be justified
(given good reasons for) before it is rational for us to believe in them.
It is rational, at least initially, to believe what our experience (or belief-
forming processes) leads us to believe.

The foundational evidentialist agrees partly with the presumptionist on this matter, but claims that some of the beliefs delivered
by these processes need not to be supported by evidence, namely
the ones that are properly basic. Foundational evidentialists disagree,
as we have seen, about which beliefs can be classified as properly
basic, but most of them would probably agree that there are, at least,
beliefs that are evident to the senses and beliefs that are self-evident
which would qualify as properly basic. So according to them a person
is rational in accepting a given belief only if that belief is either a

properly basic belief or if it can be shown (by acceptable methods of inference) to be evidentially supported by properly basic beliefs or by other already justified beliefs.

Now, one way of understanding presumptionism is to see it as a rejection of the foundational evidentialist's claim that only properly basic beliefs need no evidential support. Instead the presumptionist claims that rational people should treat *all* their beliefs as "properly basic" ones (in the sense that they do not require evidential support) until special reasons for not doing so have emerged. The presumption of rationality should be expanded to all the beliefs an agent holds. That our belief-forming processes are reliable is nothing we can prove (or disprove for that matter), since they might totally mislead us. But the presumptionist claims that even if that is possible, rational people should *bet* on the general trustworthiness of their belief-forming processes and their deliverances. What else can we reasonably do except trust the only light we have, however weak its light might be? As Rescher points out:

> [the trust's] rationale is that without it we remove the basis on which alone creatures such as ourselves can confidently live a life of effective thought and action. In such cases, pragmatic rationality urges us to gamble on trust in reason, not because it cannot fail us, but because in so doing little is to be lost and much to be gained.[30]

This means that it is *first* in situations of resistance a rational person should start to qualify this initial trust in his or her beliefs and their sources, and *only* then. And it is how a person reacts to these anomalies or defeaters that determines whether he or she is rational in his or her belief-regulation.

But notice that the presumptionist expands this presumption to cover all our beliefs not out of indifference, pure generosity, or assumed laziness. The reason is that rationality must be realistic in its demands. A rationality that cannot be implemented by us in our situation is totally pointless. Because the agents of rationality are human beings who live on this earth, we should accept this general presumption (concerning their believing). If our resources had been greater (like, for example, Superman's) or if our situation had been different (for instance, if we have had unlimited time at our disposal), *then* we could reasonably have asked for more, for example, that people always ought to have adequate evidence for their beliefs.

Rationality is a matter of cognitive economy, to adjust one's belief-regulation to one's resources and predicament.[31]

2.7   IRRATIONALITY

Before we go on and inquire more deeply what consequences presumptionism has for life-view rationality, we need to specify in what ways it is possible to be irrational on this account. How can one be irrational on the presumptionist account, and in particular, how can one be irrational in one's religious or secular life-view believing? Generally speaking, people are *irrational* if they violate or fail to meet their intellectual obligations. According to the evidentialist, this means that someone is irrational who does not have good reasons for his or her beliefs, actions, and evaluations. The presumptionist, on the other hand, claims that one is irrational not if one fails to have good reasons for what one does, but if one fails to take into account things that count against what one does.

If rationality is a matter of doing (believing, acting, and evaluating) what we intellectually ought to do and can realistically manage to do, so that in our circumstances we choose appropriate ends and means to achieve these ends, then it is possible, I will claim, to be irrational in at least three different ways: in respect to our ends, means, and situation. Let us start with the last of these.

What I have tried to emphasize is that the act of believing is always done by somebody, and that somebody has certain resources and is always in a particular situation. Therefore, rational individuals must take into account their individual resources and the environment they live in when they are doing something. So people can be irrational in the sense that what they want to do does not stand in (any reasonable) proportion to their *resources* or the *situation* they are in, and they ought to be aware of this. This might happen when somebody, for example, overestimates the time, cognitive ability, economical resources he or she has, or misrepresents the nature of the natural or the social world in which he or she lives. For instance, this happens when somebody tries to swim across the Atlantic Ocean. When some philosophers demand that they and everybody else ought to have good reasons for everything they believe, they risk being irrational in this sense, since they do not take into account their and our internal and external environment as they should. And of course, somebody who tries to follow their advice runs the same risk. People can be irrational in the sense of not adjusting their belief-regulation to their constitution and predicament.

A second way people can be irrational occurs when they adopt a *means* that they ought to know does not satisfy their ends, when, for example, an individual's aim is to pass the final exam but he or she studies only ten minutes a day.

A last way of being irrational happens when people adopt *ends* that they desire but which go against their real interests, and they ought to be aware of this. For example, when somebody just wants to have peace of mind, when he or she ought to know that such a narrow non-epistemic end goes against his or her best interest most of the time. Or individuals live irrationally if they satisfy desires (for instance, the desire to be extremely drunk everyday) that are harmful to their health in the long run. But the life-view skeptics also run the risk of being irrational in this sense, when they claim that there is insufficient evidence for life-view believing and that consequently we should not accept any beliefs of this sort, since the skeptics are not taking into account our existential interests, one of our true needs, and therefore they threaten their and our well-being.

So, on the presumptionist account, an individual or a group of them can be irrational in the following ways:

1. People can be irrational in the sense that they do not take into account their *resources* and *predicament* when they are doing (or want to do) something.
2. People can be irrational in what they are doing (or want to do) in the sense of adopting unsuitable *means* for the ends they are trying to satisfy.
3. People can be irrational in what they are doing (or want to do) in the sense of adopting *ends* unsuitable to their needs.

Let us now ask what consequences this understanding of irrationality has when it comes to religious believing.

2.8   THE PRESUMPTIONIST CHALLENGE TO RELIGIOUS BELIEVING

Does presumptionism include any challenge to religious belief? Yes, indeed it does. But the challenge is not only against religious beliefs but against all life-beliefs. And it is not strictly speaking a challenge directed against beliefs but rather towards believing—the life-view believing of human agents. The *presumptionist challenge to life-view believing* consists in the demand that:

> It is rational to accept a life-view belief only if there are no good reasons not to do so and there is no rival belief one would be better off believing.

If we want to know when religious believers are rational, this means that it is rational to accept religious beliefs only so long as there is not sufficient reason to cease from doing so. They might be, however, rational to hold on to them even then, if there are no better rival views of life available which they ought to be aware of. Consequently, to be rational in holding religious beliefs, religious people do not need evidence that supports these beliefs. That is, religious believers do not need to hold them on the (evidential) basis of *other* beliefs that they are rationally entitled to hold. This is so not because religious beliefs have a special epistemic status (for example, being properly basic beliefs, or being a special type of perceptional beliefs, or the like)[32] but because of a *presumption* a human agent is granted in favor of all his or her beliefs, that implies that those beliefs should all be treated as intellectually innocent until proven guilty. People are rationally justified in continuing to believe what they believe as long as they have no special reason to stop accepting those beliefs. This means that the evidentialist's argument for the irrationality of religious belief loses much of its force. For example it is not the case, as Kenny thinks, that belief in God is not rational unless natural theology can be carried out successfully (that is, sufficient evidence can be given for the truth of this belief), because the view of rationality he presupposes violates the axiom of reasonable demand.[33]

But *when* can we say that religious believers are irrational? Generally speaking, they are irrational when they fail to meet the demands of presumptionism. This happens, for example, when Christian fundamentalists claim that (1) the Bible is "inerrant," that is, it is free from all factual errors of any type (scientific, historical, doctrinal, or the like), and that (2) any view or literary analysis of the Bible which yields results in conflict with the first claim must be rejected.[34] They are irrational not primarily because there is sufficient evidence against the first claim, but because they do not let *anything* at all count against their view of the Bible (which is the result of the conjunction of (1) and (2))—and they ought to be aware of this. It is not that they misjudge the counter-evidence but that it is impossible even in principle for defeaters to arise against their belief. If they are wrong, they can never (even in principle) find that out. And such believing is irrational since it does not satisfy the requirements of the principle of presumption.

However, there are religious people who are rationally justified in accepting the first claim (that the Bible is inerrant), that is, people who are with respect to this belief doing what can rightly be demanded of them. But professional Christian theologians or philosophers are hardly rational in so believing, since there is sufficient counter-evidence against this claim, and they should—given their cognitive resources and predicament—be aware of that. They are not doing what can reasonably be demanded of them, therefore their believing is in this sense irrational. Such fundamentalists do not satisfy the demands of presumptionism. Religious people are irrational any time they continue to hold on to a religious belief when sufficient reasons against it have arisen.

2.9   THE END OF THE RATIONALITY DEBATE

In the end the crucial question is not, I have claimed, whether people can rationally believe in God or some other religious beliefs, because the answer is clearly "Yes, they can." The "unfriendly atheist"—in Rowe's terminology, or the "unfriendly secular believer," that is, the secular believer that thinks that no one is rationally justified in believing in God or the sacred, is wrong. But the very opposite is of course just as true, a secular believer can be rational in not believing in God or some other religious beliefs. The unfriendly theist or more generally, the unfriendly religious believer—the religious believer who thinks that no one is rationally justified in not believing in God or the sacred—is also wrong.

Our argument has led us to believe that the most reasonable position to adopt on this issue is either to be a friendly secular believer (the secular believer who thinks that some religious believers are rationally entitled to believe in God or the sacred) or a friendly religious believer (the religious believer who thinks that some secular believers are rationally entitled not to believe in God or the sacred). Of course, as Rowe points out:

If no one can be rationally justified in believing a false proposition then friendly atheism is a paradoxical, if not incoherent position. But surely the truth of a belief is not a necessary condition of someone's being rationally justified in having that belief. So in holding that someone is rationally justified in believing that the theistic God exists, the friendly atheist is not committed to thinking that the theist has a true belief. What he is committed to is that the theist has rational grounds for his belief, a belief the atheist rejects and is convinced he is rationally justified in rejecting.[35]

And as we have seen in chapter 8, the notions of rationality and truth do not entail one another. What a person believes may be rational but false, or irrational but true. Therefore, there is nothing paradoxial or incoherent in being a friendly secular or religious believer.

What does it mean that a secular or religious believer is rationally entitled to disbelieve (respectively believe) in God or the sacred? It means that they are not violating any of their intellectual duties. They are doing what can reasonably be demanded of them with respect to the regulation of their life-view beliefs. Of course there are still a lot of religious and secular believers who are irrational, people who violate their intellectual responsibilities. They are not modifying or giving up their religious or secular beliefs when sufficient counter-evidence has emerged. These people stick to their beliefs even when there are good reasons to cease believing them and there is a better alternative present that they ought to be aware of. But that is another matter, and it does not count against the fact that there are (and have always been) people who are rational religious believers. *The debate of whether people actually are rational in believing in God is over!* A lot of people are within their intellectual rights in accepting or holding on to life-view beliefs in general, and religious beliefs in particular.

Therefore, it is necessary to distinguish between questions of *rationality* (concerned with when a person or a group of persons are entitled to believe what they believe) and of *justification* (concerned with when a person or a group of persons have provided sufficient grounds for a belief to render it generally acceptable). The latter are questions which deal with the degree to which one can justify religious and secular beliefs. Can any life-view belief be justified to such a degree that it should be generally acceptable or be considered a part of our body of knowledge? If that is so, when are sufficient grounds provided that should convince other neutral or hostile people? What kinds of agreements can be reached among people when it comes to their ultimate commitments, their views of life? Another related question is whether a particular religious or secular belief is true or constitutes knowledge—the question of *warrant* (concerned with when a person's true believing constitutes knowledge).[36]

These questions of justification and warrant are indeed important issues since normally, I take it, we want not only to be rational in our believing, but also to know if what we believe is true or false (warrant) and convince other people that what we believe is the right thing to believe (justification). And here it is possible to talk on a more abstract and universal level, since truth and knowledge are not person-relative notions—at least not in the same way that rational belief is. In fact, I think that many philosophers and theologians are actually involved in this project, but they are not sufficiently aware of the distinction between rationality and justification (and warrant). They too often confuse the following questions:

(1)   What arguments can be given for or against the existence of the sacred or the truth of any other religious belief?

(2)   What arguments can be given for or against the rationality of believing in the existence of the sacred or holding any other religous belief?

A second confusion in the current discussion of religious rationality, which might be one reason why many philosophers commit the first one, arises, as we have seen, when somebody thinks that rationality is a property a belief or proposition can have or lack, in the same way a belief or proposition can have the property of being true or false. Because of this understanding of the locus of rationality they tend not to see the difference between the following two questions:

(3)   When is a belief p rational?

(4)   When is an agent rational in believing p?

This happens when philosophers ask, as we saw in chapter 4, "whether the argument from evil can establish the irrationality of religious belief . . ."[37] and when philosophers like Mackie answer the

question by claiming that "Here it can be shown, not that religious beliefs lack rational support, but that they are positively irrational . . ."[38]
Now suppose Mackie or any other natural atheologian is quite successful in arguing this. According to him, the following set of beliefs
is contradictory and therefore irrational: God is omnipotent; God is
wholly good; and yet evil exists. But now assume, which seems very
likely, that many theists are not, and cannot reasonably be blamed for
not being, aware of Mackie's Master Argument; nevertheless, they are
doing as well in their theistic believing as can rightly be demanded of
them with respect to rationality. The astonishing conclusion seems to
be that this group of people is *rational in accepting an irrational set of
beliefs!* But this is just confusing. What instead should have followed,
given that we accept the distinction between question (1) and (2), is
that Mackie has succeeded in showing that this set of religious beliefs
is probably *inconsistent* and that it is therefore unlikely that the set is
true. In other words, he should be seen as being primarily involved
in the project of giving an answer to the first question.

So to ask whether religious belief is rational is a confused or
misleading way of stating the issue of religious rationality. In fact,
question (3) could be answered *only* if all people were in the same
situation—had the same cognitive resources and training, the same
access to relevant evidence or counter-evidence, and the like. But
since not all people are even close to being in the same situation in
this sense the only really meaningful question we can ask is the second
one; or we can interpret (3), as we previously did, as a question about
what standards it is rational for people to use to govern their believing.

However, notice the difference between question (1) above, and
the following question:

(5)   What arguments can be given for or against why peo-
      ple should be religious believers?

The only good reasons that can be given to answer question (1) are
epistemic reasons, since the question concerns whether it is *true* that
the sacred exists (a purely epistemic end). But that is not true of question (5), because when we try to argue why people should or should
not be religious believers ends other than purely epistemic ones are
clearly relevant. Whether religious beliefs are true is important, but
it is also important whether being a religious believer helps one to
deal with existential constraints, live a morally good life, and so on.

Just as questions concerning life-view rationality cannot be reduced to epistemic rationality, questions concerning life-view justification cannot be reduced to epistemic justification. (Therefore it might be of importance to distinguish between questions of justification and warrant in philosophy of religion, because warrant is by definition purely epistemic.) Because of our constitution and predicament we have real interests other than trying to possess as many true beliefs as possible and to eliminate as many false ones as possible.

What has come to an end is, at least, the traditional issue concerning whether people actually are rational in believing in God, since the answer to that question should/must be affirmative. But there is unfortunately another problem left for religious believers (and to some extent also for secular believers), that seriously threatens the rationality of their believing, and that is the degree of commitment that is often present in this kind of believing. This is so because it is one thing to be entitled to accept a belief, quite another thing to be entitled to believe with a particular strength.

3.   Religious Commitment and Rationality

One can distinguish three issues when it comes to believing: *what* one believes, *why* one believes, and *how* one believes. We have seen that what one believes (the content or, in particular, the kind of belief) is of importance for rationality, though the focus in this study has mainly been on why one believes (the reasons or grounds for the beliefs accepted). But there is also a third aspect that is relevant for rational believing, namely with what *strength* (the degree of commitment) one accepts the beliefs held, or what attitude one adopts towards what is believed—how one believes. Here the issue is not primarily whether an agent needs to have good reasons for being rational in accepting a belief or not, but concerns *how strongly* a rational agent is entitled to hold a belief.

Many people have pointed out that the religious way of holding belief ("faith" in religious terminology) is different from the way we normally hold what we believe. Religious believers typically believe in God no matter what happens. It is this "no-matter-what-happens-mentality" that bothers non-religious people, and rightly so I think.

And it is here that the main problem concerning the rationality of religious believing lies. The *challenge to religious believing* in this context is not that it is based on insufficient evidence, but that the strength with which the religious believer holds these beliefs seems to be unreasonable. Gutting writes: "even if believers properly understand an article of their faith, they may assent to it in an inappropriate way. . . . I shall argue that the self-misunderstanding of traditional religions is most apparent in their insistence on decisive assent to claims that are not worthy of such assent when given their traditional interpretations."[39]

Gutting here contrasts two different types of assents, *decisive* and *interim assent*. He defines them in the following way: "Roughly, decisive assent denies the epistemic need for further discussion of the claim assented to, whereas interim assent acknowledges such a need."[40] Gutting tries to show that for many religious beliefs it is rational to give only interim assent because their evidential support is so weak. More generally, this tentativist challenge to religious belief consists in the claim that:

> even if there is sufficient evidence, or if evidence is not necessary, to support religious belief, these beliefs ought not to be held *as firmly* as religious people normally do.

An assumption of this challenge is that one can hold the same belief with different degrees of acceptance (or firmness, commitment, confidence, assent, and the like), and different beliefs with the same degree of acceptance. This is a reasonable assumption, at least, I do not find it questionable. So acceptance of a belief can be of different degrees, and we can distinguish at least two sorts of acceptance, full acceptance and more tentative acceptance.[41] We could say that a belief is *tentatively accepted* when one thinks there is a need to investigate it further, but one is willing to use it as a starting-point (a working hypothesis) for something one is doing. This further inquiry might be done in different ways. One is actively (or constantly) looking for defeaters (counter-evidence) of one view, or one is actively searching for justifiers (evidence) of it, or both. On the other hand, a belief is *fully accepted* when one thinks it is true and that there is no need to investigate it further, or no need to doubt its credibility. And we can add that a belief is *not accepted* when one thinks it is false or when, at least, one is not willing to use it as a starting-point (a working hypothesis) for something one is doing.

According to the presumptionist, it is rational to accept a belief unless there are sufficient reasons to cease from accepting it and there is a better alternative available. But *what* degree of acceptance ought to be rationally acceptable? If one is justified in believing *p* because one satisfies the principle of presumption, with what degree of assent is one permitted to hold *p*? Before we try to answer that, let us recall what we have said so far on this issue. Popper claims that it is not rational for a person to accept any scientific hypothesis fully. If we generalize this demand, it means that all beliefs should be only tentatively accepted (the principle of tentativity). One should never stop actively looking for defeaters of one's beliefs. According to classical evidentialists like Locke and Hume, one's acceptance of a belief should always stand in proportion to the strength of the supporting evidence (the proportionality principle). But this means that on this account, *if* the evidence supporting a belief is strong one might be rationally justified in fully accepting that belief. So it is possible to hold religious beliefs with full acceptance, given that one can marshall strong reasons that support them—which indeed some religious believers think is possible. In other words, one way of stating evidentialism is:

> One is rational in continuing *fully* to accept a (important non-basic) belief only if there is *strong* evidence that supports it.

And consequently:

> One is rational in continuing *tentatively* to accept a (important non-basic) belief only if there is *some* evidence that supports it.

However, we noticed in chapter 5 that a commitment to a belief that exceeds the evidence for it is not necessarily irrational, because without this kind of commitment progress in science would not be possible (or anywhere else for that matter). And this is a main reason why we should reject not only the principle of tentativity but also the proportionality principle.

But even granted that the commitment may exceed the evidence, the evidence underlying religious beliefs seems to many to be, at best, weak (that is, it is not only possible but fairly likely that religious beliefs are false), and therefore the only rational degree of acceptance must be *less than full*. That is, to be rational in accepting them religious believers must actively continue the inquiry concerning the truth of these beliefs. This demand seems to be even more reasonable on a presumptionist account, in which it is rational to accept religious beliefs without evidence (the support of other beliefs) on the basis of a presumption only. Since no evidence is needed (which, of course, does not mean that there is none) to support religious beliefs for a person to be rational in accepting them (given that there is no counter-evidence present that he or she ought to be aware of), a full acceptance of them can hardly, it seems, be justified. Gutting claims that this kind of position "may justify holding beliefs with a religious content, but it will not justify holding them in a religious way."[42] That is, presumptionism may justify a tentative, but not a full, acceptance of religious beliefs. According to such criticism, the only reasonable version of presumptionism is one that accepts only a *tentative principle of presumption:*

> One is rational in *tentatively* accepting a belief unless there are good reasons to cease from doing that and there is no better alternative available.

This would mean, for example, that someone who believes in the sacred is rational only in tentatively accepting that belief. A rational religious believer is then a person who thinks that there is a need to further (actively) investigate if the belief in the sacred is true, but despite this believes in the sacred and is willing to use it as a starting-point (a working hypothesis) for his or her way of living. But if this is all a religious believer who accepts religious belief on the basis of a presumption is granted, then those religious believers who think that their beliefs in the sacred are true and that they need not be questioned are irrational. They are holding their religious beliefs too firmly. But why should they not be allowed fully to accept their beliefs? What they seem to need in order to be rational in their religious believing is a defense of a *principle of full presumption:*

> One is rational in *fully* accepting a belief unless there are good reasons to cease from accepting it or, at least,

cease from accepting it fully, and there is no better alternative available.

Can this version of the principle be acceptable? Can a person be rational who fully accepts a belief even though it is not held on evidence—on the basis of other beliefs of his or her? I think the answer is yes, and for several reasons. One reason is that tentative acceptance is not easy. The *cognitive cost* of this kind of acceptance is much higher than that of full acceptance of beliefs, and this is probably the reason why people normally tend to accept what they believe fully rather than tentatively. As Harman points out, it takes a certain degree of sophistication and training to be able to investigate an issue by only tentatively accepting various beliefs. This is so because when one only tentatively accepts something one needs to keep in mind which tentatively accepted claims depend on others. One must try to remember what evidence there is for or against various possible outcomes of the issue. Until the investigation is completed one needs to keep a record of justifiers for various possible conclusions, possible defeaters of the justifiers, defeaters of those defeaters, and so on. Harman illustrates this by considering the situation of jurors in a trial, a situation in which we can easily imagine what effort (cognitive input) is needed for the pursuit of tentative acceptance of various claims. He concludes by saying:

> If one had unlimited powers of record keeping and an unlimited ability to survey ever more complex structures of argument, replies, rebuttals, and so on, it would be rational always to accept things only tentatively as working hypotheses never ending inquiry. But since one does not have such unlimited powers of record keeping and has a quite limited ability to survey reasons and arguments, one is forced to limit the amount of inquiry in which one is engaged and one must fully accept most of the conclusions one accepts, thereby ending inquiry. Tentative acceptance must remain a special case of acceptance. It cannot be the general rule.[43]

So if we take into account the fact that we have limited cognitive resources there is nothing irrational or strange in finding it difficult in general to accept things only tentatively, and we quickly convert this type of acceptance of various beliefs into full acceptance. It is a matter of cognitive economy to adjust how one believes to one's resources.

Another related reason is that we can give examples where we find it entirely appropriate, on the basis of a presumption, fully to accept a belief. Consider, for instance, the following two situations. Suppose somebody I have never seen before tells me that if I continue this road four blocks and then turn left I can see the bus station. Typically, in the absence of special reasons, we accept this kind of belief fully, that is, we think it is true and we do not think that we have to investigate it further. Or somebody is begging for food and a complete stranger gives him or her some bread, again in the absence of special reasons, the beggar thinks that the bread is all right and eats it. But according to the advocate of a strictly tentative principle of presumption these people are not behaving rationally. This goes, I think, strongly against our intuitions.

Perhaps the reason why many philosophers have argued so strongly for only tentative acceptance is that they tend to confuse *full* and *dogmatic* acceptance. For instance, Popper contrasts a critical (or tentative) attitude with a dogmatic one.[44] But cannot a person who fully accepts (or is firmly committed to) a belief rationally assess that belief? Does full acceptance entail *dogmatic acceptance*, that is, a disregard for future counter-evidence of what is believed? This can hardly be the case, since the assumption that there is no need to investigate a belief may be challenged and an inquiry may start. The point the presumptionist wants to make is that since a constant questioning is not desirable or even irrational (it wastes too much of our limited cognitive resources), a special reason is needed before the believer can be required to start an inquiry. Even if one thinks, at present, that a continuing reflection on the truth of a belief is unnecessary, that does not mean that it cannot be revised or rejected. Full acceptance is compatible with an openness to criticism.

The third reason is directly connected to religious believing. The character of the purported object of religious belief and the function of religious believing also affect what level of acceptance one ought to adopt toward them. If one only tentatively accepts a religious view of life it seems difficult to perform religious acts in the way that is required. It is not that this is impossible, since full acceptance is not a necessary condition of qualifying as a religious believer.[45] Only a person who does not believe in the sacred and is not willing to act on these beliefs would not qualify. In fact I think the number of tentative believers is constantly increasing, at least, in Western countries.[46] But this is not a new phenomenon, already in the Old Testament we can read about tentative believers:

> Some of the ancient Israelites were inclined to reason thus: "It seems pretty likely that our God, Yahweh, really is the one who is running the show, so by all means let's worship him, 'pay our dues,' make the appropriate sacrifices, and so on. Still, it is also true that Baal, the God of the Canaanites, has some pretty impressive credentials of his own. So, the smart thing to do is to hedge our bets a little— we will sacrifice to Yahweh, all right, but we will also do what we can to keep on the right side of Baal—just in case."[47]

Of course, according to these texts, Yahweh was not happy with this way of believing, nor are most defenders of religious views of life, but that is another matter. And by the way, these people were perhaps more sincere in their believing than this quotation seems to suggest.

However, to clarify the problem with a tentative attitude in religious believing let me illustrate by taking an example from another area of life: My love of my wife. The presumptionist thinks that, in the absence of any special reasons to believe the contrary, I am rational in believing that she loves me. The way it appears to be to me is sufficient. But the tentative principle of presumption allows me to accept that belief only if I actively try to find reasons that would falsify it. But this is deeply problematic since actively seeking such falsifying reasons seems to destroy the very foundation necessary for a loving relationship to take place—it undermines the trust and loyalty that must exist between two lovers. So at least in this area of life such tentative attitudes seem unreasonable, even destructive. This example is important for understanding religious believing since belief in human beings provides us with an analogy to what belief in the sacred is all about. To believe in the sacred is not, at least in theistic faith, just a matter of mentally assenting to a set of propositions, but of *trusting* the Divine reality. So the character and intentional object of religious belief makes full acceptance desirable and perhaps even necessary. And this is the reason, I think, religious people normally react so strongly against a tentative acceptance of faith, since in one respect it shows that one actually lacks faith. It seems to undermine the very foundation necessary for a relationship of trust between the religious believer and God.

But often religious believers are not satisfied with even full acceptance, since they say that they would believe in the sacred come what may or no matter what happened. This is, I will claim, the real problem for religious believers in matters concerning rationality: they sometimes tend toward *a dogmatic attitude or acceptance— nothing whatsoever can count against their acceptance of religious belief.* Sometimes the argument that is given (if any!) for this religious attitude is the same one as I directed against the application of a principle of tentative presumption to religious practice. But this argument is not convincing when it is directed against an application of the principle of full presumption. To see why, let us once again consider my love of my wife. A full acceptance of that belief does allow that it is nevertheless possible that she does not love me and that if there are special reasons to doubt this, I would start an inquiry. Does this means that I am less convinced of my wife's love? By no means, since realizing that I could be wrong does not mean that I am any less convinced that I am right! On the contrary, if this were not possible then there would be no way for me to determine if she actually loves me or if I am just fooling myself. The same is true, I think, of belief in the sacred. Belief in the sacred, which includes trusting the Divine reality, is not threatened by the fact that it is possible that it is wrong. It is like my belief in my wife's love, anyone is welcome—if they like—to try to find reasons to doubt it, since I am certain that they will actually fail, and so can and should it also be for the rational religious believer.

But why then do so many religious people often dogmatically accept their religious beliefs? Can we find some kind of explanation? I think that the nature of the intentional object of religious faith can give us a clue to why this is so. If the intentional object of religious faith is typically thought to be, as I argued in the last chapter, the most perfect possible reality (it is so great that we can conceive of nothing greater), then it is likely that religious people in experiencing this reality should be so overwhelmed by it that even the thought that this reality would not be real appears to be unthinkable. In fact this is what many religious believers report: Augustine says, "Far off, I heard your voice saying *I am the God who IS* . . . and at once I had no cause to doubt. I might more easily have doubted that I was alive than that Truth had being."[48] Mahatma Gandhi reports: "Often in my progress I have had faint glimpses of the Absolute Truth, God, and daily the conviction is growing upon me that He alone is real and all else is unreal." Westphal makes the following comment to these claims: "They [religious experiences] are based on a sense of the presence of something that is more real than I myself and the world of my immediate experience. I become what is relative, and in relation to this something I find myself to be suddenly doubtful, less real and not definitely there."[49]

Westphal characterizes these phenomena as experiences of "ontological inadequacy." What should we make of this? I think that it is possible that religious people who experience the sacred in this overwhelming way might, after all, be rational in believing that it is unthinkable that the sacred would not be real, *but* only in a particular cultural setting. To see why, consider an analogy. People normally believe that it is unthinkable that there is no external world. If you question this they look at you as if you were mad. Why should they be considered rational, which I think they should, in having this attitude? One reason might be that there is nobody in their environment of whom they ought to be aware and take seriously who thinks anything else.

In a similar fashion religious people living in a *monocentric culture*—that is, a culture in which there is no, or almost no, knowledge of or acquaintance with other views of life—might be rational in believing that it is unthinkable that their belief in the sacred could possibly be wrong. This is so because in such a cultural setting nobody has even thought that these things could have been different. For example, some of the believers in the so called primitive religions may be or have been in such a situation. But notice that this situation comes to an end as soon as these people meet and start to interact with other people with a different view of life. So all that is needed for these people to be irrational in dogmatically accepting their religious beliefs, is other people with different religious or secular beliefs. All that is required is a first degree of *secularization*. This occurs when people start realizing that they have a religion. They realize this because they are beginning to understand that one could actually have another view of life different from their own. In such a culture they have experiences of resistance, and in them possible defeaters could be found. Therefore, full acceptance is all a rational religious believer can be granted—despite these experiences of ontological inadequacy— in a *monopolitic culture* (one in which there is knowledge of or acquaintance with other views of life, but in which only one view of life is permitted to function), and in particular in a *pluralistic culture* (that is, a culture in which there exist different views of life and they are allowed to compete with each other).[50]

To sum up, the challenge directed against how religious beliefs are held was that: even if there is sufficient evidence, or in particular, if evidence is not necessary to support religious beliefs, these beliefs ought not to be held as firmly as religious people hold them. Now we can see that this challenge should be rejected if the advocates of it mean by "being held too firmly" that religious beliefs are fully accepted. But if they mean rather that the beliefs are dogmatically accepted they have a case, especially, in a pluralistic culture.

What we have so far *assumed* in our discussion of rationality is that it is possible to criticize what is going on in a practice from the outside—by somebody who is not involved in that kind of activity or believing. But this assumption is not unproblematic and has been challenged by many philosophers and theologians. What they all have in common is, roughly, that they deny the possibility of such criticism, because the only form of rationality available, according to them, is *practice-internal rationality*. To this issue we must now turn in more detail.

4

11

Contextualism and Human Practices

What has been of great importance for my discussion and classification of different models of rationality is the distinction introduced in chapter one: between the formal, practice-oriented, and social approaches to philosophy. So far we have discussed only the first two of these in detail, and I have been criticizing, in particular, formal—but to some extent also social—evidentialism (and thereby much of the contemporary discussion of rationality in philosophy of religion) for adopting too much of a formal approach. Now it is time to turn our attention toward the other end of this spectrum. But first a short summary of our way towards this end of the scale.

I construed formal evidentialism as an example of a formal approach to philosophy applied to questions of rationality. This means that formal evidentialists typically understand the issue of rationality as a matter of logic and conceptual analysis only. Standards of rationality can be formulated independently of the subject matter—science, religion, everyday life, and the like. These philosophers strive toward establishing a conception of rationality which would be appropriate for any reasoning being, which would be good no matter what practice the agent was involved in, and no matter what the world is like. The logic of rationality or the conceptual truths about rationality are applicable universally in any world.

Practice-oriented philosophers (both social evidentialists and presumptionists) question whether such an idealized conception of rationality really can apply to us. According to them (particularly the presumptionist), such ideals must always be grounded in facts about the agent of rationality. In this case facts about human beings, how beings like us function and how beings like us could attain our epistemic and non-epistemic ends in a world like ours, are of great relevance. What we need is a conception of rationality that is applicable to limited

301

creatures like us, and that would be effective in the actual world. A conception that allows for human limitations but can still view our behaving as rational or irrational—within that framework. This means that a conceptual analysis (*a priori* considerations) is not sufficient for completing this task, since we also need access to certain empirical facts (*a posterior* considerations).

So the advocates of the formal approach do not think it is necessary to pay any serious attention to the actual agents of rationality or the actual practices of rationality to be able to develop an appropriate model of rationality. The standards for rationality are *epistemically independent* of the actual agents and the actual practices the agents are involved in. The presumptionists, on the other hand, deny this and claim that empirical studies of our actual practices play a central role in developing an appropriate model of rationality. According to them standards of rationality are practice-dependent, that is, they are epistemically dependent on, but not exhausted by, the actual practices.

The advocates of the social approach (the contextualists) agree with the presumptionists in much of their criticism of the formal approach. But the contextualists want to go even further and claim that standards for rationality are not only practice-dependent, they are *practice-determined*. The ultimate epistemic authority when it comes to the formulation of the standards for and application of rationality is the participants of a practice themselves. The only form of rationality available is *practice-internal rationality*.

1. The Contextual Principle

I will in what follows try to develop this third approach to philosophy. When it is applied to questions of rationality, I shall call it the *contextual model of rationality* (or just *contextualism*). My aim will be to try to specify what counts for and what counts against this model, and also to determine what consequences it has for life-view rationality. In doing this I will try to show why I think we should reject contextualism and instead adopt some version of presumptionism. But even though I will claim that we should reject it as an adequate model of rationality, there are elements in it we must be able to take into account and incorporate within presumptionism. The contextual model is not new, but recently some version of it has become more and more popular because of the growing realization among scholars of all kinds that there is *a social and historical character to all kinds of reasoning—scientific included*. Hollis and Lukes give the following report from the frontiers:

> Recent upheavals in the philosophy of science have turned the historian or sociologist of science into something of an anthropologist, an explorer of alien cultures. It is as if scientific paradigms and theoretical frameworks were strung out in time like islands across an archipelago. Other minds, other cultures, other languages and other theoretical schemes call for understanding from within. Seen from within, they make us doubt whether there is anything universal under the sun. This doubt is also a challenge to the very idea of a single world. Is not the world, as interpreted in our scheme of things, but one of many? Are not our forms of reasoning and tests of truth as parochial as any other?[1]

Even though many contextualists are not ready to go as far as this quotation seems to allow, it indicates one of the basic themes of contextualism: *that rationality (and if one wants to add: truth, reality and the like) is always bound to a practice, paradigm, conceptual scheme, form of life, or the like*. There is no universal rationality, since rationality is always practice-bound. But despite this beliefs can be rational or irrational, not universally but locally. Religious beliefs and other kinds of beliefs can be rational, but the standards of rationality are embedded in the way of life to which the belief in question belongs. We can express this basic thesis (let us call it the "contextual principle") in the following way:

> *The Contextual Principle:* What is rational or irrational can be determined only internally, from within a context (practice); there exist no context-independent standards of rationality.

To put the point in a slightly different way, the main thesis is that (*a*) each practice has its own standards of rationality, and that (*b*) there is no independent basis for deciding whether one practice is more rational than another. The contextual principle, or some part of it, has been expressed and developed in many different ways by sociologists, philosophers, and theologians. Let me just quote some of these thinkers who can be classified as being more or less contextualist in their approach. MacIntyre claims:

> Each tradition can at each stage of its development provide rational justification for its central theses in its own terms, employing the concepts and standards by which it defines itself, but there is no set of independent standards of rational justification by appeal to which the issues between contending traditions can be decided.[2]

Hesse writes that "'rules of argument and criteria of truth are internal to a social system', that 'truth' and 'rationality' are to be redefined as 'internal to given societies' . . ."[3] According to Stark: "Every society has its own particular view of reality, its own universe of thought, indeed its own universe of truth."[4] And lastly, Bernstein describes a version of contextualism, when he writes that:

> Those concepts that philosophers have taken to be the most fundamental—whether it is the concept of rationality, truth, reality, right, the good, or norms—we are forced to recognize that in the final analysis all such concepts must be understood as relative to a specific conceptual scheme, theoretical framework, paradigm, form of life, society, or culture.[5]

As the quotations show, many contextualists do not restrict the contextual principles just to rationality, they also apply it to notions like truth, reality, and knowledge. These quotations also indicate that *what* rationality is supposed to be internal to varies. According to Hesse, rationality is internal to social systems, according to MacIntyre, to traditions. According to still other contextualists, rationality is internal to forms of life, language-games, paradigms, and so on. To avoid needless repetition I earlier introduced the term "practice" as an umbrella concept, to cover all these different specifications of what particular domains the contextualists might have in mind. I do this not only for that reason, but also because it is important to see that these accounts are all species of the same model of rationality. This means that we need not describe and assess all versions of contextualism. What we need to do is, first of all, to try to specify the features that all versions of contextualism have in common and then critically assess these features.

All contextualists share the view that rationality is *internal* to some practice, though they do not agree upon the specifications of practices to which rationality is internal. So the first thing we have to do is to distinguish between rationality that is internal and external to a practice. Something like the following might do:

> *Practice-Internal Rationality:* The conception of rationality that is used to determine whether or not something is rational or irrational within a practice.

> *Practice-External Rationality:* The conception of rationality that is used to determine whether or not a practice is rational to pursue or rational to participate in.

Contextualists characteristically deny that there are any forms of practice-external rationality at all. To question whether or not it is rational to accept a belief within a practice—an issue which can be decided according to standards internal to the practice to which the belief belongs—is legitimate. But it is illegitimate, or maybe even meaningless, to ask whether the whole practice is rational, or whether someone's participation in a practice is rational. To be able to see what counts for and against contextualism let us take an example of two practices that many contextualists claim are autonomous: science and religion.

Many contextualists have been inspired by the writings of Wittgenstein. Therefore let us take our starting-point in Wittgenstein before we consider more systematically developed versions of neo-Wittgensteinian contextualism. Wittgenstein claims that in religion a use of language is involved which is different from that used in science and ordinary life. Beliefs in the case of religion mean something different from what they mean in a scientific context. For instance, is the fact that scientific beliefs are held rationally if they are accepted tentatively and in proportion to the evidence available. Religious beliefs, on the other hand, are held not tentatively but in an unconditional, an all or nothing way. Wittgenstein's explanation of why this is so is roughly that religion in contrast to science has a regulative function with respect to a form of life. Since the ultimacy and unshakeability of religious belief excludes it from the "more-or-less" factors which is

typical of scientific and ordinary belief, he concludes that religious
beliefs are neither rational (reasonable) nor irrational (unreasonable);
they are not the kind of beliefs to which the notion of rationality
applies:

> . . . Am I to say they [religious beliefs] are unreasonable? I wouldn't
> call them unreasonable.
> I would say, they are certainly not *reasonable,* that's obvious.
> "Unreasonable" implies, with everyone, rebuke.
> I want to say: they don't treat this as a matter of reasonability.
> Anyone who reads the Epistles will find it said: not only that it is
> not reasonable, but that it is folly.
> Not only is it not reasonable, but it doesn't pretend to be.
> What seems to me ludicrous about O'Hare is his making it appear
> to be *reasonable.*[6]

However, this conclusion does not seem to follow from his argumentation. What follows is at most that scientific rationality (rea-
sonability) does not apply to religious belief. But given that there are
other forms of rationality available (which Wittgenstein, following the
positivists, might deny) the most his remarks give us is a reason to
think that there is *another* kind of rationality present in religion. It is
precisely this theme that some of the philosophers whom Wittgenstein
inspired try to develop. According to Winch, the contextual principle
applies to at least science and religion:

> one cannot apply criteria of logic to modes of social life as such.
> For instance, science is one such mode and religion is another;
> and each has criteria of intelligibility peculiar to itself. So within
> science or religion actions can be logical or illogical: in science, for
> example, it would be illogical to refuse to be bound by the results of
> a properly carried out experiment; in religion it would be illogical
> to suppose that one could pit one's own strength against God's;
> and so on. But we cannot sensibly say that either the practice of
> science itself or that of religion is either illogical or logical; both are
> non-logical.[7]

The difference between some practices (like science and religion) is not that some of them do and others do not conform to
standards of rationality, but that different standards are being used
within them. According to Winch then, it is a necessary condition of

rationality that there be standards (norms), but the existence of any system of standards (norms) within a practice is sufficient for rationality.[8] So rationality consists in the observation of standards that are internal to a practice. But to criticize one practice with standards taken from another is "nonsensical," "absurd," and to commit a "category-mistake."[9] External rationality is an impossibility.

Phillips is another philosopher inspired by Wittgenstein and he does not accept that there is one paradigm of rationality, science, for all forms of practices. Rather there is a diversity of standards of rationality, just as there is a diversity of contexts; one for science, another for religion, morality, art, politics, and the like. But there is not only (*a*) different standards for rationality in different practices, there is also (*b*) no practice-independent standards which can be used to assess the practice-internal ones or to assess the practices themselves. Therefore, every practice is in order as it is. However, that does not mean that the practices are static or unchangeable, it means that they can be changed only from within. According to Phillips, philosophers are supposed to try not to justify or critically assess what standards they find in a practice, but to understand them, to describe them in their own terms without imposing external standards picked up from a foreign practice. The only proper form of philosophy of religion, philosophy of science, and so on, is a *grammatical* one. The philosopher's task is not to justify or criticize these practices, because that makes no sense; rather he should give an account of the use of language involved. "He can only say that these language-games are played," or (in my terminology) that people participate in these practices.[10]

Concerning the rationality of religious belief Phillips holds that: "We may come to see that religion does lack what has already been defined as a rational basis. This is not to say that it has no basis, but simply that it lacks the kind of basis that is called rational."[11] This quotation might be interpreted as implying that religion is an *arational* practice, but I think that if we take into account other things he says it should be understood as the claim that in religion there is a different conception of rationality than in science and everyday life. For example, Phillips says that he is critical of any "attempt to show that religious belief is rational, by employing a notion of rationality which transcends belief and nonbelief."[12] So he seems to allow a rationality internal to religion. There are standards of rationality

applicable to religion, but they are internal ones. Phillips also allows a
kind of evidence for religious belief: "Religious believers, when asked
why they believe in God, may reply in a variety of ways. They may
say, 'I have had an experience of the living God', 'I believe in the
Lord Jesus Christ', 'God saved me while I was a sinner', or 'I just
can't help believing'."[13] But this evidence is, in the same way as the
standards, internal to the religious (Christian) practice. "That there is
no evidence available outside religious categories, . . . is one of the
important defining characteristics of the grammar of these religious
truths."[14]

So the claim is that "religious and other kinds of beliefs can
indeed be rational or irrational; but the criteria of rationality by which
we draw this distinction are embedded in the way of life to which
the belief in question belongs."[15] But what support can be given for
thinking that the contextual principle is correct—whether it is supposed to apply to science and religion or some other practices? First
of all, we need to see that it can actually be interpreted as consisting
of three different theses. The first point the contextual principle might
be taken to imply is:

> *The Internal Thesis:* The only kind of rationality that
> exists is internal, that is, rationality is always used in
> a practice of one sort of another.

In other words, the internal thesis consists of the claim that there
are no *context-* or *practice-independent* standards of rationality. If
this means only that one is always involved in some kind of activity
or other, that questions of rationality are always asked from some
perspective, I think the contextualist is quite right. We can never
conduct an inquiry about whether or not a particular person or group
of them are rational without doing it from the perspective of a particular domain—everyday, life-view, scientific practice, or however we
classify them. We always have to start somewhere. As Rescher points
out: "Only for someone who has no scheme or framework at all—who
is located wholly outside the realm of linguistic and epistemic and
cognitive commitments—is there an open and uncommitted choice
among alternatives. But of course none of us do or can find ourselves
in *that* position."[16] We all have a framework (our very own) from
which we assess the rationality of our own or other people's beliefs.
And there is no independent or non-contextual basis for deciding

whether one practice is more rational than another. There exists no non-practice located, or not framework-based, positions in this sense.

The second claim that the contextual principle seems to contain is the following one:

> *The Incompatibility Thesis:* It is not appropriate to assess beliefs in a particular practice by using standards of rationality that are collected from another type of practice.

In the previous discussion I have sided with the contextualist on the issue that the incompatibility thesis concerns. As I pointed out in the last chapter, it does not seem to be appropriate to apply, for example, the principle of predictability (concerning the possible predictions of new phenomena), which is used in scientific practice, to religious beliefs. On the other hand, neither is it reasonable to apply the principle of moral adequacy (concerning how people should be able to live a morally better life) to scientific claims. But even if this is true, that there are some scientific standards that are not applicable to religion, and vice versa, does it follow that it is true of *all* scientific standards? The presumptionist would say that it is true for all stan·dards, *except* for those standards of rationality the religious and the scientific practice have in common. And here we come to a *crucial difference* between the presumptionist and the contextualist, because the third thesis implicit in the contextual principle contains a denial of this, namely:

> *The Autonomy Thesis:* There are no standards of rationality that are applicable in all practices and none that are applicable to a practice itself.

That is to say that there are practices which have their own unique conception of rationality and which cannot themselves be rationally assessed. This thesis consists of two different claims. First, the contextualist claims that there are not only no practice-independent, but also no *practice-transcendent,* standards of rationality; that is, practices—like science and religion—do not have any standards of rationality in common. This shows that it is important to distinguish the claim that there are no practice-independent standards (the internal thesis) from the claim that there are no practice-transcendent ones (the autonomy thesis), because one can accept the first and still reject the second thesis. Sometimes, it seems to me, contextualists are not aware of this difference. It is one thing to say that assessments always take place within a practice, quite another to say that the assessments done within different practices have no standards in common. But as Kekes points out, "only if forms of life, linguistic frameworks, or whatnot, are entirely distinct does it become plausible that each has its own conception of reality, rationality, and proof. And only then could it be a mistake to criticize one from the point of view of the other."[17] Hence the plausibility of the autonomy thesis depends on whether or not it can be shown that practices like religion, science, and everyday life, are entirely distinct.

Second, the autonomy thesis consists of the claim that one cannot ask whether a whole practice is rational. There exists no practice-external rationality. Against this claim it has been argued that such questions can in fact be raised since some practices have been rejected as irrational. One example of this is belief in trolls and fairies.[18] Dalferth accepts this as true but claims that it is compatible with contextualism because:

> the distinction between the rational and the irrational is always drawn in terms of criteria *internal* to a form of life: if beliefs in trolls are rejected as irrational, then that occurs *within,* for example, a scientific or a Christian form of life, i.e., not in their own sense but in the sense proper to science or the Christian faith; and this is perfectly rational as long as we have reasons to assume that the scientific or Christian criteria of rationality are relevant to the beliefs in question. Thus in order to reject a whole form of life we do not need a specific ("objective") set of more fundamental external criteria of rationality by which we assess not only particular beliefs but whole modes of life. All we need are reasons for believing those beliefs to fall into the province of science or the Christian faith, i.e., some second-order beliefs about the kind and type of belief in question.[19]

Winch also accepts that at least some practices can be criticized in this way. The examples he gives are Black magic and the Black Mass because they have a parasitic relationship to the Christian practice and can be "rejected as *irrational* (in the sense proper to religion) in the system of beliefs on which these practices are thus parasitic"; and the same holds with regard to the relationship between astrology and astronomy.[20] So one can ask whether or not a practice is rational, but only by claiming that the practice is not an *autonomous* one; its beliefs do in fact fall within the proper domain of another (autonomous) practice. But then which practices are autonomous ones? In particular are science and religion examples of autonomous practices? And why is it not possible to assess an autonomous practice? Let us start with the last question.

2.   Autonomous Practices

According to still another contextualist, Malcolm, all questions about whether or not a belief is rational must be made within a context, a particular practice (in his terminology a "system"). The practice provides the boundaries within which we can meaningfully question something. Further, a practice is defined by its *practice-basic beliefs* (in his vocabulary "framework principles," another term used by contextualists is "rules"), which are beliefs that are taken for granted or seen as unquestionable by the participants of the practice. They function as the "rules" that define the "game" played.[21] Examples Malcolm and other contextualists give of practice-basic beliefs are: the physical world exists, people have brains, I have two hands, the earth has existed for many years, I was born, this is a tree, nature is continuous, God exists, and the like. These practice-basic beliefs make rational assessment possible—within a practice, but it is not possible to justify them rationally:

> A "system" provides the boundaries within which we ask questions, carry out investigations, and make judgments. Hypotheses are put forth, and challenged, *within* a system. Verification, justification, the search for evidence, occur *within* a system. The framework propositions of the system are not put to the test, not backed up by evidence.[22]

The reason why it makes no sense to try to justify practice-basic beliefs it that the notion of justification itself involves the notion of an end of justification. Malcolm quotes Wittgenstein who says about justification in calculation: "In certain circumstances . . . we regard a calculation as sufficiently checked. What gives us a right to do so? . . . Somewhere we must be finished with justification, and then there remains the proposition that *this* is how we calculate."[23] And this last remark is an example of a practice-basic belief. So without practice-basic beliefs, which are themselves *groundless* (that is, inappropriate objects of the process of justification), the whole enterprise of justification is impossible. This is the reason why, Phillips thinks, it is not possible to assess a whole practice, because we must have a "reference to a subject within which the different ways of looking at the world [can] compete."[24]

Here it becomes evident that, despite the Wittgensteinian contextualists' own loud protests, their account can be understood as a form of foundationalism or, at least, as a position closely related to foundationalism.[25] As we have seen foundationalism is roughly the view that there are two classes of beliefs, one in need of justification, the other needing no such support. What might make us hesitate to classify Wittgensteinian contextualism as a version of foundationalism is that although Wittgensteinian contextualists seem to accept the second thesis of foundationalism (that basic beliefs are not justified by appeal to non-basic beliefs) they reject the second part of the first thesis (there are two forms of justification, inferential and non-inferential). That is, they claim that basic beliefs are groundless and so cannot be justified—not even non-inferentially.[26] But if one classifies Wittgensteinian contextualism as a form of foundationalism, it is important to see that this version of foundationalism differs from the more traditional sorts in also another sense, in being a form of *local foundationalism*. This is a consequence of the contextual principle, namely that if it is the case that there exist totally distinct practices then there is no foundation (i.e., a set of practice-basic beliefs) that our practices have in common, as the traditional versions of (global) foundationalism typically hoped to establish; each autonomous practice has its own distinct foundation.

However, as we saw in the case of belief in trolls and fairies, not all distinctive practices need be autonomous practices. It is, therefore, an open question *what* practices we should regard as autonomous ones. As Gutting points out, a set of practice-basic beliefs "must not only provide a basis for a process of justification, it must also not itself fall within the scope of some more basic process of justification."[27] So the identification of a domain as a practice is not enough to establish that we cannot ask whether the whole practice is rational; what is also needed is an argument that shows that the practice *is* autonomous.

More fundamentally, we have to ask what makes a practice autonomous. In the previous chapter I pointed out that one way of investigating whether rationality is practice-relative or practice-dependent is to compare the *aims* of different practices with each other. The same way of proceeding is open when we want to investigate whether rationality is practice-determined. Another way of stating this point is to say that by focusing on the *functions* different practices fulfill we might get a clue about the characteristics of autonomous practices. And I said that we have to pay attention to what function a practice has, otherwise we might apply inappropriate standards of rationality, ask for the wrong kind of evidence, or misrepresent the beliefs of the practice. I suggest that we can determine whether a practice is autonomous by focusing on four aspects of the practice:

1. the aims of the practice (concerning *value autonomy*),
2. the subject matter of the practice (concerning *ontological autonomy*),
3. the concepts of the practice (concerning *conceptual autonomy*), and
4. the processes of assessment used in the practice (concerning *epistemological autonomy*).

We have already discussed in some detail the first aspect, which concerns *value autonomy*. In the previous chapter I contrasted three practices with each other and summarized their different aims by saying that, roughly, science and metaphysics aim to make the world theoretically intelligible, but science also aims to make it predictively intelligible. Religion on the other hand, aims primarily to make our lives existentially intelligible. The basic thought here is that if the ends of religious practice are to respond to and overcome guilt, sin, meaninglessness, alienation, and the like, and the ends of science are prediction and control, and the like, then we might have a reason to think that these two practices are distinct and even autonomous ones. I concluded that this is enough to show that they cannot be reduced to one another. But despite this I claimed that both practices have epistemic ends in common, truth and the avoidance of falsehood. However, that is of course something the contextualists can deny by claiming that a practice like religion is non-cognitive. I think the strategy they use more often is to try to argue that practices like science and religion have different conceptions of truth and falsehood. Not only rationality, but also epistemic ends, are practice-determined. (We will come back to this thesis later on.)

Practices might also be distinguished in terms of their subject matter, by what kind (or kinds) of entities the beliefs in the practice are about. Practices can be (more or less) *ontologically autonomous.* For instance, a practice might have one or more of the following entities as its subject matter: physical objects, animals, persons, numbers, values, god(s), and so on. Natural science deals primarily with physical objects, things that are relatively stable and permanent, which possess size, shape, mass, temperature, and the like. Social science typically involves not only physical objects, but also human persons, beings with a living body of a particular sort, who perform cognitive, evaluative, and conative activities, and so on.[28] Religion on the other hand, adds a third element, a divine reality (the sacred). How it is characterized depends on which religion one advocates, but the sacred can, nevertheless, be seen as the basic entity of the religious practice. If these examples of subject matter (physical objects, human persons, a divine reality) cannot be reduced to one or two of the other, then practices that just range over one kind of entity are ontologically autonomous; and practices that involve two or more of them are partly autonomous. The practices we are involved in are of one or the other kind, consisting of either a monistic or pluralistic ontology. As Alston points out:

> Large stretches of our discourse range over entities of a single type. We can envisage the possibility of a totally self-enclosed physical-object discourse that never mentions relations to other sorts of things whereas language-games that have to do centrally with purposive agents, whether human, divine, or otherwise, cannot be concerned just with purposive agents, for it is essential to, or at least typical of, agents, that their purposes extend to things that are not of their own kind.[29]

One strategy the contextualist can use to argue that practices like science and religion are ontologically autonomous is to claim that the subject matters of the religious practice is of a kind ontologically distinct from the ones in the scientific practice. For example, they could maintain that religious practice focuses only on the divine reality, whereas science is occupied exclusively with physical objects. But more common is another strategy, because the obvious objection to the first line of argumentation is that, of course, the religious practice is not just about the sacred, but also about human beings and the world in which they live. Phillips claims: "Coming to God is not a change of opinion, but a change of direction; a reorientation of one's whole life" nor is it to include one more entity in one's belief system. "The realisation he [the converted] comes to is a realisation of something new, something in the light of which his former life is reassessed."[30] This reorientation is to start seeing the whole world in a new light, to see it *as* God's creation, *as* the place for redemption and so on. So the thought here is that when one becomes a participant of a religious practice all objects are perceived in a different way from before, a way totally distinct from the scientific way of viewing reality. But even if Phillips is right in that becoming a religious believer is *more* than adding one item to one's ontology, it seems—*pace* Phillips— to include *at least* that. He is here, I think, creating a false dichotomy, trying to force us to make a choice we do not have to make.

More typically, however, at least for the philosophers and theologians inspired by Wittgenstein, the contextualists have, rather than focusing on ontology, put their energy into showing that practices like science and religion are *conceptually autonomous*. But what does this mean? As Alston points out the basic idea seems to be that there are certain kinds of concepts that can be applied to one particular subject matter but not to others. Certain concepts do or do not apply to physical objects, human persons, divine beings, and so on. He exemplifies this idea by saying that it is a meaningful question to ask whether a person is thinking about the weather, but not whether a stone or a sense-datum is doing so; further, we can wonder what the back of a house looks like but not what the back of a number or Euclidean triangle look like.[31] If it is not possible to define all or some of the concepts of a practice in terms of the concepts of another practice, then the practice is (completely or partly) conceptually autonomous. Well known attempts to define concepts of one kind in terms of another kind are, the efforts to define theoretical statements in terms of observation statements, ethical concepts psychologically, god as a father figure, and so on. The attempt to use non-religious discourse to explain or assess the use of religious discourse is seen as involving a reductionism that cannot be accepted.

Both Winch and Phillips claim that we should be able to see that religion has its own unique conception of rationality if we pay enough attention to the nature or the grammar of the religious language. Hence the essential structure of their argument seems to be that: *a different conception of rationality (epistemological autonomy) follows from conceptual autonomy.* The thought is that there is a connection between the meaning of a statement and the proper assessment of it. This is, I think, an important observation. The meaning that beliefs in a religious practice have will affect what the appropriate standards of rationality and evidence are. As Abraham points out, if the statement "God exists" is a piece of poetry, it is surely inappropriate to try to support this statement by giving the kind of arguments used in (classical) natural theology.[32] Before we try to evaluate what conclusions it is appropriate to draw from this observation, let us try to specify the kind of autonomy, epistemological autonomy, that is supposed to follow from conceptual autonomy.

The fourth aspect of a practice we have to take into account when we want to determine whether a practice is autonomous is the process of assessment used in the practice—the issue of *epistemological autonomy*. A practice is epistemologically autonomous if, for example, the rationality or justification of its beliefs (actions or evaluations) do not depend on support from other practices. Such support can be of three different kinds: concerning certain beliefs, standards, or reasons (evidence). For instance, if the religious practice must be built on, or be related in anyway to, scientific theories, if it must be justified by scientific standards, or if it needs to be supported by scientifically acceptable evidence, it is not epistemologically autonomous.

I have been focusing on rationality, and the claim for epistemological autonomy has been understood as an acceptance of the autonomy thesis: that there are no standards of rationality that are applicable across autonomous practices, or to a whole practice. So let us, with these clarifications in mind, go back to the issues of whether religion is an entirely distinct practice and whether we should accept the autonomy thesis. A basic claim of Winch and Phillips seems to be that:

> A proper understanding of the distinctive features of a religious practice will show that the ordinary conception of rationality is inappropriate to use on (and in) the religious practice.

What a proper analysis of a religious practice shows, among other things, is that it has, in general, no factual content—that religious beliefs are not really factual claims. Winch admits, as Gutting points out, that if the Zande beliefs are taken as hypotheses about the causes of things (in our scientific sense of "cause"), then they *are* irrational.[33] However, the Zande beliefs have a different meaning, and therefore scientific standards of rationality cannot apply to them:

> [MacIntyre] thinks that the Zande "belief" is a sort of *hypothesis* . . . MacIntyre believes that he is applying as it were a neutral concept of "A affecting B", equally applicable to Zande magic and western science. In fact, however, he is applying the concept with which *he* is familiar, one which draws its significance from its use in scientific and technological contexts. There is no reason to suppose that the Zande magical concept of "A affecting B" has anything like the same significance. . . . there is every reason to think that their concept of magical "influence" is quite different.[34]

A different conception of rationality is being used since the Zande beliefs are not meant as descriptions of the world (factual claims). Rather, they "express an attitude to contingencies; one, that is, which involves recognition that one's life is subject to contingencies, rather than an attempt to control these."[35]

Phillips argues in a similar way. According to him, religious belief in literal survival is superstitious; it is an irrational belief. However, that is not what the doctrine of immortality really means: rather religious belief in immortality is concerned with the quality of one's present life, a quality indicated by expressions like "participating in the life of God" or "living in God's presence." And he offers a similar analysis of other central religious beliefs concerning such things as petitionary prayer and the last judgment.[36] So Winch's and Phillips's strategy is, essentially, to show that:

> religious beliefs have, in general, a *meaning different* from that of scientific beliefs, otherwise they would be irrational (superstition), and because of this special meaning a different conception of rationality is needed in religious practice.

This means that whether the religious practice is autonomous depends on how one understands the meaning of religious beliefs. If one construes them as factual claims they fall within the scope of the scientific practice, and then they would be superstitious. However, according to Winch and Phillips, they are not factual claims, and they are therefore properly basic beliefs (or groundless beliefs) of an autonomous practice. In other words, if religious beliefs are factual then their epistemological autonomy can be denied, since one can then argue that they fall into the province of science. In that case one can ask whether the whole religious practice is rational, but then one does not apply practice-independent or practice-transcendent standards of rationality since these beliefs belong, in fact, to scientific practice. But this argument, Phillips thinks, can be rejected because it seriously misrepresents the nature and function of religious belief. "The philosophical scandal . . . consists precisely in this: we are asked to accept as the only appropriate philosophical method for establishing the rationality of religious belief, a method which actually distorts the character of religious belief."[37]

3.   The Issue of Incompatible Conceptions of Rationality

Should we accept the contextualist's general claims that there are no practice-transcending standards of rationality and that there are autonomous practices? That is, should we agree with the contextualist in saying that there are practices that have their own unique conception of rationality and which cannot themselves be rationally assessed (the autonomy thesis)? In particular, should we accept the more specific claim of Winch and Phillips that religion and science are examples of two autonomous practices? Complicating the issues is the fact that typically the contextualists (but also their opponents) have been unclear about what they mean by "rationality." For example, they do not state what exact standards of rationality they have in mind. They sometimes talk about *the* scientific standard of rationality, but they do not specify what the standard consists in. This is in fact a peculiar feature of much of the debate that has been going on between contextualists and non-contextualists. It seems unlikely that we will be able to evaluate which of them, if any, is correct in these matters since they all fail to explicate the concept and standards of rationality.[38] So unfortunately a part of our task will have to be to try to figure out what the contextualists mean when they claim that each different practice has its own unique conception of rationality.

First, it is clear that, according to contextualists, rationality consists in the observation of standards that are internal to a practice. Does this mean that every practice characterizes the *nature* of rationality differently (that is, there are distinct kinds of rationality)? Not necessarily. If rationality is a matter of conforming to (social) norms this *can* be interpreted as a version of deontological rationality. In other words, the contextualists can be taken to claim that:

> *rationality* consists in fulfilling one's intellectual obligations as these are specified within a particular practice.

This means further that:

> an *individual is rational* in accepting a belief if it conforms to the norms internal to the practice to which the belief in question belongs.

If this is correct, what the contextualists deny is that this intellectual duty is the same in all practices, whereas that is something non-contextualists typically affirm. But despite this disagreement they can all, it seems, agree on the question of what rationality *is*—an intellectual duty with respect to what one does (believes, acts, and evaluates). So the contextualists should probably not be taken to claim that the nature of rationality is different in autonomous practices. This means that we can distinguish between two fundamental issues on which the advocates of different models of rationality can disagree with each other. The first is the one we have discussed almost exclusively before this chapter, namely, the *question of in what our intellectual obligations actually consist*. Are they a matter of following rules or of performing judgments? Are they a matter of having good reasons for what one does or of only doing something as long as there are no good reasons to cease from doing it, or are they something else? The second issue is the one we have now started to discuss in more detail. The *question of the range of these obligations (however they are specified)—whether or not these obligations are the same in all practices or contexts*. Non-contextualists assume that all or many of these obligations are the same in all practices or contexts; and that is, of course, what contextualists challenge.

Second, contextualists cannot build their case on the claim that different things count as *evidence* (or good reasons) in different practices, since this is nothing non-contextualists (at least, not presumptionists) need deny. This is so because what should count as a good reason depends on what it is supposed to be a reason *for,* which in turn depends on what aims the practice has. However, that is not necessarily something controversial. After all, that is one of the reasons why we talk about different practices at all and are able to identify them. So the fact that practices like science and religion have different *aims* need not mean that they automatically have different conceptions of what rationality is or entirely distinct standards of rationality. Third, it seems as if their position stands or falls with the question of *whether each practice has its own standards of rationality and whether practices therefore cannot be rationally justified themselves*—the only form of rationality that is available is practice-internal. This is how I have interpreted contextualism, by focusing on the contextual principle. However, as we have seen, the only element in that principle non-contextualists (at least, presumptionists) have to deny is the autonomy thesis. So should we accept it or not? As far as I can see there are basically two arguments the Wittgensteinian contextualists give to support the autonomy thesis, what we might call the *meaning* and the *basicality arguments.*

3.1   THE MEANING ARGUMENT

As I have already indicated above, the meaning argument consists of the claim that *since religious beliefs have a meaning different from scientific beliefs, these two practices have no standards of rationality in common.* So if we apply scientific standards (or any other external standards for that matter) to religious beliefs we distort their character, since we make them into something other than what they really are. Again what makes it difficult to assess the meaning argument is that these contextualists say only that different standards apply, and they do not make any serious attempt to identify or specify them. This makes me suspect that this argument is, at least to some of them, partly *a priori:* since the meaning of the statements in science and religion is not the same, they *must* have different standards of rationality, therefore, we need not specify exactly what they are or compare them. If this is the case, they are not as practice-oriented as they say. Rather they become advocates, on this point, of a version of the formal approach to philosophy.

But what is so problematic about assuming that religious beliefs are typically factual claims? I have argued that religious beliefs are *more* than factual beliefs (more specifically, they are existential or life-orienting beliefs). But is there any reason to think that in general they do not contain a factual element at all? Phenomenologically speaking, it seems as if ordinary religious believers typically think and talk as though religious beliefs were a kind of factual belief. Many of their attitudes and activities also seem to make no sense if they do not think that it is factually true that the God in whom they believe exists. So I think Wainwright is correct in claiming that the best way of reading at least Phillips's account of the meaning or nature of religious belief is as a *recommendation* and not as a description, since his view seems far from being just a simple description of what devout people mean or think when they speak of God.[39] However, is this view that religious beliefs in general should be understood as factual claims just a naive form of religious realism? There seem to be certain anomalies or problems with taking what ordinary religious believers think and say about their religious beliefs at face value. What are these anomalies? The contextualist wants to point them out by arguing in the following way: suppose that religious beliefs are factual, and that they can therefore be wrong. We could then see them as *hypotheses,* with a certain degree of *probability*. However, we hesitate to call these beliefs hypotheses because they seem to have a greater *security* in the life of the religious believer than that description allows; therefore we should not interpret them as factual claims. Phillips says: "Strong [religious] belief is not tentative or hypothetical. Believers do not pray to a God who probably exists." And:

> Because the evidence is never as good as we would like, religious beliefs, . . . are matters of probability. It then seems that we should reformulate religious beliefs so that the natural expressions of them become less misleading. On this view, should we not say from now on, "I believe that it is highly probably that there is an almighty God, maker of heaven and earth", "I believe it is highly probably that God forgives sins", and so on? Do these reformulations do justice to the nature of religious belief? Hardly.[40]

So the anomalies are (*a*) our discomfort in calling these beliefs "hypotheses," and that (*b*) they then become tentative beliefs. It is also the case that (*c*) religious beliefs (belief in God) become *defeasible* if they are interpreted as factual claims. What should we say of this? First, as we have seen in the last chapter, it is completely proper to believe with full acceptance what has less than maximal probability on one's total evidence, or even what is believed only on the basis of a presumption. So neither the social evidentialist nor the presumptionist who claims that religious beliefs have a factual element need be committed to the view that religious beliefs must be only tentatively accepted.

Sometimes Phillips seems to think that *any* belief that could be wrong or defeasible should be only tentatively accepted. This becomes evident when he criticizes Plantinga's account of the rationality of religious belief. Even though Plantinga thinks that religious beliefs are factual, he is (like Phillips) critical of calling religious beliefs hypotheses. At the same time, however, he thinks that even if religious beliefs are properly basic (held immediately), they are in principle nonetheless defeasible. Phillips writes: "Just as in his [Plantinga's] analysis of 'I see a tree', the possibility of being mistaken is maintained, so also in the analysis of 'God exists', the possibility of error is allowed." He continues: "Having noted Plantinga's criticisms of foundationalism, do we not have to say, when we come to consider his own discussion, that he, too, introduces a tentativeness, a necessary tentativeness, into the nature of religious belief?"[41] Phillips thinks that answer must be yes, and this is one of the reasons why he rejects Plantinga's analysis. So his view seems to be that if one claims that religious belief is defeasible then it becomes tentative in character. His way of arguing seems to be: factual claims are defeasible, and defeasible claims should always be only tentatively accepted; however, belief in God is not normally accepted tentatively by the mature religious believer; therefore, belief in God cannot be a factual claim, since it cannot be mistaken.

But why should we think that what can possibly be wrong must be tentatively accepted? Recall the discussion in the last chapter about my belief that my wife loves me. If I admit, as I do that it is *possible* that she might not love me, on Phillips's analysis, I can no longer say that "My wife loves me," rather I should say that "I am married to a woman who probably loves me" or "I believe that it is highly probable that my wife loves me." But why? If there is anything I am sure of, this is it, but despite this my belief *could* be wrong. However, as a presumptionist I am still rationally entitled to believe it with full acceptance until special, *very* special, reasons have arisen to think otherwise. Defeaters can arise, as when I or one of my best friends sees her dating another man, or the like. And this applies also to belief in the sacred. If belief in the sacred is factual and defeasible it can still be fully accepted by a rational religious believer, and the character of religious belief would not be threatened. Religious people do not have to say "I believe that it is highly probably that there is an almighty God, maker of heaven and earth." Perhaps that should be true of religious people who accept formal evidentialism, but that is another matter. Here again, Phillips's analysis makes more sense if we see it as a normative and not a descriptive account (as he himself claims) since, as Wolterstorff points out:

> *Within* religious practice believers regularly surrender, in the face of objections raised, beliefs which they hold immediately; and even the most cursory glance shows that religious believers do not in fact treat cultural developments outside religion as irrelevant to the tenability of their religious convictions.[42]

Obviously something that counts against religious belief (especially Christian belief) is the existence of evil, and because of that many religious believers have surrendered their religious faith. So it seems, phenomenologically speaking, that when some religious people encounter instances of evil, these experiences are taken by the believers themselves as reasons that count against their faith— they function as defeaters. Hence the fact that religious beliefs are defeasible (can be mistaken), rather than being an anomaly, seems to be at least compatible with how religious people often seem to think and act. Perhaps the reason Phillips makes these connections between factual and defeasible claims on the one hand and tentativity on the other is, as Banner suggests, that he confuses the fact that all factual beliefs *are provisional,* in the sense that they depend on what is the case or what happens in the world, with the fact that all factual claims *can be tentatively* accepted, that is, held with little confidence.[43]

I think, however, that Phillips and Plantinga are on to something when they question the possibility of treating religious beliefs as hypotheses. But what exactly is problematic here? To be able to answer that we must focus on how "hypothesis" has been used and defined. It is problematic for Phillips, and in this respect also for Winch, that when religious beliefs are treated as hypotheses, they should be only tentatively accepted. This means that one thinks that there is a need to investigate them further, but one is nonetheless willing to use them as a starting-point (a working hypothesis) for an inquiry. (See chapter 10.) But this is not the way religious people normally understand their faith. So religious belief should not be seen as a hypothesis. Recall MacIntyre's objection against Crombie:

> [Crombie's account] suggests that religious belief is a hypothesis which will be confirmed or overthrown after death. But, if this is correct, in this present life religious beliefs could never be anything more than as yet unconfirmed hypotheses, warranting nothing more than a provisional and tentative adherence. But such adherence is completely uncharacteristic of religious belief. A God who could be believed in in this way would not be the God of Christian theism. For part of the content of Christian belief is that decisive adherence has to be given to God. So that to hold Christian belief as a hypothesis would be to render it no longer Christian belief.[44]

Not all hypotheses, however, are *working hypotheses*. As we saw when we discussed the practice-oriented view of science, not even all scientific hypotheses are held tentatively: some of them are embraced by scientists with a strong commitment, and they are treated as paradigms—the very (unquestionable) foundation for research going on in the practice. However, they share one feature with working hypotheses: they can be seen as something that explains some phenomena or data. Could we then not even say that religious belief can be seen as what we might call a (more or less) *stable hypothesis?* If we think that religious beliefs include factual elements (as I have tried to argue), I am inclined to think that the answer must be "yes, we can," because any factual belief can in principle by itself or in conjunction with other beliefs be viewed as hypotheses. If by "hypothesis" we mean something that can be designed to explain or test some phenomena or data.

Is there something problematic if somebody—religious or nonreligious—treats belief in the sacred as a hypothesis, designed to explain and test some body of evidence or phenomena? Plantinga seems to think so. Discussing Mackie's book *The Miracle of Theism* he says that: "The most important and debilitating of these [Mackie's questionable presuppositions] is his taking it for granted that theism or belief in God is a scientific hypothesis, or a quasi-scientific hypothesis, or relevantly *like* a scientific hypothesis." So Plantinga objects to the way the advocates of the religious hypothesis typically set up the issue: "On this way of looking at the matter, there is a relevant body of evidence shared by believer and unbeliever alike; theism is a hypothesis designed to explain that body of evidence; and theism is rationally defensible only to the extent that it is a good explanation thereof."[45]

But on this issue we must distinguish between what "is" and what "can" be the case. Let me illustrate what I have in mind by once again focusing on my belief that my wife loves me. Is it a hypothesis? Not for me, since I do not put that belief forward to explain or test phenomena. For me it is not a belief designed to explain something, and it is not the case that this belief is rationally defensible only to the extent that it is a good explanation of something which can be established by using a body of evidence shared by me and everybody else alike. That is the way it appears to me, and I am rational in continuing to hold that belief in the absence of special reasons to do otherwise. However, can it, at the same time, be a hypothesis for somebody else? I see no reason why it could not be so. Suppose, for example, two persons hear me say that my wife loves me. One of them believes me, the other does not. So they decide to treat my belief as a hypothesis and try to collect evidence for or against its truth that they both could accept. I can see nothing problematic about that.

In a similar fashion belief in the sacred for many religious believers is not seen as a hypothesis, a belief put forward to explain or test some things. But from this it does not follow that somebody else cannot, at the same time, treat it as a hypothesis and start an inquiry. However, if the claim is that religious believers must treat belief in the sacred as a hypothesis to be rationally justified in accepting it, this can be rejected on a presumptionist account, but that is another issue. So it is possible that belief in the sacred is not a hypothesis for the religious believer and at the same time a hypothesis for somebody else, without destroying the character of the belief in question. In other words, we must distinguish between two issues here, one concerning whether a religious believer *must* treat his or her belief in the sacred as a hypothesis, the other concerning whether religious belief *can* be seen as a hypothesis. Religious belief is typically not a hypothesis for the believer, but it can be for other people.

However this is not, I think, Plantinga's main objection. He asks us to consider whether factual beliefs like our beliefs about the past, about material things, and about other minds really can or should be seen as hypotheses. He gives an illustration of what he has in mind by reminding us how Thomas Reid responded to Hume's skepticism about the external world:

> Suppose it is proposed that my belief in material objects is "rationally defensible" only if it is more probable than not with respect to a body of knowledge that includes no physical object propositions but only, say, self-evident truths together with experiential propositions specifying how I am appeared to. Add (as the history of modern philosophy strongly suggests) that it is impossible to show that physical object statements are more probable than not with respect to such a body of evidence; or add, more strongly, that in fact physical objects propositions are *not* more probable than not with respect to such propositions. What would follow from that? It is one of Reid's most important and enduring contributions to point out that nothing of much interest would follow from that. In particular it would not follow that belief in physical objects ought to be discouraged as somehow improper, or irrational, or intellectually out of order. But why, then, should we think it follows in the case of theism?[46]

But here again Plantinga oscillates between the two issues I distinguished above. This could definitely be seen as an objection against the traditional version of evidentialist challenge to religious belief, but how can it be an objection against the *possibility* of treating belief in God as a hypothesis? Perhaps we should understand him the following way. Consider belief in the past, material objects or other minds; why do we generally hesitate to call these hypotheses, to treat them as beliefs designed to explain or be tested by a body of evidence or counter-evidence? I think the reason is that we do not know what could count as evidence in these cases. There is nothing we are more certain of that could constitute evidence for or against our claims in this context. There is nothing we believe that is more sure than these beliefs that could be used as justifiers or defeaters. Plantinga's point would then be that many religious believers (at least mature believers) hesitate for similar reasons to call belief in the sacred a hypothesis. For them nothing could be more certain which could function as evidence for or against. Therefore, theism is not a hypothesis.

It might be true that many religious believers react in this way, and this may even be a rationally acceptable position to adopt from their point of view; however, since so many people (non-religious *and* religious) do not feel the same hesitation in *this* case as in the other, this cannot function as a forceful argument against the *possibility* of treating belief in the sacred as a hypothesis. And consider again my belief that my wife loves me. From my point of view it is not a hypothesis, but that is not an argument against the possibility that the very same belief might be understood as a hypothesis, and properly so, by other people.

Let us consider one further anomaly with understanding religious belief as including a factual element. According to contexualists, if we interpret religious people's beliefs as factual claims, hypotheses, explanations, or the like, they become irrational beliefs. This would make these people look unintelligent; but surely how could all these people be so stupid? "You might say: 'For a blunder, that's too big.' "[47] So the fourth anomaly is (*d*) that we, if we interpret religious beliefs in this way, have to attribute systematic irrationality to these people, which does not seem to be a plausible move.

Wittgenstein, Winch, and Phillips react strongly against anthropologists like Frazer, Levy-Bruhl, and Evans-Pritchard who make people of the past or of other cultures look stupid and irrational. Instead we should do our best to make their beliefs and actions seem reasonable. We should apply a principle of charity. If we apply such a principle, we can avoid concluding that their beliefs are irrational by presupposing that they have their own unique conception of rationality and that their apparently literal sentences should be interpreted as symbolic speech. So our choice is either to attribute irrationality to them or to claim that their beliefs have only a non-factual content and because of this a different conception of rationality applies. And surely faced with this choice we should choose the latter view. Anything else would be an insult to these people. But to argue in such a way is a mistake, which the contextualists commit because they in fact *share* a certain view about rationality with the people they criticize. The *thesis* they all seem to have in common is:

> If we are rationally justified in believing what we believe, then somebody else (from the past or another culture) cannot be rationally justified in disagreeing with us,

but to this, these contextualists claim that there is an exception:

> unless we have different and incompatible concep-
> tions of rationality.

The assumption seems to be that if we share the same conception of rationality, what is rational for us must be rational for them. But according to contextualists we do not share the same conception, so people of other cultures cannot be said to be irrational just because they do not conform to *our* conception of rationality. Rescher seems to accept that different cultures have different conceptions of rationality, but objects that the conception of rationality that has priority (for us) is our own, otherwise it would not be our own. And according to our conception of rationality these beliefs of other (primitive) cultures are irrational. He asks us to consider whether the beliefs of primitive, pre-scientific cultures indeed are less rational than ours:

> A resounding negative is maintained in Peter Winch's widely cited article on "Understanding a Primitive Society", which maintains vividly that Azande beliefs about witchcraft and oracles cannot be rejected as rationally inappropriate despite their clear violation of the evidential canons of modern Western scientific culture. Winch maintains that the Azande can quite "rationally" see those occult beliefs to be justifiable in their own (deviant) way. But just here lies the problem. The answer you get depends on the question you ask. If we ask "Do they hold their beliefs rationally?" we, of course, mean "*rationally* on our understanding of the matter". And the answer here is clearly "*No*", because in fact this sort of rationality does not figure in *their* thinking at all. The fact that they deem their beliefs somehow "justified" by some considerations or other (which in fact provide no rational adequate justification at all) is going to cut no ice in *our* deliberations.[48]

I would say that Winch, and not Rescher, is right but for the wrong reason. These beliefs are (possibly) rational not because the Azande have their own unique conception of rationality, but because they are doing what can rightly be demanded of them, given *their* resources and *their* situation. Rescher claims that their beliefs are obviously not rational since these people violate the "canons of modern Western scientific culture." But this fact, if it is true, is not an argument—it "cuts no ice"—against the rationality of these people's believing. It can be such an argument only if we can reasonably claim that they should know about the content of these evidential canons, but that is absurd.

It is not only that the answer to Rescher's question (as to whether the beliefs of primitive, pre-scientific cultures are less rational than ours) is not a clear "no," strictly speaking, we cannot even ask the question; beliefs cannot be rational or irrational as such. However, what we can ask (and that is the way I reinterpreted this question above) is whether, given their and our historical and cultural situations, they are doing what can rightly be demanded of them less satisfactorily than we are. But to this there is no obvious answer, because it depends on, among other things, a case-by-case assessment of reasons available for us and them. So the question of rationality in this context is really:

> Are these people of the past or of other cultures doing what one can rightly demand of them in regulating their believing?

If so, their beliefs were or are rational irrespective of what it is rational for us to believe on these matters. And if we want to compare them with ourselves, the question we should ask is:

> Are people of the past or of other cultures doing worse or better than we are when it comes to satisfying what can reasonably be demanded of them in regulating their believing?

More specifically, according to the presumptionist, if we want to determine whether people of the past or of other cultures are rational in their believing, we have to ask if they proceeded (or proceed) against good reasons when they believed the way they did, reasons that they ought to have been aware of; if not, we should attribute rationality to them. However, by "good reasons" we mean reasons *available* to them in their situation. To ask for any other kind of reason is completely unrealistic. So two *mistakes* both the contextualists and the anthropologists they criticize make are, first to assume that if we share or had shared the same conception of rationality, what is rational for us must be rational for them, and vice versa; and second, to ignore the fact that some reasons are available to us which are not available to these people. On our normative conception of rationality (the presumptionist one), if we are rationally justified in believing what we believe, then somebody else (from the past or another culture) *can* be rational in disagreeing with us. But we have—irrespective of which culture we belong to or during which historical period we live under—the same intellectual duty. So for these people, unless there are special reasons available to them that they ought to be aware of that count against what they believe, they are rational in believing what they believe, even if the very same beliefs would be irrational for us to accept.

However, even if Phillips and Winch are right in saying that religious beliefs do have a special meaning, it does not even then follow that religious practice does not share some standards with the scientific and the everyday life practice. Even if the meaning of religious belief is non-factual and its function is pragmatic, that does not mean that the people who accept these beliefs do not have to satisfy the principle of presumption. In fact, as we have seen, this principle applies even to practices which have non-epistemic ends (as it does to those which have only epistemic ends or to those with both sorts of ends).

So the first argument, the meaning argument, the contextualists give for the autonomy thesis is not convincing. Let us now consider the second one.

3.2   THE BASICALITY ARGUMENT

The second argument given to support for the autonomy thesis (its second part) is the basicality argument. It consists essentially of the claim that *it is meaningless to ask whether religious practice (and thereby the basic beliefs of the practice, such as "God exists") is rational because that question cannot (grammatically speaking) be properly raised.* No evidence can support religious practice and no counter-evidence can arise against it since it constitutes an autonomous practice. Evidence can exist for or against a belief only *within* the practice. This does not mean, as we have seen, that religious beliefs cannot be rational or irrational, because there is a rationality internal to the religious practice. It means only that the practice-basic beliefs are not rationally assessable:

> *Within* a language-game there is justification and lack of justification, evidence and proof, mistakes and groundless opinions, good

or bad reasoning, correct measurements and incorrect ones. One cannot properly apply these terms to a language-game itself. It may, however, be said to be "groundless," not in the sense of a groundless opinion, but in the sense that we accept it, we live it. We can say, "This is what we do. This is how we are." In this sense religion is groundless; and so is chemistry.[49]

The reason it is meaningless to ask whether a practice is rational to pursue is that justification must stop somewhere. Questions must always be asked within a context. I have not challenged that questions of rationality must always be asked within a context (the internal thesis), nor that justification must stop somewhere. However, *where* justification should stop is an open question. It is one thing to say that there are autonomous practices (practices which cannot be rationally assessed as a whole), quite another to say which practices are autonomous in this way. So what I shall question in what follows is the contextualists' claim that religion is an autonomous practice. Let us see where the presumptionist and the contextualist differ on these matters. Malcolm writes:

> The obsessive concern [in philosophy of religion] with the proofs [of the existence of God] reveals the assumption that in order for religious belief to be intellectually respectable it *ought* to have a rational justification. *That* is the misunderstanding. It is like the idea that we are not justified in relying on memory until memory has been proved reliable.[50]

Presumptionists agree with Malcolm in so far as they also reject the claim that religious beliefs ought to have a rational justification, if by that one means satisfying the evidential principle. Religious believing, just like our trust in our memory, ought to be treated as intellectually innocent until proven guilty. However, Malcolm is saying more than this. He claims that we cannot ask whether religious belief or our trust in our memory is rational, since they are just there as a part of life; they are groundless and autonomous. Why is it not possible to ask whether it is rational to trust in our memory? Malcolm does not say, but I guess he has something like the following in mind. Memory seems to be necessary for our reasoning. Unless we trust our memories we cannot reason at all, because in all processes of inference we have to remember our premises on our way to the conclusions we draw.

Suppose we want to justify or criticize our reliance on memories. To be able to do that we have to use our memory, we have to remember the arguments we try to give for or against that reliance of ours. So we have to assume the truth of what we try to justify or criticize. And consequently, we cannot find *any* non-circular evidence in either direction. Our belief in our memory is, in Malcolm's terminology, groundless. For Phillips and maybe also for Malcolm, it is not just something we cannot justify or criticize, it is even meaningless to ask the question. And so is it, Malcolm claims, also with religious belief. But how could that be the case? These activities do not seem to be on a par. Whereas it seems difficult, perhaps even impossible, to deny our belief in our memories, that is not so when it comes to the denial of religious belief. A lot of people deny religious belief without being cut off from reason, and they can reject it without having to assume the truth of what they deny. So it may not be possible rationally to assess our trust in our memories, but from that it does not follow that we cannot ask whether it is rational to participate in religious practice, because the former cannot be denied but the latter can. Phillips is aware of this difference:

> In discussing Wittgenstein's treatment of basic propositions we saw how, with regard to many of them, they could not be denied without our being cut off from reason. This is one difference, and an important one, between basic propositions such as "This is a tree," "I was born," "There is a corridor outside my door", etc., etc., and religious beliefs. The latter *are* denied.[51]

So why is it not proper to ask whether religious practice is rational, if religion can properly be denied, without cutting oneself off from reason? Further, it looks as if there are other alternatives present in this case, secular views of life, and it seems as if we could assess and compare these views of life by using, for instance, the principle of presumption. Phillips think that we should deny this temptation. But why? His answer is far from satisfying, but essentially he claims that Wittgenstein has *shown* why it is not possible, by giving the following example:

> Suppose someone is ill and he says: "This is a punishment," and I say: "If I'm ill, I don't think of punishment at all." If you say: "Do you believe the opposite?"—you can call it believing the opposite, but

it is entirely different from what we would normally call believing the opposite.

I think differently, in a different way. I say different things to myself. I have different pictures.

It is this way: if someone said: "Wittgenstein, you don't take illness as punishment, so what do you believe?"—I'd say: "I don't have any thoughts of punishment."

There are, for instance, these entirely different ways of thinking first of all—which needn't be expressed by one person saying one thing, another person another thing.[52]

Phillips does not explain how this quotation from Wittgenstein shows that it is not possible critically to assess and compare different views of life. The point seems to be, however, that the advocates of different views of life do not believe contradictory propositions. However, most people (at least in pluralistic societies) seem to understand perfectly well that different views of life (like atheism and theism) compete and often contradict each other. But even if they, say an atheist and a theist, do not contradict each other, how does this show that we cannot ask whether it is rational to pursue religious practice? What it seems to cast doubt on, at the most, is that we could apply exactly the same standards to these non-contradictory practices. But much more argumentation is needed to show even that this is so.

Perhaps what Phillips is after is the following. What makes the question of rationality inappropriate in the context of our trust in our memories is that, if it were doubted, it would be had to see how someone could go on living. Why that question is not proper when it comes to religious belief is that this is a case where "changes may enable you to go on, [if it were doubted,] but not in the same way as you went on before." The convert "comes to something new, something which does not stop him [from] going on, but which nevertheless *demands that he does not go on in the same way.*" So the case in which somebody cannot go on in the same way if he or she rejects religious belief (or some other view of life) shows that the question of rationality cannot properly be raised in this context. But how could the fact that the changing of a view of life is "a reorientation of one's whole life" make it inappropriate to ask whether it is rational to adopt that view of life?[53] I suppose that leaving the conservative party and

becoming a socialist is a radical reorientation of a person's whole life
and that it demands that the person "does not go on in the same
way." But to conclude from this that we cannot ask whether his or
her participation in the socialist party is rational seems, at least, very
strange. How could that follow?

However, sometimes giving up one's religious faith does in fact
stop one from, in a sense, going on living. In some cases of so called
primitive religion this might be so, when religion is an inseparable
part of these societies. One cannot refrain from holding such religious
beliefs without becoming an outsider to the society, which would be
the same as ceasing to exist as a person. In such a situation it might be
meaningless to ask whether the religious practice is rational because
that question cannot be properly raised. Gutting writes:

> If Winch's account is correct, there is no way of being an Azande
> without believing in witchcraft and poison-oracles. So no one born
> into the Zande form of life can give up such beliefs without be-
> coming an outsider to Zande society—for example, by becoming
> westernized or going mad. But a twentieth-century American given
> the most devout and pervasive religious upbringing does not be-
> come an outsider to American society by ceasing to believe in God.
> The American has not abandoned a form of life but rather a way
> of thinking and acting *within* a form of life. This is because for us
> religion exists not as a form of life but as a challenge and option
> within our form of life. And this is why even the most committed
> believer must, as their religion itself will insist, see nonbelief as a
> real possibility for them.[54]

So as Gutting points out, Winch's scenario of the Zande's form of
life is typically not the type of situation that the great world religions
are in, and it is in particular not representative of views of life in the
Western world. They challenge and transform societies rather than
being woven into the very fabric of autonomous practices. If our
religions were autonomous in the sense that some primitive religions
are, then the practice-basic beliefs of our religions might well be
properly groundless. But then they would lose their "distinctive and
invaluable character as a call to transform—without renouncing—
our human condition."[55] However, all that is probably needed for
believers of primitive religions to be able to see the appropriateness
of asking whether it is rational for them to participate in their religious
practice is some serious interaction with people who hold views of

life other than themselves. Therefore, even granted the exception
of some primitive religions, the conclusion must be that neither the
meaning argument nor the basicality argument should convince us
that we cannot properly ask whether it is rational to pursue religious
(or secular) practice.

4.   The Autonomy of Life-View Practice

Implicit in Phillips's view we can instead find some thoughts that
might lead us to see why the question of rationality can meaningfully
be asked in matters concerning religion and what really might be
autonomous or groundless in this context. Let us start by noticing
that Phillips does not think that religion is an "esoteric game" isolated
from the rest of life: "Religion has something to say about aspects
of human existence which are quite intelligible without reference to
religion: birth, death, joy, misery, . . . fortune and misfortune."[56] For
him the question of whether one should hold religious beliefs is a
matter of adopting a way of life. "To ask someone whether he thinks
these beliefs are true is not to ask him to produce evidence for them,
but rather to ask him *whether he can live by them,* . . ."[57] Here he
focuses on the regulative function of the religious practice, which is
its life-directing role. Religion provides life with depth and meaning
and so equips us better to deal practically with it. And sometimes he
seems to think that the religious way of life provides the best and most
authentic human life. But this is open to challenge because secular
views of life make similar claims.
So religion provides life with depth and significance, but here
we have one of the grounds on which the presumptionist claims that
both religious and secular views of life try to provide convincing
alternatives. All views of life try at least to come to grips with our
existential concerns. And here good reasons (or evidence) become
relevant. There might exist good reasons (or evidence) to think that
adherents of a particular view of life *cannot live by* their life-view
beliefs, and this might indicate that their acceptance of this view of life
is irrational and that they should therefore try to abandon it. Further,
if the religious practice includes a factual element (has a theoretical
as well as regulative function) and this does not distort the character
of these beliefs, then truth (or other epistemic ends) is another end
secular and religious views of life have in common.

However, Phillips thinks that these practices have no standards (no "evaluative yardstick") in common, so the fact that they have some ends in common does not help; therefore, it is still misleading to speak of adopting or rejecting a religion as rational or irrational.[58] But this is wrong, since all religious and secular practices can have a standard in common, namely the principle of presumption, and the very same principle might even apply to everyday life and to science (at least as a necessary condition for rationality), and perhaps even to all other practices we are involved in.

There are, I think, certain elements of our previous discussion we can introduce to clarify the issues at stake here. First, consider the locus of rationality and the discussion concerning what can and cannot be rational. Contextualists make the same mistake as many other philosophers and talk about "rational beliefs" and "rational practices." This is a misleading way of talking about rationality because it is not certain that beliefs and practices *per se* can or cannot be rationally justified. Rather, it is what someone believes and someone's participation in a practice that can be rational or irrational themselves. On such an analysis, what contextualists are, strictly speaking, claiming is that:

> We cannot properly ask whether or not people's participation in the religious practice is rational.

Or more broadly speaking, they claim:

> We cannot properly ask whether or not people's participation in autonomous practices is rational.

So it is neither beliefs nor practices that are rational, but *believing*—believing in the context of a practice of some sort. Scientific rationality is concerned with believing in scientific practice. Life-view rationality is concerned with believing in religious and secular practices. Other forms of rationality are economical and political rationality, and so on.

Once we change the locus of rationality we can see that the distinction contextualists make between internal and external rationality needs to be clarified, and what is external and internal is not as static as it seems to be in their account. Recall that I first introduced the distinction to be able to distinguish between how an agent ought to regulate his or her internal affairs (concerning the rational regulation of already accepted beliefs), and his or her external affairs (concerning the rational regulation of the relation between, on the one hand, already accepted beliefs and, on the other hand, their grounds, other people's beliefs, new experiences encountered, etc.). Let us call this *agent-internal* and *agent-external rationality.* (See also chapter 3.) However, the way the contextualists use the distinction it is not meant to distinguish between what is external and internal to an *agent's belief system,* but to distinguish between what is external and internal to a *given practice,* such as science or religion:

> *Practice-Internal Rationality:* The standards of rationality used to determine whether what some agents believe within a practice are rational.

> *Practice-External Rationality:* The standards of rationality used to determine whether the participation of some agents in a practice is rational, or whether it is rational to pursue a practice.

So we have to distinguish between agent-internal and practice-internal and agent-external and practice-external rationality. But this means that it is possible that what is internal to a person's belief system might be external to the set of beliefs that constitutes a practice. And consequently what might seem to be an internal standard from the perspective of the religious practice might be an external standard from the personal point of view. The same ambiguity is present when we talk about basic beliefs (or non-basic beliefs for that matter). Do we mean practice-basic or agent-basic beliefs—the foundational beliefs of a practice or of an agent's belief system? Further, whereas the beliefs a practice contains are relatively homogenous (they are not of completely different kinds), this is not so for an agent's belief system—assuming he or she participates in many different practices, which is likely. If we take into account these observations a more dynamic picture of belief-regulation or revision emerges. People move in between different practices, meet certain standards of rationality in one practice and other standards in another practice, and so on. But the uniting element is the agent (or agents), and the ultimate locus of rationality is not beliefs nor practices, but the agent him or herself.

This can help us locate what might be autonomous in this context. Not all people enter a religious practice (even less the Christian practice), however, all people have to enter the domain of a lifeview practice—without one, it would be hard to see how someone could go on living. Here a life-view practice is on the same level as everyday practice. A religious person may abandon his or her faith, a scientist may quit being a scientist, an artist may give up art, and in so doing cease to participate in a practice. But if someone were to stop participating in everyday life or holding a view of life, that person would give up *life*.[59] Such a person would cease to be a properly functioning human. In a life-view practice we try at least to deal with our existential experiences of resistance (like experiences of grief, anxiety, meaninglessness, suffering), and we try to find a way through the barriers that block the road toward a happy and good life or toward ultimate fulfillment. Suppose someone asked: "Is it rational to do that?" All we could say I think is, as Wittgenstein, that: "Then I am inclined to say: 'This is simply what I do.'"

So characteristic of both life-view and everyday practice is that they are *non-optional,* it is a practical necessity that we participate in these practices. (Science, on the other hand, is an example of an optional practice.) Therefore, what we could claim is not that religion, or even more narrowly Christianity or Buddhism, are (entirely) autonomous practices, but that they rather belong to a more fundamental (autonomous) practice, the *life-view practice,* which not only includes different religious views of life but also secular ones, like Marxism and Ecosophy. We may not be able to ask whether it is rational to participate in a life-view practice, and in this sense there might be no practice-external rationality. But we can ask whether it is rational to participate in optional and alternative practices (such as Christian or Buddhist practices) *within* the life-view practice; in this sense there is a practice-internal rationality. And we can apply standards like the principle of presumption to try to determine whether an agent's (or agents') life-view beliefs or participation in a particular view of life is rational or irrational.

However, for the sake of argument, suppose that the contextualist is right after all concerning the first part of the autonomy thesis: there are no practice-transcendent standards of rationality. Our different practices do not share one single standard of rationality with each other. Does it follow even in such a situation that we cannot determine whether it is rational for someone in a practice to hold a particular belief or whether it is rational at all to participate in a practice? Not necessarily. To see why consider the following scenario. Let us suppose that scientific standards of rationality are completely unique and that they have nothing in common whatsoever with standards used in any other human practices. The reason why this is so is that the subject matter of science is special and that scientific claims have a specific meaning. Suppose further that some people, say philosophers, who are not themselves scientists start thinking about what standards of rationality are appropriate to use in scientific practice. They learn how scientists normally work, what the aims of scientific practice are, and what meaning scientific claims have. However, they come to the conclusion that some of the standards used in science should be abandoned and replaced with some other standards; and perhaps they themselves propose what standards these should actually be. In such a case it seems possible to criticize what is going on in scientific practice from the outside—by somebody who is not involved in that practice, even though the set of standards is completely unique for this practice.

So it is not enough that contextualists can show that our practices have no standards in common to conclude that rationality is not only practice-dependent (as presumptionists claim) but *practice-determined*. They also have to block the possibility that somebody who is not participating in the practice can establish or propose appropriate standards for whether it is rational for a person to accept a belief in that domain. Contextualists must claim that it is the preferences of the participants that have *epistemic authority,* and typically I think that this is what they, at least implicitly, claim. What is needed for rationality to be practice-determined is, therefore, an additional thesis, namely:

> *The Authority Thesis:* It is only the participants of a practice who can decide what standards of rationality are appropriate to use in that practice.

If this is correct then implicit in the contextual principle (that what can be rational or irrational can be determined only internally, from within a context, since there exists no trans-contextual standards of rationality) we can also find the authority thesis.

However, contextualists can choose to use another strategy to sustain the claim that rationality is practice-determined instead. Because even if people who are not involved in the practice can assess what standards it is appropriate to use, contextualists can still hold on to their position by claiming:

The Participation Thesis: It is only the participants of
a practice who can appropriately apply the standards
of rationality to beliefs in that practice.

Therefore, only those taking part in a practice can in the end
assess when a particular person's beliefs are rational in that domain.
This last possibility is open to at least those contextualists who reject
the rule principle (that rationality is rule-determined) and who accept
the claim that the basic mode of rational justification is judgment.
What should we say of this?

There is certainly some truth in the authority and participation
theses; for instance, people trained in a practice like science are
normally better skilled to assess what is rational to do or believe in
scientific practice than other people. On the other hand, we know
that sometimes it is helpful to bring in people from the outside when
we have to settle a conflict, solve an issue, or the like. This is not
just true of negotiators called upon to negotiate between the union
(or the employees) and the employers, but it applies to all areas
in life. So I find it unlikely that these theses are true, and to me
it seems even dangerous to accept them as true. It is dangerous
since it makes it possible for members of a practice to decide to
accept just *any* set of beliefs they like, without it being possible for
other people rationally to assess such decisions. On such an account
to explain the rationality of practices like science and religion is to
explain the actual preferences (whatever they are and however they
have been arrived at) of the scientific and religious community. In
the end the very possibility of democracy seems to be threatened,
since it, as far as I can understand, presupposes that people can and
have a right to rationally assess what other people believe, do, or
participate in.

So contextualists have to be able to build a strong case before we
should feel obligated to accept the authority and participation theses
because such an acceptance seems to undermine the very foundation
our society stands on. This has not yet been done to my knowledge,
and therefore my conclusion is that contextualism in this form should
be rejected. However, we are all participants in the life-view practice
so we can all be experts at least in this field, and therefore these two
theses do not have much force in this area, nor in any other non-
optional practices for that matter.

5.   Contextualism and Truth

I have so far consciously avoided including the familiar contextualist claim that each practice embodies its own distinctive or unique concepts of truth and reality, since it is not necessary to hold this view to be a contextualist in matters concerning rationality. And I think personally that the strongest version of contextualism is one that restricts the scope of the contextual principle to rationality, since we will see that an expanded version has problems being internally consistent. However, many contextualists do not hesitate to apply the contextual principle not only to rationality but also to truth and reality:

> What is rational, true, and real can be determined
> only internally, from within a context (practice), so
> there exists no rationality, truth, or reality that is trans-
> contextual.

Not only rationality but also truth and reality are said to be practice-determined. Let us see why these contextualists think that different practices come equipped with their own distinctive notions of truth and reality. One could say that contextualism starts with an empirical observation, and this position is an attempt to come to grip with this fact. The empirical observation is that people construe their worlds radically differently; our world is far from being the same as the medieval world or the worlds of other cultures. People throughout history have created different conceptual schemes and organized their reality in different ways. Different communities of, for example, scientists and religious believers—living in the same or different cultures— seem to be living in divergent worlds. So contextualists take their starting-point in our "growing awareness of the way in which all our ideas are shaped by the cultural and symbolic framework of orientation within which we are living and thinking."[60]

What should we make of this? One possible explanation is the one offered by the *critical realists,* namely, that it is not as easy as we might have thought to come in touch with reality or find the truth. The world does not constrain what we believe to the extent we had previously expected. However, reality is what it is and people's different ways of describing it should be understood as more or less successful attempts to get in touch with that reality. But contextualists claim that the realists have got things backwards, and these fundamental disagreements among people of the past and of the present should be understood in a different way. This is so because a central thesis of the contextualist is:

> *The Conceptual Thesis:* The only reality we know anything about is the reality we encounter through the framework of our language.

According to Winch: "Our idea of what belongs to the realm of reality is given for us in the language that we use. The concepts we have settle for us the form of the experience we have of the world. . . . The world *is* for us what is presented through those concepts. That is not to say that our concepts may not change; but when they do, that means that our concept of the world has changed too."[61] So language in some sense determines our reality. In an important way we human beings are responsible for the structure and nature of reality by way of our linguistic or symbolic activity. In other words, these contextualists seem to accept some version of what I previously called *creative anti-realism* (the view that reality, or some aspect of it, is dependent on the way human beings think believe, or speak).[62] Reality is our own construction. But as we have noticed, we do not all construct the same world. Religious believers construct their world differently from scientists, Swedes different from the Azande, and so on.

However, if the only reality we know anything about is the reality we encounter through our language, then, as Brown points out, people with different languages live in different *worlds,* and "can legitimately be described as knowing different *truths* in the sense in which a true statement must conform to reality."[63] So science and religion provide us with two different languages, and thus two different realities and sets of truths. But these realities are real, and these truths are true, only *for* the participants in these practices, for those who speak the language of science and of religion. Therefore Sapir can claim that:

> The "real world" is to a large extent unconsciously built upon the language habits of the group. The worlds in which different societies live are *distinct* worlds, not merely the same world with different labels attached. We see and hear and otherwise experience very largely as we do because the language habits of our community predispose certain choices of interpretation.[64]

So religious practice constitutes a world of its own, with its own reality and its own truth; and the word "God" used in religious practice (or any other word used in any other practice for that matter) does not refer to a language-independent reality. Phillips thinks Lindbeck is "absolutely right" in claiming "that we misunderstand the logic of theological doctrines if we think of them as descriptions of an object, a phenomenon, given *independently* of them."[65] In general, our words should not at all be thought of as referring to a practice-independent reality, but be seen as the way words are used in a given practice.

But do Phillips and Lindbeck really think that religious people in general would agree that God's basic structure or even existence depends on human practices or on our linguistic activities? Is not rather Alston right when he claims that for them this would be seen as a failing in faith, "to deny that God is what He is and does what He does, whatever we may think or feel about it"?[66] I think the answer must be "yes" indeed. So again, to make sense of what these contextualists say we should understand them as recommending to religious believers a way in which they should understand their faith rather than a description of faith. However, thinking about how actual religious believers might react shows that this version of the contextual principle in the end becomes counter-intuitive and makes of us something more than we really are. Consider Plantinga's provocative responses:

> Until you feel the grip of this way of looking at things, it can seem a bit presumptuous, not to say preposterous. Did *we* structure or create the heavens and the earth? Some of us think there were animals—dinosaurs, let's say—roaming the earth before human beings had so much as put in an appearance; how could it be that those dinosaurs owed their structure to our noetic [or linguistic] activity? What did we do to give *them* the structure they enjoyed? And what about all those stars and planets we have never even heard of: how have we managed to structure them? When did we do all this? Did we structure ourselves in this way too? And if the way things are is thus up to us and our structuring activity, why don't we improve things a bit?[67]

Although it is undeniable that our *processes* of thinking are always done in a historical and social context, the *results* of our thinking might have practice-transcending significance and so be true in all practices. Would we not agree that claims that are true independently of the linguistic structure of different cultures or practices are: that we need food to survive, that we have to look after our hygiene in order not to catch different diseases, that many diseases depend on our genes, that certain ecological disasters depend on certain agricultural techniques. And it does not help if all the members of a practice agree that these are not true in their practice or are not at all aware of these truths. Cancer does not disappear just because we decide to drop a concept from our repertoire.[68] These observations lead naturally over to what is really problematic about this version of contextualism.

The source of this problem for contextualists is their claim that each different practice has its own unique conceptions of rationality, truth, and reality; that different societies have radically different conceptions of reality; that the world is accessible to us only through our linguistic activity, and so on. But how should we interpret these other than as claims that *it is true* that different practices have their own unique conceptions of rationality, truth, and reality; that *it is true* that different societies have radically different conceptions of reality; that *it is true* that the world is accessible to us only through our linguistic activity? On such an interpretation these claims are thought to be universally true. But then their position is false, because it consists of the claim that there exists no trans-contextual, trans-social, practice-transcending, or universal truths. Their position becomes *self-defeating*.

However, they can avoid this internal inconsistency by claiming that these claims are true only for people who share their cultural or social context—participate in their practice. But then they cannot say that the people who reject their contextualism and even the advocates of the most absolute universalism are claiming something false, because according to their own theory they must accept that these views are true for the people who accept them, even if these views are false for them. Both contextualism and universalism are equally true, and each is true for those who accept them. In other words, contextualists can disagree only with each other, not with people who disagree with them, since they have different and incompatible conceptions of truth.

Much more could be said about these things, but I think this is sufficient to show that the most plausible version of contextualism is one that limits the scope of the contextual principle to rationality. In such an account one could say, without being self-defeating, that it is *true* that rationality is practice-determined. However, we have seen that there are reasons to believe that this version of contextualism is *false*. But before we close our discussion of contextualism I think we have to consider one more version of it. This is a version which may be the most interesting of them all because it seriously tries to come to grips with conflicts between different practices. This version is presented by MacIntyre in his recent book *Whose Justice? Which Rationality?* It is a form of contextualism that I will call "dynamic contextualism" for reasons that will soon become clear.

6. MacIntyre's Dynamic Contextualism

I find myself in agreement with much of what MacIntyre writes about rationality, but despite this I inclined to understand it as a form of contextualism, which means that I, in the end, reject his position.[69] This shows, again, that there is no clear demarcation between formal, practice-oriented, and contextual approaches to rationality. They can all be seen as located on a spectrum with formalism and contextualism at each end. But where exactly the borders between formalist and contextualist positions, on the one hand, and practice-oriented positions, on the other hand, go is hard to determine. So in a sense MacIntyre's dynamic contextualism can be seen as a test case which helps us see where the border might be between a practice-oriented position like presumptionism and contextualism.

The purpose of MacIntyre's inquiry into the conceptions of rationality and justice given throughout our history is to arrive at "a true account of justice and of practical rationality." During this inquiry, MacIntyre writes, he came to recognize "that different and incompatible conceptions of justice are characteristically closely linked to different and incompatible conceptions of practical rationality." Underlying people's diverse judgments upon issues concerning justice are a set of conflicting and incompatible conceptions of justice and rationality. He writes that we "inhabit a culture in which an inability to arrive at agreed rationally justifiable conclusions on the nature of justice and practical rationality . . ." is manifest.[70] There are among people of our culture radical disagreements on what standpoint to adopt on central issues. Here we can see that MacIntyre shares with contextualism its focus on how much disagreement there is between people of the same or of different cultures. People construe their worlds in radically different ways. And he wants to explain this in the same way as the contextualists we have considered, not by a hypothesis that traditions share the same conception of rationality, but rather that different practices incorporate often conflicting and incompatible conceptions of rationality.[71] His main thesis seems to be that:

> Our inability to arrive at *agreed* (rationally justifiable) *conclusions* on the nature of rationality and justice, and issues like abortion and the Vietnam war, should be explained by the fact that we belong to different practices (in his terminology traditions)[72] which embody different and incompatible conceptions of rationality and justice.

MacIntyre wants to replace the Enlightenment's (in my terminology one version of the formal) view of rationality with a *tradition-bound account of rationality,*[73] that is, with "a conception of rational enquiry as embodied in a tradition, a conception according to which the standards of rational justification themselves emerge from and are part of a history in which they are vindicated by the way in which they transcend the limitations of and provide remedies for the defects of their predecessors within the history of that *same* tradition."[74] So MacIntyre seems to accept the contextual principle (at least the first part of it)—that what can be rational or irrational can only be determined internally, from within a context (practice), there exist no context-independent standards of rationality—as an explanatory principle. Which of the theses we have distinguished implicit in the contextual principle does he accept? It is clear, from the quotation above and the following one, that MacIntyre in one sense accepts the first part of the autonomy thesis (that there are practices that have their own unique conceptions of rationality):

> Each tradition can at each stage of its development provide rational justification for its central theses in its own terms, employing the concepts and standards by which it defines itself, but there is no set of independent standards of rational justification by appeal to which the issues between contending traditions can be decided.[75]

But he qualifies his acceptance of this thesis, because he agrees with the evidentialist and presumptionist that there are *some* practice-transcending standards of rationality. At least, the practices he has examined share some set of standards. They all accept that logic has certain authority. But the basic laws of logic constitute only a necessary and not a sufficient condition for rationality. Hence these practices have insufficient common standards of rationality to resolve their disagreements. This is probably true not only for the moral practices he examines (the Plantonic-Aristotelian, the Augustianian, and the Scottish) but for all practices we participate in, since he thinks that ". . . Aristotle was successful, . . . in showing that no one who understands the laws of logic can remain rational while rejecting them."[76]

For MacIntrye the truth of the autonomy thesis is not an *a priori* truth, since it is possible that we all could have the same conception of rationality—*if* we did not disagree as much and as fundamentally as we do. But even then, I take it, he would claim that *rationality is possible only within a practice*. In other words, he would accept the internal thesis (that the only kind of rationality that exists is internal; rationality is always used in a practice of one sort or another) even if the autonomy thesis could not be empirically supported. That is: "There is no standing ground, no place for enquiry, no way to engage in the practices of advancing, evaluating, accepting, and rejecting reasoned argument apart from that which is provided by some particular tradition or other."[77] And he says: "Every such form of enquiry begins in and from some condition of pure historical contingency, from the beliefs, institutions, and practices of some particular community which constitute a given."[78] In this sense there is no rationality as such. Rather rationality itself, whether theoretical or practical, is a concept with a history. Rationality is always practice-laden. We have to begin where we stand, with what we know and then proceed. So *rational believing* always begins from contingently given beliefs, beliefs which are ours simply because we participate in some practice. And *rational belief-regulation* depends on the conceptual resources available in that practice, for both stating the problems and providing standards of what may count as acceptable solutions to them.

What sets him apart from the other contextualists we have considered is that he denies that it follows from the fact that the standards of rationality are practice-determined that no practice can claim rational superiority to any other. It appears that no practice can claim rationality to any other. It appears that no practice can claim rational superiority because if each tradition has internal to itself its own view of what rational superiority consists in, then its adherents can always claim that their practice is rationally superior since they themselves decide which standards competing practices should be evaluated against. So it seems as if no rational debate between traditions can occur at any fundamental level. This MacIntyre calls the "relativist challenge": roughly, it could be stated as the claim that if each practice embodies its own specific conception of rationality, then "no issue between contending traditions is rationally decidable."[79]

Before we see how he attempts to overcome this challenge let us notice that implicit in this way of arguing, questioning, or responding, there lies a rejection of the second part of the autonomy thesis, that it is inappropriate to ask whether a practice is rational to pursue. I think that for MacIntyre it is both possible and important to ask whether or not someone's participation in a practice is rational. However, the problem is not that we ask this kind of question, but that we do not (as a matter of fact) have a sufficient set of standards of rationality available to help us determine which one of two or more competing practices is to be preferred. So the version of the autonomy thesis that he accepts is something like the following. There are some standards of rationality applicable to all practices but they are insufficient to resolve issues on which these practices disagree. Therefore we have to make use of practice-specific standards to be able to rationally justify our beliefs and actions. The other contextualists' answer to the relativist challenge—if they do not accept it themselves—is, roughly, that this is how we proceed. It is meaningless to ask, for example, which secular or religious practice it is rational for a person to accept. MacIntyre, on the other hand, claims that the solution to the challenge is that:

> A practice can by its own standards of rationality recognize that another practice is rationally superior.

Practices can cease to be progressive by their own lights. When a practice stagnates or degenerates it enters a period of *epistemological crisis*. And a practice can in such a situation defeat another if the alien practice can (*a*) construct an explanation, which is cogent and illuminating by the standards of the practice in crisis, of what it was that made the practice in crisis stagnate or degenerate, and (*b*) itself solve the problems that the defeated practice could not come to grips with. MacIntyre says that: "In this kind of situation the rationality of tradition requires an acknowledgment by those who have hitherto inhabited and given their allegiance to the tradition in crisis that the alien tradition is superior in rationality and in respect of its claims to truth to their own."[80] (This is why I label his view "dynamic" contextualism, since on his account a practice can meet not only internal but also external challenges, and the external challenges are real ones because a practice can be defeated by another. Practices can compete and overcome each other.)

Notice that MacIntyre introduces here a practice-transcending standard, which is applicable to all practices that are in such an epistemological crisis as the one sketched above. We might call it, to have a label, the *principle of progressivity*. It requires that, independently of which practice we belong to, if we are in this kind of situation—when conditions (a) and (b) are satisfied—then we must switch our allegiance to the rival practice if our own has ceased to be progressive. However, the principle of progressivity presupposes that MacIntyre rejects the authority thesis (that it is only the participants of a practice themselves who can decide what standards of rationality are appropriate to use in their practice). Otherwise, nothing stops the adherents of the practice in crisis from changing or modifying the standards of their practice so as to render incoherent (according to the modified standards) the explanation of the rival practice of what it was that rendered their practice non-progressive.

However, the problem, as MacIntyre is quick to point out, is that defeat is just one of the possible outcomes of a confrontation between two practices. If that is the case, the relativist can reply that this might be true of some conflicts but most of the time conflicts between practices do not end with defeat; examples from theology, science, politics, and so on, are not hard to find. Hence MacIntyre has only partly responded to the relativist challenge, and more is needed to overcome it. He attempts to provide that by creating a *dilemma* for the relativist, a dilemma that will show that the challenge cannot properly be raised. And he does this by drawing out some of the implications that the internal thesis has. The question we have to ask the relativist is: "Who is in a position to issue such a challenge (to claim that if each practice embodies its own specific conception of rationality, then no issue between contending traditions is rationally decidable)?" MacIntyre's conclusion is that the relativist at least is not in such a position. For a person who would raise the challenge "must during such period of time *either* be him or herself an inhabitant of one of the two or more rival traditions, owing allegiance to its standards of inquiry and justification and employing them in his or her reasoning, *or* be someone outside all of the traditions, him or herself traditionless."[81]

But in the former alternative, in the absence of severe epistemological crisis in the practice the person belongs to, a person will be committed to its rationality since he or she would have no good reason to question his or her allegiance to the practice. In such case, his or her situation precludes him or her from having a rational basis for the challenge. In the latter alternative, a person tries to issue the challenge by adopting a standpoint outside all practices but this is an impossibility since rationality is practice-bound (the internal thesis). Therefore, such persons lack "sufficient rational resources for enquiry and *a fortiori* for enquiry into what tradition is to be rationally preferred."[82] So in neither case can the challenge be properly raised. It does not seem possible that the challenge is itself rational for someone to issue.

MacIntyre's argument against relativisim seems to be successful, but I think its scope is more limited than what he believes. He is quite right, I think, to claim that all kinds of criticism (including the relativist challenge) must be directed from some kind of perspective, from some kind of practice—that is the essential content of the internal thesis. This means that his argument is successful against a general relativisim that consists of the claim that most issues between *all* contending practices is rationally undecidable. But his argument lacks force against a local relativisim, one that consists of the claim that most issues between *some* rival practices are rationally undecidable. And most of the criticism we have discussed has taken this form, for example, both the scientific and the evidentialist challenge to religious belief can be understood in this way. The scientific challenge is raised *within* a practice—science—against religious practices. And a similar challenge against contending moral practices (like the ones MacIntyre discusses) can be issued *from* some other kind of practices. Since these challenges are raised within practices of one kind and directed towards rival practices of another kind, MacIntyre's dilemma is not applicable, and his argument against this form of relativism fails. The dilemma is not applicable because the person who issues the relativist challenge is not directing it against all practices nor against the practice that he or she belongs to (hence the first horn of the dilemma is avoided), neither is this person traditionless (hence the second horn is also avoided); the person in question belongs to a practice, but of a kind other than the one challenged.

As we have seen, MacIntyre's main argument for his hypothesis, that different practices embody incompatible conceptions of rationality (that is, that rationality is practice-determined), is not identical with the meaning or the basicality argument, but is a kind of *non-consensus argument*:

> Because we do not arrive at agreed conclusions when
> we use only practice-transcending standards we must
> accept the fact that the practices to which we belong
> have incompatible conceptions of rationality.

He does not deny that there are practice-transcending standards of rationality, but only that they are sufficient for universal and rational convergence. So in a sense MacIntyre's model of rationality is compatible with presumptionism, since he can accept the principle of presumption and yet claim that it is just another necessary but not a sufficient condition for rationality since it resolves neither our disagreements nor the disagreements between the practices we participate in.

But why should we think that we must, if we have the same conception of rationality, be able to agree on which of the rival practices is (rationally) superior? Why should we think that we have a sufficient condition for rationality only if all rational people would in fact accept the same conclusion? Here he makes the same mistake as other contextualists (and many non-contextualists for that matter) in thinking that if we are rationally justified in believing what we believe, then somebody else cannot be rationally justified in disagreeing with us, unless we have different and incompatible conceptions of rationality. The assumption is that what is rational for us must be rational for them if we share the same conception of rationality. But this does not follow, because agreement does not seem to be a necessary condition for a general or practice-transcending conception of rationality.

Before I try to show why I think this is so, it is important to notice that MacIntyre has the same problem in his own backyard, because even *within* a practice people do not always agree that some beliefs have "vindicated themselves as superior to their historical predecessors."[83] For instance, within the Christian practice, Christians do not agree on what the practice-constituting principles of rationality are. Is conformity with the Bible such a principle? Some say so, others deny it. Nor do they agree on what beliefs it is rational to hold as a Christian. Must one believe that God was literally incarnated in Christ? Some say so, others deny it. On these and similar issues there is no consensus among the participants of Christian practice. Does this mean that the people who disagree belong to different sub-practices with incompatible conceptions of rationality, and the people who disagree in the sub-practices belong to sub-sub-practices, and so on? This does not seem to be a promising way of understanding rationality.

Instead we should reject the non-consensus argument. We can still share the same conception of rationality even though we do not arrive at agreed conclusions. In fact, many times if we arrived at the same conclusions we would be irrational since we normally do not have access to the same evidence and have not had the same experiences. But this does not count against a general or practice-transcending conception of rationality. It requires only that one accept that what is rational for one person to believe must be rational for anyone else in the same situation. The universal claim is that what is rational for someone is also rational for everybody else were they in his or her shoes. The demand of rationality is for everyone and everywhere the same, that *we ought to do what can rightly be demanded of us with the limited means at our disposal and in the particular situation in which we find ourselves.* And according to the presumptionist, what can be rightly demanded of us is that we have a willingness to test our beliefs (actions and evaluations) in situations of resistance. But in the absence of special reasons to the contrary we are rationally entitled to continue fully to believe what we believe. However, the ways (standards, methods, or the like) we use to fulfill this demand change with time and cultural setting, and it all depends on what resources are available to us where we are. For example, some societies have access to statistics and computers, others not, and this affects what it is rational to do in fields where such tools are applicable.

This means that MacIntyre is in an important way right in connecting rationality to consensus. Because if we were in the same situation (had the same opportunities, capacities, objectives, needs, wants, access to evidence, values, and the like) and we satisfied the demands of rationality in the way we should, we would accept the same beliefs. But his mistake is that he does not distinguish between *actual* and *ideal* consensus. Only ideal consensus can be considered a necessary condition for a unified conception of rationality. As Rescher says:

> Rationality itself is, after all, a project that we are bound to pursue by variable means amongst the varied circumstances of a difficult world, where the consesnsus that objectivity ideally involves may well be unattainable in practice. (The extent to which reality cooperates with the demands of rationality is limited.) Rationality must, for us, remain something of an ideal which we can only realize to the limited extent that the circumstances of our situation permit.[84]

But of course, on the other hand, the conception of rationality we employ must not be *too* idealized, since it must be applicable in a meaningful way to human agents living, not in an ideal, but in the real world. Rationality cannot demand more of us than we reasonably can do with our resources and in our predicament.[85]

To sum up, we should agree with MacIntyre that rationality is *practice-bound,* if by that we mean that we accept the internal thesis. However, there is no need for us to accept his claim that rationality is essentially *practice-determined* (or accept the autonomy thesis) because we are frequently unable to arrive at consensus regarding of issues like abortion or the Vietnam war, since rationality, properly understood, does not require that kind of convergence. Hence a general model of rationality, more specifically, presumptionism, is after all to be preferred.

12

Some Concluding Remarks

I have tried to argue that rationality has to do with an agent's proper (reasonable or intelligent) exercise of his or her cognitive equipment or intelligence. Rationality tells us how one ought to regulate what one is doing (believing, acting, and evaluating). Consequently, the theory of rationality tries to lay down principles or suggestions for how we or other beings should conduct our cognitive (practical and evaluative) affairs. However, principles or suggestions should take into account the agent's capacities and situation. This thesis that rationality should be realistic is based on the axiom of reasonable demand: One cannot reasonably demand of a person what that person cannot do.

Traditional theory of rationality has often ignored this constraint on rationality. The proposed standards of rationality seem to address ideal cognizers without any consideration for their general usefulness and applicability; they seem not to be directed toward human beings with their limited cognitive resources and location in this world. I have tried to show that behind this way of understanding rationality is a particular view of how proper philosophy should be conducted, namely the formal approach to philosophy. The formalist claims that the formulation of the adequate standards for evaluating some aspect (in this case rationality) of a practice can be done independently from the actual practice. The standards of rationality are assumed to be epistemically independent of the actual agents and the actual practices the agents are involved in.

I have on the contrary argued that standards of rationality cannot be stated properly without taking into consideration who the agent is. Therefore, logic or *a priori* considerations are not sufficient for generating appropriate standards of rationality, as we need also to know the characteristics of the agent and his or her situation. Our concern has been human rationality and the specification of appropriate standards for deciding when people should be considered rational in believing what they believe. In this context the question of rationality is essentially: What can one reasonably demand of human beings when it comes to regulating their believing processes or regulating their accepting and holding on to beliefs? Behind this way of understanding the question of rationality is another view of philosophy, a practice-oriented approach to philosophy. The practice-oriented philosopher claims that the formulation of adequate standards of rationality is epistemically dependent on the actual agents and the actual practices in which these agents participate. An examination of the actual past and contemporary practices of, for instance, science or religion is needed as a basis for a recommendation regarding proper standards of scientific or religious rationality.

Characteristic of our situation is (among other things) that we are finite beings with limited cognitive abilities and only a limited amount of time to exercise these abilities, and we have, because of our predicament, certain needs that we must try to fulfill or encounter certain experiences of resistance we have to try to overcome. Our limited cognitive resources and our location in this world are two crucial aspects of the predicament of human beings. So who and where we are affects under what circumstances we are rationally justified in accepting our beliefs, getting involved in a practice, and regarding what ends it is rational for us to adopt. People who do not take into account the limitations of their cognitive resources or the situation they are in, are acting irrationally; and standards of rationality that do not take this into account are inadequate. Such standards are not relevant to assessing human rationality (or irrationality).

What should one then demand of people when it comes to the rational regulation of their believings? According to the formal evidentialist, a belief is rationally acceptable only if it is obtained by following the appropriate rules. We need rules to be able to determine whether a belief is rational to accept. The social evidentialist, on the other hand, rejects the rule principle, claiming that rationality is not necessarily a rule-governed process, but rather a process that is first of all guided by the exercise of informed judgments. A belief is rationally acceptable only if it is obtained by a person who exercises an informed judgment, and, further, if it is exposed to peer evaluation.

However, both the formal and the social evidentialist share a commitment to evidentialism, since they claim that people are entitled to accept a belief only if there are good reasons for holding it. Hence the proper initial attitude towards our beliefs, and thereby also our belief-forming and regulating processes, is one of skepticism. We are not supposed to accept beliefs until we have good reasons for thinking that they are properly basic beliefs or that they are evidentially supported by other already rationally acceptable beliefs. What I have tried to show is that it is not rational for real people to try to satisfy the demand of the evidential principle, and this principle is, therefore, an inappropriate standard of rationality. It is not rational for people to conform to the evidential principle because they do not have the time nor the resources needed. In their situation, it would be irrational not to start by trusting their belief-forming and regulation processes and their deliverances (beliefs). Instead of being evidentialists, people ought to have confidence in their cognitive faculties and their deliverances, unless experience provides them with substantial grounds for questioning that confidence. These processes and their deliverances do not first need to be justified before it is rational for us to believe in them. Rather we are rational in accepting a belief as long as there is no special reason to do otherwise (the principle of presumption). So our initial attitude toward our beliefs should not be skepticism, as evidentialism implies, but trust. According to the presumptionist, we have a right to take all things which we find ourselves believing at face value unless we have a special reason not to do so.

But is there really—as the formal evidentialist the social evidentialist, and the presumptionist assume—a universal rationality, a rationality that is applicable in all areas of human life? The contextualist denies this and claims that rationality means one thing in one practice (or context, tradition, culture, etc.) and something completely different in another practice. Each practice has its own standards of rationality, and there is no independent basis for deciding whether one practice is more rational than another. Behind this understanding of rationality is a third approach to philosophy, the contextual approach. It states that the formulation of adequate standards for assessing some aspect of a practice (such as rationality) is totally determined by the actual practice. The standards of rationality are neither practice-independent (as the formalist thinks) nor only practice-dependent (as the practice-oriented philosopher thinks), but practice-determined. The ultimate epistemic authority when it comes to the formulation of the standards for rationality and the application of them is the participants of a practice themselves.

However, the mistake many contextualists make is to think that different practices have different rationalities because their participants pursue different ends by different means. But all a unified conception of rationality requires is that in any area of life we ought to do what can rightly be demanded of us with the limited means at our disposal and in the particular situation in which we find ourselves. The means we use to fulfill this universal demand of rationality change with time and cultural setting, since it all depends on what resources are available to us where we are. But the nature of rationality is the same; rationality is a matter of doing (believing, acting, and evaluating) what we intellectually ought to do and can realistically manage to do, so that in our circumstances we choose appropriate ends and means to achieve these ends.

I have argued that it can reasonably be demanded of us in all areas of life that we continue to believe something only as long as we have no special reason to stop believing it. Hence the principle of presumption is applicable not only to areas such as science and everyday life but also to religious practice. However, I have tried to show that much of the discussion of rationality in philosophy of religion is, in fact, religiously irrelevant because it does not take into account the actual aim or function of religious practice or the actual situation in which it is pursued. In our lives we encounter experiences of suffering, death, guilt, meaninglessness, and the like. In that situation we value a practice that makes sense out of these experiences, diagnoses them, and helps us find a way through these existential constraints. The practice that fulfills this function is life-view practice, and the actual end of life-view believing is this—to make our life and the world existentially intelligible. To have this end in one's believing could be irrational only if trying to overcome or deal with experiences of grief, anxiety, alienation, meaninglessness, suffering, and so on, is not among human beings' intrinsic needs, is not a part of our true interests, but clearly it is. Therefore, the end of life-view practice (secular or religious) is rational.

This also means that ultimately the acceptance of religion (or some secular alternative) is an existential choice. What is at stake is not only whether some beliefs are true or what conclusions we should draw regarding certain arguments, but how we actually should live our lives. It is not just a matter of making up one's mind, it is also a matter of choosing a way of living. Hence only standards of life-view rationality that take into account this function of life-view believing can be adequate. So in order to assess and weigh properly the rationality of what the adherents of a view of life tell us, we not only have to assess and weigh what they say (the theoretical adequacy), but also how they live (the existential adequacy). And the existential adequacy of a view of life can be determined only by focusing on how successful it is in actually guiding its adherents in their concrete lives, in overcoming existential constraints. Hence the rationality of religious believing can be evaluated properly only if we take into account how it does things, overcomes guilt and alienation, creates forgiveness and meaning, and so on.

But is it then rational for people to have—in their predicament—religious beliefs? Since all human beings have to deal with existential experiences of resistance, the issue is not "Shall we have a view of life?" but "Which view of life should we choose?" because we have to make a choice (consciously or unconsciously) no matter what. If we do not vote with our head, we vote with our feet. So the question is neither whether religious beliefs are scientifically acceptable nor whether religious beliefs can be supported by sufficient evidence, but whether one should be a religious or secular believer of one kind or another. If our answer is "no, people are not rational in accepting religious beliefs," then probably also secular believers fail to be rational. But then it could be asked whether it would not be irrational for these people to try to satisfy such standards of rationality because it is in their real interest to try to deal with their existential concerns. If that is correct, the only reasonable conclusion we can draw is that people are rational in accepting religious beliefs. They are doing what can reasonably be demanded of them with respect to the regulation of their life-view beliefs. Of course there are still a lot of religious and secular believers who are irrational, people who violate their intellectual responsibilities. They fail to modify or give up their religious or secular beliefs when sufficient evidence against their beliefs has emerged. These people stick to their beliefs even when there are good reasons to cease from believing them and there is a better alternative available. But that is another matter, it does not count against the fact that there are (and have always been) people who are rational religious believers. The debate on whether religious beliefs are rationally acceptable is over.[1]

Notes

1. Introduction

1 Putnam 1990:176.

2 Rescher 1988:2.

3 See, for example, Chisholm 1977:5.

4 Most of the time I will talk about a person, an individual or an agent. That does *not* mean that rationality is individualistic, and my suggestions can apply just as well to persons, individuals, or agents.

5 There is, unfortunately, one serious shortcoming of this study that I am well aware of. It focuses almost exclusively on "analytic philosophy" and the discussion of rationality going on there; no attempt is made to survey the discussion of rationality in "continental philosophy." The reason for not bringing in this material is not that I do not think it is of great importance; it definitely is. The reason is only my own lack of ability to cover such a wide philosophical territory—I, unfortunately, have already had to leave out relevant literature in analytic philosophy. However, that does not, of course, stop somebody else from bringing in such material, and so, I hope, a fruitful discussion of these important issues can continue.

2. The Nature of Rationality

1. The same is true of the less used term "reasonableness." Hence "rational," "justified," and "reasonable" are also often used interchangeably.

2. Bennett 1989:5.

3. Føllesdal 1986:122, 123.

4. de Sousa 1990:160

5. Chisholm 1977:6.

6. See Plantinga 1983 and 1990c.

7. *An Essay Concerning Human Understanding,* Essay IV, xvii, 24.

8. Chisholm 1977:14.

9. Blanshard 1974:400.

10. BonJour 1985:7–8.

11. Plantinga 1983:30–31.

12. Plantinga 1983:33. See also Chisholm 1977:14.

13. Foley 1988:131.

14. Chalmers 1990:24.

15. Elster 1986:1.

16. Cf. Nordin 1988:16–18.

17. Foley 1991:366.

18. Rescher 1988:29.

19. Chisholm 1977:15.

20. Some of these difficulties are discussed in Hempel 1966:40–45.

21. I am not saying that the issue is settled. This view of simplicity as a nonepistemic end only functions as an illustration in this chapter. See, for example, BonJour 1985:183, for an attempt to construe simplicity as an epistemic concept.

22. Elster 1986:1.

23. Compare with Foley 1991:376: " . . . *A* provides you with an evidential [in my terminology epistemic] reason to believe *B* only if you stand in an appropriate relation to *A* and only if, in addition, from some presupposed perspective *A* seems to be a mark of *B's* truth. The appropriate relation that you must bear to *A* can be left open for the discussion here—perhaps you must know *A* or, perhaps, you must rationally believe it or, perhaps, it is enough for you to have some sort of access to its truth."

24. As, for example, Boundon has pointed out, some ends can be explained in terms of means, especially in those cases when the evaluation of the ends depends on the evaluation of the means. If this is so, then means-end rationality can take into account the rationality of some ends. See Boudon 1993:7.

25. Simon 1983:7–8.

26. Russell 1954:viii.

27. See also, for instance, Ellul 1964 and Bernstein 1988.

28. von Wright 1988:17–18.

29. *A Treatise on Human Nature,* bk. II. pt. iii. sect. 3.

30. Berlin 1964:221–223.

31. Nathanson 1985:102.

32. Rescher 1988:103.

33. For a more comprehensive and detailed discussion of the short-comings of means-end rationality see Baier 1958, and especially Nathanson 1985.

34. von Wright 1988:140.

35. Nathanson 1985:118.

3.   Science and Formal Evidentialism

1. Carnap 1937:xiii.
2. McMullin 1988:1.
3. McMullin 1988:5.
4. Giere 1988:2.
5. Pap 1962:3.
6. Russell 1984:514.
7. Clifford 1970:159.
8. Chalmers 1983:3.
9. See, for example, Chisholm 1977:17–19.
10. Foundationalism is on this account understood as a component of a theory of rationality. However, it can be used in other contexts as well; it may, for instance, be formulated as a part of a theory of knowledge or a theory of ethics.
11. Plantinga 1986a:117.
12. Wittgenstein 1969.
13. See Dancy 1985:62.
14. The formalist can, of course, reject foundationalism and instead adopt a coherentist position. However, I will assume that the formalist is a foundationalist because that is the position that has dominated episte-mology in the West.
15. Foundationalism and coherentism are meta-positions with re-spect to the classical options available in epistemology, namely ratio-nalism and empiricism. We now recognize that both rationalism and empiricism have traditionally been given the same meta-structure, foun-dationalism, their disagreement being about what beliefs the foundation should contain.
16. Plantigna 1983:72.
17. On this account perceptual beliefs are rational beliefs only if they can be derived from incorrigible beliefs about how things seems to us.
18. Dancy 1985:54.

19. Plantinga 1983:79.

20. Wainwright 1988:155.

21. Plantinga 1983:58–59.

22. Stout 1981:25.

23. Schrag 1992:23 (emphasis added).

24. Also in, for example, Rorty 1979, Murphy and McClendon 1989, Lindbeck 1984, and to some extent Brown 1988, can we find this kind of understanding of foundationalism.

25. See for instance, Alston 1976, Chisholm 1989, Plantinga 1983 and 1986a.

26. Wolterstorff 1984:65–69.

27. Plantinga 1983:78–82.

28. Kenny 1983:10.

29. See for example Pap 1962:24f.

30. Putnam 1990:125.

31. Brown 1988:80.

32. Hempel 1965:10.

33. Carnap 1966:35.

34. See, for instance, Jeffrey 1956, Swinburne 1973 and 1985. Critical discussions of Bayesian decision models can be found in Brown 1988, Giere 1988, and Putnam 1990.

35. Popper writes: "But real support can be obtained only from observations undertaken as tests (by 'attempted refutations'); and for this purpose *criteria of refutation* have to be laid down beforehand: it must be agreed which observable situations, if actually observed, mean that the theory is refuted." Popper 1985:38*n*.

36. Lakatos 1978:168–69.

37. Scheffler 1967:9–10.

38. Zahar 1982:407.

39. I am much in debt to Harold I. Brown for this characterization of rule-rationality. See his book *Rationality,* especially chapter 1.

40. Brown 188:5.

41. Douglas Hofstadter, quoted in Brown 1988:4.

42. Brown 1988:14.

43. Brown 1988:20 and Newton-Smith 1981:115.

44. Lakatos 1985:122.

45. Hempel 1979:58.

46. One can basically distinguish between a realist and anti-realist view of science. Roughly, according to the *realist* the aim of science is truth or the avoidance of falsehood, or something in this neighborhood. Popper, for example, would say that the aim of science is the production of true explanatory theories. But *anti-realists* claim, again roughly, that

the aim is not truth but the production of theories that are useful to predict different phenomena or solve different problems. See Johansson 1991:429, and especially Leplin (ed.) 1984.

47. Newton-Smith 1981:4.

48. Ayer 1946:35.

49. Popper 1985:40.

50. Popper 1985:38.

51. Lakatos 1978:1.

52. Lakatos 1978:88.

53. Feldman and Conee 1985:15.

54. Swinburne 1981:33.

55. Gärdenfors 1988:9. (See also the quotation of Hintikka below on pp. 80–81.)

56. Brown 1988:19 (emphasis added).

57. Wolterstorff 1983b:183 n.

58. Hintikka 1962:36.

59. Horwich 1982:12.

60. Elster 1982: 111–127.

61. See, for example, Føllesdal 1986:111–112.

62. Gärdenfors 1988:8, 22.

63. Only if we develop a body of rules (develop a logic) that does not allow one to deduce anything from an inconsistency, might it be possible to (rationally) tolerate inconsistency.

64. See also Hintikka 1962:16–39.

65. Gärdenfors 1988:22.

4. The Scientific and the Evidentialist Challenge to Religious Belief

1. For a more detailed account of this discussion see, for example Diamond 1974, Franck 1988, and Stanesby 1988.

2. Russell quoted in Smith 1979:58.

3. Putnam 1990:105.

4. Reichenbach 1951:305.

5. Ayer 1946:41.

6. Stanesby 1988:25.

7. Ayer 1946:31.

8. Ayer 1946:115, 120.

9. See, for instance, Flew's contribution in Flew, Hare, and Mitchell 1983, and Flew 1966.

10. Maybe the most well-known and most influential collection of essays that deals with this issue is *New Essays in Philosophical Theology,* edited by A. Flew and A. MacIntyre and published in 1955.

11. For examples of the first strategy see Mitchell's contribution in Flew, Hare, and Mitchell 1983 and Hick 1983, and for the latter one see Hare's contribution in Flew, Hare, and Mitchell 1983, Phillips 1983 and Braithwaite 1983. For a more detailed discussion of these strategies see Herrmann 1991:224–228.

12. Plantinga 1990a:156–183 (first printed in 1967).

13. Notice that this kind of objection cannot be directed against Popper's falsification principle, because he never claims that the only kind of cognitively meaningful statements that exist are either analytic or synthetic ones.

14. Mackie 1986:1.

15. Mackie 1986:4.

16. Flew, Hare, and Mitchell 1983:13–15, 20–22.

17. Wolterstorff 1983a:6.

18. Scriven 1966:103.

19. Branshard 1974:401.

20. Flew 1984:22–23.

21. Clifford 1970:159 (emphasis added).

22. Wolterstorff 1983b:163.

23. Flew 1984:23.

24. Mackie 1990:25.

25. Mackie 1986:12, 253.

26. Plantinga 1983:27.

27. Russell 1979:13–26.

28. Swinburne 1985:10.

29. It is of course possible to make a corresponding distinction between negative and positive natural theology.

30. An alternative strategy is to restrict the evidential principle to non-basic beliefs which involve only positive existence claims. This is the way Morris understands the principle, though he calls it the *Hanson-Scriven thesis.* It consists of the claim that: "For any rational subject S and any positive existence claim P, if S is in possession of no good evidence or any other positive epistemic ground for thinking that P is true, then S ought to adopt the cognitive relation to P of denial." Morris 1985:219. See also Plantinga 1983:28–29.

31. Swinburne 1977:2.

32. Mackie 1986:1.

33. See Swinburne 1973.

34. Swinburne 1985:2–3.

35. Mackie 1986:4–5. For his acceptance of confirmation theory see p. 9–10.

36. Mackie 1986:10.

37. Swinburne 1985:51.

38. Swinburne 1985:90, 107–108.

39. Swinburne 1985:68.

40. Swinburne 1985:106.

41. Swinburne 1985:9.

42. Swinburne 1985:7.

43. MacIntyre 1959:63.

44. Flew 1966:62–63.

45. Gutting 1982:7–8.

46. Mackie 1986:7. See also Swinburne 1985:13–14.

47. Wainwright 1988:170, and Newman 1955:235–237.

48. Swinburne 1985:291.

49. Swinburne 1983:386.

50. Whether Hume and Kant thought this themselves can be disputed. What cannot be disputed, however, is that philosophers and theologians have attributed this kind of view (or something similar) to them.

51. Swinburne 1985:2.

52. For a similar way of arguing see Lucas 1987.

53. To say that the probability of a hypothesis is equal to one, that is, $P(h) = 1$ is to say that the hypothesis is certainly true, and to say that it is equal to zero, i.e., $P(h) = 0$ is to say that the hypothesis is certainly false. And if $P(h) = 1/2$, the hypothesis is just as likely to be true as false, and if $P(h) > 1/2$, then the hypothesis is more likely to be true than false.

54. Wittgenstein 1966:55ff.

55. MacIntyre 1970:171.

56. Price 1983:143–167.

57. Mackie 1986:3–4.

58. Mackie 1986:253.

59. Swinburne 1985:290–91.

60. In all fairness it must admitted that it puts some constraint on Swinburne's evidentalist case. One of his reasons for excluding the ontological argument is that he thinks it is a purely philosophical construction, it cannot be found among ordianry believers. Swinburne 1985:10.

61. Abraham 1985:100.

62. Alston states his position clearly in Alston 1983.

63. Plantinga 1983:18–19.

64. Plantinga 1983:17.

65. Plantinga 1983:59.

66. However, strictly speaking, it is not belief in God that Plantinga claims is properly basic. Instead it is propositions about some of God's attributes or actions, like "God is speaking to me" and "God has created all this." But propositions of this sort do of course self-evidently entail the proposition that "God exists." So Plantinga sees no harm in speaking of belief in God as properly basic. Plantinga 1983:81–82.

67. Plantinga 1983:80.

68. Plantinga 1983:76.

69. Plantinga 1983:77.

70. Gutting 1982:79–92.

71. Wainwright 1988:156, 157–158.

72. Plantinga 1979:51–52.

73. Hick 1989:229n.

74. Hick 1989:36.

75. For a more profound critical discussion of the proper basicality of belief in God see, especially, Audi 1986, Gutting 1982, Kenny 1983, and Quinn 1985.

76. To some people this might sound surprising and confusing. Does not Plantinga say that he rejects evidentialism, that he is not an evidentialist but a reformed epistemologist? That is true. However, the confusion is caused by Plantinga himself because he uses the term in a very special and context-dependent way. For him the evidentialist is the one who claims that it is irrational to accept theistic belief in the absence of sufficient evidence. Hence "evidentialism" refers to the thesis that belief in God is irrational unless it is based on the evidence of other beliefs. But the way I have used the notion, the evidentialist does not take a stand on the issue whether belief in God is a basic or non-basic belief; the evidentalist can believe either way.

77. Plantinga 1983:79.

78. Plantinga 1983:54, 72.

79. Plantinga 1986b:132–133.

80. Plantinga 1990a:271.

5.   The Practice-Oriented View of Science

1. Giere writes: "With a quarter century of hindsight it is now clear that Kuhn's *Structure of Scientific Revolutions* (1962) is, by any measure, the most influential book on the nature of science yet to be published in the twentieth century." Giere 1988:32.

2. Kitcher 1992:56–57.

3. McMullin 1988:22.

4. Giere 1988:149.

5. Moser 1991:562.

6. Kuhn 1970:v.

7. Kuhn 1970:81–82. See also the examples given in Brown 1988: 90–93, 210–222, and Chalmers 1983:66–75.

8. Many of his critics accept this point of his account. See Lakatos 1985 and Laudan 1977.

9. Kuhn 1970:175, viii.

10. Brown 1988:109.

11. Laudan 1977:129.

12. Laudan 1981.

13. Shapere 1984:210.

14. Brown 1988:112.

15. Giere 1988:149.

16. Giere 1988:156.

17. Giere 1988:149–156.

18. Lakatos 1985:178 (the second sentence is italicized in the original version).

19. Kuhn 1985b:264.

20. See, for instance, Feyerabend 1975.

21 Kuhn 1985b:235.

22. Brown 1988:79.

23. Giere 1988:11.

24. Kuhn 1985b:262.

25. Kuhn 1985b:261.

26. Lakatos 1985:93.

27. Lakatos 1985:178 (the quoted phrases are italicized in the original version).

28. Gutting 1980:7–8.

29. McMullin 1988:24.

30. Newton-Smith 1981:234. See also McMullin 1983:14–18, and Putnam 1990, chap. 8,

31. Brown 1988:137.

32. Brown 1988:139–149.

33. Polanyi 1962:101.

34. See Kuhn 1985a:16. Gutting gives the following comment: "But at the heart of his analysis is always the idea that all these rules are relevant to the practice of science only to the extent that they are embodied in some concrete scientific achievement and that this achievement is not reducible to the rules implicit in it." Gutting 1980:1.

35. Brown 1988:149.

36. Brown 1988:149.

37. Kuhn 1985b:237–238.

38. Brown 1988:190.

39. For discussion on whether the practice-oriented view of scientific rationality also should (as Kuhn seems to think) include a consensus requirement, see the following two chapters.

40. See Shapere 1984 for an interesting discussion of this issue.

41. Shapere 1984:205.

42. Laudan 1977:123.

43. Brown 1988:185.

44. See also chapter 10 for a discussion of the relationship between evidence and (basic and derived) standards of rationality.

45. Brown 1988:146.

46. Lakatos 1985:92.

47. Kuhn 1977:236 (emphasis added).

48. Kuhn 1977:228–229.

49. Kuhn 1977:226

50. Newton-Smith 1981:75.

51. Newton-Smith 1981:75.

52. Chalmers 1990:9.

53. Chalmers 1983:169. Also quoted in Chalmers 1990:10.

6.   Social Evidentialism

1. Jeffner 1987:7.

2. Brown 1988:186.

3. Brown 1988:183–84.

4. Cherniak 1986:6.

5. Brown 1988:187.

6. Gutting 1982:83. Gutting discusses in this context only religious beliefs, but I think he takes this social requirement to hold of any type of belief.

7. Brown 1988:187.

8. Brown 1988:196.

9. Brown 1988:148–49.

10. Brown 1988:185.

11. Putnam 1990:179.

12. Gutting 1982:76

13. See, for instance, Kuhn 1970:19.

14. Gutting 1982:83.

15. Gutting 1982:86.

16. Gutting also runs the risk that his position becomes self-defeating. He seems to be saying that "one cannot rationally hold a view without convincing argument if there are competent others who disagree." Call that *p*. However, there are competent others who disagree with *p*. So according to *p* Gutting should either give some convincing arguments for *p* or give it up.

17. Brown 1988:192.

18. See Kuhn 1981, for a detailed discussion.

19. Internal rationality will not be discussed in connection with this model of rationality because the social evidentialists we have considered do not address the question concerning what the appropriate standards of internal rationality are. (See chapter 3 for a discussion of internal and external rationality.)

20. Brown 1988:40, 54–58,

21. Gutting 1982:83.

22. Brown 1988:201.

23. Brown 1988:202.

24. Putnam 1990:x.

25. Putnam 1990:55.

26. Putnam 1990:55.

27. Brown 1988:198 (emphasis added).

28. Alston 1978:793.

29. Plantinga 1982:48.

30 Roughly, this seems to be the position of van Fraassen. See van Fraassen 1987.

31. Putnam 1990:49, 50.

32. Plantinga 1982:48.

33. Creative anti-realism can be interpreted in either an intersubjective or a relativistic way. On an *intersubjective* account the world is the same for all human beings because all of them have the same cognitive equipment. But from a *relativistic* perspective the world is not the same for all human beings because we do not construct the world in the same way, each individual therefore lives in a different world.

34. See Plantinga 1982, for a more complete discussion of this issue.

35. One important *difference* between this definition and the former one seems to be that the former definition leaves the question about the *scope* of its application opened. This latter definition seems to commit the creative anti-realist to a universal application.

36. Putnam 1990:56. Elsewhere (p. 49) he claims: "'Truth', in an internalist view, is some sort of (idealized) rational acceptability—some sort of ideal coherence of our beliefs with each other and with our experiences *as those experiences are themselves represented in our belief*

system—and not correspondence with mind-independent or discourse-independent 'states of affairs.' "

37. Putnam 1990:49.

38. See also Gutting 1982:164–168.

39. Hempel 1966:14.

40. Brown 1988:183.

41. Brown 1988:183, 185.

42. Newton-Smith 1981:4.

43. Brown 1988:228.

7.   Social Evidentialism and Religious Beliefs

1. Gutting 1982:1.

2. Gutting 1982:3.

3. Gutting 1982:2–3.

4. Gutting 1982:2.

5. Plantinga 1984:268.

6. See chapter 4 for a discussion of the strong, differentiation, and irrational response to the scientific challenge.

7. Gutting 1982:5–6.

8. See chapter 4 for a discussion of the difference between one-dimensional and multi-dimensional arguments.

9. Mitchell 1981:40–42.

10. Gutting 1982:8.

11. Gutting 1982:8.

12. See, for instance, Abraham 1985:104–7.

13. Mitchell 1981:99.

14. See Barbosa da Silva 1982:72, and Holte 1984:45.

15. Yandell 1984:155.

16. See especially Banner 1990, Barbour 1974, Mitchell 1981, and Wolterstorff 1984.

17. Gutting 1982:111–112.

18. Gutting 1982:113.

19. Gutting 1982:124.

20. Wolterstorff writes that it is "a form of evidentialism which has emerged not so much from an articulate epistemology as from the intuitive conviction that the phenomenon of fundamental religious diversity in our societies places on believers the obligation to justify themselves." Wolterstorff 1988:58.

21. Brown 1988:195.

22. Brown 1988:194–195.

23. Wykstra 1990b:146.

24. Jeffner 1981:48 (my translation). See also pp. 40 and 63–64.

25. The consensus principle or requirement could, of course, also be added.

26. Kuhn 1977:225–239.

27. In doing that I will also consider Gutting's distinction between decisive and interim assent.

8.   Presumptionism

1. This axiom needs to be qualified so it does not follow from it that people who, for instance, are insane or whose cognitive equipment malfunctions can be rational. This qualification is added in the end of this chapter.

2. Hermann 1991:236.

3. The two other meta-criteria are discussed in chapter 6. They state that: (1) All else being equal, the broader the scope or field of application a model of rationality has the better it is. (2) An adequate model of rationality must do better than chance in the long run.

4. Brown 1988:207.

5. Furberg 1987:204.

6. I suspect one reason why ordinary people do not pay much attention or spend little time listening to analytic philosophers like me has to do with the fact that we work too much with idealizations which are not directly or indirectly applicable to situations in ordinary life. Another reason is of course the kind of quasi-scientific, formalistic language analytic philosophers have a predilection to use. It is hard to disagree with MacIntyre when he writes that: "The attempted professionalization of serious and systematic thinking has had a disastrous effect upon our culture." MacIntyre 1988:x.

7. Cherniak 1986:53. I am in debt to Cherniak for much of this discussion of human memory and cognition.

8. Cherniak 1986:93.

9. Cherniak 1986:81.

10. See for example Tversky and Kahenman 1974, and Nisbett and Ross 1980.

11. Cherniak 1986:82.

12. Cherniak 1986:67.

13. Cherniak 1986:67.

14. Goldman 1978:514.

15. For a further discussion of the relation between logic and standards of rationality, see Goldman 1978 and Harman 1986.

16. Andersson and Furberg 1986:197.

17. These examples do not necessarily count as trivial in general, because they could be important for somebody else, in a given situation. So the triviality of beliefs is often, but not always, person-relative.

18. Presumptionism is a theory of rationality, but a similar approach has also been developed in theory of knowledge, where such an approach is sometimes called *methodological* or *epistemic conservatism*. See, for instance, Harman 1986.

19. Andersson and Furberg 1986:197 (My translation).

20. Harman 1986:32.

21. Wolterstorff 1983b:163.

22. Wolterstorff 1983b:164.

23. Normally, of course, fideism is restricted to a particular domain, typically, to religious beliefs.

24. Hermann 1991:236.

25. Gettier 1967.

26. Deontological because internalism, typically, has to do with what can be demanded of an agent, or with what epistemic duties or obligations an agent has. See Plantinga 1990c.

27. Probably the best known way of spelling out externalism is *reliabilism*. On this account a true belief is justified when it is produced by a "reliable process," a process that reliably produces true beliefs whether or not the knowing subject is aware of this. (See for instance Goldman 1979.) So a true belief constitutes knowledge if it is produced by a reliable belief producing mechanism. (For a discussion of internalism, externalism, and reliabilism see, for example, Dancy 1985 and BonJour 1985.)

28. The thought is that we need a *higher* degree of justification for knowledge than for rationality. A certain (high) degree of justification—together with true belief—is (or is nearly) necessary and sufficient for knowledge. The degree of justification that is needed for rational acceptability is less, but of the same kind, as the one needed for knowledge.

29. Hanson 1971:313–314.

30. This seems also to be Hanson's own view, at least, sometimes. See Hanson 1971:318.

31. See Kuhn 1970:102 and Brown 1988:81–82.

32. See Plantinga 1990c:51.

33. Mavrodes 1983:216.

34. Rowe 1990:135–136. (Whether Rowe himself is a social evidentialist, is, of course, another question.)

35. Brown 1988:201.

36. Andersson and Furberg 1986:198–199 (My translation).

37. Wolterstorff 1983b:171.

38. The example is taken from Wykstra 1990a:153.

39. For an interesting account of proper function, see Plantinga 1988.

40. Wolterstorff 1983b:155.

41. Brown makes a similar remark. See Brown 1988:196.

42. This way of understanding scientific justification is not uncommon in philosophy of science. Consider, for instance, what Moser writes: "A scientifically justified belief, roughly characterized, is a belief appropriately warranted to be a component of scientific knowledge." Moser 1991:557.

43. Brown 1988:187.

9.   The Nature and Function of Religious Belief

1. Batson and Ventis 1982:7.

2. For a similar understanding of religion see Smith 1979:56–57.

3. See for example Bråkenhielm 1990.

4. One could say that these people's views of life are often unconscious. They do not exist as conscious or intellectual systems of thought. Rather, as Jeffner points out, they exist as cognitive and emotional reaction dispositions or inclinations that are triggered in certain situations. Jeffner 1988:11–12.

5. Perhaps what is characteristic for many post-modern thinkers today is that they have chosen to be fragmentists, since they reject any attempt to create a comprehensive and coherent picture of life.

6. Therefore, one can be an agnostic or skeptic with respect to certain questions or parts of a view of life, but one can never be skeptical with respect to all questions or parts, that is, of course, given that one wants to function appropriately as a human being.

7. Jeffner 1988:7 (my translation). Jeffner has discussed this definition in various publications, most of which have been published in Swedish.

8. Jeffner 1992:138.

9. See also Bråkenhielm 1990:107–121 for a discussion of Jeffner's definition, of the possibility of applying the concept in social science, and of the relationship between views of life and theology.

10. Malcolm 1977:155.

11. Jeffner 1988:9 and Holte 1984:37.

12. Hick on the other hand does not think that this is possible. See Hick 1989:3–5.

13. See Barbosa da Silva 1982:175–196, for a discussion of different aspects of the notion of the "sacred"—with special reference to Mircea Eliade.

14. Haught 1990:159.

15. This is a rough outline of religion in general but I think it is enough for my purpose here. For a more detailed account of what religion is all about see, for example, Westphal 1987.

16. Westphal 1987:39.

17. See for example, Schlesinger 1983, for an illuminating discussion of the difference between science and metaphysics.

18. Compare with Brümmer 1981:1–3.

19. Gyllensten 1980:277 (my translation).

20. This discussion about an agent's question, an agent-question, and an urgent question is based on Furberg 1987, chapter 7 and 8.

21. Gutting 1982:106.

22. Tillich 1951:211–215.

23. Wainwright 1988:2.

24. The sacred is then a *maximally perfect reality*. According to Wainwright: "Something is maximally perfect only if no actual *or possible* reality is greater. Thus, to claim that something like God or Brahman is maximally perfect is to claim not only that nothing in the actual world surpasses it but also that nothing in any possible world does so." Wainwright 1988:6.

10.   Religious Rationality

1. Rescher 1988:105.

2. The holistic conception of the nature of rationality and this axiological standard of rationality are discussed in chapter 2.

3. The holistic conception and presumptionism are connected in the following way. Presumptionism is a thesis about what can be rightly demanded of us, that is, about the *standards* of rationality. Holistic rationality is a thesis about the *nature* of rationality or about what rationality is. The way I have expressed the standards of presumptionism, they presuppose the holistic account of the nature of rationality—but, of course, this is not necessary.

4. Wykstra drew my attention to this fact. See Wykstra 1990b:137.

5. See Hempel 1965:40–45, Foley 1988:136–47 and 1991:378–82, and Wykstra 1990b:130–31. See also the discussion of simplicity in chapter 2.

6. Alston 1989:8.

7. Yandell 1984:vii.

8. Plantinga 1983:18.

9. This is the same problem as the one discussed earlier in regard to science. How can the philosophical discussion be *scientifically relevant,* if the standards of scientific rationality are unconstrained by the goals and assumptions of actual scientific practice? Why should the scientist pay any attention at all to what the philosopher of science is saying?

10. Perhaps what I have here been arguing against in contemporary philosophy of religion is what Kaufman is after when he tries to explain why theologians are not so interested in taking part in the philosophical discussion of religious belief. He says: "[But] wider questions, about the nature of traditions or worldviews themselves and how these function in human experience and thinking, do not ordinarily come up for direct consideration in these discussions." Kaufman 1989:39.

11. Peacocke seems to be of a similar opinion when he claims that the scientific and religious (theological) enterprises have in common "their search for *intelligibility,* for what makes the most coherent sense of the experimental data with which they are each respectively concerned. What proves to be intelligible is applied, in science, to prediction and control and, in theology, to provide moral purpose and personal meaning and to enable human beings to steer their path from birth to death." Peacocke 1981:xii. See also Wykstra 1990b:137.

12. Previously we have considered the negative version of this standard. See chapter 2, and the beginning of this chapter.

13. Bowker 1973:82f.

14. Gandhi quoted in Dupré 1989:260.

15. John 3:21 (New American Standard Bible).

16. Dupré 1989:260.

17. MacIntyre 1988:5.

18. This is also true in the context of moral traditions where Mac-Intyre's remark is meant to apply. People may want to hold correct moral views, but primarily they want to know *how to live* a morally good life, and therefore persons who exemplify a way of living morally or a way of dealing with moral experiences of resistance matter greatly.

19. Rolston 1987:7 (emphasis added).

20. Wykstra 1990b:138 (emphasis added).

21. See again, for instance, Brown 1988 and Rescher 1988.

22. See for instance, Abraham 1985: 239–51, Mavrodes 1986, and Wolterstroff 1990.

23. See Wykstra 1990b:135–57 for an interesting discussion of some adequate standards for religious (Christian) rationality.

24. Russell 1979:44 (emphasis added).

25. Provine 1988:10.

26. Lakatos 1985:115.

27. We might, of course, disagree about what it should *mean* to say that one belief would make one better off than another, but that is another question. Maybe we should say that a theory *T'* is better than theory *T*, if *T'* is more comprehensive than *T, T'* explains everything that *T* explains, *T'* predicts novel facts that are improbable in the light of *T*, or the like. But it is also plausible to think that what it means to be better off will vary to some degree from practice to practice.

28. Alternatively, one could omit the qualification of the principle of presumption and claim instead that there are no good or sufficient reasons to refrain from accepting a belief until there is at least a better rival belief present, that is, the qualification is taken to be implicit in the principle as it is originally stated.

29. Klemke 1981:168.

30. Rescher 1988:54.

31. This argument might, of course, not convince the skeptics, but that is *their* and not our problem. We do not need, on a presumptional account, to convince the skeptics that they are wrong, to be rationally entitled to *our* belief.

32. See Plantinga 1983 and Alston 1983.

33. Kenny 1983:63–65.

34. See for example Geisler 1980, especially the article by J. Barton Payne "Higher Criticism and Biblical Inerrancy."

35. Rowe 1990:135.

36. There is a difference between justification and warrant only if justification (together with true belief) is not, or at least not always, sufficient for knowledge.

37. Adams 1990:210.

38. Mackie 1990:25.

39. Gutting 1982:4.

40. Gutting 1982:4.

41. See Harman 1986:47.

42. Gutting 1982:108.

43. Harman 1986:50.

44. Popper 1985:49.

45. For example Clayton defends this possibility. See Clayton 1989: 138–43.

46. See, for instance, the discussion of quest-oriented believing in Batson and Ventis 1982.

47. Peterson, Hasker, Reichenbach, and Basinger 1991:43.

48. Augustine, *Confessions,* VII, 10.

49. Westphal 1987:27–28. (The quotation from Gandhi is also taken from these pages.)

50. The distinction between monocentric, monopolitic, and pluralistic cultures is from Geels and Wikström 1985:42–43.

11. Contextualism and Human Practices

1. Hollis and Lukes (eds.) 1982:1.

2. MacIntyre 1988:351.

3. Mary Hesse quoted in Hollis and Lukes (eds.) 1982:13.

4. W. Stark quoted in Brown 1988:122.

5. Bernstein 1989:8.

6. Wittgenstein 1966:58.

7. Winch 1990:100–101.

8. Winch 1991:99–100, Kekes 1976:97.

9. Winch 1991:93.

10. Phillips 1976:41.

11. Phillips 1976:7.

12. Phillips 1981:62–63.

13. Phillips 1971:13.

14. Phillips 1988:79.

15. Dalferth is here referring to Winch's and Phillips's position, but he also seems to accept it himself. Dalferth 1988:6.

16. Rescher 1988:140.

17. Kekes 1976:100–1.

18. Nielsen 1967:207 and Kellenberger 1985:13.

19. Dalferth 1988:7.

20. Winch 1991:84.

21. Malcolm 1977:143–44.

22. Malcolm 1977:146.

23. Wittgenstein quoted by Malcolm 1977:147.

24. Phillips 1988:66.

25. Consider also what Wittgenstein writes: "when Moore says he *knows* such and such [for instance that he has two hands], he is really enumerating a lot of empirical propositions which we affirm without special testing; propositions, that is, which have a peculiar logical role in the system of our empirical propositions." Wittgenstein 1969, § 136.

26. However, sometimes Phillips seems to be arguing for coherentism, for example, when he quotes Wittgenstein saying: "What stands fast does so, not because it is intrinsically obvious or convicing; it is rather held fast by what lies around it." (Phillips 1988:xiv, 40) But he

does not develop his position enough to say for certain whether he is a foundationalist or a coherentist.

27. Gutting 1982:32.

28. Alston 1981:131–32.

29. Alston 1981:140n.

30. Phillips 1988:118, 121.

31. Alston 1981:132.

32. Abraham 1985:10.

33. Gutting 1982:33.

34. Winch 1991:103.

35. Winch 1991:104–5

36. Phillips 1970.

37. Phillips 1988:12.

38. See for example the discussion between Winch and MacIntyre, in Winch 1991 and MacIntyre 1991.

39. "Sophisticated Christians or Muslims who no longer believe that their creeds express factual truths may still find the Christian or Muslim stories nourishing and the Christian or Muslim way of life rich and deep. People of this sort can continue to use religious language if they construe it as expressing profound and moving pictures and a commitment to live by them." Wainwright 1988:145.

40. Phillips 1988:xiii, 49–50.

41. Phillips 1988:49, 50.

42. Wolterstorff 1992.

43. Banner 1990:112.

44. MacIntyre 1970:171.

45. Plantinga 1986b:127, 133.

46. Plantinga 1986b:133.

47. Wittgenstein 1966:61–62.

48. Rescher 1988:146.

49. Malcolm 1977:152.

50. Malcolm 1977:154–55.

51. Phillips 1988:117.

52. Wittenstein 1966:55.

53. Phillips 1988:118.

54. Gutting 1982:78.

55. Gutting 1982:78.

56. Phillips 1971:97.

57. Phillips 1970:71 (emphasis added)

58. Phillips 1981:62.

59. I am partly in debt to Kekes for this observation. See Kekes 1976:101.

60. Kaufman 1989:42.

61. Winch 1990:15.

62. See chapter 6.

63. Brown 1988:121 (emphasis added).

64. Sapir 1929:209.

65. Phillips 1988:202 (emphasis added).

66. Alston 1989:7.

67. Plantinga 1992:301.

68. Brown 1988:180.

69. The reason why I find myself in agreement with much of what MacIntyre says may be my great admiration of Kuhn's work in philosophy of science. There is a striking resemblance between MacIntyre's tradition-bound rationality and Kuhn's paradigm-bound rationality. This is so striking that I find it surprising that MacIntyre nowhere in *Whose Justice? Which Rationality?* mentions Kuhn's view of rationality. MacIntyre's view also has a lot in common with Lakatos's theory of research programs, and he does not refer to Laktos either.

70. MacIntyre 1988:389, ix, 5–6.

71. It is worth mentioning that MacIntyre primarily discusses practical rationality and not as I have done theoretical rationality. However, in several places he claims that his view also applies to theoretical rationality, so I think it is quite appropriate to treat it as I will do here as also a model of theoretical rationality. See, for example, MacIntyre 1988:4, 9.

72. I will in what follows use mainly my umbrella notion "practices" to describe his view.

73. MacIntyre has also inspired other thinkers to develop similar accounts of rationality, see for instance, Stout 1981, Hauerwas and Burrell 1989, and D'Costa 1993.

74. MacIntyre 1988:7 (emphasis added).

75. MacIntyre 1988:351.

76. MacIntyre 1988:4, see also p. 351.

77. MacIntyre 1988:350.

78. MacIntyre 1988:354.

79. MacIntyre 1988:352.

80. MacIntyre 1988:365.

81. MacIntyre 1988:366–67.

82. MacIntyre 1988:367.

83. MacIntyre 1988:360.

84. Rescher 1988:175.

85. See also the discussion of rationality and consensus in chapter 6 and 7.

12.   Some Concluding Remarks

1. However, a deeper analaysis of actual religious practice is needed than the one I have been able to give in this study. But I will, in a Kuhnian fashion, claim that what we need is a reorientation of philosophy of religion, a paradigm shift, we need to follow our colleagues in philosophy of science. The dominant formal research program must be abandoned and a new practice-oriented one must come in its place (without in the process becoming contextualist). Further, the scope of the debate must be expanded in two ways, first, we must bring in material from religions other than theistic ones, and second, secular views of life must also be considered.

Bibliography

Abraham, W. J. 1985: *An Introduction to the Philosophy of Religion* (Englewood Cliffs, New Jersey: Prentice-Hall, Inc.)

Abraham, W. J., and S. W. Holtzer (eds.) 1987: *The Rationality of Religious Belief* (Oxford: Clarendon Press)

Adams, M. M., and R. M. Adams (eds.) 1990: *The Problem of Evil* (Oxford and New York: Oxford University Press)

Adams, M. M. 1990: "Horrendous Evils and the Goodness of God" in Adams and Adams (eds.)

Alston, W. 1976: "Has Foundationalism Been Refuted?" in *Philosophical Studies*, Vol. 29.

———. 1978: "Yes, Virginia, there is a Real World" in *Proceedings and Addresses of the American Philosophical Association*, Vol. 52, No. 1.

———. 1981: "The Christian Language-Game" in Crosson (ed.)

———. 1983: "Christian Experience and Christian Belief" in Plantinga and Wolterstorff (eds.)

———. 1989: *Divine Nature and Human Language* (Ithaca and London: Cornell University Press)

Andersson, J., and M. Furberg 1986: *Om världens gåta* (Lund: Doxa AB)

Audi, R. 1986: "Direct Justification, Evidential Dependence, and Theistic Belief" in Audi and Wainwright (eds.)

———. 1988: *Belief, Justification and Knowledge* (Belmont, California: Wadsworth Publishing Company)

Audi, R., and W. J. Wainwright (eds.) 1986: *Rationality, Religious Belief, and Moral Commitment* (Ithaca and London: Cornell University Press)

Ayer, A. J. 1946: *Language, Truth and Logic* [1936] (London: Victor Gollancz Ltd.)

Baier, K. 1958: *The Moral Point of View* (Ithaca, NY.: Cornell University Press)

Banner, M. C. 1990: *The Justification of Science and the Rationality of Religious Belief* (Oxford: Clarendon Press)

Barbosa da Silva, A. 1982: *The Phenomenology of Religion as a Philosophical Problem* (Lund: CWK Gleerup)

Barbour, I. G. 1974: *Myths, Models, and Paradigms* (New York: Harper & Row)

Batson, C. D. and W. L. Ventis, 1982: *The Religious Experience* (New York and Oxford: Oxford University Press)

Beaty, M. D. (ed.) 1990: *Christian Theism and the Problems of Philosophy* (Notre Dame and London: University of Notre Dame Press)

Bennett, J. 1989: *Rationality* [1964] (Indianapolis and Cambridge: Hackett Publishing Company)

Berlin, I. 1964: "Rationality of Value Judgments" in C. J. Friedrich (ed.), *Rational Decision,* (New York: Atherton Press)

Bernstein, R. J. 1988: "The Rage Against Reason" in McMullin (ed.) 1989: *Beyond Objectivism and Relativism* [1983] (Oxford: Basil Blackwell)

Blanshard, B. 1974: *Reason and Belief* (London: Allen & Unwin)

BonJour, L. 1985: *The Structure of Empirical Knowledge* (Cambridge, Massachusetts, and London: Harvard University Press)

Boundon, R. 1993: "Toward a Synthetic Theory of Rationality" in *International Studies in the Philosophy of Science,* Vol. 7, No. 1.

Bowker, J. 1973: *The Sense of God* (Oxford: Clarendon Press)

Braithwaite, R. B. 1983: "An Empiricist's View of the Nature of Religious Belief" in Mitchell (ed.)

Bråkenhielm, C-R. 1990: "Constructive Theology and the Study of Popular Life-Philosophies" in *Studia Theologica,* Vol. 44.

Brink, G. van den, L. J. van den Brom, M. Sarot (eds.) 1992: *Christian Faith and Philosophical Theology* (Kamen: Kok Pharos)

Brown, H. I. 1979: *Perception, Theory and Commitment* [1977] (Chicago and London: University of Chicago Press)

———. 1988: *Rationality* (London and New York: Routledge)

Brown, S. C. (ed.) 1977: *Reason and Religion* (Ithaca and London: Cornell University Press)

Brümmer, V. 1981: *Theology and Philosophical Inquiry* (London and Basingstoke: Macmillan Press)

Carnap, R. 1937: *The Logical Syntax of Language* (London: Routledge & Kegan Paul)

———. 1966: *Philosophical Foundations of Physics* (New York: Basic Books)

Chalmers, A. F. 1983: *What is this Thing called Science?* 2nd ed. [1978] (Milton Keynes: Open University Press)

———. 1990: *Science and Its Fabrication* (Milton Keynes: Open University Press)

Cherniak, C. 1986: *Minimal Rationality* (Cambridge, Massachusetts and London: MIT Press)

Chisholm, R. 1977: *Theory of Knowledge,* 2nd ed. (Engelwood Cliffs: Prentice Hall)

———. 1989: *Theory of Knowledge,* 3rd ed. (Engelwood Cliffs; Prentice Hall)

Clayton, P. 1989: *Explanation from Physics to Theology* (New Haven and London: Yale University Press)

Clifford, W. K. 1970: "The Ethics of Belief" in *The Rationality of Belief in God,* Mavrodes (ed.) (Englewood Cliffs: Prentice Hall). Originally published in W. K. Clifford *Lectures and Essays* (London: Macmillan and Co. 1886)

Crosson, F. (ed.) 1981: *The Autonomy of Religious Belief* (Notre Dame and London: University of Notre Dame Press)

Dalferth, I. U. 1988: *Theology and Philosophy* (Oxford: Basil Blackwell)

Dancy, J. 1985: *Introduction to Contemporary Epistemology* (Oxford and New York: Basil Blackwell)

D'Costa, G. 1993: "Whose Objectivity? Which Neutrality? The Doomed Quest for a Neutral Vantage Point From Which to Judge Religions" in *Religious Studies,* Vol. 29.

Delaney, C. F. (ed.) 1979: *Rationality and Religious Belief* (Notre Dame and London: University of Notre Dame Press)

Diamond, M. L. 1974: *Contemporary Philosophy and Religious Thought* (New York: McGraw-Hill Book Company)

Dupré, L. 1989: "Reflections on the Truth of Religion" in *Faith and Philosophy,* Vol. 6, No. 3.

Ellul, J. 1964: *The Technological Society* [1954] (New York: Vintage Books)

Elster, J. 1982: "Rationality" in G. Fløistad (ed.) *Contemporary Philosophy. A New Survey.* Vol. 2. (The Hague: Martinus Nijhoff Publishers)

———. 1986: "Introduction" in J. Elster (ed.) *Rational Choice* (Oxford: Basil Blackwell)

Feldman, R., and E. Conee, 1985: "Evidentialism" in *Philosophical Studies,* Vol. 48.

Feyerabend, P. 1975: *Against Method* (London: NLB)

Flew, A. 1966: *God and Philosophy* (London: Hutchinson & Co.)

———. 1984: *God, Freedom, and Immortality* (Buffalo: Prometheus Books)

Flew, A., R. M. Hare, and B. Mitchell. 1983: "Theology and Falsification" in Mitchell 1983 (ed.). Also printed in Flew and MacIntyre (eds.) 1955.

Flew A., and A. MacIntyre (eds.) 1955: *New Essays in Philosophical Theology* (London: SCM)

Foley, R. 1988: "Some Different Conceptions of Rationality" in McMullin (ed.)

———. 1991: "Rationality, Belief and Commitment" in *Synthese,* Vol. 89.

Føllesdal, D. 1986: "Intentionality and Rationality" in Margolis, J., M. Krausz, R. M. Burian (eds.)

Fraassen van, B. C. 1987: *The Scientific Image* [1980] (Oxford: Clarendon Press)

Franck, O. 1988: *The Criteriological Problem* (Stockholm: Almquist & Wiksell Int.)

Furberg, M. 1987: *Allting en trasa?* [1975] (Lund: Doxa)

Gärdenfors, P. 1988: *Knowledge in Flux* (Cambridge and London: MIT Press)

Geels, A., and O. Wikström, 1985: *Den Religiösa Människan* (Löberöd: Plus Ultra)

Geisler, N. L. (ed.) 1980: *Inerrancy* (Grand Rapids: Zondervan Publishing House)

Geraets, T. F. ed. 1979: *Rationality Today* (Ottawa: University of Ottawa Press)

Gettier, E. L. 1967: "Is Justified True Belief Knowledge?" in *Analysis,* 23.

Giere, R. N. 1988: *Explaining Science* (Chicago and London: University of Chicago Press)

Goldman, A. I. 1978: "Epistemics: the Regulative Theory of Cognition" in *The Journal of Philosophy,* Vol. LXXV, No. 10.

———. 1979: "What is Justified Belief?" in Pappas (ed.)

Gutting, G. (ed.) 1980: *Paradigms and Revolutions* (Notre Dame and London: University of Notre Dame Press)

Gutting, G. 1980: "Introduction" in Gutting (ed.)

———. 1982: *Religious Belief and Religious Skepticism* (Notre Dame and London: University of Notre Dame Press)

Gyllensten, L. 1980: "Varför inte kristendom?" in *Signum,* No. 9–10.

Hanson, N. R. 1971: *What I do not Believe, and Other Essays,* S. Toulmin and H. Woolf (eds.) (Dordrecht: Reidel Publishing Company)

Hauerwas, S., and D. Burrell, 1989: "From System to Story: An Alternative Pattern for Rationality in Ethics" in Hauerwas and Jones (eds.)

Hauerwas, S., and L. G. Jones (eds.) 1989: *Why Narrative?* (Grand Rapids, Mich.: Eerdmans)

Haught, J. F. 1990: *What is Religion?* (New York and New Jersey: Paulist Press)

Harman, G. 1986: *Change in View* (Cambridge, Massachusetts and London: MIT Press)

Hempel, C. G. 1965: *Aspects of Scientific Explanation* (New York: Free Press)

———. 1966: *Philosophy of Natural Science* (Englewood Cliffs: Prentice-Hall)

————. 1979: "Scientific Rationality: Analytic vs Pragmatic Perspectives" in Geraets (ed.)

Herrmann, E. 1991: "The Rationality of Ideologies and Religions" in *Nederlands Theologisch Tijdschrift*, July.

Hick, J. 1983: "Theology and Verification" in Mitchell (ed.)

————. 1989: *An Interpretation of Religion* (New Haven and London: Yale University Press)

Hintikka, J. 1962: *Knowledge and Belief* (New York: Cornell University Press)

Hollis, M., and S. Lukes (eds.) 1982: *Rationality and Relativisim* (Cambridge, Mass.: MIT Press)

Holte, R. 1984: *Människa, Livstolkning, Gudstro* (Lund: Doxa AB)

Horwich, P. 1982: *Probability and Evidence* (Cambridge: Cambridge University Press)

Jeffner, A. 1981: *Vägar till teologi* (Arlöv: Skeab förlag)

————. 1987: *Theology and Integration* (Uppsala: Almqvist & Wiksell Int.)

————. 1988: *Livsåskådningar i Sverige* (Uppsala)

————. 1992: "A New View of the World Emerging among Ordinary People" in van den Brink, van den Brom and Sarot (eds.)

Jeffrey, R. C. 1956: "Valuation and Acceptance of Scientific Hypotheses" in *Philosophy of the Social Sciences*, Vol. 23.

Johansson, I. 1991: "Pluralism and Rationality in the Social Sciences" in *Philosophy of the Social Sciences*, Vol. 21. No. 4.

Kaufman, G. D. 1989: " 'Evidentialism': A Theologian's Response" in *Faith and Philosophy*, Vol. 6. No. 1.

Kellenberger, J. 1985: *The Cognitivity of Religion* (London: Macmillan Press)

Kekes, J. 1976: *A Justification of Rationality* (Albany: State University of New York Press)

Kenny, A. 1983: *Faith and Reason* (New York: Columbia University Press)

Kitcher, P. 1992: "The Naturalists Return" in *The Philosophical Review*, Vol. 101, No. 1.

Klemke, E. D. 1981: "Living Without Appeal: An Affirmative Philosophy of Life" in E. D. Klemke (ed.) *The Meaning of Life*, 1981 (New York and Oxford: Oxford University Press)

Kuhn, T. 1970: *The Structure of Scientific Revolutions* 2nd ed. (Chicago and London: University of Chicago Press)

————. 1977: *The Essential Tension* (Chicago and London: University of Chicago Press)

————. 1981: *The Copernican Revolution* [1957] (Cambridge, Mass., and London: Harvard University Press)

———. 1985a: "Logic of Discovery or Psychology of Research?" in Lakatos and Musgrave (eds.)

———. 1985b: "Reflections on My Critics" in Lakatos and Musgrave (eds.)

Lakatos, I. 1978: *The Methodology of Scientific Research Programmes,* (eds.) J. Worrall and G. Currie (Cambridge: Cambridge University Press)

———. 1985: "Falsification and the Methodology of Scientific Research Programmes" in Lakatos and Musgrave (eds.)

Lakatos, I., and A. Musgrave (eds.) 1985: *Criticism and the Growth of Knowledge* [1970] (Cambridge and London: Cambridge University Press)

Laudan, L. 1977: *Progress and its Problems* (Berkeley: University of California Press)

———. 1981: *Science and Hypothesis* (Dordrecht: D. Reidel Publishing Company)

———. 1984: *Science and Values* (Berkeley, Los Angeles and London: University of California Press)

Leplin, J. (ed.) 1984: *Scientific Realism* (Berkeley and London: University of California Press)

Lindbeck, G. A. 1984: *The Nature of Doctrine* (Philadelphia: Westminster Press)

Lucas, J. R. 1987: "Reason Restored" in Abraham and Holtzer (eds.)

Mackie, J. L. 1986: *The Miracle of Theism* [1982] (Oxford: Clarendon Press)

———. 1990: "Evil and Omnipotence" [1955] in Adams and Adams (eds.)

MacIntyre, A. 1959: *Difficulties in Christian Belief* (London: SCM Press)

———. 1970: "The Logical Status of Religious Belief" in Toulmin, Hepburn, and MacIntyre (eds.)

———. 1988: *Whose Justice? Which Rationality?* (Notre Dame and London: University of Notre Dame Press)

———. 1991: "Is Understanding Religion Compatible with Believing?" [1964] in Wilson (ed.)

Malcolm, N. 1977: "The Groundlessness of Belief" in Brown (ed.)

Margolis, J., M. Krausz, and R. M. Burian (eds.), 1986: *Rationality, Relativism and the Human Sciences* (Dordrecht: Martinus Nijhoff Publishers)

Mavrodes, G. I. 1970: *Belief in God* (New York and London: University Press of America)

———. 1983: "Jerusalem and Athens Revisited" in Plantinga and Wolterstorff (eds.)

———. 1986: "Intellectual Morality in Clifford and James" in McCarthy (ed.) McCarthy, G. D. (ed.) 1986: *The Ethics of Belief Debate* (Atlanta: Scholars Press)

McMullin, E. (ed.) 1988: *Construction and Constraint* (Notre Dame: University of Notre Dame Press)

McMullin, E. 1983: "Values in Science" in *The Philosophy of Science Association,* Vol. 2.

————. 1988: "The Shaping of Scientific Rationality: Construction and Constraint" in McMullin (ed.)

Mitchell, B. (ed.) 1983: *The Philosophy of Religion* [1971] (London and New York: Oxford University Press)

Mitchell, B. 1981: *The Justification of Religious Belief* [1973] (London and New York: Oxford University Press)

Morris, T. V. 1985: "Agnosticism" in *Analysis*

Moser, P. K. 1991: "Justification in the Natural Sciences" in *British Journal for the Philosophy of Science,* Vol. 39.

Murphy, N., and J. Wm. McClendon, Jr. 1989: "Distinguishing Modern and Postmodern Theologies" in *Modern Theology,* Vol. 5. No. 3.

Nathanson, S. 1985: *The Ideal of Rationality* (Atlantic Highlands, NJ: Humanities Press International, Inc.)

Newman, J. H. 1955: *A Grammar of Assent* (New York: Doubleday)

Newton-Smith, W. H. 1981: *The Rationality of Science* (London and New York: Routledge and Kegan Paul)

Nielsen, K. 1967: "Wittgensteinian Fideism" in *Philosophy,* Vol. 42.

Nisbett. R., and L. Ross, 1980: *Human Inference* (Englewood Cliffs: Prentice-Hall)

Nordin, I. 1988: *Teknologins rationalitet* (Göteborg: Timbro)

Pap, A. 1962: *An Introduction to Philosophy of Science* (London: Free Press)

Pappas, G. (ed.) 1979: *Justification and Knowledge* (Dordrecht: Reidel)

Peacocke, A. R. (ed.) 1981: *The Sciences and Theology in the Twentieth Century* (London: Oriel Press)

Peterson, M., W. Hasker, B. Reichenbach, and D. Basinger, 1991: *Reason and Religious Belief* (New York and Oxford: Oxford University Press)

Phillips, D. Z. 1970: *Death and Immortality* (London: Macmillan Press)

————. 1971: *Faith and Philosophical Enquiry* (New York: Schocken Books)

————. 1976: *Religion Without Explanation* (Oxford: Basil Blackwell)

————. 1981: "Belief, Change, and Forms of Life" in Crosson (ed.)

————. 1983: "Religious Beliefs and Language Games" in Mitchell (ed.)

————. 1988: *Faith After Foundationalism* (London and New York: Routledge)

Plantinga, A. 1982: "How to be an Anti-Realist" in *Proceedings and Addresses of the American Philosophical Association,* Vol. 56, No. 1.

———. 1983: "Reason and Belief in God" in Plantinga and Wolterstorff (eds.)

———. 1984: "Advice to Christian Philosophers" in *Faith and Philosophy* Vol. 1, No. 3, also in Beaty (ed.)

———. 1986a: "Coherentism and the Evidentialist Objection" in Audi and Wainwright (eds.)

———. 1986b: "Is Theism Really a Miracle?" in *Faith and Philosophy,* Vol. 3, No. 2.

———. 1988: "Positive Epistemic Status and Proper Function" in *Philosophical Perspectives,* Vol. 2: *Epistemology,* James Tomberlin (ed.) (Northridge: California State University)

———. 1990a: *God and Other Minds* [1967] (Ithaca and London: Cornell University Press)

———. 1990b: "Justification and Theism" in Beaty (ed.)

———. 1990c: "Justification in the 20th Century" in *Philosophy and Phenomenological Research,* Vol. L, Fall 1990.

———. 1992: "Augustinian Christian Philosophy" in *The Monist,* Vol. 75, No. 3.

Plantinga, A., and N. Wolterstorff (eds.) 1983: *Faith and Rationality* (Notre Dame and London: University of Notre Dame Press)

Polanyi, M. 1962: *Personal Knowledge* [1958] (Chicago and London: University of Chicago Press)

Popper, K. 1959: *Logic of Scientific Discovery* (London: Hutchinson & Co.)

———. 1985: *Conjectures and Refutations* [1963] (London and Henley: Routledge and Kegan Paul)

Price, H. H. 1983: "Belief 'In' and Belief 'That' " in Mitchell (ed.)

Provine, W. 1988: "Scientists, Face It! Science and Religion are Incompatible" in *The Scientist,* Sept. 5.

Putnam, H. 1990: *Reason, Truth and History* [1981] (Cambridge: Cambridge University Press)

Quinn, P. 1985: "In Search of the Foundations of Theism" in *Faith and Philosophy,* Vol. 2, No. 4.

Ratzsch, D. 1986: *Philosophy of Science* (Downers Grove and Leicester: InterVarsity Press)

Reichenbach, H. 1938: *Experience and Prediction* (Chicago: University of Chicago Press)

———. 1951: *The Rise of Scientific Philosophy* (Berkeley: University of California Press)

Rescher, N. 1988: *Rationality* (Oxford: Clarendon Press)

Rolston III, H. 1987: *Science and Religion* (Philadelphia: Temple University Press)

Rorty, R. 1979: *Philosophy and the Mirror of Nature* (Princeton: Princeton University Press)

Rowe, W. L. 1990: "The Problem of Evil and Some Varieties of Atheism" in Adams and Adams (eds.)

Russell, B. 1954: *Human Society in Ethics and Politics* (London: Allen and Unwin)

———. 1979: *Why I Am Not a Christian* [1957] (London: Unwin Paperbacks)

———. 1984: *A History of Western Philosophy* [1946] (London: Unwin Paperbacks)

Sapir, E. 1929: "The Status of Linguistics as a Science" in *Language,* Vol. 5.

Scheffler, I. 1967: *Science and Subjectivity* (Indianapolis: Bobbs-Merrill)

Schlesinger, G. H. 1983: *Metaphysics* (Oxford: Basil Blackwell)

Schrag, C. O. 1992: *The Resources of Rationality* (Bloomington: Indiana University Press)

Scriven, M. 1966: *Primary Philosophy* (New York: McGraw-Hill)

Shapere, D. 1984: *Reason and the Search for Knowledge* (Dordrecht: D. Reidel Publishing Company)

Simon, H. A. 1983: *Reason in Human Affairs* (Oxford: Basil Blackwell)

Smith, J. E. 1979: "Faith, Belief, and the Problem of Rationality in Religion" in Delaney (ed.)

Sousa de, R. 1990: *The Rationality of Emotion* (Cambridge, Massachusetts and London: MIT Press)

Stanesby, D. 1988: *Science, Reason and Religion* [1985] (London and New York: Routledge)

Stout, J. 1981: *The Flight from Authority* (Notre Dame and London: University of Notre Dame Press)

Suppe, F. 1977: *The Structure of Scientific Theories,* 2nd. (Urbana and Chicago: University of Illinois Press)

Swinburne, R. 1973: *An Introduction to Confirmation Theory* (London: Methuen & Co.)

———. 1977: *The Coherence of Theism* (Oxford: Oxford University Press)

———. 1981: *Faith and Reason* (Oxford: Clarendon Press)

———. 1983: "Mackie, Induction, and God" in *Religious Studies,* Vol. 19.

———. 1985: *The Existence of God* [1979] (Oxford: Oxford University Press)·

Tillich, P. 1951: *Systematic Theology* (Chicago and London: University of Chicago Press)

Toulmin, S. E., R. W. Hepburn, and A. MacIntyre (eds.) 1970: *Metaphysical Beliefs* [1957] (London: SCM Press)

Tversky, A., and D. Kahneman, 1974: "Judgment and Uncertainty: Heuristics and Biases" in *Science,* 185.

Wainwright, W. J. 1988: *Philosophy of Religion* (Belmont: Wadsworth Publishing Company)

Westphal, M. 1987: *God, Guilt, and Death* [1984] (Bloomington: Indiana University Press)

Wilson, B. R. (ed.) 1991: *Rationality* [1970] (Oxford: Basil Blackwell)

Winch, P. 1990: *The Idea of a Social Science and Its Relation to Philosophy* 2nd ed. [1958] (London: Routledge)

———. 1991: "Understanding a Primitive Society" in Wilson (ed.)

Wittgenstein, L. 1966: *Lectures and Conversations on Aesthetics, Psychology and Religious Belief,* (ed.) C. Barrett (Oxford: Basil Blackwell)

———. 1969: *On Certainty* (eds.) G. E. M. Anscombe and G. H. von Wright (Oxford: Basil Blackwell)

Wolfe, D. 1982: *Epistemology* (Downers Grove: InterVarsity Press)

Wolterstorff, N. 1983a: "Introduction" in Plantinga and Wolterstorff (eds.)

———. 1983b: "Can Belief in God be Rational?" in Plantinga and Wolterstorff (eds.)

———. 1984: *Reason within the Bounds of Religion,* 2nd. [1976] (Grand Rapids: Eerdmans)

———. 1988: "Once Again, Evidentialism—This Time, Social" in *Philosophical Topics,* Vol. XVI, No. 2.

———. 1990: "The Assurance of Faith" in *Faith and Philosophy,* Vol. 7, No. 4.

———. 1992: Review of "Faith After Foundationalism" by D. Z. Phillips in *The Philosophical Review,* Vol. 101. No. 2.

Wright von, G. 1988: *Vetenskapen och förnuftet* [1986] (Stockholm: Mån-Pocket)

Wykstra, S. J. 1990a: "The Humean Obstacle to Evidential Arguments from Suffering" in Adams and Adams (eds.)

———. 1990b: "Reasons, Redemption, and Realism" in Beaty (ed.)

Yandell, K. E. 1984: *Christianity and Philosophy* (Grand Rapids: Eerdmans)

Zahar, E. 1982: "Feyerabend on Observation and Empirical Content" in *British Journal for the Philosophy of Science* 33.